WEED-CROP ECOLOGY

PRINCIPLES IN WEED MANAGEMENT

R.J. ALDRICH

Agronomist, U.S. Department of Agriculture
Professor of Agronomy, University of Missouri–Columbia

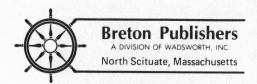

Breton Publishers
A DIVISION OF WADSWORTH, INC.
North Scituate, Massachusetts

This book is dedicated to my wife, June, for her enduring patience, under standing, and encouragement.

Breton Publishers
A Division of Wadsworth, Inc.

© 1984 by Wadsworth, Inc., Belmont, California 94002. All rights reserved. No part of this book may be reproduced, stored in a retrieval system, or transcribed, in any form or by any means, electronic, mechanical, photocopying, recording, or otherwise, without the prior written permission of the publisher, Breton Publishers, a Division of Wadsworth, Inc., North Scituate, Massachusetts 02060.

Library of Congress Cataloging in Publication Data

Aldrich, R.J. (Richard J.), 1925–
    Weed crop ecology principles in weed management.

    Includes index.
    1. Weed control.   2. Weeds.   3. Weeds—Ecology.
I. Title.
SB611.A4   1984   632'.58   83-10005
ISBN 0-534-02833-0

Printed in the United States of America
1 2 3 4 5 6 7 8 9–88 87 86 85 84

Weed–Crop Ecology was prepared for publication by the following people:
    Sponsoring editor: Jay P. Bartlett
    Copy editor: Shirley H. Pitcher
    Interior designer: Mary S. Mowrey
    Cover designer: Ellie Connolly
    Cover photo: Elanco Products Company

CONTENTS

PREFACE

The emergence and development of selective weed control may well be the most important advance of the century in agriculture. It has had a direct impact on nearly every aspect of plant production from trees to turf to crops and an indirect impact on such other activities as highway maintenance, industrial site maintenance, water recreation, and many more.

As significant as the accomplishments have been, the full potential of weed science is yet to be realized. Weed science can help show the way in moves to shape and improve our systems of plant production and management—not just as the source of information for minimizing losses from weeds each year in a given crop. When seen in the larger sense, weed science can be a powerful factor in responding to two major challenges facing agriculture and all of society: enough energy and enough food.

For the full potential of weed science to be realized, prevention must have a place alongside control in our mindset toward weeds. The discovery of the selective weed control properties of 2,4–D fueled a flurry of research and development in the chemical industry leading to a large number of additional selective herbicides. There was a concurrent rapid growth in demand from farmers and others for information on how best to use the new herbicides to control weeds in their particular situations. This left little time for weed scientists to seek answers to such basic questions as: Why do we have weeds? Why do we have the weeds we do? What is the nature of competition? What is the relationship between weeds and cultural practices? What are the possibilities for predicting future weed problems?

Thus, it has taken longer than one might have hoped to accumulate enough information on these ecological questions for prevention to become a part of our thinking. Enough information has been obtained to justify preparation of a book that articulates the concepts suggested and supported by the available data even though much additional research is needed.

This book is written to fill that area between weed control and weed biology/demography. There are several good texts on weed control and some on weed biology/demography, but none that relate knowledge on weed biology/demography to approaches for preventing or minimizing losses from weeds.

The book is aimed at college students enrolled in introductory courses in weed science or weed–crop ecology. A basic botany or plant science course (or a general biology course that covers the fundamental principles of plant science) is the only recommended prerequisite. Instructors desiring more specific coverage of chemical weed control procedures might supplement this text with publications from the USDA, the chemical industry, and especially their own Extension Services. Such bulletins contain more thorough, timely, and locally appropriate information than any general textbook.

For the student pursuing weed science, the book provides an understanding of ecological relationships between weeds and the environment provided by agricultural and other uses of land. The weed science student with this background should bring to the profession of weed science an expanded view for dealing with weeds.

For the student interested in integrated pest management, the book provides the coverage of weed–crop ecological relationships needed to place treatment of weeds on a par with that of the other major plant pests. The absence of such a book has been a major deterrent to more effective treatment of weeds in emerging IPM curricula.

For those with a general interest in agriculture or the plant sciences, the book will help provide a better perspective of the relationship between weeds (and weed science) and the other factors (and disciplines) involved in plant production.

Additionally, the book should help weed scientists and other plant scientists identify opportunities for cooperative effort. There are many fruitful areas for multi- and interdisciplinary effort. One is in utilizing allelopathy in preventing/minimizing problems with weeds. Geneticists and plant breeders will need to build such characteristics into available varieties for the potential to be realized. Another is in crop systems analysis. Such efforts will be less effective than they could be until the weed–crop relationships are understood and factored in. For its part, weed science will fall short of effectively predicting weed problems for changes in production practices without the benefit of systems analysis.

Much material was drawn from the research of colleagues, many of whom generously provided photographs and drawings used as illustrations in the book. Many in the private sector also graciously provided material used in the illustrations. Comments and suggestions to an early draft of the manuscript by Diane Kintner, John Smith, and John Albright, weed science graduate students in the Agronomy Department of the University of Missouri–Columbia, helped identify critical omissions, clarify certain points, and develop a tone appropriate to a student audience. Valuable council and advice on some aspects was also obtained from Dr. Laurel Anderson, Dr. O. Hale Fletchall, and Dr. Harold Kerr in the Agronomy Department and from Dr. Elroy Peters of the USDA. The publisher's review board, which included Kriton K. Hatzios of Virginia Polytechnic Institute and State University and Richard D. Ilnicki of Rutgers, The State University of New Jersey, offered many useful criticisms during the development of the manuscript. I am sincerely grateful for all of these important contributions.

INTRODUCTION 1

Have you ever wondered why we have weeds and why we have the ones we do? Why is chickweed (Stellaria media) a particular problem in fall-seeded alfalfa in the Northeast, giant foxtail *(Setaria faberii)* a particular problem in corn and soybeans in the Midwest, cocklebur *(Xanthium strumarium)* a plague to cotton producers from the early days of cotton production in the South, and kochia *(Kochia scoparia)* commonly a problem in sugar beets in the West? A quick answer might be that these are weeds that herbicides do not effectively control. Only a little deliberation tells us this answer is inadequate. Available herbicides can control each of these weeds and, in fact, are providing good control on many acres each year. Indeed, wherever they occur, there are very few weeds that cannot be satisfactorily controlled with one or more of the herbicides available today.

Since the widespread availability of selective herbicides has only occurred in the second half of this century, is it possible that there simply has not been enough time for these herbicides to have their full effect? Given time, will the storehouse of weed seeds, rhizomes, and other reproductive parts be used up, with a consequential disappearance of weeds? Both the explanation and the projection must also be rejected. Weed control has been practiced from the very beginning of our managed production of food. Hand removal and cultivation used prior to the modern herbicide era provided enough control on many farms for full crop yields to be realized. Weeds have persisted in spite of control. Why? Must it always be so? As a student of weed science, you will find that answers to these questions can do more than simply satisfy your curiosity about such puzzles of the plant world. The answers provide the necessary background to explore and understand competition of weeds with crops; to identify appropriate roles for allelopathy, biotic agents, cropping and tillage practices, and herbicides in preventing losses from weeds;

and to better relate weeds and weed science to the many other areas of plant science studied.

SCOPE OF THE BOOK

Nature of Weeds and Competition

Chapter 2 of this book provides answers to why we have weeds, why we have those we do, and why they have persisted. The ecological concepts explored that apply to weed–crop relationships tell us why. Chapters 3 and 4 consider the weed's remarkable capacity for survival even under very adverse conditions. For annual weeds, seeds are the vehicle for survival. Thus, long-term control—*prevention*—must focus on the seed. Most perennial weeds reproduce by both seeds and vegetative parts. However, it is the protection offered by the vegetative reproductive parts during both climatic and crop-competition stress that makes perennial species especially troublesome. Thus, long-term control, or prevention, must focus on such reproductive parts. Factors affecting production and longevity are identified and explained.

Chapter 5 looks specifically at factors that affect the resumption of growth from seed and from perennating parts. Resumption of growth, either of seed or of vegetative parts, is a key phase for crop production in the life history of weeds since its timing and numbers in relationship to the crop life cycle determines the severity of competition or whether there is competition at all. Chapters 6 and 7 examine the nature of competition between weeds and crops; when weeds compete and a perspective of weed numbers and weed weights as indices of competition are developed.

Weeds in Crop Production Systems

With an understanding of the nature and competition of weeds as background, the remainder of the book explores ways of dealing with weeds in crop production systems. There is much evidence that metabolites of many weeds and crops have an adverse effect on the growth of other weeds and of crops. In Chapter 8, allelopathy, as this effect is known, is considered as a possible factor in the persistence of certain weeds, in the shift in composition of weed communities following changes of cultural practices, in the direct interference with production of a given crop, and as a potential tool for preventing losses from weeds.

It is a rare organism that has no natural enemies, if indeed such an organism exists. Weeds are no exception. Chapter 9 draws upon this fact to identify the role of biotic agents in preventing losses from weeds. Concepts involved in their successful use are listed and discussed.

Discovery of the auxin-type herbicides in the 1940s has led to the widespread use of herbicides common throughout agriculture today. Whereas most herbicides prior to the 1940s were inorganic chemicals, all those of the modern era are organic. The majority of the latter are systemic—that is, readily translocated in plants. Chapter 10 examines the current usage of systemic herbicides and introduces their broader potential role in weed management. Chapter 11 develops a general understanding of entry, transport and gross effects as they relate to plant anatomy and to the environment. With this knowledge as background, Chapters 12 and 13 discuss the place of herbicides in each of the three broad approaches to weed management: (1) preventing emergence of weeds with crops, (2) minimizing competition from weeds growing with crops, and (3) reducing the number of viable propagules in the soil. Both the physical environment and characteristics of the weeds themselves are discussed as they influence successful use of herbicides.

It has been said that the history of weeds is essentially the history of human beings. The significance of this statement for weed–crop ecology is the implication that weeds are associated with disturbed environments. Production agriculture involves repeated disturbance of the environment. Chapter 14 examines specific effects of cropping practices, tillage practices, and weed control practices on weed numbers and species. Understanding these effects is a necessary first step in predicting future weed problems and in designing more effective ways of dealing with them.

The preceding chapters provide a sequence of subject matter coverage that builds logically from the constraints of our current emphasis on control to the expanded opportunities of weed management. The concepts developed are brought together in Chapter 15. The need to base weed management on prevention is explained, and the relationship between prevention and control in such an approach is discussed. In effect, Chapter 15 provides the necessary foundation for establishing weed management as the next higher level in a hierarchy of approaches to weeds.

A NEW MINDSET TOWARD WEEDS

For weed management to assume its proper place in the evolutionary process, there must be a change in our mindset towards weeds. For the most part, weed control, as practiced today, is geared toward dealing with the specific weed(s) in a given crop in a single year. Within this overall approach, a number of different methods for dealing with weeds have been developed in response to different weed problems faced. Preemergence and preplant-incorporated applications of herbicides thus are based on the expectations that there will be a competing population of weeds—mostly annuals—with the crop. Machines have been adapted and new ones built to remove weeds growing with the crop. Sprayers have been designed to place chemicals selectively on the weeds and not on the crop.

Under this year-to-year approach, a new problem resulting from a change in weed composition or from a change in an individual species is dealt with only after the new problem is established. The result can be a need for drastic changes in weed control methods with associated costs to the farmer. Further, this approach implies that some measure of loss is to be accepted as a result of a change in the weed community before an effective control is developed. Finally, as we shall see, the year-to-year approach unnecessarily restricts the technology that can be used to minimize losses from weeds.

Changes in Weeds

There is much evidence to show that weeds do change in response to weed control and other crop production practices. Shifts in weed composition in the Corn Belt of the United States provide a striking example of such changes over a broad area. Following its introduction in the late 1940s, the herbicide 2,4–D was widely used in corn throughout the Corn Belt. It selectively controlled many of the broadleaf annual weeds, causing a shift in the weed community by the late 1950s to one dominated by annual grasses. Herbicides especially effective against annual grasses (such as the triazines) were developed and widely used in the 1960s. By the 1970s, species such as fall panicum *(Panicum dichotomiflorum)* and honeyvine milkweed *(Ampelamus albidus)* had become prevalent because by germinating and making their growth later in the season, they escaped the effects of the commonly used preemergence and early postemergence herbicides.

Need for a Changing Approach

Even though the prediction of future weed problems and the development of corresponding prevention programs are still only goals, weed science has much to gain by developing an understanding of the ecological relationships among weeds, crops, and production practices. Current approaches to control can be improved if there is a better understanding of such relationships.

What is needed is recognition and acceptance of an appropriate companion role for prevention in dealing with weeds. A simple analogy identifies the change in mindset needed. Our historical approach, which has been to deal with weeds when and where we have them, was built upon the view that weed vegetative growth must be kept out or controlled if crop losses are to be avoided. In this view, weed reproductive parts—that is, seeds, rhizomes, and so forth—are viewed as simply the vehicles for producing more plants. Conversely, the preventive view focuses on production of seed and perennating parts and on their germination. This view sees the plant as a vehicle for producing reproductive parts.

The former, or historical, view is adequate when competition from weeds is the only focus. It is inadequate for a perspective broadened to encompass changes in the weed community in response to changes in production practices. The first view recognizes that numbers of individual weeds determine the consequences of weeds for a particular crop. The latter, or preventive, view recognizes that it is the individual plant and its fitness for both the natural environment and the environment we provide that determine shifts in the weed community and changes within the individual weed species. The reason is that the individual, not the population, transmits the genetic message. Under a preventive mindset, accumulation of knowledge about the individual weed's response to our imposed environment will ultimately be enough to make forecasting a reality.

CONCEPTS AND DEFINITIONS

Weeds are constant associates of our cultivated plants. Anyone familiar with plants has a perception of what is a weedy and what is a clean crop, lawn, vegetable garden, or other managed use of plants. Yet, as we shall see, it is not easy to determine the degree of weediness that represents a threat to crop yield or to survival of a lawn. Neither is it easy to define a weed in terms that clearly distinguish it from cultivated plants and from other wild plants.

We will see, however, that weeds do have important characteristics different from cultivated plants. Also, out of 250,000 plant species in the world, fewer than 250 species (1%) account for the readily apparent weediness often seen. Thus, weeds are hardly synonymous with wild plants. Having in mind a clear definition of a weed and a grasp of weediness is important to a full appreciation and understanding of the concepts and principles this book encompasses.

Weed Defined

How should a weed be defined? Numerous definitions can be found in the literature. Such common definitions as a plant out of place, a plant interfering with man's intended use of the land, and a plant with negative value fairly well describe a weed in a vegetation control context. That is, they are adequate when our focus is only on the problems posed by the growth of unwanted plants at a particular point in time. Further, these definitions embrace the key fact that a plant appropriately is a weed *only in reference to us*. The problem comes when we try to use these definitions beyond a point in time and a particular place. Put another way, the definitions do not fit the dynamic aspects implied in a focus on ecological relationships. Rather, these definitions imply that a weed is fixed in time in a static state. As we shall see, weeds are continually changing. We will also see, contrary to the first definition, that we have weeds because our production practices provide a place for them.

The second definition poses a definitional problem for those plants that are present but become an interfering associate only when we change crops or production practices. Dandelion *(Taraxicum officinale)*, which infests lawns in subdivisions developed on land removed from agricultural use, is one of many examples that could be cited. Under a strict interpretation of the second definition, a dandelion in a field used for food or feed production would not be called a weed because it is probably not interfering, while a dandelion in the lawn would. Calling one dandelion a weed and not the other is not based on any inherent difference between the plants, only on a difference in when and where they occur. Similarly, negative value can only apply to plants when they are present where they are not wanted. This definition accommodates cultivated plants that escape or volunteer to interfere with our intended use of the land. This loophole in itself suggests a weakness in the definition since it becomes confounded with the definition of a crop.

A more useful definition of a *weed* for weed–crop ecology is a plant that originated under a natural environment and, in response to imposed and natural environments, evolved, and continues to do so, as an interfering associate with our crops and activities. Such a definition continues to relate to us as it should, but as contrasted with previous definitions, it provides both an origin and continuing change perspective. Recognizing that weeds are part of a dynamic, not static, ecosystem helps expand our thinking on how best to prevent losses from them. Excluding plants developed by us for our uses properly recognizes inherent differences between such plants and weeds with respect to seed dormancy, seed longevity, and length of the life cycle. This definition of a weed is used throughout the text.

Cultivated plants as weeds. The new definition of a weed leaves the question of what to call escaped ornamental and volunteer cultivated plants. It is suggested that they be called exactly what they are—that is, *volunteer* corn, *volunteer* wheat, or some other *volunteer* crop, growing where it is not wanted. Similarly, plants introduced as ornamentals that have escaped to interfere with our activities would be identified as *escapes*. For example, *escaped* Japanese knotweed *(Polygonum cuspidatum)*, escaped prickly-pear cactus *(Opuntia* spp.), or some other *escaped* ornamental.

Weediness Defined

Identifying as volunteer or escaped cultivated or ornamental plants that behave like weeds helps us to grasp what is meant by weediness. *Weediness* is defined as "the state or condition of a field, flower bed, lawn, and so forth, in which there is an abundance of weeds" (Winburne, 1962). Thus, weediness connotes a *condition*. By contrast, under the definition proposed in this book, a weed is a particular *biological entity*. It follows that it is appropriate to refer to soybeans as being weedy with corn and to a flower bed as being weedy with bluegrass.

Costs of weeds. Weediness also connotes "numbers." That is, to suggest that a crop is weedy implies that it has many weeds—enough to reduce crop yield. Although weeds have many other negative aspects, it is this threat to yield, to the production of food, that accounts for most of the effort devoted to their control since the beginning of agriculture. Still, crop losses due to weeds are very large. In the United States alone, as shown in Table 1–1, the estimated average annual loss was nearly $8 billion in the 1973–1977 period (Chandler, 1980).

Weeds represent a cost in many other respects. They directly affect human health through allergies and poisoning. Weeds adversely affect livestock production: Animals die from eating poisonous weeds, off-flavor is imparted to milk and other dairy products when weeds such as wild garlic *(Allium vineale)* are eaten, and hides and carcasses are physically damaged by weeds. Weeds may harbor insect and disease organisms that affect cultivated plants. Finally, weeds entail a cost for their control in fields and on such nonagricultural sites as along highways, around buildings, and in waterways. Nearly all of these aspects imply the occurrence of excessive numbers. It is understandable, therefore, that the most commonly used definitions for a weed are also synonymous for weediness. This is one more reason why the traditional definitions are inadequate in a weed–crop ecology context because, as we shall see, the focus must frequently be on the *individual*, not the group, in order to understand properly the ecological forces involved.

TABLE 1-1

Estimated average annual losses due to weeds in all crops in the United States, 1973-1977.

Commodity Group	Average Annual Monetary Losses ($1,000)
Field crops	$5,735,821
Vegetables	450,093
Fruits and nuts	299,498
Forage seed crops	38,763
Hay	676,221
Pasture and rangelands	788,805
Total	$7,989,201

Source: Data from Chandler, 1980.

Weed Management Defined

Simply stated, *weed management* is an approach in which weed prevention and weed control have companion roles. It implies a systems context in which all available tools are used to reduce the propagule seedbank, prevent weed emergence with crops, and minimize competition from weeds growing with crops. Thus, weed management has both immediate and long-term objectives. This approach also implies a consideration of weeds in the broader context of their interactions with production practices. It follows that weed management requires knowledge of weeds themselves and of the ecological principles that involve them. The remainder of this book provides the necessary knowledge for such an expanded approach to weeds.

WEED NOMENCLATURE AND CLASSIFICATION

Scientific Classification

Binomial names. Because weed species have ecological characteristics unique to each, it is essential that they be identified by a standard system. Further, the entire science of weeds and weed management is built upon the weed species present or anticipated. The standard of plant nomenclature in use throughout the world today gives the name in Latin and is based upon the 1753 publication *Species Plantarum* by Linnaeus in which a two-part, or *binomial*, naming system was used. The first part identifies the genus, or generic name, and the second part identifies the specific epithet.

For example, in the binomial name of giant foxtail *(Setaria faberii)*, *Setaria* identifies the genus, and *faberii*, the specific epithet. Under the *International Code of Botanical Nomenclature*, only one genus can have the name *Setaria* and only one epithet within this genus can have the name *faberii*, although the same specific epithet may be used for plants of different genuses. Since reading is easier when common names are used, the generic name is used in this book only the first time the species is referred to in the body of the text. The binomial name of every species referred to by common name is listed in Table 1 of the Appendix.

Hierarchy of the plant kingdom. Using lambsquarters *(Chenopodium album)* as an example, the major subdivisions of the taxonomic hierarchy of the plant kingdom include the following rank of taxa:

Kingdom—Plantae
  Division—Tracheophyta
    Subdivision—Spermatophytina
      Class—Angiospermae
        Order—Caryophyllalés
          Family—Chenopodiaceae
            Genus—*Chenopodium*
              Species—*Chenopodium album*

The ranks used most often in weed science are family, genus, and species. There are about 450 families of flowering plants in the world. A relatively few families contain the majority of the approximately 200 species that account for most of the losses in food production worldwide. The main contributing families and number of weed species in each are as follows: Poaceae (44 species), Cyperaceae (12 species), Asteraceae (32 species), Polygonaceae (8 species), Amaranthaceae (7 species), Brassicaceae (7 species), Leguminosae (6 species), Convolvulaceae (5 species), Euphorbiaceae (5 species), Chenopodiacea (4 species), Malvaceae (4 species), and Solonaceae (3 species). The first three families contain 44% of the problem weeds, and the twelve combined, 68% (Holm, 1978). Some families and representative weed species of each are shown in Table 1–2.

Common Systems of Classification

Grasslike and broadleaf weeds. The seed-producing plants (Spermatophytina) have two classes: Angiospermae (covered seed) and Gymnospermae (naked seed). Most weeds are in the Angiospermae class. The Angiospermae class is further separated into two subclasses based upon the number of cotyledons (seed leaves). *Monocotyledoneae* are those weeds whose embryo has one cotyledon. *Dicotyledoneae* have two cotyledons. The name *grassy*, or *grasslike*, is commonly applied to the monocotyledons, and the name *broadleaf*, to the dicotyledons. The common names are descriptors of both leaf shape and growth form. The monocotyledons commonly have a nonbranched growth form with leaves that are usually narrow or linear in shape with parallel veins. The dicotyledons commonly have a branched growth form with leaves that are usually broader and net-veined. As we shall see later, these differences in leaves and growth form may have far-reaching implications for a weed's competitive ability and for its control or management.

Annual, biennial, and perennial weeds. Weeds are also commonly classified according to their life cycles. *Annuals* are species that can complete their life cycle in one year or less from seed germination to seed production. There may be two kinds: winter annuals and summer annuals. *Summer annuals* germinate in the

TABLE 1-2

Some plant families and a representative weed species of each.

Family		Representative Weed	
Common Name	Latin Name	Common Name	Latin Name
Amaranth or pigweed	*Amaranthaceae*	Redroot pigweed	*Amaranthus retroflexus*
Buckwheat or smartweed	*Polygonaceae*	Pennsylvania smartweed	*Polygonum pennsylvanicum*
Chickweed or pink	*Caryophyllaceae*	Common chickweed	*Stellaria media*
Composite	*Compositae*	Common ragweed	*Ambrosia artemisiifolia*
Goosefoot	*Chenopodiaceae*	Lambsquarters	*Chenopodium album*
Grass	*Gramineae*	Quackgrass	*Agropyron repens*
Mallow	*Malvaceae*	Velvetleaf	*Abutilon theophrasti*
Milkweed	*Asclepiadaceae*	Common milkweed	*Asclepias syriaca*
Morning-glory	*Convolvulaceae*	Field bindweed	*Convolvulus arvensis*
Mustard	*Cruciferae*	Wild mustard	*Brassica kaber*
Nightshade	*Solonaceae*	Jimsonweed	*Datura stramonuim*
Parsley	*Umbelliferae*	Wild carrot	*Daucus carota*
Plantain	*Plantaginaeceae*	Buckhorn plantain	*Plantago lanceolata*
Purslane	*Portulacaceae*	Common purslane	*Portulaca oleraceae*
Sedge	*Cyperaceae*	Yellow nutsedge	*Cyperus esculentus*
Spurge	*Euphorbiaceae*	Leafy spurge	*Euphorbia esula*

spring, produce seed, and die later that same year. *Winter annuals* germinate in the fall of one year, overwinter, then resume growth, produce seed, and die the next year. Annuals represent by far the largest number of weed species that compete with annual row crops. The reason is that completion of their life cycle is interfered with less in the production of annual crops than is that of biennials or perennials. This statement is further emphasized by the fact that summer annuals, such as pigweed, foxtails, and lambsquarters, are most commonly associated with spring-seeded crops, such as soybeans, corn, and spring wheat. Winter annuals, such as chickweed and pepperweed (*Lepidium* spp.), are most common with fall-seeded crops, such as legumes and winter wheat.

Biennials may complete their life cycle in 2 years. They germinate one year, overwinter, then resume growth the next year and may produce seed, after which they usually die. There are only a few biennial weeds. Among the common ones are wild carrot, mullein *(Verbascum Thapsus)*, and bull thistle *(Cirsium vulgare)*. Because more than one year is required to complete the life cycle, such species are not a common problem with annual row-crops but may be with perennial crops used for hay and pasture. In nature, many individual plants of so-called biennial species may take more than 2 years to complete the cycle. For example, if flowering and seed production of wild carrot are prevented in the second year, it has been shown that the plants continue vegetative growth into subsequent years, continuing possibly for 4 to 5 years (Holt, 1972). The terminating feature is seed production, not years from germination.

Perennials, as the name implies, are species that may live more than 2 years. A distinguishing feature is that many such species can reproduce from vegetative parts, as well as from seed, in the same and subsequent years. At any given time, new plants may be arising both as a result of regeneration from the perennating parts and from seed. It is the perennating characteristic that makes some perennials so difficult to prevent from interfering with crop production. Vegetative reproduction is discussed in detail in Chapter 4. Note here, however, that such reproduction may occur from roots (dandelion), tubers (yellow nutsedge), rhizomes (quackgrass), stolons (bermudagrass—*Cynodon dactylon*), and bulbs (wild garlic).

Some care must be exercised in classifying weeds according to life cycle. Life cycle itself is not fixed; rather, it is greatly influenced by the environment. As mentioned earlier, the life cycle of the biennial wild carrot can be extended beyond 2 years. Also, plants of some biennials may behave as annuals. Plants of some species commonly classified as annuals can be made to live for more than one year by providing conditions that encourage vegetative growth and discourage flowering. Younger (1961) observed that crabgrass *(Digitaria sanguinalis)*, classified as a summer annual, behaved otherwise in bermudagrass turf in southern California. Some plants in the turf, which was regularly mowed to 2.5 cm (1 in.), overwintered, and if allowed to do so, flowered and produced seed the next spring. At the other extreme, plants of some species commonly classified as perennials can be forced to behave as annuals. This situation is illustrated by the fact that bermudagrass, widely used as a perennial forage species in the southeastern United States, fails to become a perennial if overgrazed. In fact, the objective of cultural practices used to check perennial weeds is to prevent the production of perennating parts, which prevention, in effect, causes them to behave as annuals. In summary, it is helpful to view classification by life cycle as applying to the entire population of a species. In this way, general behavior is emphasized rather than behavior of individuals. Plasticity of life cycle of individual specimens should be borne in mind, however.

FRAMEWORK OF THE BOOK

Metric Units

The metric system is used throughout the body of the text. Where data in references cited are presented in the English system, the English unit is shown in parentheses after the metric unit. This method is used to avoid the confusion that would otherwise occur in switching back and forth from metric to English units, depending upon the system used in the data cited. Conversion to metric units of data published in English units results in some awkward numbers in the text. For example, a depth of 3 inches reported in a tillage study becomes 7.62 centimeters. To improve readability, only one decimal place is used in such transformed figures. In this case, the depth as given in the text is 7.6 cm. To correctly reproduce figures and tables taken from other publications, the system used in the other publication is retained. Transformation in the text to metric units with English units in parentheses minimizes the need for conversion.

Literature Treatment and Key Points

A large body of literature has accumulated on weed science. This book is not intended as a review of that literature. Only that literature needed to establish the concepts and principles covered is cited. Because there is limited literature on some important concepts and principles, some citations necessarily go back many years. However, these citations should not be construed as a review of that particular literature. Similarly, some recent publications on particular subjects are not cited simply because they neither add new concepts nor modify concepts already established from earlier publications.

A list of the important concepts and conclusions developed within each chapter is given at the end of each chapter. This list will help you to recognize and retain as a reference the key points in each chapter. It is important to grasp the concepts in each chapter as you go along because each succeeding chapter, to some extent, builds upon the concepts and principles of the preceding chapter(s).

CONCEPTS AND CONCLUSIONS

1. Monocotyledonous (grasslike) and dicotyledonous (broadleaf) weeds have a different aboveground growth form (upright versus branched/spreading) that

affects both their competition with crops and approaches for their management.

2. A preventive approach to weeds calls for a mindset geared to the reproductive part: the seeds of annuals and biennials and the seeds and perennating parts of perennials.

3. A weed must be defined in terms that relate it to its ecological heritage, establish it as a biological entity, and recognize its continuing potential to change.

4. Weediness connotes a condition related to numbers.

5. To deal with weeds most effectively, prevention must have a companion role with control; these approaches are the two components of weed management.

REFERENCES

Chandler, J.M. 1980. Assessing losses caused by weeds. In Proceedings of E.C. Stakman Commemorative Symposium, miscellaneous publication no. 7, pp. 234–40. Agricultural Experiments Station, University of Minnesota, St. Paul.

Holm, L.G. 1978. Some characteristics of weed problems in two worlds. Proc. West. Soc. Weed Sci. 31:3–12.

Holt, B.R. 1972. Effect of arrival time on recruitment, mortality, and reproduction in successional plant populations. Ecology 53:668–73.

Winburne, J.N. 1962. A dictionary of agricultural and allied terminology. E. Lansing: Michigan State University Press.

Younger, V.B. 1961. Winter survival of *Digitaria sanguinalis* in subtropical climates. Weeds 9 (4):654–55.

ECOLOGICAL CONCEPTS FOR WEED–CROP RELATIONSHIPS

2

WEED–CROP RELATIONSHIPS

Historical Perspective

Weeds are part of a dynamic system. However, our approach to dealing with them, especially in recent times, has failed to recognize this fact adequately. This failure is largely a consequence of rapid advances in herbicide technology. Historically, the need to deal with weeds has been an important factor in farm machinery development and use. The first such machine, the plow, was recognized as an effective implement for interrupting growth or destroying weeds by cutting them off and turning them under.

The design of most tillage equipment that followed the plow took weeds into account. Some, such as the field cultivator, the rotary hoe, and the row cultivator, were designed specifically for weed control. The primary reason for planting crops such as cotton, corn, and soybeans in rows was so that machines could be used to remove weeds during the growing season. The choice of what crop to plant and in what sequence in the field was influenced by the need for weed control during the production of that crop and the crops to follow. Perennial forage crops grown for hay, especially alfalfa, were used to check some problem weeds. In fact, the long-standing practice of rotating crops itself was an important way to minimize losses from weeds prior to the modern herbicide era.

The discovery of 2,4–D as an effective herbicide to selectively control many broadleaf weeds in grain crops ushered in the modern era of weed control.[1] The discovery and development of additional selective herbicides progressed rapidly, and there are now well over one hundred. Prior to this widespread availability of herbicides, prevention was involved in many of the practices used to deal with weeds. The availability of a herbicide to selectively remove nearly any weed from any crop has reduced the pressure to gear tillage and crop choice, crop sequence, and crop spacing to weed control. Herbicide use served to mask the importance of prevention and the need to understand weed–crop ecological relationships.

Ecological Perspective

A number of events have served to emphasize the need for more and better information about the ecological aspects of weed–crop relationships. The shifts in weed composition that have occurred where weeds were differentially controlled with herbicides is one. Weed problems associated with crop monoculture is another. The weed problems associated with reduced tillage systems is yet another. Multiple cropping and intercropping in themselves require knowledge of ecological concepts. These challenges cannot be satisfactorily met without an understanding of reproduction of weeds, dormancy of reproductive parts, and competition as these phenomena relate to the environment imposed by our production practices. The move to develop such an understanding begins with the system of which weeds are a part.

WEED–CROP ECOLOGY

Definitions

Ecology by definition is concerned with the relationship between organisms and the environment. Understanding the relationship between structure (growth form, species makeup, and other growth characteristics) and function (role in the system) is the ultimate goal of a study of any level of a plant system. Understanding the relationship between the weeds associated with a given set of production practices and the function of that ecosystem is the goal of *weed–crop ecology*.

The weed–crop relationships are depicted schematically in Figure 2–1. This schematic representation shows that there are four key components: (1) the weed,

---

[1]The common names of herbicides accepted by the Terminology Committee of the Weed Science Society of America are used in this text. A list of accepted common names and their chemical names are included as Table 2 in the Appendix.

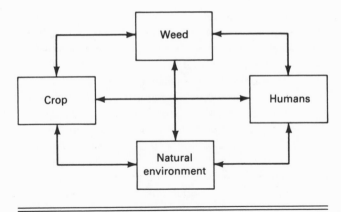

FIGURE 2–1. Weed–crop ecosystem. Each part has a potential impact on all other parts.

(2) the crop, (3) the natural environment, and (4) human beings. Our more traditional viewpoint and approach have been to focus mainly on the weed and the crop in this four-part system. In this chapter and those that follow, we will see that weeds also influence the environment. Thus, the four components create a dynamic system called the *weed–crop ecosystem*.

Hierarchy of biosystems.   Developing weed science around the ecosystem presented schematically in Figure 2–1 logically necessitates its being founded upon ecological concepts and principles. In ecological terms, there is a hierarchy of biosystems that begins at the lowest level with genetic systems and ends with the largest systems, ecosystems. These systems, composed of both biotic and abiotic components, are shown in Figure 2–2. Our primary concern in weed–crop

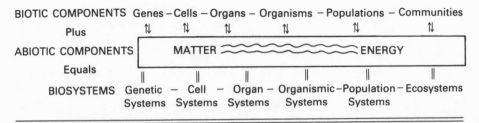

FIGURE 2–2. Levels of organization spectrum.
Source: Odum, 1971. From Fundamentals of ecology, 3rd ed., by Eugene P. Odum. Copyright © 1971 by W.B. Saunders Co. Copyright 1953 and 1959 by W.B. Saunders Co. Reprinted by permission of Holt, Rinehart & Winston, CBS College Publishing.

ecology, as with ecology in general, is species (organisms), populations, communities, and their corresponding systems in this spectrum of levels of organization. Note the two-way relationship between the biotic and abiotic components. This two-way relationship serves as a reminder that the biosystem is a product of the interactions of these two components. Note also that one level is not independent of another. No sharp line can be drawn separating them. In terms of weed science, this fact simply recognizes that an individual weed cannot survive—at least not for long—independent of its population anymore than a population can survive without the individual as the means for the production of seed or other reproductive parts. However, each level has unique characteristics that hold significance for weed science. Therefore, it is important to examine some of the characteristics of individual organisms, populations, and communities.

Weed's-Eye View

To understand the weed–crop ecological relationships discussed, it is helpful to have a weed's eye view—that is, to see the several factors to be discussed from the perspective of the weed. How does a weed view intensive versus minimum tillage, corn versus soybeans, and Williams soybeans versus Amsoy soybeans, for example? Only through an awareness of the weed's-eye view can we fully appreciate the extreme heterogeneity of the environment and of the individual plant growth form interacting with that environment.

Environmental heterogeneity.   The environment where we are apt to find a particular weed is indeed extremely heterogeneous when viewed by the plant growing in it. The diversity extends both laterally and vertically. This concept may run counter to our initial view of the environment; for example, an environment provided for cotton and weeds in a newly planted cotton field. After all, the field was uniformly tilled and the fertilizer used applied as uniformly as possible. Depending upon the size of the field, each hectare received the same amount of rainfall as each neighboring hectare. Thus, from our view, there is environmental uniformity in the lateral dimension.

The individual cotton seed or seedling or weed seed or seedling sees quite a different picture. On a microscale level, minor differences in elevation across the field create differences in temperature and in wetness and dryness, depending upon the direction of slope. The final tillage operation itself creates a series of ridges and furrows that are deep valleys and hills to a weed seed. The relatively small ridges, 7.5 cm, shown for a newly planted wheat field in Figure 2–3 are fairly

FIGURE 2–3. Relatively small ridges in a newly planted wheat field.

FIGURE 2–4. Large ridges in a ridge-planted cotton field.

representative of millions of hectares of crops. Figure 2–4, showing a ridge of about 25 cm for cotton, indicates an extreme, but one nonetheless used for many hectares of cotton and some other field and vegetable crops. A height difference between the top of a ridge and the bottom of a furrow of only 5 cm represents a height factor of 250 to 1 for our smallest weed seeds. Thus, even though the growth factors of water and nutrients the plant must get from the soil may be relatively evenly distributed laterally, the conditions under which they are presented to the germinating seed and developing seedling may vary greatly.

In the vertical dimension, there may be diversity in both the growth factors and the conditions under which they are available to the plant. In the soil, water and nutrients typically are unevenly distributed throughout the soil profile, at least on the scale pertinent to a germinating weed seed. These differences are further influenced by microsite differences in other environmental conditions, such as temperature.

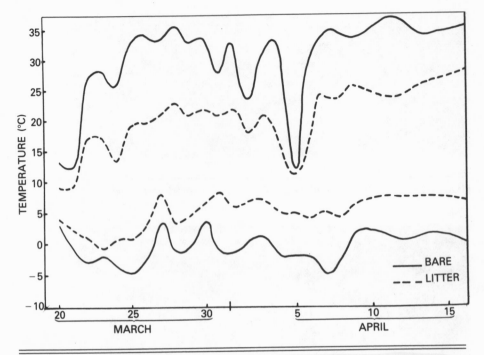

FIGURE 2–5. Influence of soil cover (litter) on maximum and minimum soil temperatures at the soil surface.
Source: Evans and Young, 1970. Reproduced with permission of the Weed Science Society of America.

Studies by Evans and Young (1970) on medusahead *(Taeniatherum asperum)* ecology suggest the magnitude of differences at the weed seed site. In gross terms, the temperature range at the surface of bare soil was about twice that of soil with litter (plant residue) on it (Figure 2–5). In a more general study of plant residue effects on environmental conditions, Van Doren and Allmaras (1978) found measurable differences in temperature for as little as 20% cover of soil with residue. Thus, there is at least circumstantial evidence suggesting that weed seeds at the soil surface under a disked-down corn stalk or other plant residue are exposed to quite a temperature difference from neighboring weed seeds germinating at or just beneath bare soil.

The moisture environment may also be influenced by litter, as shown in Figure

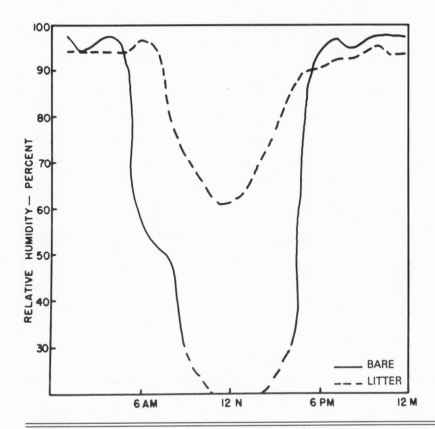

FIGURE 2–6. Influence of soil cover on relative humidity at 0 to 3 cm above the soil surface. Daily patterns are the average of readings in March and April 1969. Values below 30% are extrapolated.

Source: Evans and Young, 1970. Reproduced with permission of the Weed Science Society of America.

2–6. Even at midday, the relative humidity did not fall below 60% where there was plant litter, whereas it was below this level for much of the daylight period over bare soil. As we shall see later, because seeds of many weeds germinate at or slightly below the soil surface, such minor temperature and moisture differences may well have a significant effect on germination.

Plants obtain light and carbon dioxide (CO_2) through their aboveground portion. Here, too, from the developing plants' perspective, considerable variation may exist, depending upon the amount and type of vegetation present. Representa-

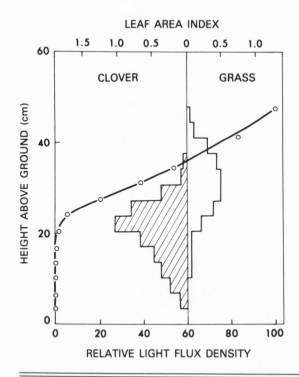

FIGURE 2–7. Light extinction with height in a mixed clover–grass sward.

Source: Trenbath, 1976. Reproduced from Multiple cropping, ASA Special Publication no. 27, 1976, by permission of the American Society of Agronomy, Crop Science Society of America, and Soil Science Society of America.

tive variations of these two factors are shown in Figures 2–7 and 2–8. In Figure 2–7, light intensity drops rapidly with depth in the canopy. Also the *leaf area index* (LAI)—that is, the area of leaf blades relative to the soil surface—shows that clover provides more than twice as much leaf area for light interception as does the grass. Although not as dramatic as light, CO_2 content may vary as much as 15 ppm, depending upon the level within the canopy (Figure 2–8).

Clearly the *abiotic environment* is extremely heterogeneous at the level being sampled by an individual weed seed or seedling. Because the environment is so varied, weeds with quite different requirements may occupy a given area, which helps explain why we usually have a mixture of weeds.

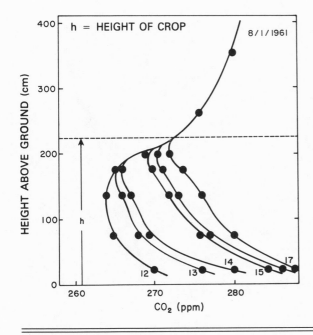

FIGURE 2–8. CO_2 profiles within and above a maize crop for the period 1200–1700 hours.

Source: Wright and Lemon, 1966. Reproduced from Agron. J., vol. 58, 1966, pp.265–68, by permission of the American Society of Agronomy.

Differences in growth form.   Growth form varies considerably from weed species to weed species and from plant to plant within a species. In Figure 2–9, we see that the aboveground portions vary from single-stemmed to multiple-branched and from upright to prostrate to climbing. The form of root growth may be equally as varied, from a single taproot to a network of root fibers (Figure 2–10). These differences in aboveground and belowground growth forms impart different capabilities to the weed to sample the varied abiotic factors of the environment. Differences in the environment and in the individual weed's ability to sample the environment further explain why we usually have a mixture of weeds. That is to say, in almost any weed–crop situation that can be envisioned, there will be differences in environment from the weed's perspective that can be differentially sampled by different individuals or different species of weeds.

A. Upright, branched, broad leaves of lambs-quarters

B. Upright, nonbranched, narrow leaves of giant foxtail

C. Prostrate growth of carpetweed

D. Climbing growth of wild buckwheat

FIGURE 2–9. Different aboveground growth forms of weeds.

A. Taproot of giant ragweed   B. Fibrous roots of crabgrass

FIGURE 2–10. Different belowground growth forms of weeds.

Weed's ecological niche. If we add to the differential sampling ability of individual weeds their effect on environment, we have defined the weed's *ecological niche*. The reader is referred to Odum's *Fundamentals of Ecology* (1971) for a detailed treatment of ecological niche. Here we simply need to recognize that weeds do change the environment. Their germination, growth, and death change moisture, temperature, nutrient, and ultimately organic matter of the soil. That is to say, they are active not passive participants in the weed–crop ecosystem. Thus, removal of a weed by whatever means creates a void in the ecosystem. The void is soon filled by another weed unless the environment of which the niche is a part is itself changed by a change in the production system. Recognition of this ecological principle is fundamental to a management approach to weeds.

At this point, it may be helpful to remind ourselves that the net effect and response is at the individual plant level. A mustard plant, or any other individual weed plant, may differ greatly from a neighboring mustard plant, depending upon microscale differences in the environments available to the two plants. Further, the growth within an individual plant varies with location on the plant. A leaf at the top of a plant has more light available to it than one in a lower portion of the plant. The CO_2 level may well be different for the two leaves. Temperatures can vary within the canopy. These facts have particular significance for weed science in understanding and interpreting results of research on individual species.

We have seen that environments are heterogeneous and that a weed's ability to sample different environments depends upon its growth form, which also varies greatly. For this reason, we commonly have a mixture of weeds. This mixture is not static. It changes in response to imposed changes in the environment. To understand why and how the mixture of weed species changes, it is first necessary to understand how new species arise.

SPECIES

Definitions

A *species* is the natural biological unit, or organism, (Figure 2–2) tied together by the sharing of a common gene pool (Merrell, 1962). In simple terms, *speciation* is the product of natural selection and genetic mutation, resulting in a new gene pool to be shared. This definition tells us *what* happens. To understand *why* it happens, it is necessary to examine the processes in terms of the forces exerted by the environment.

Concept of Limiting Factors

The concept of *limiting factors* is a good place to begin. Odum (1971) points out that organisms are controlled in nature by: (1) the quantity and variability of materials for which there is a minimum requirement and physical factors that are critical, and (2) the limits of tolerance of the organisms themselves to these and other components of the environment. Thus, organisms are controlled by both too little and too much of the factors needed for growth and the conditions under which they are available. The weeds' response to limiting factors is the beginning of speciation. As we have already learned, a plant is an actor in the game of evolution, not just a passive observer. Its very presence modifies the physical environment and it itself changes. These dynamic aspects of a plant's presence serve to lessen the effects of limiting factors. In ecological terms, such lessening of effects is known as *factor compensation*. Compensation for temperature and light or other factors outside the optimum range may involve fixation in new genetic combinations or simply a wide range of growth responses (plasticity).

Allopatric and Sympatric Speciation

Keeping in mind the weed's-eye view of the environment, it can be seen that factor compensation may be operable within a relatively restricted geographic area. Therefore, examination of time and space aspects are especially important to a full understanding of speciation in weeds. Ecology uses the term *sympatry* to describe speciation in a very local situation and *allopatry* to describe that situation where segments of a species—that is, individual plants or groups of plants—are widely separated geographically. (An example of allopatry is the introduction of weeds into North America from other continents.) In time, compensation for conditions of the new environment becomes fixed in the genetic makeup to the point that interbreeding can no longer occur. In a sense, allopatry is speciation in response to influence outside the plant.

Sympatry, by contrast, may be thought of as the result of changes from within. That is, isolation of the gene pool occurs as a result of polyploidy, hybridization, self-fertilization, and asexual reproduction, all of which can occur in a very local situation. Clearing the forests and plowing the prairies provided a rich setting for *interspecific hybridization*—that is, the crossing of two species—by bringing together closely related species previously well isolated. Such natural hybridization is common among weeds, more so than for other groups of plants. Also common among weeds is *introgressive hybridization*, the gradual infiltration of the germ plasm of one species into that of another by hybridization and repeated backcrossing. In both allopatry and sympatry, speciation is the result of interruption in gene movement within the common pool, illustrated in Figure 2–2.

An obvious time difference is implied between allopatry and sympatry. Allopatric speciation is assumed to be a relatively long-term process, whereas sympatry may be a short-term process. For example, duplication of chromosome sets in polyploidy brings about immediate genetic isolation.

It is important to emphasize that weeds have had and continue to have thrust upon them conditions that encourage speciation. They have been moved from continent to continent and from place to place within agricultural regions (allopatric influences). Continual disturbance of the land and everchanging agricultural practices provided repeated opportunities for hybridization and for selection in response to all genetic phenomena (sympatric influences). Thus, we expect a given weed species to be different today from what it was in the past and to be different in the future from what it is today. There is much evidence in the weed research literature to show that this indeed is so.

Ecotypes

Many studies have shown that the same weed species differs from one location to another. *Ecotype* is the term used to describe such locally adapted populations. The presence of ecotypes is well documented for a wide variety of weed species, including johnsongrass *(Sorghum halepense)* (McWhorter, 1971; Burt, 1974; Wedderspoon and Burt, 1974; and McWhorter and Jordan, 1976); Canada thistle *(Circium arvense)* (Hodgson, 1964); common ragweed (Dickerson and Sweet, 1971); yellow nutsedge (Yip, 1978); purslain (Gorske, Rhodes, and Hopen, 1979); annual bluegrass *(Poa annua)* (Warwick and Briggs, 1978); creeping buttercup *(Ranunculus repens)* (Soane and Watkinson, 1979); and medusahead (Young, Evans, and Kay, 1970).

Differences in growth form of ecotypes may be relatively large. In a study by McWhorter (1971) of johnsongrass ecotypes, 55 morphologically distinct ecotypes from Mississippi and from selected other states were grown at Stoneville, Mississippi. The data for growth form in Table 2–1 show about a two-fold range for leaf length (31 to 59 cm), leaf blade width (1.7 to 3.4 cm), width of clumps (99 to 156 cm) and plant height (128 to 212 cm). The range in density of culms is even greater (65 culms to 226 culms per square meter).

Ecotypes may occur within relatively small geographic areas. For example, Burt (1974) found that ecotypes of johnsongrass from northern Maryland had nearly completed flowering (96%) 7 weeks after planting, compared with only 46% flowering of the ecotypes from southeastern Maryland. The linear distance between the two regions is about 100 kilometers and the latitudinal distance is approximately 2 degrees. Data from McWhorter's (1971) study of johnsongrass ecotypes also show large variation. In fact, the comparison in Table 2–2 shows the range in variation for ecotypes from within the state of Mississippi to be larger than the range in these measurements for ecotypes from outside Mississippi for all measurements except culms per square meter.

From these studies, it is not possible to identify the specific processes involved in the development of a particular ecotype. They do provide the basis for some interesting speculation. Local variations support the established ecological principle for species in close association to diverge. Caution is necessary in doing more than simply speculating that this is the explanation in these instances since the studies were not established to test the principle and, of course, the sample size and time are probably too small. Irrespective of the specific mechanism involved, it is significant that differences occurred in a comparatively small geographic area, serving to emphasize the need for care in interpreting results of studies on individual weed species by different researchers in different locations. The researchers may not, in fact, be working on precisely the same species. This possibility is reinforced by a study of population differences in annual bluegrass by Warwick and Briggs (1978). They found two very different types of annual bluegrass in bowling greens in England and in the associated flower beds along the greens. The ecotype in the green was mainly of prostrate growth form. The flower

TABLE 2-1

Average seasonal growth of johnsongrass ecotypes in 1964 and 1965 at Stoneville, Mississippi.

Ecotype Source	Leaf Length (cm)	Leaf Blade Width (cm)	Width of Clumps (cm)	Plant Height (cm)	Culm Density (culms/m^2)
Arkansas	41	2.1	118	154	226
Arizona	37	1.8	123	174	182
California	40	1.9	120	160	114
Georgia	43	1.8	117	146	118
Illinois	37	3.0	133	171	81
Louisiana–BR	39	1.8	155	165	88
Louisiana–H	39	2.5	122	192	101
Missouri–1	47	2.4	140	178	65
Missouri–2	40	2.0	130	170	113
North Carolina	40	1.9	153	160	107
Texas	44	1.9	140	163	140
Washington	39	2.0	119	142	66
Mississippi S1	36	1.7	132	172	112
Mississippi S2	40	3.1	112	162	105
Mississippi S3	46	3.4	152	189	111
Mississippi S4	42	1.9	139	188	100
Mississippi S5	35	1.9	129	170	117
Mississippi S6	31	1.8	116	175	163
Mississippi S7	44	2.0	124	168	111
Mississippi S8	59	2.7	109	212	87
Mississippi S9	42	2.2	119	146	110
Mississippi S10	38	2.1	130	140	123
Mississippi S11	57	2.4	155	177	108
Mississippi S12	46	2.2	121	182	90
Mississippi S13	44	1.9	124	180	96
Mississippi S14	43	1.9	128	185	85
Mississippi S15	48	2.3	123	178	73
Mississippi S16	41	1.9	124	166	96
Mississippi S17	43	1.9	135	170	110
Mississippi S18	41	1.9	156	162	82
Mississippi S19	53	2.3	146	192	114
Mississippi S20	46	2.2	128	177	140
Mississippi S21	40	2.1	126	163	81
Mississippi S22	39	1.9	128	158	104
Mississippi S23	45	2.6	132	141	91
Mississippi S24	42	2.0	99	131	73
Mississippi S25	35	2.0	112	128	151

Source: McWhorter, 1971. Reproduced with permission of the Weed Science Society of America.

TABLE 2-2

Range in measurements of growth characteristics for johnsongrass ecotypes from within and outside Mississippi when grown in Stoneville, Mississippi.

	Range				
Ecotype Source	Leaf Length (cm)	Leaf Width (cm)	Clump Width (cm)	Height (cm)	Culm Density (culms/m²)
Within Mississippi	31–59	1.7–3.4	99–156	128–212	73–165
Outside Mississippi	37–47	1.8–3.0	117–155	142–192	65–226

Source: Adapted from McWhorter, 1971.

bed contained an ecotype that was upright in growth form. The difference was shown to be genetically controlled.

The development of ecotypes has far-reaching implications for weeds and their management or control. As we have seen, ecotypes vary markedly in growth form. For example, johnsongrass ecotypes within Mississippi had approximately a two-fold range in leaf length, leaf width, clump width, height, and culms per unit area. As we shall see in Chapters 6 and 7, these differences can be expected to influence the ability of the particular ecotype to compete for growth factors. Later (Chapter 11), we shall see that these differences influence the extent of herbicide contact and penetration. Finally, although internal biochemistry is not identified as differing in these studies, most likely there are differences as pronounced as those in growth form. Such differences can be expected to influence the total response to specific herbicides. Together, the external and internal differences of ecotypes can be expected to influence the entire range of interrelationships of the ecotype in the weed–crop ecosystem depicted in Figure 2–1.

Ploidy Relationships

The inherent genetic makeup of a species, as expressed by ploidy level (multiple of the basic chromosome number) and by life cycle (annual, biennial, perennial), also influences the extent and rate of natural selection in response to changes in the environment. Mulligan (1960) made a detailed analysis of polyploidy in Canadian weeds that provides genetic background information significant for speciation. The study included 151 common weeds widespread in Canada. As shown in the top graph of Figure 2–11, it was found that there was a difference in the distribution in *diploids*—2 times the basic chromosome number—and *polyploids*—more than 2 times the basic chromosome number—for different habitats.

Diploids were more common to grain fields and polyploids were more common

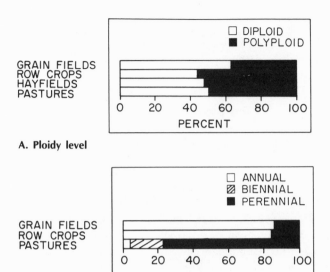

A. Ploidy level

B. Life cycle

FIGURE 2–11. Different ploidy levels and life cycles of weeds for different crops.
Source: Data from Mulligan, 1960.

to row crops, pastures, and hayfields. The predominance of polyploids in hayfields and pastures was explained on the basis that such crops have more perennial than annual weeds, as shown in the bottom graph of Figure 2–1. Nearly 80% of the weeds in pastures are perennials, compared with less than 20% in grain fields and row crops. Polyploidy is more common with perennials than with annual species. Because the same 5 perennial species occurred in grain fields and row crops, the differences observed for these two habitats are presumed to lie with the annual species. The higher incidence of polyploidy in row-crop than in grain-field weeds was ascribed by Mulligan to the selection pressure imposed by different agricultural practices.

In grain fields, selection is presumed to be for weeds with their maximum germination in the spring and with a life cycle and growth habit similar to the grain. Thus, it would be advantageous to be homogeneous for these characteristics. Since diploids are usually more uniform than polyploids, they might be expected at high frequency in grain fields where strong selection pressure for homogeneity occurs. In annual row crops, cultivation provides selection pressure for weeds with variable dormancy, germination periodicity, and photoperiod, thus favoring the less uniform nature of polyploids. Thus, it would appear that the type of agriculture within a given area does influence speciation through the relationship with ploidy. In summary, compensation in growth form and modification in genetic makeup on the part of individual plants within a species in response to alterations in the environment cause new species to arise.

POPULATION

Population, the accumulation of organisms of a single species, is the level of ecological organization around which weed control programs and recommendations are built. Because *density*—that is, the number of plants on a given area—is the attribute of a weed population that figures most prominently in the development of control efforts, some of the ecological concepts associated with it are examined here. However, a population has many characteristics other than density that are unique to it, including age distribution, growth form, adaptiveness, persistence, reproduction fitness, birth and death rates, and dispersion. Thus, an individual weed germinates but does not have a germination rate as does a population, a weed has age but does not have an age ratio, and so forth. Refer to Odum (1971) for a detailed review of the several characteristics unique to a population. The emphasis in this book is on density.

Inherent Variability of Weeds

Before moving to a discussion of density, it is helpful to consider briefly the cross-fertilization heritage of weeds. Some knowledge of this evolutionary background of weeds will contribute to our understanding of the significance of density aspects, particularly survival strategy. The key question is: How do we explain the fact that many weeds survive under a range of environments? The answer lies in their evolutionary background. Most weeds evolved, and continue to do so, under hostile environments. They have had to survive unfavorable conditions imposed by both the natural environment—for example, drought and low temperature—as well as the manipulated environment—for example, disruption from tillage and competition with crops.

The product of these ecological forces is what Baker (1965 and 1974) terms *general-purpose genotypes*. These are genotypes that allow a wide range of growth responses (phenotypic plasticity) from an individual while still maintaining the ability to evolve new forms through genetic recombinations. As discussed later in the chapter, such attributes are particularly important to annual weeds, commonly the early colonizers in ecological succession. Most weeds, especially annuals, are normally self-pollinated with, however, the potential for some cross-pollination. Self-pollination assures the seed production of weeds invading an area even if plants are widely scattered or even if only a single individual is present. It also allows the rapid accumulation of individuals as well suited to that environment as the immigrant parent. Vegetative reproduction in perennial species also accomplishes this purpose. The risk, of course, is the development over time of a very uniform population poorly suited to a different environment. Cross-pollination provides variability in offspring that improves the chances for surviving such changes in the environment.

The ability to cross-pollinate has also contributed to variability in weed species through the crossing of segments of populations introduced at different times and from different sources. The movement of weed seed, coincidental to human migration and to trade, introduced new species and genotypes to new areas over a long period of time. Such movement provided repeated opportunities for introgressive and interspecific hybridization, described earlier.

Density Concepts and Relationships

As previously mentioned, weed density is an important determinant of the need for weed control. Several aspects of population density influence weed–crop ecology. Among them are the survival strategy of weeds, the effects of physical and biological factors on density, the relationship between density levels and carrying capacity, and the effects of agriculture itself.

K– and r–survival strategies. Weeds have two broad strategies with respect to survival. In general terms, one strategy is based on numbers and the other is based on exploitive ability. These strategies are founded on the two parameters r and K that together identify population behavior in response to disturbance. The *parameter r* identifies the potential rate of increase of a population for a given set of environmental conditions and is a measure of the rate at which population will increase where there is no shortage of resources or constraints on population growth. The *parameter K* identifies an upper limit beyond which a population cannot go. This upper limit is determined by available resources and constraints of the population itself. For a species, the r–survival strategy, or *r-strategy*, is one that relies on the production of a large number of seeds (or vegetative reproduction units) and high dispersability. The K–survival strategy, or *K-strategy*, relies upon fewer reproduction units, relatively low dispersability, and strong exploitive ability. Further, in r-strategy species, a larger portion of resources is allocated to seed production.

The r-strategy is representative of many of the annual weeds with which we deal in agriculture. It is an important factor to keep in mind in our efforts to develop a predictive and preventive posture towards such weeds, which are discussed in greater detail in later chapters. That is, the r-strategy comes into play in competitive ability, germination, dormancy, and longevity of weed seeds. The larger-seeded annual weeds and perennial weeds are characteristic of the K-strategy. Such species are usually not first colonizers but enter after there has been some amelioration of the environment.

Of course, many perennials produce seed as well as perennating parts. Such species may exhibit either the r- or the K-strategy for both seed production and the production of perennating parts. For example, in a study of five perennial Compositae, it was found that Canada thistle was the most r-strategic in vegetative reproduction but quite K-strategic in seed production (Bostock and Benton, 1979). Dandelion, on the other hand, was strongly r-strategic in seed production and intermediate in vegetative reproduction. Thus, the strategy for both seed production and vegetative reproduction must be considered in designing control and prevention approaches.

Survival vs. competition.   In considering r- and K-strategies, care must be taken to distinguish survival strategy from competition of weeds towards crops. Otherwise, the r-strategy ascribed to survival of many annual weeds and the K-strategy of many perennial weeds may seem contradictory. It is common knowledge that annual weeds can be very damaging to crop yield, frequently more so than perennials. This is so largely because their r-survival strategy assures a large number of potential individuals on every hectare of a field of a given crop. As we shall see when we examine competition in Chapters 6 and 7, individual weed plants may well be poor competitors with the crop plants under equal conditions. By contrast, many perennial weeds are restricted to patches within a field. The individual plants of such weeds commonly are more competitive for growth factors available to the patch area than individual plants of either the crop or of most annual weeds. For the entire field, however, collective losses from the perennial weed plants may well be much less than collective losses from the annual weed plants.

Physical and biological factors.   The upper limit beyond which density cannot go is determined by both physical and biological factors. Further, the imposition of these factors may be both independent of and dependent upon density of the population. Physical factors such as light, water, and nutrients tend to exert their influence independent of the density of the population. That is, the amount of these factors is outside the control of the population itself. For example, the amount of light available to the plants in 1 square meter is the same whether there is 1 plant or 100 plants in that area. Biological factors, on the other hand, such as growth form, seed production, and competitive ability are all influenced in their effect by the density of the population. It must be kept in mind, however, that these effects are not mutually exclusive. Although the population cannot govern the amount of a physical factor available to it, it can modify its influence. For example, as we shall see later, stem extension, leaf area, and leaf arrangement

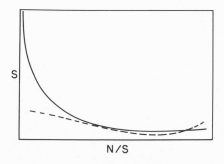

FIGURE 2–12. General density relationship between number of species (S) and number of individuals per species (N/S).

Source: Odum, 1971. From Fundamentals of ecology, 3rd ed., by Eugene P. Odum. Copyright © 1971 by W.B. Saunders Co. Copyright 1953 and 1959 by W.B. Saunders Co. Reprinted by permission of Holt, Rinehart & Winston, CBS College Publishing.

influence a plant's ability to compete for light. Conversely, a physical factor can influence the growth form and other characteristics of the plant.

The broad overall principles of density relationships can be applied to weed–crop situations to help explain observed differences in weed population density for different crops. The general relationship between number of species and their density is shown graphically in Figure 2–12. The solid line is representative of undisturbed plant communities. Such communities have a few species in large numbers and many species in small numbers. The dotted line is representative of communities in disturbed environments. Such communities have a large variety of species with none predominating.

The implication for weed–crop ecology is that we would expect the relationship between species number and individuals per species to be like that represented by the dotted line. That is, tillage imposes a physical stress that can be expected to flatten the relationship curve. Such a flattening, in fact, has happened in Germany as reported by Koch and Hess (1980). On the experimental farms of Hohenheim University, intensive farming is credited for the reduction by more than half in the number of weed species from 1860 to 1980. Since the greatest loss of species occurred prior to 1940, herbicides were not an important factor. Further, in comparing the weed flora in an area in southwest Germany, the number fell from 124 species in 1948–1949 to 61 species in 1975–1978, when cereals were grown.

The density-dependent relationships established in these ecological principles support the following generalizations: (1) The density of the population tends to be controlled by physical factors in low-diversity, physically stressed agroecosystems representative of row-crop agriculture; and (2) biological factors are the controlling influence in higher-diversity agroecosystems, such as permanent pasture.

Density levels and carrying capacity.   In considering density relationships, it is necessary to distinguish between densities that can be maintained (supported over time) and densities that exceed this level as a consequence of a large flush of seed germination, which may be caused by any number of factors. A term commonly used in agriculture to describe the density level that can be maintained over time is *carrying capacity*. Carrying capacity can be exceeded both by us in our agricultural production practices and by the weed populations. Overshooting the carrying capacity is followed by fluctuations before ultimately settling down to a density level that can be maintained. In weed–crop situations, the development of ecotypes and of plasticity is likely to cause weed numbers to stabilize at a somewhat lower level than the carrying capacity.

Overshooting carrying capacity has implications for weeds in still another aspect. There is evidence from limited studies that the mortality rate is high during the seedling period and then constant at a lower rate for the rest of the weed's life cycle. The flush of weed seed germination, especially that associated with row-crop agriculture, provides a large number of individuals from which natural selection can choose those best fitted to the particular set of cultural practices imposed by the agricultural production system.

Effects of agriculture on density.   Although there is a fixed upper limit to density for any given weed, as we have seen, wide fluctuations are common both above and below this limit before the population settles back to this level. The maturity of the agroecosystem and the cultural practices followed in agriculture affect the density relationships, especially the fluctuation above and below the carrying capacity. The most violent fluctuations tend to be associated with the most simple agroecosystems, which are those of row-crop agriculture. In this regard, it should be emphasized that systems of production that have been used for long periods of time, even though the practice itself is unsettling, can nevertheless be assumed to have a stabilizing aspect. For example, the common practice of plowing, used throughout agriculture for many years, although disruptive, can be said to have a stabilizing aspect. The recent move to reduced or minimum tillage represents a departure from this long-used practice. Because of this change, we can anticipate even more drastic fluctuations in our weeds than before.

Individual Plant as a Population

Before leaving a discussion of population, it is helpful to consider Harper's (1977) concept that an individual plant is also a population in a certain sense. An individual plant actually has an age structure in that the first-formed leaves are older than more recently formed leaves, and it can respond to stress usually by altering the number of its parts. Thus, Harper suggests viewing populations as having two structures. One structure is described by the number of individuals (N) that come from original zygotes (genets). The other structure is a unit (n) of the genet—for example, a leaf with its bud, a tiller, a rhizome, and so forth. N and n combined identify the number of modular units and describe behavior of a population occurring through changes in N or n or some combination of the two. These structures have special significance for weed science. Weed numbers (N) are often used in measuring effectiveness of weed control practices. Although N provides a valid measure of herbicide efficacy, it may provide relatively little information about weed competition because it fails to take n into account. Also, as we shall see later, N especially may provide little information about seed production because it fails to identify the number of potential reproductive units (n structure).

COMMUNITY

The *community*, or mixture of weeds, has special significance for weed science because it represents the organizational level at which change in response to agricultural practices most commonly occurs. Further, a community of weeds is the most usual situation faced in agricultural use of land. There are instances of a single weed being the predominant problem in a given crop situation. For example, milkweed in wheat in Missouri at harvest time is often the only weed problem in many fields. However, these instances are exceptions.

The characteristic of a community to change in response to changes in production practices is of special concern to weed science. The foundation in ecological principles and theory for these changes needs to be understood to better predict future weed problems and prepare to deal with them. Two mechanisms can bring about a change in a community of weed species: (1) A change can occur within a species (such as ecotype development, mutation, and so on), and (2) one species can be replaced by another. As we have seen, changes do occur within an individual weed species as a result of the processes of allopatry and sympatry. The growing list of ecotypes for weeds attests to this fact. Nevertheless, the replacement of one species by another is much the more obvious mechanism and probably the more important one in the short run. A primary reason is found in the fact that the practice of agriculture provides repeated opportunities for selection of those species best suited to a particular practice. This opportunity is amplified by the observed common tendencies for populations to overshoot the carrying capacity. The shifts in weeds referred to earlier for corn in response to different herbicides provide an excellent example of species replacement in response to production practices.

Two ecological principles are at work in a mixture of weed species to influence the makeup of the community: (1) the competitive exclusion principle and (2) the factor compensation principle. The *competitive exclusion principle* is the process that expresses the ecological concept of closely related or otherwise similar species to separate ecologically. This process clearly operates essentially to minimize the number of different species within a community. The *factor compensation principle* is exemplified by coexistence of different species.

Coexistence of Different Weed Species

The fact that a single species has not won out in the struggle for adaptation to conditions imposed by particular agricultural practices indicates the importance of coexistence as a type of change. Harper (1977) has identified four mechanisms that may allow two species to persist together: (1) different nutritional requirements, (2) different causes of mortality, (3) differing sensitivity to toxins, and (4) different time demands on growth factors. The most common example of the first mechanism is that of legumes persisting with nonleguminous species because of their different requirements for nitrogen. Selective grazing by livestock of the forage species, leaving ungrazed such weeds as Canada thistle, is an example of coexistence because of different mortality. The differential responses of plants to allelochemicals (plant chemicals produced and introduced into the environment that inhibit other plants), which is discussed in greater depth in Chapter 8, is an example of differing sensitivity to toxins.

Different time demands.   Differences among populations in the time of their demands on environmental factors is much the most common source of coexistence. A long-term crop rotation study established on the University of Missouri campus at Columbia, Missouri, provides an excellent example of coexistence. Timothy *(Phleum pratense)* has been grown continuously for 37 years on one of these plots. In this plot, little barley *(Hordeum pusillum)* has become almost the sole weed species. It appears to be living as a winter annual. Thus, it germinates in the fall after the timothy has ceased active growth, overwinters, then completes its growth and seed production in the spring prior to the early flush of timothy growth.

In effect then, these two species coexist by making their main demands upon moisture, light, and plant nutrients at different times of the year, thus avoiding competition. Such differences in time demands are common in the weed–crop world. This phenomenon has particular implications for a system of control geared to the entire rotation and for preventive approaches because it implies that the weed may originate (from seed or perennating parts) at a different time or in a different crop from the one in which it is a problem.

Edge Effect

Another ecological concept, known as the edge effect, has significance in explaining diversity of weed populations in weed–crop situations. The *edge effect* in ecology is the tendency for greater diversity of species at junctures of communities. The junction zone, or *ecotone*, contains some species common to both adjoining communities. The practice of agriculture in itself presents many edges. In the United States, for example, settlement involved "islands" of farms surrounded by forest or prairie from which the farm was taken. This settlement created two broad types of ecotone: (1) the forest–agricultural use ecotone, and (2) the prairie–agricultural use ecotone. In more recent years, placement of land in the so-called soil bank in the 1950s and removal of much of that same land from the soil bank in the 1970s created ecotones in broad agricultural belts within the United States and even on individual farms. Many additional edge effects can be visualized as the result of the type of farming, including the relationship between farmed land and roadsides, ditchbanks, and so forth. Thus, the edge effect is no doubt a major source of diversity in weed–crop communities, especially in the United States.

WEED–CROP ECOSYSTEM

The *weed–crop ecosystem,* also called the agroecosystem, is the weed–crop community and nonliving environment functioning together. This system is the overall focus of this book, a focus that recognizes we cannot effectively deal with weeds unless we understand their relationship with the crop and the environment, including humans. Further, it recognizes that the weed community is the reflection of the history of crops grown, tillage performed, and the environment. If we are ever to reach the point where the effect of changes in practices on weed populations can be predicted, we must have an understanding of both the currently interacting forces and the effects of past treatments.

Ecological Succession

Ecological succession is an orderly change in species resulting from modification of the physical environment by the community. In nature, it culminates in a stabilized ecosystem dominated by a few species. *Primary succession* is succession that begins on newly exposed rock, bare sand, or lava flow. *Secondary succession* is succession on an area from which a community has been removed. Secondary succession is the type in mind for the discussion that follows because some principles involved in secondary ecological succession provide important information for understanding the historical interactions of the weeds with which we deal.

A common thread in succession, of course, is the replacement of species. It should be emphasized that replacement is the result of action by the community, that is, by the living part of the system. Water, nutrients, and other physical factors of the environment may affect the rate of change and the ultimate balance or climax attained; but it is the living portion that modifies and changes the environment, thus triggering succession. Modification of the environment, which is the driving force for succession, has its foundation in the aspect of the ecological niche concept that dictates that each species has its particular requirements, with no two species being able to occupy exactly the same niche, at least not for long. Thus, in a natural ecosystem, the presence of populations results in new niches being formed that are occupied by different populations, which in turn result in new niches being formed. These same forces are at work in agroecosystems.

A commonly used method for evaluating the modifying effects of the community during succession is the study of abandoned fields. The abandoned wagon roads made by the pioneers as they crossed the Great Plains in the movement west provided an early opportunity for identifying succession in this region of the United States. The pattern observed involved four stages: (1) annual weed stage, (2) short-lived grass stage, (3) early perennial grass stage, and (4) climax grass stage. Although the species differ with geography, the pattern holds everywhere in the Great Plains. The species common to the four stages for Oklahoma and southern Kansas are shown in Table 2–3.

Dominants.   Dominance by a few species is a common characteristic of plant communities. Species that strongly affect the environment of all other species are termed *dominants*. For weeds, of the hundreds that might be present in a weed–crop situation, relatively few occur; and of these, a very few species are usually dominant in a given crop situation.

One of the established principles relating to removal of a dominant has special implications for weed ecology: Removal of a dominant is more disruptive of the environment than is removal of a nondominant. By intent, weed control focuses on the dominants in view of their overriding influence on crop yields. Thus, control in

TABLE 2-3

Dominant species for each of the four stages of plant succession in old fields in central Oklahoma.

Stage 1 Pioneer Weed (2-5 years)	Stage 2 Annual Grass (3-10 years)	Stage 3 Perennial Bunch Grass (10-20 years or more)	Stage 4 True Prairie
Common sunflower *(Helianthus annuus)* Western ragweed *(Conyza* *canadensis)* Lambsquarters Johnsongrass Crabgrass Plus several others	Triple-awned grass *(Aristida* *oligantha)*	Little bluestem *(Andropogon* *scoparius)*	Little bluestem Big bluestem *(Andropogon* *gerardi)* Switchgrass *(Panicum* *virgatum)* Indiangrass *(Sorghastrum* *nutans)*

itself creates a diversity of environments to be filled by other weeds unless it is filled by a crop. Any time effective control of a dominant weed is realized, we should be alert to the probability of its being replaced.

Biomes. The thrust, or function, of succession from the pioneer stage on is to try to achieve stability. If succession goes to completion, the vegetation present, known as the *climate climax*, will be representative of broad climate zones. These broad, worldwide areas, known as *biomes*, are shown in Figure 2–13. The names in the key signify the dominant species and general characteristics for the climax and represent the end towards which succession is reaching in each broad area. Within each of these large areas, there are climaxes called *edaphic climaxes* that are modified by local conditions (soil type, nutrient availability). Note that annual weeds are the first stage in succession for all of the climatic and edaphic climaxes. These annuals are r-strategy species that rely upon large numbers and high dispersibility for survival. In this regard, it is significant for weed science that seeds of such species dominate the reservoir of seeds in the soil, even under permanent pasture or mature agroecosystems.

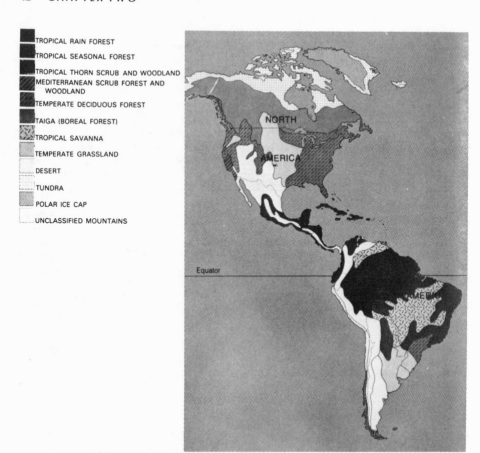

TROPICAL RAIN FOREST
TROPICAL SEASONAL FOREST
TROPICAL THORN SCRUB AND WOODLAND
MEDITERRANEAN SCRUB FOREST AND WOODLAND
TEMPERATE DECIDUOUS FOREST
TAIGA (BOREAL FOREST)
TROPICAL SAVANNA
TEMPERATE GRASSLAND
DESERT
TUNDRA
POLAR ICE CAP
UNCLASSIFIED MOUNTAINS

FIGURE 2–13. Major biomes of the world.

Source: Starr and Taggart, 1981. From Biology, the unity and diversity of life, 2nd ed., by Cecie Starr and Ralph Taggart. © 1981 by Wadsworth, Inc. Reprinted by permission of Wadsworth Publishing Company, Belmont, Calif. 94002.

The striving for stability implies a progressive lessening of the impacts of disturbances. This situation is represented diagrammatically in Figure 2–14 for a two-species community. Competition is shown by a minus (−) sign, neutral effects by a zero (0), and synergism (helpful effects) by a plus (+) sign. The interactions that occur range from those in which each species is hurt (− and −) by association with one another to those in which each is helped (+ and +). Further, disturbance (agriculture) tends to create unstable, competing relationships. The challenge facing weed science in this regard is to do what it can to cause agroecosystems to

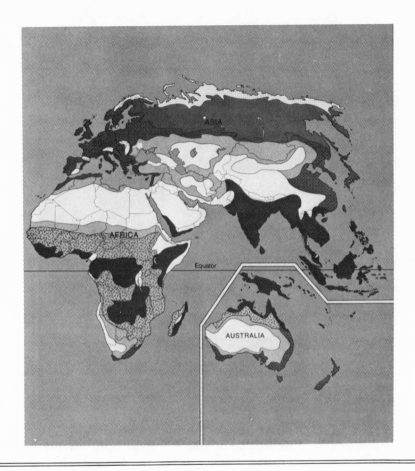

behave more like natural ecosystems—that is, to move the weed–crop relationship in the direction of reduced competition and greater stability. Reduced tillage (facilitated by adequate chemical weed control) is a move in this direction. Weed management—in contrast to weed control—can also be seen to have a stabilizing influence.

Two key phrases with respect to succession have implication for weed science: *orderly change* and *predicted end*. As we learn more about the changes in weed composition associated with particular agricultural practices, it seems reasonable

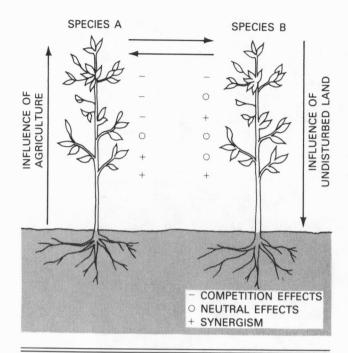

FIGURE 2–14. Diagrammatic representation showing the possible interactions between two species and the general influence of land use on such interactions.

to expect that we can achieve fairly accurate predictions of what our weed problem will be in the future. The tremendous contributions such predictions from weed science can make to agriculture are many. For weed science itself, intelligent predictions are an important first step towards effective preventive weed control.

CONCEPTS AND CONCLUSIONS

1. Weeds exist because there are ecological (biological) niches for them.
2. Weeds, within a species and within a community, change in response to crop production practices.
3. Most problem annual weeds have a survival strategy based upon production of a large number of seeds.
4. Most problem perennial weeds have a survival strategy based upon strong competitive ability.

5. Modern agriculture encourages weed populations to overshoot the carrying capacity of the land.

REFERENCES

Baker, H.G. 1965. Characteristics and modes of origin of weeds. In H.G. Baker and G.L. Stebbins, eds., The genetics of colonizing species, pp. 147–72. New York: Academic Press.

———. 1974. The evolution of weeds. Ann. Rev. Ecol. Syst. 5:1–24.

Bostock, S.J., and R.A. Benton. 1979. The reproduction strategies of five perennial Compositae. J. Ecol. 67 (1):91–107.

Burt, G.W. 1974. Adaptation of johnsongrass. Weed Sci. 22 (1):59–63.

Dickerson, C.T., Jr., and R.D. Sweet. 1971. Common ragweed ecotypes. Weed Sci. 19 (1):64–66.

Evans, R.A., and J.A. Young. 1970. Plant litter and establishment of alien annual weed species in rangeland communities. Weed Sci. 18 (6):697–703.

Gorske, S.F., A.M. Rhodes, and H.J. Hopen. 1979. A numerical taxonomic study of Portulaca oleracea. Weed Sci. 27 (1):96–102.

Harper, J.L. 1977. Population biology of plants. New York: Academic Press.

Hodgson, J.M. 1964. Variations in ecotypes of Canada thistle. Weeds 12 (3):167–71.

Koch, W., and M. Hess. 1980. Weeds in wheat. In Wheat, technical monograph, pp. 33–40. Basle, Switzerland: CIBA-GEIGY.

McWhorter, C.G. 1971. Growth and development of johnsongrass ecotypes. Weed Sci. 19 (2):141–47.

———, and T.N. Jordan. 1976. Comparative morphological development of six johnsongrass ecotypes. Weed Sci. 24 (3):270–75.

Merrell, D.J. 1962. Evolution and genetics. New York: Holt, Rinehart and Winston.

Mulligan, G.A. 1960. Polyploidy in Canadian weeds. Can. J. Gen. Cyt. 2 (2):150–61.

Odum, E.P. 1971. Fundamentals of ecology, 3rd ed. Philadelphia: Saunders.

Soane, I.D., and G.R. Watkinson. 1979. Clonal variation in populations of Ranunculus repens. New Phyto. 82 (2):557–73.

Starr, C., and R. Taggart. 1981. Biology, the unity and diversity of life, 2nd ed. Belmont, Calif.: Wadsworth.

Trenbath, R.R. 1976. Plant interactions in mixed crop communities. In Multiple cropping, ASA special publication no. 27, pp. 129–69. Madison, Wis.: American Society of Agronomy, Crop Science Society of America, and Soil Science Society of America.

Van Doren, D.M., and R.R. Allmaras. 1978. Crop residue management systems. In Effect of residue management practices on the soil, physical environment, microclimate, and plant growth, ASA special publication no. 31, pp. 49–83.

Madison, Wis.: American Society of Agronomy, Crop Science Society of America, and Soil Science Society of America.

Warwick, S.I., and D. Briggs. 1978. The genecology of lawn weeds, 1. Population differentiation in *Poa annua* in a mosaic environment of bowling green lawns and flower beds. New Phyto. 81 (3):711–23.

Watson, A.K., and M.G. Sampson. 1982. Weed biology and control: a laboratory manual. Ste-Anne-de-Bellevue, Quebec: McGill University Press.

Wedderspoon, I.M., and G.W. Burt. 1974. Growth and development of three johnsongrass selections. Weed Sci. 22 (4):319–22.

Wright, J.L., and E.R. Lemon. 1966. Photosynthesis under field conditions, IX. Vertical distribution of photosynthesis within a corn canopy. Agron. J. 58:265–68.

Yip, C.P. 1978. Yellow nutsedge ecotypes, their characteristics and responses to environment and herbicides. Diss. Abstr. Int. B 39 (4):1562–63.

Young, J.A., R.A. Evans, and B.L. Kay. 1970. Phenology of reproduction of medusahead. Weed Sci. 18 (4):451–54.

REPRODUCTION FROM SEED

3

The weed seed, especially of annual species, holds the key to success for both a control and a prevention approach to weeds. The number of seeds that germinate and survive control efforts largely determines crop loss for a given year. The number of seeds both in the soil (seedbank) and returned to the soil in a new crop determines whether the species will survive to pose a potential threat to future crops. For this reason, as discussed in Chapter 1, it is important to adopt a mindset that views the plant as a vehicle for producing seeds. Only with such a mindset can there be appropriate focus on the seed commensurate with its key role. Its role is larger than simply serving as the vehicle for multiplication, however, important as that role is.

Four additional roles are played by the seed in a weed's life cycle: (1) dispersal, (2) protection during conditions unfavorable for germination and development (dormancy), (3) a temporary source of food for the embryo, and (4) a source for transfer of new genetic combinations. All five roles come into play in the natural selection of individuals best suited to specific conditions. In the remainder of this chapter, we examine multiplication, dispersal, and longevity. Dormancy and its particular effect on longevity are examined in Chapter 5.

WEED SEED CHARACTERISTICS

The seed is an interesting package indeed. By definition, a *seed* is a fertilized, mature ovule having an embryonic plant, stored food material (rarely missing), and a protective coat or coats. Thus, it contains all that is necessary to transmit the genetic material provided by the parents and sustain, at least temporarily, the new seedling that carries this genetic information.

External Characteristics

The seed varies tremendously in its external characteristics, as can be seen in Figures 1 through 30 in the appendix at the end of the chapter. It may vary in size from a 10 kg coconut to a seed of false pimpernell (*Lindernia* spp.) so small that approximately 300 million are required to weigh 1 kg. Its shape may vary from round to trapezoidal and from spherical to flat. It comes in all colors of the rainbow. Its surface may be smooth, rough, coated with mucilage, or covered with a variety of appendages important to widespread dispersal.

Internal Characteristics

Internal characteristics of seeds are equally variable. Differences include embryo characteristics, quantity of food reserve stored, and chemical composition. One obvious difference in embryo characteristic is in the number of cotyledons. Monocot embryos in the seed have one cotyledon, and dicot embryos, two cotyledons. The quantity of stored food in a coconut may be a billion times greater than that in an orchid seed. Seeds of corn are high in starch, and soybean and cotton seeds are high in protein and in oil.

Seed Numbers

Weeds vary greatly in their potential seed production capacity. Table 3–1 shows the relative potential seed production capacity per plant and per gram for a number of common weeds. The actual production per plant will vary greatly from the potential indicated depending upon environmental conditions under which the plant is grown. For example, seed production in the poppy (Papaver Rhoeas) varied from 1 capsule containing only 4 seeds up to 400 capsules, each containing 2000 seeds (Bleasdale, 1960). The significance of the figures in Table 3–1 lies in showing the large production *potential* of many of our weed species. For many species, a single plant has the potential to produce a competitive infestation if all the seeds are evenly distributed over an area and all germinated in a given season.

On a population basis, weeds have the ability in the production of seed to compensate greatly for loss in numbers. For example, it was observed with

TABLE 3-1

Seed production capacities of selected weeds.

Common Name	Number of Seeds	
	Per Plant	Per Gram
Barnyardgrass	7,160[1,2]	714
Buckwheat, wild	11,900	143
Charlock	2,700	526
Dock, curly	29,500	714
Dodder, field	16,000[2]	1,299
Kochia	14,600	1,176
Lambsquarters	72,450	1,428
Medic, black	2,350	833
Mullein	223,200	11,111
Mustard, black	13,400[3]	588
Nutsedge, yellow	2,420[1]	5,263
Oat, wild	250[1]	57
Pigweed, redroot	117,400[1]	2,632
Plantain, broadleaf	36,150	5,000
Primrose, evening	118,500	3,030
Purslane	52,300	7,692
Ragweed, common	3,380[1]	253
Sandbur	1,110[1]	148
Shepherdspurse	38,500[1,2]	10,000
Smartweed, Pennsylvania	3,140	278
Spurge, leafy	140[3]	286
Stinkgrass	82,100[1,2]	14,286
Sunflower, common	7,200[1,2]	152
Thistle, Canada	680[1,2]	637

[1] Calculated immature seeds also present.

[2] Many seeds shattered.

[3] Yield of one main stem.

Source: Data from Stevens, 1932.

corncockle *(Agrostemma githoga)* that a 90% reduction in stand reduced the seed production of that population by only 10% (Bleasdale, 1960). Very large seed production potential and the ability to produce some seed even under very adverse conditions are two important difficulties facing a weed prevention approach. The weed numbers may be below the level to compete with the crop but still sufficient to produce enough seed to assure a competing population in subsequent crops. As shown in Figure 3–1, this situation simply reflects the allocation of more of the resources of such plants to production of seed than is true of perennial weed species and expresses the r– and K–survival strategies discussed in Chapter 2. The figure also shows that plants that produce only one seed per carpel (mono-carpy) allocate proportionately more resources to seed production than do those that produce two or more seeds per carpel (polycarpy). A *carpel* is an individual segment of the ovary.

Relative Freedom from Pests

Seeds of most annual weeds apparently have fewer insect and disease pests than seeds of other species. As new colonizers, such species would not have been as exposed to such pests as later, more permanent residents in succession. For these annual species to have insect and disease pests, an alternate host would probably have been necessary. It can be speculated that the yearly occurrence of some of these species in agriculture has provided opportunity for the selection of pests that indeed have such alternate host traits. However, the tendency for pioneer species to have fewer native disease and insect pests suggests that biological control may be more difficult with them than with perennial species. This matter is expanded upon in Chapter 9 when we consider biological control.

Entry of Weed Seeds

The significance of additions to the *seedbank*—that is, the reservoir of viable seeds in the soil—from outside a given site must be understood for the importance of weed seed production and longevity to be fully appreciated. Of concern here is the addition of numbers sufficient to significantly increase the size of the seedbank. Thus, we are not concerned at this point with the spread of weeds from place to place over relatively great distances; this topic is covered in Chapter 11.

In the past, the contamination of crop seed with weed seed was a major source of additions to the seedbank. With the general use of high-quality seed today, this problem is not major, although it may be for selected weed species. For example, eastern black nightshade *(Solanum ptycanthum)* is increasing as a problem in soybeans, in part because the fruit is comparable in shape and size to the soybean seed and therefore cannot easily be separated during seed cleaning. Nevertheless, ample supplies of clean seed are usually available for all crops and thus should not be an important source of addition to the seedbank.

Birds and other animals, water, and wind are vehicles for the movement of weed seeds into an area. Weeds and weed seeds have a number of unique

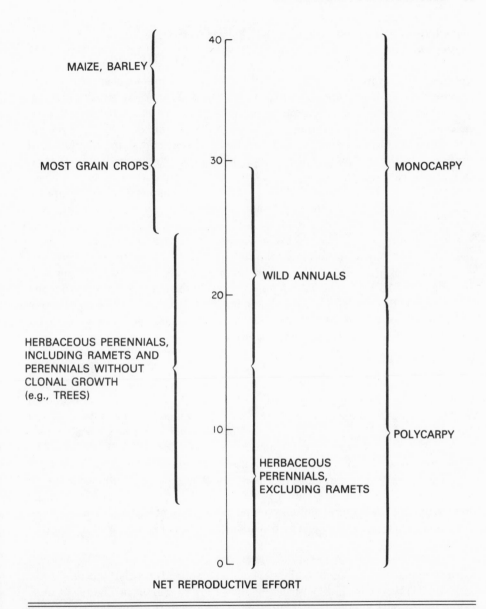

FIGURE 3–1. Proportions of annual net assimilation involved in allocation to reproduction in different groups of flowering plants.

Source: From Ogden, as reported by Harper, 1977. Reproduced courtesy of J.L. Harper, © copyright 1977.

characteristics that aid such movement. Some of these characteristics are shown in Figure 3–2.

Animals.   Many weed fruit or seed readily attach to animals and can, in that way, be moved into a clean area (Figures 3–2C and 3–2D). Many weed seeds can survive passage through the digestive tract of birds and other animals and thus be the source of establishment in new sites. Nevertheless, although such movement may be important in the spread of species from a given source, and, therefore, in reinfestation, it is not an important source of additions to the seedbank. That is, individual, scattered plants may arise, but not in sufficient numbers to be a factor in competition. Thus, wind and water are left as the vehicles that add significant numbers of weed seeds to the seedbank.

Water.   Kelley and Bruns (1975), in studies of irrigation laterals of the Yakima and Columbia rivers in Washington, showed that irrigation water could indeed be a major source of introduction of weed seeds. In three separate years of sampling, they identified 137, 84, and 77 separate species in the irrigation water. The total number of weed seeds found was such that if evenly distributed in average rates of irrigation, it would contribute 94,500, 10,400, and 14,000 seeds per hectare for the three years, respectively. From what we will see about numbers and competition in Chapters 6 and 7, if all the seeds germinated at one time, the resulting weed stand of about 9.5, 1.0, and 1.4 weeds per square meter, respectively, could be competitive, depending upon the weed and the corp. Water from the North Platte River Project was also found to deliver potentially competitive numbers of weed seeds to cropland (Wilson, 1980). On nonirrigated land, movement with runoff water can be visualized as resulting in the concentration of seeds of certain weeds on new sites. For example, many seeds, such as common milkweed in Figure 3–2B, readily float on water. Even though these examples indicate that significant numbers of weed seeds may move into an area with water, these circumstances are rather unusual. Further, these numbers are much less than the numbers already present in most agricultural soils. From the perspective of agriculture as a whole, therefore, influx with water must be considered as a minor source of addition to the seedbank.

Wind.   Some weeds, such as dandelion, have appendages that aid movement with wind. The umbrella-like structure shown for dandelion in Figure 3–2A is called a *pappus*. A pappus is characteristic of seeds of the Compositae family. The pappus of dandelion acts like a parachute, thus allowing it and the attached seed to literally float with the wind. Pappi vary in their efficiency to aid dispersal, depending mainly on their diameter compared to the diameter of the seed. Although such structures clearly can result in individual seeds being moved some distance, the important question in terms of the seedbank for a given area is: How

A. Parachute-like pappus of dandelion seed that floats with the wind

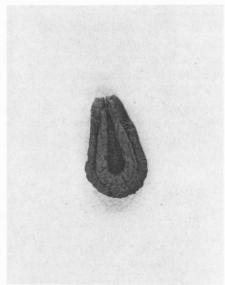

B. Flat and light common milkweed seed that readily floats on water

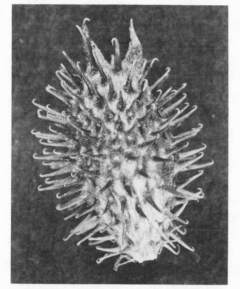

C. Common cocklebur seed with appendages that attach to animals

D. Beggarticks seed with appendages that attach to animals

FIGURE 3–2. Some unique characteristics that aid dispersal of weed seeds.

many seeds enter in this way? Studies, such as the one shown in Figure 3–3, clearly indicate that dispersal falls off rapidly with distance from the source. For the weed shown, tansy ragwort *(Senecio jacobaea)*, 60% of all the seeds were at the base of the plants, and only about 0.4% were beyond 4.6 m. Regardless of wind direction, the preponderance of seeds was close to the source. Where movement was with the wind, the number of seeds moved to about 35 m was approximately 10 per square meter. If all survived to become a part of the viable seedbank, they would represent a significant addition. Beyond this distance, additions would be relatively insignificant.

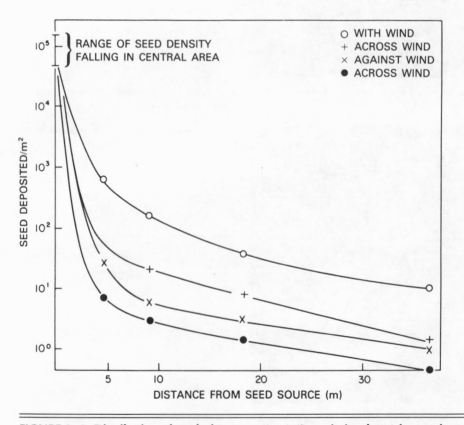

FIGURE 3–3. Distribution of seed of tansy ragwort *(Senecio jacobaea)* from a dense population about 20 m², measured in relation to the direction of the prevailing wind. Note that curves are eye-fitted.

Source: Harper, 1977. Reproduced courtesy of J.L. Harper, © copyright 1977.

Relative importance of seed entry.   In spite of evidence for movement of significant numbers of weed seed by water and by wind, the fact remains that invasion from outside is a relatively minor source of additions to the seedbank under most agricultural conditions. This fact is well illustrated by the vastly different community of weeds in the different treatments in the long-standing crop production treatments in Sanborn Field at Columbia, Missouri. For example, the weeds on the plot that has been in continuous wheat since 1888 are almost exclusively shepherdspurse, pepperweed, and pennycress *(Thlaspi arvense)*, even though plots in other cropping systems only a few meters away are infested with a host of other species. Similarly, the soil in Broadbalk Field at the Rothamsted Station in England contained very different flora for the differences in manure applications on wheat, indicating invasion from neighboring plots was relatively unimportant (Brenchley and Warington, 1930).

Thus, except for cropland immediately adjacent to fence rows, ditch banks, roadways, and similar sources, invasion from outside does not add significant numbers to the seedbank. This factor is very significant for prevention in weed management. It means that efforts can be concentrated on seed production of those weeds occupying the area and on those seeds already present. Present approaches to weed management usually underemphasize the value of prevention, partly because the significance of infestation from outside is overemphasized. This statement, of course, does not mean that such additions from outside are unimportant because they may result in reinfestation and in new species becoming established that if not controlled, could become a problem. As we shall see in the next chapter, outside additions may be particularly significant for perennial species that spread relatively slowly by their vegetative parts.

FACTORS AFFECTING WEED SEED PRODUCTION

At the outset of this section, it is important to emphasize two characteristics common to many annual weeds that further complicate preventive approaches. These characteristics are: (1) the relatively short period from emergence to first production of seed (precocity), and (2) the ability to produce viable seeds even when the flowering part is severed or the parent plant is destroyed before the seeds reach maturity.

Precocity

Many annual weeds produce seed comparatively quickly. Such precociousness, where it occurs, is a major reason these species persist with cultivated plants.

Annual bluegrass, shepherdspurse, and groundsell are examples of weeds with a very short juvenile period. These weeds may produce viable seed in about 6 weeks from the time their seed is planted. Such weeds, where they occur in row-crop agriculture, may produce viable seed before the crop with which they are growing is harvested. Therefore, escaped plants from a weed control or management effort successful in reducing or keeping numbers below a competitive level could contribute significant new additions of seed to the seedbank in the soil.

Common chickweed is an example of many weeds that may produce seed before a perennial crop, such as alfalfa, is harvested. Common chickweed in alfalfa germinates in the fall with a fall seeding or in an established stand. In either case, it flowers in the late winter or early spring and produces seed before the first cutting of alfalfa is harvested. Common ragweed following wheat harvest in central United States is one example of many weeds that produce seed following crop harvest. In Missouri, winter wheat is usually harvested in June, leaving about 4 months of growing season. This time is more than ample for the many precocious weeds, such as ragweed, to produce a seed crop.

Precociousness may also allow a weed to produce seed in spite of management practices that control or prevent seed production of most weeds. Annual bluegrass in golf course turf is a good example. During ideal growing conditions, seedheads can appear within hours after mowing and may develop to the point that some viable seeds are present by the next mowing.

Maturity

As is true with crop seeds, viability of weed seeds increases with maturity. However, with many weeds—for example, wild oats *(Avena fatua)*—even very immature seeds may be viable. The data in Table 3–2 show that by the time the parent plants had begun to head, some seeds were able to produce a new plant even if the plants were cut. Clearly, viability increases with maturity, to the point where in the late milk to early dough stages, more than 50% emergence occurred. In view of the very large seed production potential of many annual weeds, even a rather low viability percentage on destroyed plants could contribute significant additions to the seedbank. It is therefore important in a preventive weed management program to know the effect of maturity on seed viability for the species involved. Whichever practice is used to prevent seed production needs to be timed to precede the stage after which significant numbers of seeds may be produced.

Nutrients and Moisture

It is a common characteristic of many weeds to produce some seeds even under very poor conditions. This characteristic is understandable in view of their

TABLE 3-2

Percent emergence, 2 weeks after planting, of wild oat seedlings from seeds harvested from mowed parent plants.

Stage of Parent Plants When Mowed*	Percent Emergence
Late joint	0.0
Early boot	0.0
Boot	0.0
Early head	0.3
Early milk	18.0
Late milk to early dough	53.7

* Simulated by removing the panicles and storing dry at room temperature until planted in the greenhouse.

Source: Adapted from Anderson and Helgeson, 1958.

evolutionary background. That is, many of them as early colonizers faced circumstances of low nutrient and moisture availability and low organic matter. This situation provided for the selection of individuals that could tolerate such conditions.

We would expect the total yield of weed seeds for a given area to be greater under adequate supplies of nutrients and moisture, much as crop yields respond to such growth factors. Although no discrete data are available to support or reject this supposition, there is circumstantial evidence that weeds respond relatively less than crops. The reduction in corn cockle seed production of only 10% for a stand reduction of 90% referred to earlier is one such piece of evidence. There are data for additional weeds that also show the production of seed *for a given area* to be relatively constant over a wide range of plant densities (Palmblad, 1968; and Harper, 1961). Although most crops also exhibit plasticity of seed production and density, the extent is appreciably less than for the weeds cited. The relevance to moisture and nutrients is simply that the population densities used were so high that some competition for these growth factors could have been expected. For example, in one study (Harper, 1961), there were 200 plants per each 15 cm pot. The relatively shorter life cycles of many annual weeds than the life cycles of crops with which they are growing is another piece of such evidence.

Thus, under conditions often encountered in agriculture, weeds may well obtain enough nutrients and water to assure production of a full seed crop before competition from the crop occurs. Further, because their life cycles are relatively shorter, they may experience fewer instances of moisture stress than the crop may face over its longer growing season.

Environmental differences under which weeds and crops developed provide additional theoretical evidence. Crops have been bred and selected under conditions of more or less adequate nutrient supply and sometimes even under supplemental irrigation. Thus, crops have been purposely selected for the ability to perform best under good conditions. For their part, as we know, weeds, especially the early colonizing annuals, evolved under conditions of inadequate supply of nutrients and moisture. Because their survival strategy is based on numbers, a premium is placed on the ability to perform (produce seed) well under such adverse conditions.

Light

The evolutionary background provides reason to believe that light might have a greater effect on seed production of weeds than of crops. The reasoning is that as early colonizers, such species basically establish themselves in open areas without selection pressure for light. Although there is some work on the effect of shading on the growth of weeds, very little data exist concerning the effect on seed production. What data are available indicate that seed production is very much reduced by shade.

Knake (1972) obtained data on the effects of shading on seed production in connection with a competition study on giant foxtail. Different levels of shading using a plastic shade cloth were initiated when foxtail plants were 30 cm tall (leaves extended). Light shade caused the foxtail to be taller (Figure 3–4A) and to have more tillers, or stems, (Figure 3–4B) at the last measurement date. The latter effect probably kept the plants vegetative longer since those under no shade actually produced more tillers, but tillering occurred earlier in the test period. Shade of 70% or more reduced both height and number of tillers, with 98% shade ultimately being lethal. The effect on numbers of seedheads per plant was relatively greater than on growth (Figure 3–4C compared with 3–4A and 3–4B). Seedhead production was cut about 50% by 60% shade, whereas height was actually increased and stems per plant decreased only about one-third by this level of shading. Under 80% shade, the number of seedheads was only about one-fifth of the unshaded.

Shade also greatly reduced the number of seed in each head and, thus, seed weight, as can be seen in Figure 3–5. Under 80% shade, seed numbers were reduced about 50% and the weight of seed by about 70%. In this study, 98% shade was lethal to the foxtail plant, so, of course, no seed was produced.

To relate these findings under controlled conditions to what might occur under field conditions, light measurements were made in 50 corn fields selected at random in Illinois between July 8 and August 6, 1964. Table 3–3 shows the percent shade that occurred under corn canopies of different populations. Even the

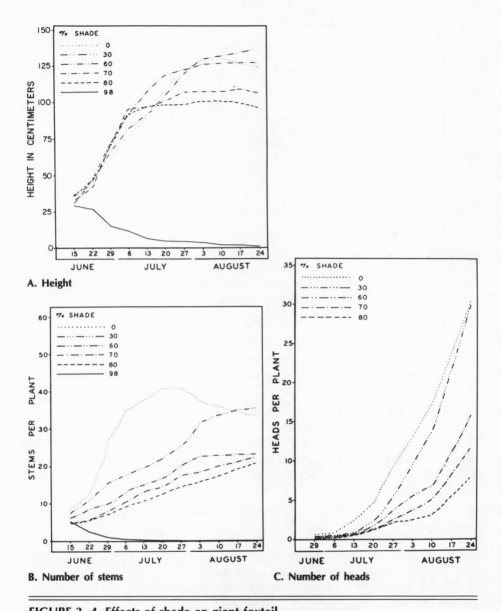

A. Height

B. Number of stems

C. Number of heads

FIGURE 3–4. Effects of shade on giant foxtail.
Source: Knake, 1972. Reproduced with permission of the Weed Science Society of America.

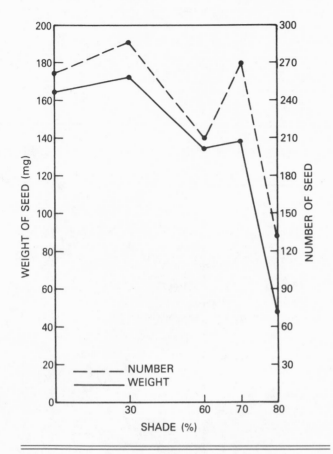

FIGURE 3–5. Effect of shade on seed production of giant foxtail.
Source: Data from Knake, 1972.

lowest population provided shade well above the 80% level and approaching the level found to be lethal to the foxtail plant itself.

Recent work with itchgrass *(Rottboellia exalta)* has shown that this weed is capable of producing seed under relatively dense shade. In corn, which provided 92% shade, itchgrass produced 35 seeds per plant (Fisher and Burrill, 1981). Itchgrass, a native of India, is a weed of warm season crops. Since giant foxtail is apparently a young, and itchgrass an old, species to agriculture, the contrasting response between it and foxtail with respect to shading suggests an interesting speculation. If given crop production and weed control programs are maintained long enough, will species such as foxtail, young in ecological terms, adapt their

TABLE 3-3

Percent shade provided by different stands of corn under field conditions in Illinois between July 8 and August 6, 1964.

Number of Fields	Range in Population between Fields		Population Mean (plants/ha)	Mean Shade (%)
	From	To		
8	50,400	68,000	56,300	97.3
8	44,500	47,700	46,000	96.2
15	40,000	43,700	42,300	95.9
12	35,800	39,000	37,600	95.8
7	30,400	34,300	32,900	92.4

Source: Knake, 1972. Reproduced with permission of the Weed Science Society of America.

seed production to heavy shading? What we have learned about speciation suggests that they could.

SEEDBANK

At any given time, the soil contains viable weed seeds produced in previous years. As we will see later, the number may be very large. The seeds that may, under favorable conditions, germinate and emerge to interfere with our use of the land constitute the seedbank. The seedbank consists of seeds of different ages, some of which are dormant (development arrested), with some being exposed to favorable and some to unfavorable conditions for germination. Seeds several meters deep may be a part of the seedbank because they can be brought to the surface by excavating, by burrowing animals, or by other means. Ordinarily, however, those seeds of the seedbank in the tilled surface soil layer are of primary concern in weed management since they largely determine the number and species of weeds present to interfere with our use of land each year.

Safe Sites

After a weed seed is produced, many things can happen to it to prevent it from becoming a part of the seedbank and a potential source for production of new seeds. The concept of safe site for germination and seedling establishment developed by Harper (1977) can be adapted to seed survival. A *safe site* for seed survival, thus, is one that provides: (1) protection against specific hazards before reaching the soil (predation, harvesting, and so forth), (2) a place for physical residence on the soil surface, (3) protection against effects of predators in the environment after reaching the soil, and (4) conditions unfavorable for germination.

A large part of a weed seed crop can be lost before it ever reaches the soil. While still on the parent plant, there is an ever-present threat from birds, other animals, insects, and disease. Harvesting of the crop may physically remove the weed seeds from the area. With wild oat, for example, it was indicated that only 40 seeds of each 1000 produced in cereal grain actually reached the soil (Sagar and Mortimer, 1976). The remainder were in the straw or in harvested grain.

Once the seed reaches the soil, establishing residence is dependent upon a matchup of seed size and shape with like size and shape of a site on the soil surface. Otherwise, the seed can physically move off the soil with wind or water unless it has a mucilaginous surface, such as that of Mediterranean sage *(Salvia aethiopis)* shown in Figure 3–6. The magnitude of such movement was measured for selected species by Mortimer and reported by Harper (1977). The movement of seeds sown on soil prepared to give different degrees of surface roughness was followed. Seeds

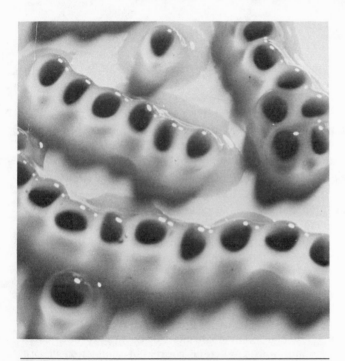

FIGURE 3–6. Mucilage surrounding seeds of Mediterra-nean sage to help hold them in place on the soil surface.
Source: Young and Evans, 1973. Reproduced with permission of the Weed Science Society of America.

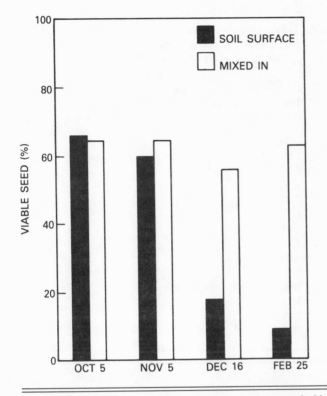

FIGURE 3–7. Viability of wild oat seed greatly extended by mixing in soil.

Source: Data from Sagar and Mortimer, 1976.

of oat-grass *(Arrhenatherum elatius)* moved as far as 37 cm per day. This distance could be significant in dispersal but would be of only minor importance in terms of the seedbank on the macroscale of our interest in agriculture.

Seeds that find a physical place to reside face additional threats of both a physical and biological nature. They may be preyed upon, they may be moved by birds or by burrowing animals, or their viability may be substantially reduced by exposure to the elements. In the latter context, Sagar and Mortimer (1976) cited work by Wilson showing that viability was rapidly lost by wild oat seeds resting on the soil surface. A summary of their data, shown in Figure 3–7, shows that only 10% of the seeds sown in September were still viable the following February where they overwintered on the soil surface. In a related study of a natural infestation, the number of viable seed dropped from 294 per square meter (246 per square yard) on September 3 to 44 per square meter (37 per square yard) on November 29. Other work (Papay and Thompson, 1979; and Chepil, 1946a) has also shown that some protection, such as litter or physical burial, is necessary to avoid marked loss of viability in those seeds that reach the soil.

TABLE 3-4

Average number of viable weed seeds by species in the upper 15.2 cm (6 in.) layer of cultivated soil in England.

Weed Species	Millions of Seeds per Hectare
Scarlet pimpernel	0.20
Parsley-piert	1.09
Mouse-ear cress	0.82
Shepherdspurse	1.73
Lambsquarters	0.27
Fumitory	1.33
Wild chamomile	0.44
Poppy	0.72
Annual bluegrass	16.06
Prostrate knotweed	1.33
Common groundsel	2.96
Common chickweed	3.21
Birdseye speedwell	1.68
Total	32.38

Source: Data from Roberts, 1968.

Thus, sizable losses can occur in the weed seed crop before it has a chance to become a part of the seedbank in the soil. Some of the hazards faced may be exploitable in designing weed management programs to reduce the renewal of the seedbank. Such possibilities are examined in Chapter 15.

Size of the Seedbank

Many studies have shown that the size of a seedbank is very large. Some of the earliest work was done at the Rothamsted Station in England. Table 3–4 shows the millions of seeds per hectare for several species found in the top 15.2 cm (6 in.) layer of soil. The number of seeds indicates the magnitude of the task facing a clean or preventive approach.

Longevity of Weed Seeds in the Seedbank

Longevity of weed seeds in the soil has long been a matter of continuing concern to weed science because of its obvious implication for potential weed numbers in crops. There have been anecdotal reports of weed seeds remaining viable for thousands of years.

Studies initiated by Beal in 1879 and Duvel in 1902 of retention of viability in weed seeds buried in soil in containers provided the first firm data on weed seed longevity. In Beal's study, 3 species of the 23 started still showed some viability after 100 years (Kivilaan and Bandurski, 1981). One, common mullein, had 2% germination, which was the first germination in 80 years. Another, dwarf mallow *(Malva rotundifolia)*, also had 2% germination and was the first in 65 years. The third, moth mullein *(Verbascum blattaria)* had 42% germination, which represented a more or less steady decline over the years. In Duvel's study, more than one-third of 107 species buried showed some viability after 39 years. These studies provide valuable data on potential longevity. Of course, they are not representative of what happens under field conditions because the seeds were somewhat protected from the soil elements and from tillage.

More recent work by Egley and Chandler (1983), in which seeds were buried in plastic screen bags, provides conditions more like those that would be faced by newly arrived seeds to a seedbank. In these studies (Table 3–5) that were initiated in 1972 and 1973, weeds common to the Stoneville, Mississippi, area varied greatly in their retention of viability. Redvine *(Brunnichia cirrhosa)*, chickweed, and barnyardgrass had lost all viability after 5.5 years. At the other extreme, johnsongrass still had nearly 50% viability and spurred anoda *(Anoda cristata)*, velvetleaf, and purple moonflower *(Ipomoea turbinata)* about one-third of their initial viability after 5.5 years. Of course, such data still does not tell us what the situation would be if we were to begin with a population containing both new and old seeds in the seedbank (the situation faced when a preventive weed management program is initiated). Nor does it tell us what the viability would be if the soil were tilled each year in association with crop production. Finally, it does not tell us how many seeds will have *germinated* after specified periods.

Calculated longevity. The drawdown of the seedbank can be mathematically calculated if assumptions are made on germination and seedbank additions. Such calculations provide an indication of the time needed to accomplish a given seedbank reduction under a planned propagule reduction program. Ennis (1977) calculated what the population of weed propagules would be under different assumed levels of germination and seedbank renewal. The age distribution of the seedbank is immaterial to the calculations. The resulting curves (Figure 3–8) show that it would take more than 30 years to deplete the soil of all propagules if 75% of the seeds present germinated each year and as few as 0.5% escaped control and produced new propagules. If, on the other hand, none of the 75% that germinated were allowed to produce new propagules, all of those in the soil would be depleted in 14 years. If it were possible to induce 98% of the propagules to germinate each year and no weeds produced seed, all of the propagules would be eliminated from the soil in a 6-year period.

TABLE 3-5

Mean percentage of original population of weed seeds still viable after burial for up to 5.5 years.

Species	Mean Percent Viability after Burial for Indicated Years			
	0	1.5	3.5	5.5
Spurred anoda	99	89	71	30
Velvetleaf	100	87	65	36
Prickly sida	100	45	21	< 1
Purple moonflower	100	84	65	33
Pitted morning-glory	100	36	23	13
Hemp sesbania	100	77	60	18
Sicklepod	100	13	16	6
Florida beggarweed	88	9	11	5
Common cocklebur	99	27	10	< 1
Redroot pigweed	96	24	2	1
Common purslane	99	21	2	< 1
Common evening primrose	95	36	12	4
Prostrate spurge	77	20	11	3
Redvine	66	5	2	0
Chickweed	100	1	< 1	0
Johnsongrass	86	75	74	48
Goosegrass	97	39	15	4
Large crabgrass	97	48	4	< 1
Texas panicum	89	39	15	5
Barnyardgrass	96	1	< 1	0

Note: Seeds were buried in 1972 and 1973 at depths of 8 cm, 23 cm, and 38 cm.

Source: Adapted from Egley and Chandler, 1983.

When the calculated longevity of Figure 3–8 and actual germination of Table 3–5 are considered together, it can be seen that even if no weeds produce seed, natural loss of viability requires several years to reduce the seedbank of all weeds to the point where it does not pose a threat to crop production. However, they also show that much can be gained by preventing seed production. For some species, such as redvine and barnyardgrass, preventing additions to the seedbank for 2 years would effectively eliminate them as threats to crops. Further, preventing seed production simplifies the weed control task over time by narrowing the weed base. For example, if soil was uniformly infested with the 20 species shown in Table 3–5, only 6 would remain as problems after 5 years if seed production was prevented during that time. Finally, preventing seed production, coupled with the

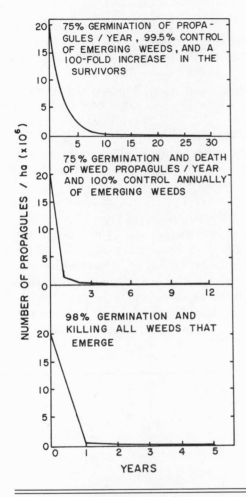

FIGURE 3–8. Calculated time needed to eliminate viable weed seeds from soil under different levels of germination and control.

Source: Ennis, 1977. Reproduced courtesy of University of Tokyo Press.

hastening of seed germination, can very much shorten the time needed to reduce weed numbers to a noncompeting level. Against this background, we examine the influence of tillage in the remainder of this chapter. Hastening germination is considered in Chapter 13.

Effects of tillage. Much evidence exists that tillage hastens depletion of the seedbank. The situation most usually faced is where some tillage occurs each year.

Figure 3–9, which compares reduction of velvetleaf under tillage and no tillage, is indicative of the magnitude of the effect of tillage. In this case, reduction was more than twice as rapid under tillage. Roberts (1970) suggested that the annual reduction from tillage is exponential for a given species and falls within the range of 30% to 60% for most weeds. For some, it is more rapid. Wilson (1978) found the annual rate of reduction of wild oat seeds to be about 80%. Standifer (1979) eliminated all viable barnyardgrass seeds with 2 years of continuous cultivation, which is about a 90% annual rate of reduction.

There is some evidence that the amount (frequency) of tillage in any one year has some effect on rate of reduction of the seedbank. However, differences are less, if they occur, between levels of tillage than between no tillage and tillage. For example, Roberts and Dawkins (1967) found 12.1, 16.5, and 25.7 million viable weeds in soil after 5 years for 4, 2, and 0 cultivations per year. Lueschen and Anderson (1980) found nearly identical reductions for 1 and 2 plowings per year. Less effect for amount of tillage may not be too surprising in view of the fact that many weed seeds require light for germination (one tillage might be enough to meet this need) and many also have a fixed period of maximum germination. These aspects are considered in greater detail in Chapter 5.

An early study (Chepil, 1946a) of weed seed longevity under tillage provided data showing the extent of first-year germination. Weed seeds were planted in three different soil types, then alternately fallowed or cropped to cereals. Tillage

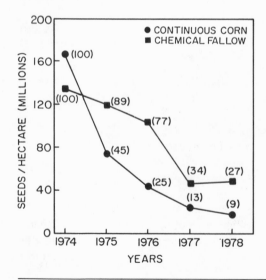

FIGURE 3–9. Reduction of velvetleaf seed in soil under tillage and no tillage with seed production prevented for both conditions. Numbers in parenthesis are number of viable seeds remaining of the population in 1974.
Source: Redrawn from Lueschen and Anderson, 1980.

was done only to a depth of 7.6 cm (3 in.) so as not to bring up other weed seeds. Since the number of viable seeds was known at the outset, emergence each year allowed the accumulated percentage to be calculated. Table 3–6 shows the accumulated emergence and first-year portion at the end of 5 years for the clay soil. There were some differences in germination and longevity between clay and the other two soils, but the results in clay serve to illustrate the depletion relation-

TABLE 3-6

Emergence of weeds from seed planted in a clay soil then alternately fallowed and cropped to cereals.

Weed	Accumulated Percent Emergence at the End of 5 Years[1]	First-Year Emergence as a Percentage of the Total[2]
Falseflax spp.	46.9	100.0
Corn cockle	77.0	100.0
Flatseed falseflax	48.7	100.0
Kochia spp.	26.0	100.0
Smallseed falseflax	17.7	100.0
Western salsify	30.9	100.0
Quackgrass	82.8	99.6
Russian thistle	87.6	99.5
Hare's ear mustard	88.2	99.4
Downy brome	33.4	98.6
Mexican dock	41.6	98.0
Green foxtail	75.5	97.9
Garden orach	66.8	97.6
Cow cockle	62.9	97.4
Indian mustard	35.8	97.4
Broadleaf plantain	28.7	97.2
Prickly lettuce var.	81.2	96.9
European sticktight	27.0	96.8
Canada thistle	70.0	96.4
Foxtail barley	76.0	96.1
Showy milkweed	47.8	94.5
Tumble mustard	8.8	91.8
Halberleaf orach	77.1	87.6
Prickly lettuce	86.0	86.8
Redroot pigweed	44.9	86.5
Stinking clover	82.2	82.2
Dog mustard	51.6	81.9
Tumble pigweed	65.0	78.7
Wild mustard	61.7	78.5

(continued)

TABLE 3-6 continued

Weed	Accumulated Percent Emergence at the End of 5 Years[1]	First-Year Emergence as a Percentage of the Total[2]
Wild oat	98.2	75.8
Prostrate pigweed	96.8	74.0
Beach cocklebur	79.6	73.1
Perennial sowthistle	10.4	72.0
Bladder campion	29.0	71.4
Tickseed spp.	27.0	66.4
Russian pigweed	56.4	66.4
Bindweed spp.	6.5	64.9
Corn spurry	11.1	64.9
Field pennycress	45.2	60.7
Nightflowering catchfly	43.7	60.6
Marshelder spp.	30.4	60.0
Common purslane	6.8	60.0
Wormseed mustard	31.7	55.0
Yellowflower pepperweed	15.8	51.9
Greenflower pepperweed	16.6	50.6
Povertyweed	9.1	47.8
Shepherdspurse	6.0	33.3
Dandelion	7.0	31.2
Evening primrose spp.	11.4	25.6
Lambsquarters	18.5	23.5
Greenweed spp.	11.7	22.6
Flixweed	10.3	9.7
Black medic	53.9	6.0

[1] Total number of seedlings emerged divided by the number of viable seeds planted.

[2] First-year emergence (not shown) divided by 5-year accumulated emergence (shown).

Source: Data from Chepil, 1946a.

ships. The first-year emergence shows that for many species, most of the germination that is going to occur does so by this time under cultivation. In fact, for the 54 species, 30 had 75% of their emergence or more the first year, and 21 had 90% or more. There were 6 species in which 100% of the germination occurred the first year. These data are important to weed management for they suggest that a majority of the seeds of many species may be prevented from becoming a part of the seedbank if given conditions conducive to germination the year following their production.

Thus, there are clearly large differences among species in the survival of their seeds under tillage. However, in all species, tillage hastens depletion of the seedbank. The significance of this fact for weed management is considered in Chapter 15.

Effects of burial depth.   Much of the research on persistence of weed seeds in soil has considered the effect of depth of burial. The most consistent result is that longevity is increased if seed is incorporated rather than left on the surface, although there are some exceptions (Williams, 1978). This effect can be seen for 4 species in Figure 3–10. The most striking difference is between seeds left on the

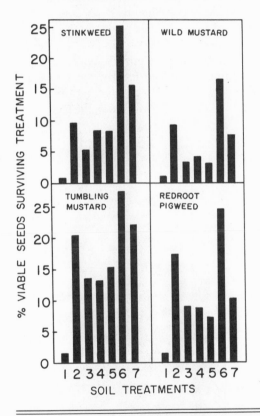

FIGURE 3–10. Effect of tillage on weed seed viability. This effect is shown by survival of seeds of four different weeds after one year of the following treatments: (1) seeds scattered on the surface, no tillage; (2) seeds mixed in the top 6.4 cm, no tillage; (3) seeds mixed in the top 6.4 cm, cultivated 6.4 cm deep 4 times; (4) same as 3 plus packed; (5) same as 3 plus kept continuously moist; (6) seeds mixed in the top 15.2 cm, no tillage; and (7) seeds mixed in the top 15.2 cm, plowed June 1, cultivated 6.4 cm deep 3 times.

Source: After Chepil, 1946b. Reproduced with permission of Agricultural Institute of Canada.

surface (treatment 1) and those mixed into the soil. However, survival was also greater with seeds mixed in the top 15.2 cm (6 in.) than if only mixed in the top 6.3 cm (2.5 in.) (treatment 2 compared with treatment 6). Part of this difference, of course, could be due to conditions in the top 6.3 cm being more favorable for germination. Germination would serve to reduce the number of viable seeds remaining. Other research (Figure 3–11) shows a direct relationship between depth and viability at the end of one year.

However, Egley and Chandler (1983) found that species varied in the effect of burial depth on longevity (see note, Table 3–5). Nine of the 20 species had increased longevity with increased depth of burial at some time during the test period. Depth had no effect on the other 11 species. Note that the shallowest depth used was 8 cm. This depth may have been deep enough to provide a majority of the effects of burial, thus leaving little additional effect to be realized for deeper burial. Clearly, some incorporation of most weed seeds extends their life expectancy in soil. Also, the relationship is likely to approach linearity in the top 15 cm.

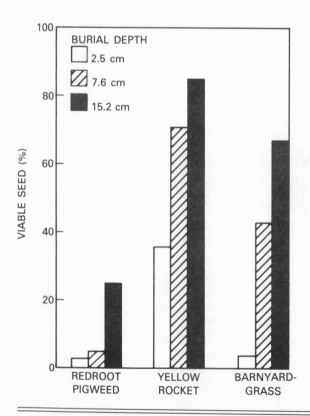

FIGURE 3–11. Retention of viability closely tied to depth of burial in some weed seeds.
Source: Data from Taylorson, 1970.

Recovery and Importance of Current Weed Crop

In addition to knowing how long seeds may remain viable under different tillage or other treatment of the soil, it is important to know something about how quickly the seedbank rebuilds following drawdown and the relative importance of each year's addition to the seedbank in terms of competition for a crop. Cords (1960) found that for foxtail barley *(Hordeum jubatum)*, the major source for reinfestation is the current season's crop. In a more detailed study of blackgrass *(Alopecurus myosuroides)* in winter wheat, Moss (1980) found that 80% to 90% of the weeds in the second year were from seeds produced in the first year where the wheat was *direct-drilled*—that is, where the soil was not plowed or cultivated to bring the previous year's weed seeds to the surface. Earlier work at the Rothamsted Station showed how quickly the seedbank could rebuild following fallowing. Note in Figure 3–12 that the seedbank actually grew more rapidly following fallowing than it was reduced with fallowing.

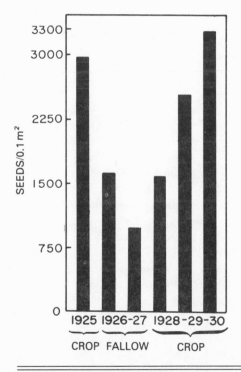

FIGURE 3–12. Quick recovery of weed seed numbers in soil following drawdown from fallowing.

Source: Modified from Brenchley and Warington, 1936. Reprinted courtesy of Blackwell Scientific Publications, Ltd.

In considering the combined implications of weed seed production and persistence in the soil, it is clear that they pose sizable challenges for preventive weed management approaches. However, it appears that programs could be planned based upon current knowledge that would, in a reasonable time, lessen the problem posed by weeds. Some of these possibilities are examined in Chapter 15.

CONCEPTS AND CONCLUSIONS

1. The seed holds the key to success in both weed control and weed prevention.
2. Most problem annual weeds have the capacity to produce a large number of seeds per plant.
3. Most problem annual weeds can adjust seed production per plant to compensate for losses in plant numbers over a relatively wide range.
4. Many annual weeds can produce some seed even under very adverse conditions.
5. Light is the growth factor to which seed production is most sensitive in many weeds; production of seed is commonly retarded and may even be prevented completely by degrees of shading that have much less effect on vegetative growth.
6. Invasion of weed seeds from outside is of only minor importance as a source of additions to the seedbank on a given area.
7. Many weeds, especially annuals, have a relatively short period from emergence to flowering and quickly reach the point of having viable seed.
8. Seeds of many weeds suffer sizable losses in viability if left on the soil surface for extended periods of time.
9. The number of seeds in the seedbank is commonly on the order of several million for the plow layer.
10. The seeds of some weeds may remain viable for many years in the soil, but for many, germination the year following production accounts for a majority of total germination for the life of the seed in the seedbank.
11. Tillage reduces the longevity of weed seeds in soil.
12. For most weed seeds, longevity is extended by incorporation in the soil and the relationship is likely to approach linearity with depth in the top 15 cm.

REFERENCES

Anderson, R.N., and E.A. Helgeson. 1958. Control of wild oats by prevention of normal seed development with sodium 2,2–dichloropropionate. Weeds 6 (3):263–70.

Bleasdale, J.K.A. 1960. Studies on plant competition. In J.L. Harper, ed., The biology of weeds, pp. 133–42. Oxford: Blackwell Scientific.

Brenchley, W.E., and K. Warington. 1930. The weed seed population of arable soil, II. Influence of crop, soil, and methods of cultivation upon the relative abundance of viable seeds. J. Ecol. 21:103–27.

―――――. 1936. The weed seed population of arable soil, III. The reestablishment of weed species after reduction by fallowing. J. Ecol. 24:479–501.

Chepil, W.S. 1946a. Germination of weed seeds, I. Longevity, periodicity of germination, and vitality of seeds in cultivated soil. Sci. Agr. 26:307–46.

―――――. 1946b. Germination of weed seeds, II. The influence of tillage treatments on germination. Sci. Agr. 26:347–57.

Cords, H.P. 1960. Factors affecting the competitive ability of foxtail barley *(Hordeum jubatum)*. Weeds 8 (4):636–44.

Egley, G.H., and J.M. Chandler. 1983. Longevity of weed seeds after 5.5 years in the Stoneville 50-year buried-seed study. Weed Sci. 31 (2):264–70.

Ennis, W.B., Jr. 1977. Integration of weed control technologies. In J.D. Fryer and S. Matsunaka, eds., Integrated control of weeds, pp. 227–42. Tokyo: University of Tokyo Press.

Fisher, H.H., and L.C. Burrill. 1981. The increasing problem of itchgrass *(Rottboellia exaltata* L.f.). Abstract ⅛307. Proc. Annual Meeting of WSSA, Las Vegas, Nevada.

Harper, J.L. 1961. Approaches to the study of plant competition. In F.L. Milthorpe, ed., Mechanisms in biological competition. New York: Academic Press.

―――――. 1977. Population biology of plants. New York: Academic Press.

Kelley, A.D., and V.F. Bruns. 1975. Dissemination of weed seeds by irrigation water. Weed Sci. 23 (6):486–93.

Kivilaan, A., and R.S. Bandurski. 1981. The one-hundred-year period for Dr. Beal's seed viability experiment. Am. J. Bot. 68 (9): 1290–92.

Knake, E.L. 1972. Effect of shade on giant foxtail. Weed Sci. 20 (6):588–92.

Lueschen, W.E., and R.N. Anderson. 1980. Longevity of velvetleaf seeds in soil under agricultural practices. Weed Sci. 28 (3):341–46.

Moss, S.R. 1980. A study of populations of blackgrass *(Alopecurus myosuroides)* in winter wheat, as influenced by seed shed in the previous crop, cultivation system, and straw disposal method. Ann. Appl. Biol. 94 (1);121–26.

Palmblad, I.G. 1968. Competition studies on experimental populations of weeds with emphasis on the regulation of population size. Ecology 49:26–34.

Papay, A.I., and A. Thompson. 1979. Some aspects of the biology of *Cordeus nutans* in New Zealand pastures. In Proc. 7th Asian-Pacific WSS Conference, pp. 343–46. Sydney, Australia.

Roberts, H.A. 1968. The changing population of viable weed seeds in an aerable soil. Weed Res. 8:253–56.

―――――. 1970. Viable weed seeds in cultivated soils. In National Vegetable Research Station Annual Report 1969, pp. 25–38. Wellesbourne, Warwick, England.

―――――, and P.A. Dawkins. 1967. Effect of cultivations on number of viable seeds in soil. Weed Res. 7 (4):290–301.

Sagar, G.R., and A.M. Mortimer. 1976. An approach to the study of the population dynamics of plants with special reference to weeds. Appl. Biol. 1:1–47.

Standifer, L.C. 1979. Some effects of cropping systems on soil weed seed populations. Abstract 160. Proc. 32nd Annual Meeting of SWSS.

✗ Stevens, O.A. 1932. The number and weight of seeds produced by weeds. Am. J. Bot. 19:784–94.

Taylorson, R.B. 1970. Changes in dormancy and viability of weed seeds in soil. Weed Sci. 18 (2):265–69.

Watson, A.K., and M.G. Sampson. 1982. Weeds: Biology and control. Quebec: Department of Plant Science, Macdonald Campus of McGill University.

Williams, E.A. 1978. Germination and longevity of seeds of *Agropyron repens* and *Agrostis gigantea* in soil in relation to different cultivation regimes. Weed Res. 18 (3):129–38.

Wilson, B.J. 1978. The long-term decline of a population of *Avena fatua* with different cultivations associated with spring barley cropping. Weed Res. 18 (1):25–31.

Wilson, R.G., Jr. 1980. Dissemination of weed seeds by surface irrigation in western Nebraska. Weed Sci. 28 (1):87–92.

Young, J.A., and R.A. Evans. 1973. Mucilaginous seed coats. Weed Sci. 21 (1):52–54.

APPENDIX TO CHAPTER 3

Shape, Size, and Surface Characteristics of Various Weed Seeds

Source: Watson and Sampson, 1982. Reproduced with permission of Department of Plant Science, Macdonald Campus of McGill University.

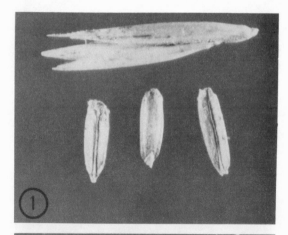

1. Quackgrass (*Agropyron repens* [L.] Beauv.), 4.5X

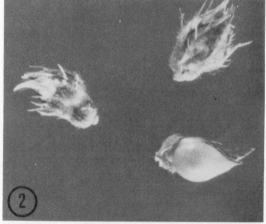

2. Barnyardgrass (*Echinochloa crusgalli* [L.] Beauv.), 7.5X

3. Yellow foxtail (*Setaria glauca* [L.] Beauv.), 7.5X

4. Wild buckwheat (*Polygonum convolvulus* L.), 6.7X

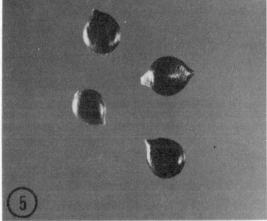

5. Ladysthumb (*Polygonum persicaria* L.), 7.5X

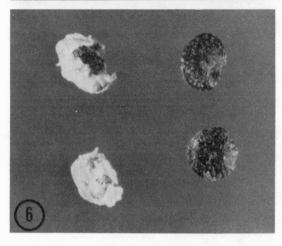

6. Lambsquarters (*Chenopodium album* L.), 11X

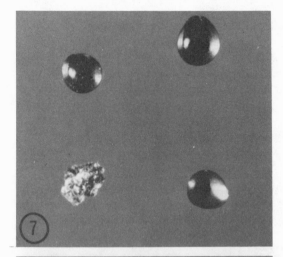

7. Redroot pigweed (*Amaranthus retroflexus* L.), 10X

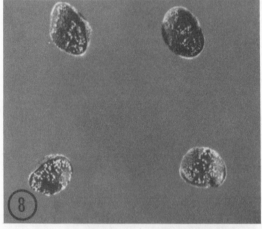

8. Corn spurry (*Spergula arvensis* L.), 11X

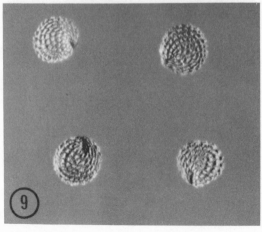

9. Common chickweed (*Stellaria media* [L.] Vill.), 11X

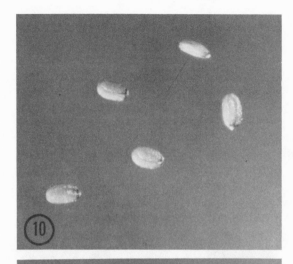

10. Shepherdspurse (*Capsella bursa-pastoris* [L.] Medic.), 10X

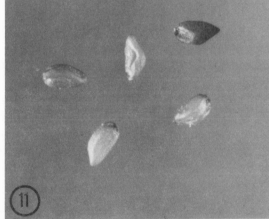

11. Wormseed mustard (*Erysimum cheiranthoides* L.), 9X

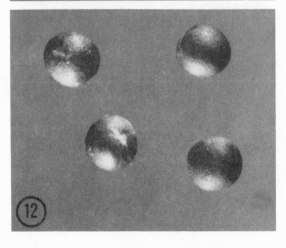

12. Crunchweed (*Sinapis arvensis* L.), 12X

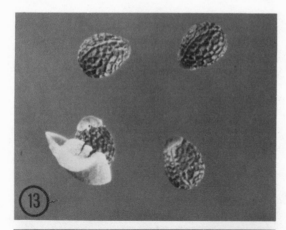

13. Leafy spurge (*Euphorbia esula* L.), 9X

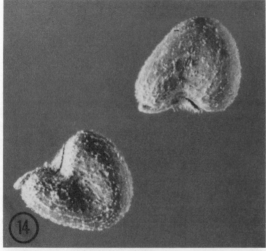

14. Velvetleaf (*Abutilon theophrasti* Medic.), 8X

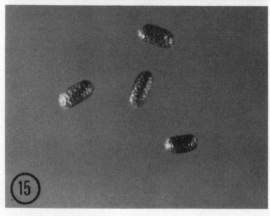

15. St. Johnswort (*Hypericum perforatum* L.), 9X

16. Common milkweed (*Asclepias syriaca* L.), 5.3X

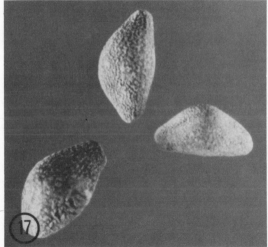

17. Field bindweed (*Convolvulus arvensis* L.), 5X

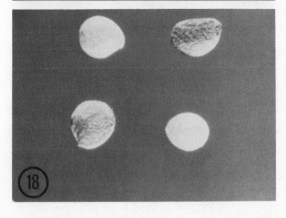

18. Dodder species (*Cuscuta* spp.), 10X

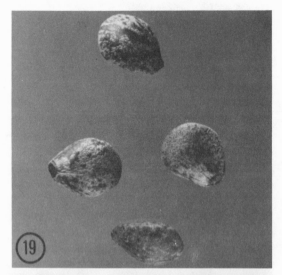

19. Hempnettle (*Galeopsis tetrahit* L.), 7X

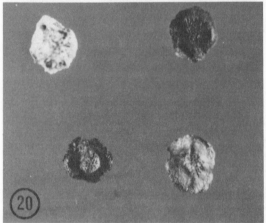

20. Yellow toadflax (*Linaria vulgaris* Mill.), 8X

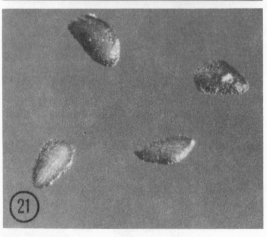

21. Broadleaf plantain (*Plantago major* L.), 9X

22. Spotted knapweed (*Centaurea maculosa* Lam.), 6.7X

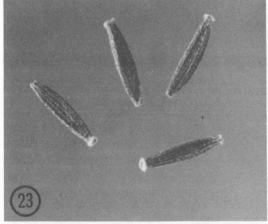

23. Common groundsel (*Senecio vulgaris* L.), 10X

24. Canada goldenrod (*Solidago canadensis* L.), 9X

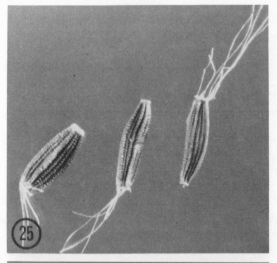

25. Perennial sowthistle (*Sonchus arvensis* L.), 8X

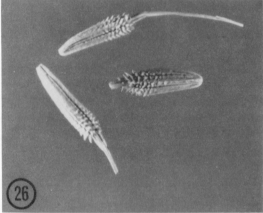

26. Dandelion (*Taraxacum officinale* Weber), 6.7X

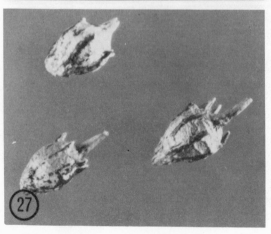

27. Common ragweed (*Ambrosia artemisiifolia* L.), 5.3X

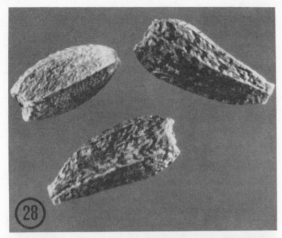

28. Common burdock (*Arctium minus* (Hill) Bernh.), 5X

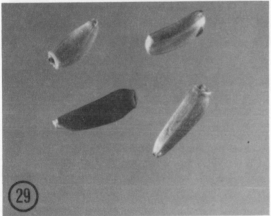

29. Canada thistle (*Cirsium arvense* [L.] Scop.), 6.7X

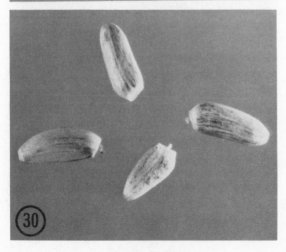

30. Bull thistle (*Cirsium vulgare* [Savi] Ten.), 4.5X

REPRODUCTION FROM VEGETATIVE PARTS

4

The ability of perennial weeds to regenerate from vegetative parts makes them highly competitive and difficult to control. Most annual weeds, with some notable exceptions, are destroyed if the plant is severed at the soil surface. On the other hand, once a herbaceous perennial weed has developed the specialized structure for vegetative regrowth, called the perennating part, it can regenerate, even if severed at or below the soil surface. In fact, severing the aboveground portion may increase the number of new shoots.

The dandelion serves as an extreme example of this phenomenon. As long as it is not disturbed, it does not vegetatively reproduce additional plant units. If, however, it is severed at or below ground level, numerous adventitious buds form at the cut surface from which several new shoots may arise. Even small segments of roots in the soil can reproduce new shoots in this way. Thus, it is important to understand the effects of the natural and human-imposed environment on the production and longevity of perennating parts.

TYPES OF PERENNATING PARTS FOR VEGETATIVE REPRODUCTION

Vegetative reproduction of perennial weeds is achieved through the production of various types of perennating (vegetative) parts. Perennating parts can be produced in both stem and root tissues of perennial weeds. The types produced in stem tissue include bulbs, corms, rhizomes, stolons, and tubers. Some of these reproductive parts and representative weeds possessing them are shown in Figures 4–1 and 4–2. A *bulb* is an underground bud consisting of a short stem axis with fleshy scales (leaves) enclosing a growing point. A *corm* is the swollen base of a stem axis and is distinguished from a bulb by its solid stem structure with distinct nodes and internodes. *Rhizomes* are specialized horizontal stems that grow belowground or just at the soil surface. *Stolons* are similar in habit but are usually aboveground and produce adventitious roots when in contact with soil. A *tuber* is a specialized structure that results from the swelling of the subapical portion of an underground stem. The reproductive function in all of these stem structures is quite easily identified because each structure contains one or more buds.

Rootstock is a type of perennating part that is produced in the root tissue of perennial weeds. It is the general term for roots that have the capability to develop adventitious buds. Rootstock cannot always be distinguished for its reproductive function. Indeed, in many species, such as dandelion, the root *assumes* the reproductive function only following injury. That is, only if a dandelion plant is cut below the surface of the ground will adventitious buds develop at the cut surface, from which new plants develop. In other species, such as leafy spurge shown in

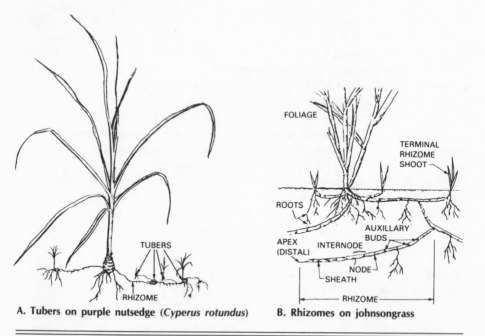

A. Tubers on purple nutsedge (*Cyperus rotundus*)   B. Rhizomes on johnsongrass

FIGURE 4–1. Stem tissue perennating parts.

Source: Part A from Agricultural Research Service, 1970. Reproduced courtesy of USDA; Part B from Beasley, 1970. Reproduced with permission of the Weed Science Society of America.

A. Clump of plants

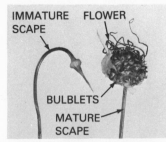

B. Aerial bulblets on a scape

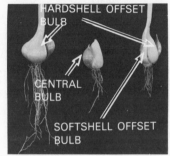

C. Different types of below-ground bulbs

FIGURE 4–2. Stem tissue perennating parts on wild garlic.
Source: Reproduced courtesy of E.J. Peters, USDA, Columbia, Missouri.

Figure 4–3, buds form on rootstocks in the soil and develop to send up new shoots or to extend laterally. Except for roots such as described for dandelion, all reproductive parts shown in Figures 4–1, 4–2, and 4–3 may be considered as being designed for regeneration. Thus, they are readily distinguished from segments of stems or leaves that for some species under proper conditions can form roots and develop into a new plant. Nonetheless, it is well known that many weeds, such as crabgrass and purslane, have the ability to develop adventitious roots at nodes and, thus, become reestablished after the plant is severed at the soil surface. Therefore, vegetative specialization for regeneration must be recognized as a relative rather than an absolute process.

Some perennial weeds utilize more than one type of perennating part for vegetative reproduction. Wild garlic, for example, reproduces from both aerial bulblets and underground bulbs. The bulbs may be central or offset, hardshell or softshell. Bermudagrass has both aboveground and belowground reproductive stems.

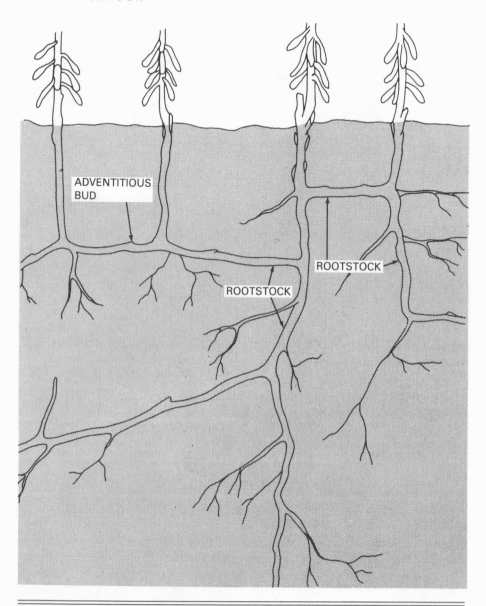

FIGURE 4–3. Root tissue perennating parts (rootstock) on a leafy spurge clone.
Source: Redrawn from Myers et al., 1964. Reproduced with permission of the Weed Science Society of America.

Potential Production Capacity
of Perennial Weeds

A single perennial plant may produce a large number of regeneration units, as can be seen in Table 4–1. For each species, the amount of reproduction is for a single growing season or less. Except for those units moved away by tillage, burrowing animals, or other outside influences, all such units remain close to or physically attached to the parent. Thus, a dense stand capable of fully exploiting resources within the area occupied can soon develop if steps are not taken to prevent it.

Although the production capabilities shown in Table 4–1 are quite remarkable in view of the relatively large size of the units produced and the short time available to produce them, the numbers are still orders of magnitude less than the seed production capacity of some annual species (Table 3–1). Furthermore, lateral spread of even the most aggressive perennial seldom exceeds 3 m (10 ft) or so in a year. Seeds may be moved much greater distances by wind, surface water, birds, and other animals. Remember, the reference here is only to the distance of dispersal, without regard to the likelihood of establishment. Because the regeneration units of perennials remain close to the parent, whereas seeds of annuals may be more widely dispersed, it follows that the perennating parts have relatively more safe sites for reestablishment. Recall from the previous chapter that seeds face many hazards.

TABLE 4-1

Vegetative reproduction capacity reported for some representative perennial weeds.

Species	Extent of Production
Yellow nutsedge	One tuber resulted in 1918 new plants and 6864 tubers in 1 year.
Cattail *(Typha latifolia)*	One plant in 6 months developed a network of rhizomes 3.0 m (10 ft) in diameter.
Johnsongrass	One plant at 14 weeks had 25.9 m (85 ft) of rhizomes.
Quackgrass	One plant in a single season produced more than 200 new rhizome buds.

Source: Nutsedge data from Tumbleson and Kommedahl, 1961; cattail data from Yeo, 1964; johnsongrass data from Anderson, 1977; quackgrass data from Sagar and Mortimer, 1976.

FACTORS AFFECTING PRODUCTION
OF PERENNATING PARTS

An understanding of factors that influence production of perennating, or vegetative reproduction, parts provides useful insights into ways to minimize or prevent crop losses from species having this capability. Age, light, plant density, nutrition, temperature, and growth regulators each have an effect, as do some interactions among these factors. The emphasis here is on the relationship with environmental factors and not on the biochemical or physiological processes themselves. However, we need to be aware of the fact that the production of vegetative reproductive parts involves the storage of carbohydrates. We would then expect factors that affect the production of carbohydrates—that is, factors that affect photosynthesis—to influence the production of these reproductive parts. In this respect, there is little difference between the seed and the vegetative offshoot because both depend, for a time, on food material supplied by the mother plant.

Age

The age at which a new perennial weed plant, either from seed or from a vegetative part, begins to produce vegetative reproductive parts is very important. Until that time, the plant is no different than an annual species in terms of its sensitivity to top growth removal.

Sensitivity to early top growth removal is shown in Table 4–2 for johnsongrass. In this study, plants from seed and rhizomes in the greenhouse were clipped weekly after the aboveground growth attained the height indicated. In only 3 weeks after emergence, plants from seed had produced sufficient storage in rhizomes,

TABLE 4-2

Effect of interval between emergence and top growth removal on survival of johnsongrass seedlings from seed and from rhizomes.

	Dates of Clipping			
Plant Material	May 14 Ht. (in.)	May 21 Ht. (in.)	May 28 Ht. (in.)	July 9 Ht. (in.)
Plants from seed	6	Dead 12	— 6	— 2
Plants from rhizome	3	1 9	Dead 8	— 4

* Plants emerged from seed May 1 and from rhizomes May 2.
Source: Adapted from McWhorter, 1961.

which first appeared 18 days after emergence, for them to survive weekly clippings thereafter. When only 2 weeks old, however, removing the top growth killed the plants. New rhizomes first appeared 21 days after emergence on plants from rhizome sections and removal of top growth 2 and 3 weeks after planting was lethal. If removal was delayed until 3 weeks, these plants survived as they did from seed.

Other studies with johnsongrass reported somewhat different ages when rhizome initiation commenced. Anderson et al. (1960) found that initiation began 4 to 5 weeks after emergence. Keeley and Thullen (1979) found that date of initiation was influenced by the date of planting and varied from 3 weeks to 6 weeks. In curly dock *(Rumex crispus)*, plants were able to regrow from rootstock when clipped after about 40 days of growth (Monaco and Cumbo, 1972). In common milkweed, small seedlings in the 1 to 1 3/4 leaf-pair stage were able to produce new shoots after being clipped (Jeffrey and Robison, 1971). In Canada thistle, seedlings 19 days old with 2 true leaves were able to resprout from mowing (Wilson, 1979). In yellow nutsedge, tuber initiation was found to begin 4 to 6 weeks after emergence (Keeley and Thullen, 1975) or 8 weeks after planting (Tumbleson and Kommedahl, 1961). The variable juvenile period with johnsongrass indicates that the age when vegetative reproduction is initiated in perennials is plastic. Nevertheless, this juvenile period is relatively short for most perennial weeds. Thus, there is a comparatively short time when new plants of most perennial species may be treated as annuals.

Density

To fully understand the effect of density on production of perennating parts, a distinction needs to be made between production on a per plant basis and on a population basis. In terms of behavior as a weed, the number of regenerating units produced per unit of surface area is the critical factor.

The effect of density on the individual plant basis appears to be quite clear-cut. Figure 4–4 shows that for two species with very different types of vegetative reproduction, such reproduction is reduced as density increases. In fact, practically no rhizome production occurred in johnsongrass (Figure 4–4A) under the highest density of 8 plants per pot. If there was only 1 plant per pot, it produced about 10 g of rhizomes. The effect on purple nutsedge tuber production (Figure 4–4B) was somewhat less drastic, but pronounced nonetheless.

When the same two species are examined on the population (area) basis, a very different effect is found (Figure 4–5). For johnsongrass, (Figure 4–5A), the production of rhizomes decreased as density increased, just as it did on a per plant basis. Ogden (1974) observed decreased allocation of dry matter to vegetative reproduction as density increased in *Tussilago farfara*, which agrees with observations on johnsongrass. Just the opposite effect occurred for tubers in purple nutsedge (Figure 4–5B). Nearly twice as many tubers were produced in the pot containing 25 plants as in the pot with only 1 plant. Thus, in johnsongrass and

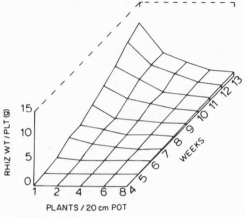

RHIZ WT / PLT (g)

PLANTS / 20 cm POT

A. Weight of rhizomes in johnsongrass

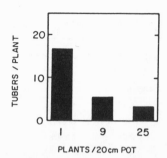

TUBERS / PLANT

PLANTS / 20 cm POT

B. Number of tubers in purple nutsedge 9 weeks after planting

FIGURE 4–4. Effect of intraspecific density on vegetative reproduction per plant.
Source: Part A from Williams and Ingber, 1977; Part B data from Williams et al., 1977. Reproduced with permission of the Weed Science Society of America.

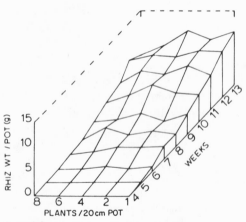

RHIZ WT / POT (g)

PLANTS / 20 cm POT

A. Weight of rhizomes in johnsongrass

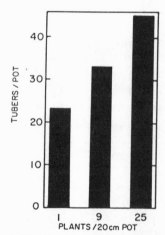

TUBERS / POT

PLANTS / 20 cm POT

B. Number of tubers in purple nutsedge 9 weeks after planting

FIGURE 4–5. Effect of intraspecific density on vegetative reproduction on an area basis.
Source: Part A from Williams and Ingber, 1977; Part B data from Williams et al., 1977. Reproduced with permission of the Weed Science Society of America.

Tussilago farfara, the density–vegetative reproduction relationship follows the general bell-shaped relationship typical of seed production. That is, vegetative reproduction increases as density increases up to a point, after which it decreases with further increases in density. In purple nutsedge, the relationship follows the straight-line density relationship typical of vegetative growth.

Not enough weed species have been studied to indicate the relative extensiveness of these two responses to density. However, there are probably many species in each category. Therefore, the implications for weed management need to be considered. Perennial weeds whose response to density is like that of purple nutsedge—that is, a straight-line relationship between density and numbers of regenerating units produced—can be expected to be somewhat less competitive towards crops than species like johnsongrass that shift towards vegetative growth at high densities. The reason is that the growing plant, not the vegetative reproductive part, is the immediate source of competition. In species such as johnsongrass, competition causes most of the resources to go into the production of roots and shoots to compete with crops. In species like purple nutsedge, some of the resources continue to go into tubers that in themselves do not compete with crops. Another way of looking at it is from the survival strategy perspective. Species like purple nutsedge express an r-strategy by giving priority to the production of regenerating units, while those like johnsongrass express a K-strategy by relying upon competitive ability.

From the weed's perspective, competition from crops can be expected to reduce production of perennating parts, regardless of whether production follows the relationship represented by nutsedge or by johnsongrass. The reason is that an increase in total density under field conditions is a result of the crop's presence. That is, all of the weed's parts in position to resume growth in all likelihood will do so, whether or not the crop is present. When the crop is added, there is, of course, an increase in the combined number of plants occupying the area. Since the weed cannot increase in numbers, the production of vegetative reproduction units will be like that observed on an individual plant basis in Figure 4–4. That is, it is reduced as density increases. Such a response is readily understandable for species like johnsongrass in which production of perennating parts is *decreased* on both an individual plant and on an area basis by an increase in density.

An example will clarify why this response is also true of a species like purple nutsedge, in which tuber production *increases* with an increase in numbers of nutsedge plants. Assume there is a nutsedge infestation comparable to 1 plant per pot in Figure 4–4B and that crop plants are added to make a density comparable to that shown for 9 plants in the figure. The resulting tuber production can be expected to be similar to that shown for 9 plants, a reduction of about two-thirds. Thus, although the general effect of adding a crop is to decrease production of perennating parts, the relative effect is less in species like purple nutsedge. This fact has implications for weed management that are expanded upon later.

Light

Quantity of light.   Because carbohydrate production is dependent upon photo-synthesis, we would expect light quantity to have an important influence on the production of vegetative reproduction parts. Indeed, this is the case, as shown in Figure 4–6. There is a direct and straight-line effect of shading on the production of tubers, in this case yellow nutsedge. With maximum shading, practically no tubers were produced. Because competition for light could be expected under increased density, the results with yellow nutsedge might at first seem to contradict the results for density effects on purple nutsedge presented in the previous section. Actually, they do not. In the case of shading on yellow nutsedge, it may be assumed that the population is constant. The results, therefore, essentially measure effects on a per plant basis. On a per plant basis, the results are similar to those shown for purple nutsedge in Figure 4–4B. The situation of a constant population is more representative of what would be faced under field conditions, although it must be remembered that numbers of plants can change in response to competition. The specific effects of competition are discussed in Chapter 7.

Tuber production in purple nutsedge is also sensitive to shading (Patterson, 1982). Tuber numbers in this species were reduced 96% by 85% shade. Although

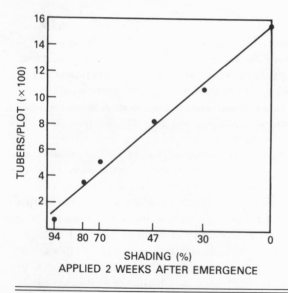

FIGURE 4–6. Relationship between shading and tuber production in yellow nutsedge.

Source: Keeley and Thullen, 1978. Reproduced with permission of the Weed Science Society of America.

precise data are lacking for other species, there is ample circumstantial evidence that light restricts production of vegetative reproductive parts in many species. As already mentioned, the effects of density on rhizome production in johnsongrass and *Tussilago farfara* implicate light as the factor involved. Light is also implicated in the sensitivity of leafy spurge to competition from a crested wheatgrass *(Agropyron cristatum)* and smooth bromegrass *(Bromus inermis)* sod (Morrow, 1979). Although moisture may have been the primary factor, leafy spurge in the sod did not spread during two growing seasons, whereas leafy spurge in plowed soil spread more than 3 m. Finally, the numerous reports of improved control of such perennials as Canada thistle (Derscheid et al., 1961; and Hodgson, 1958), field bindweed *(Convolvulus arvensis)* (Russ and Anderson, 1960; and Derscheid et al., 1970), and leafy spurge (Derscheid et al., 1960), where so-called competitive crops are used in conjunction with tillage and herbicides, implicate light quantity since this factor is the most logical one to be influenced by the competing crops.

Shading may also decrease the size of the perennating part. In purple and yellow nutsedge, for example, 85% shade reduced the average size of tubers 60% and 55%, respectively (Patterson, 1982). These results have implications for management approaches that seek to prevent losses from such species since size influences the depth from which emergence occurs, as we shall see in the next chapter.

Quality of light. Evidence exists that light quality, in addition to quantity, is a factor in production of vegetative reproductive parts. Aleixo and Valio (1976) found that white, red, and blue light inhibited rhizome formation in purple nutsedge, whereas far-red stimulated rhizome formation. As detailed later in Chapter 7, a canopy of leaves tends to filter out the white, red, and blue and allow the far-red to transmit. Therefore, the reducing effect of shading on tuber production could be expected to be offset somewhat by the far-red passing through the canopy to understory nutsedge plants. Far-red enrichment, in part, may account for continued but limited production of tubers under increase in density, discussed in the previous section.

Day length. Day length has also been found to influence tuber production in yellow nutsedge (Jansen, 1971). Tuber formation was found to be inversely related to day length, with maximum production occurring at day lengths from 8 to 10 hours in yellow nutsedge. As the day length increased, tuber formation decreased.

Thus, there is extensive direct and indirect evidence that light has a marked effect on production of perennating parts in perennial weeds. The use of such information to develop effective weed management programs is considered in Chapter 15.

Nutrition

The general effect on crops of added fertility, especially of nitrogen (N), is to encourage vegetative growth rather than the storage of carbohydrate. Thus, we would expect production of perennating parts in weeds to be decreased by added fertility. Results are available from studies of the effects of added nitrogen but not other nutrients.

Figure 4–7 shows that nitrogen does indeed affect production of perennating parts. The reduction from added nitrogen was consistent for different forms of perennating parts represented by the species, even though the studies themselves differed greatly. The studies with yellow nutsedge (Figure 4–7A) were conducted in the greenhouse where nitrogen was controlled at the indicated fractions of Hoaglund's nutrient solution. *Tussilago farfara* (Figure 4–7C) was studied outdoors, but in containers where high or low nitrogen was coincidental to high and low fertility obtained with different quantities of a planting compost medium. The quackgrass studies (Figure 4–7B) were conducted in the field where nitrogen was added to some plots and not to others.

Other results with quackgrass (Seyforth et al., 1978; McIntyre, 1971; and Dexter, 1936) and with johnsongrass (Meyers and Caso, 1976) also show an inverse relationship between nitrogen supply and vegetative reproduction. The importance of this relationship for management of such weeds is based on the fact that rhizome production and shoot growth are alternative options open to the weed. This fact can be demonstrated in yellow nutsedge and johnsongrass. In nutsedge, the basal bulb area from Figure 4–1 is the area from which rhizomes are produced. These rhizomes may differentiate either into tubers or shoots. An adequate or excess supply of nitrogen can provide the amount needed for vegetative growth, thus supporting differentiation into shoots (Garg et al., 1967). A similar situation exists for johnsongrass, where the axillary buds can develop either as rhizomes or as tillers. Adequate nitrogen supported the development of the buds as tillers (Meyers and Caso, 1976).

Since the effect of nitrogen is so consistent, it should be possible to manipulate its supply in order to minimize production of perennating parts. Nitrogen manipulation is discussed in Chapter 15.

Interactions of Factors

Most of the research on the individual factors affecting vegetative reproduction shows the effects to be relative rather than absolute. That is, the degree of effect is modified by another factor or factors. Thus, we see in Figure 4–7A that fewer nutsedge rhizomes differentiated to tubers at 21°C than at higher temperatures under restricted nitrogen, but not under the highest level of the nutrient.

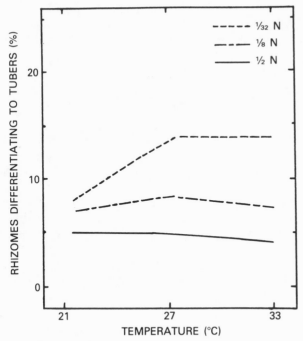

A. Yellow nutsedge

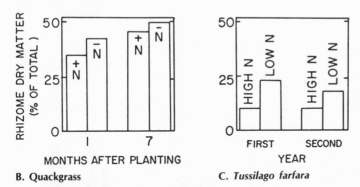

B. Quackgrass   C. *Tussilago farfara*

FIGURE 4–7. Effect of nitrogen (N) level on vegetative reproduction of three perennial weeds.

Source: Part A from Garg et al., 1967; Part B data from Johnson and Dexter, 1939; Part C data from Ogden, 1974. Reproduced with permission of the Weed Science Society of America.

It has also been found that plant growth hormones interact with other factors to affect tuber production in nutsedge (Garg et al., 1967). Figure 4–8 indicates the complexity of these interactions. In yellow nutsedge, rhizomes developing from basal bulbs (Figure 4–1A) may differentiate either to tubers or to shoots. Each of

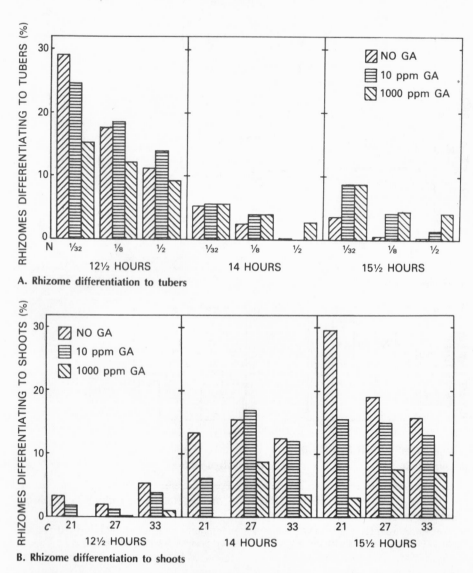

FIGURE 4–8. Interactions among photoperiod (Hrs), nitrogen (N), and gibberellin (GA) on yellow nutsedge development.

Source: Garg et al., 1967. Reproduced with permission of the Weed Science Society of America.

the variables—photoperiod (Hrs), gibberellic acid (GA), nitrogen (N), and temperature (°C)—was influenced in its effect upon rhizome differentiation by its interaction with the other variables. The effect of nitrogen was greatest under the shortest photoperiod; at this same light level, gibberellin had an apparent inhibitory effect. Under the longer day length, gibberellin appeared to be stimulatory. At the shortest photoperiod, there was little effect of temperature on differentiation of rhizomes to shoots. At the longest photoperiod, differentiation was reduced with increases in temperature. Such interactive relationships increase the ways in which the environment may be manipulated to assist in weed management. Such manipulations are considered in Chapter 15. At this point, however, we need to recognize that manipulation of types of growth may offer contradicting results. For example, manipulation to encourage shoot growth, although effective in reducing an infestation the following year, also increases the number of shoots that compete with the current crop.

FACTORS AFFECTING LONGEVITY AND SURVIVAL

The length of life of vegetatively produced reproductive parts is clearly important to control and prevention of loss from perennial species. How much of one year's growth is continued into subsequent years varies greatly among herbaceous perennials. The range varies from plants that flower within a year or two after germination and then die, to those that may not flower for many years after germination, to those that flower over a period of several years, to those that have a single flash of flowering. The range also includes plants that renew their vegetative body every year and sluff the older tissues and plants in which the rhizome persists for many years.

Most of the recent research on longevity and survival deals with rhizomes and tubers of grass or grasslike perennials, rather than with rootstocks common to broadleaf perennials. At least in the United States, this focus is partly explained by the earlier development of herbicides more effective in controlling broadleaf than grass weeds. This development, along with an increase in crop monoculture in some regions, has lessened problems posed by some broadleaf perennial species. The shift to minimum or reduced tillage, begun in the second half of this century and still continuing today, may well change this picture since there is evidence some broadleaf perennial weeds may increase under such practice.

The longevity of reproductive organs for a particular species appears to differ from place to place. For example, Palmer and Sagar (1963) indicate that quackgrass rhizomes may survive for many years in England, while Johnson and Buchholtz (1962) imply that the rhizomes live for only about one year in Wisconsin. Such differences in reports on longevity simply serve to point up the fact that longevity is a relative rather than a discrete matter and another example of plasticity on the part of the plants. Thus, it is not realistic to attempt to identify the precise term of longevity for vegetative reproductive parts. However, the relative longevity is important. In this sense, the longevity of vegetatively reproduced parts for most perennial species that we deal with in weeds is relatively short and much shorter than for most seeds. The purpose here is to identify the overall relationships between the environment and relative persistence. An understanding of the relationship between such factors as temperature, desiccation, and depth of burial may well suggest ways of improving our ability to cope with such weeds.

Depth of Burial

Much evidence verifies a direct relationship between the depth to which reproductive parts are buried in the soil and their retention of viability. Figure 4–9 shows this relationship for three perennial species and for the two types of vegetative reproductive organs, tuber and rhizome. Quackgrass and johnsongrass were compared in a different study from nutsedge, but burial of reproductive parts for all three was in November. Also, burial depths were comparable. Viability of quackgrass and johnsongrass rhizomes was measured the following January and March and that of nutsedge tubers the following May through September. Viability for quackgrass and johnsongrass was the emergence from rhizome sections removed from the soil and germinated in the greenhouse. Viability for nutsedge was emergence in the field up to September 7 plus germination of the remaining tubers removed from the soil on that date and germinated in the greenhouse. For all three, burial below 2.0 cm to 2.5 cm increased viability, although quackgrass was only minimally affected. Quackgrass rhizomes retained much of their viability at all depths, although viability was lower on March 13 for rhizomes buried only 2 cm than if buried more deeply. Johnsongrass rhizomes lost all of their viability over winter except where buried 20 cm. Viability of nutsedge tubers was also increased by burying.

    The duration of viability was also measured. The half-life for tubers buried 20.3 cm was calculated to be 5.8 months, and for 10.2 cm, 4.4 months. Even though these half-life studies indicate that most tubers germinate or lose their viability within one year from when they are produced, enough tubers will survive, especially with deep burial, to repopulate the area rather quickly.

Temperature

The effects of burial depth implicate temperature and moisture as causal factors. Indeed, examination of temperature effects on nutsedge tubers in Figure 4–10A

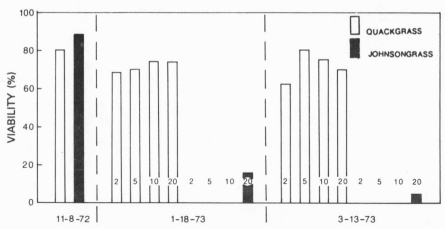

A. Quackgrass and johnsongrass rhizomes buried November 1972

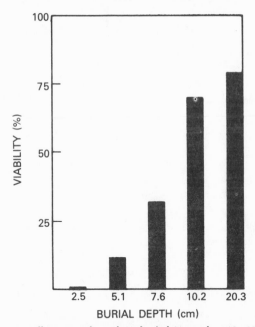

B. Yellow nutsedge tubers buried November 13, 1970

FIGURE 4–9. Effects of depth of burial on viability of vegetative reproductive parts of three perennial weeds.

Source: Part A from Stoller, 1977; Part B data from Stoller and Wax, 1973. Reproduced with permission of the Weed Science Society of America.

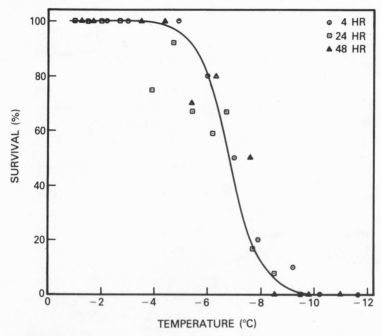

A. Survival of tubers exposed to various temperatures for 4, 24, and 48 hours in the laboratory

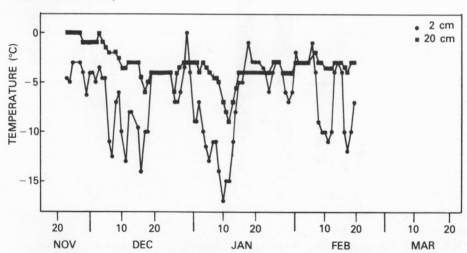

B. Soil temperatures recorded at 2 cm and 20 cm in plots at Urbana, Illinois, during winter 1972–73

FIGURE 4–10. Intolerance of yellow nutsedge tubers to cold temperature.

Source: Stoller, 1977. Reproduced with permission of the Weed Science Society of America.

shows the tubers to be extremely sensitive to low temperatures. At a temperature of −4°C, all of the tubers survived, whereas at a temperature of −10°C, none survived. The soil temperature information in Figure 4–10B indicates that soil temperature at Champaign, Illinois, exceeded that critical minimum several times during the winter of 1972–73 at the 2 cm depth. The lowest soil temperature recorded at 20 cm depth was about −8°C, whereas the lowest temperature at 2 cm was about −18°C. The relatively greater sensitivity of nutsedge tubers and johnsongrass rhizomes to low temperature than is true for most seeds should be noted.

Desiccation

Dexter (1942), working with quackgrass rhizomes in the 1930s, showed rhizomes to be sensitive to desiccation. In the ensuing years, work on many other species has shown them to be sensitive to drying. With johnsongrass, for example, drying to less than 40% of the original moisture content was lethal to all the rhizomes (Anderson et al., 1960). Reduction in moisture to 14% killed rhizomes of African feathergrass *(Pennisetum macrourum)* (Harradine, 1980). Desiccation of *Digitaria scalarum* for four days at 7°C to 27°C completely killed the rhizomes (Mshiu, 1978). Both yellow nutsedge tubers and bermudagrass buds rapidly lost viability in air-dry soil (Thomas, 1969).

An interaction between desiccation and previous nitrogen fertilization was shown for quackgrass by Dexter (1937). He found that rhizomes from plants grown under added nitrogen were damaged more from drying than were those from unfertilized plants. The widespread and pronounced sensitivity of some perennating parts to desiccation suggests opportunities for their control through management, which are considered in Chapter 15.

Food Reserves

Data obtained in conjunction with research on control of perennial weeds provide an insight into the relationship between the physiological age of the perennating part and its likelihood of survival. Prior to the widespread availability of effective selective herbicides, control of such weeds relied heavily upon the proper timing and frequency of tillage. Thus, data for many species exist showing that the extent to which food reserves (carbohydrates) are depleted in the perennating part greatly influences the part's ability to regenerate.

The relationship shown in Figure 4–11 for perennial sowthistle *(Sonchus arvensis)* is typical for species with rootstocks and rhizomes. As can be seen in 4–

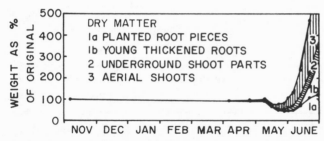

A. Changes in dry matter of undisturbed reproductive root pieces following planting on November 7, 1966

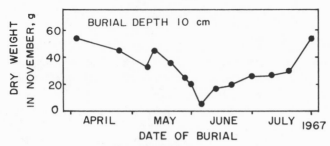

B. Effect of a single burial during 1967 on dry weight of reproductive roots in November 1967

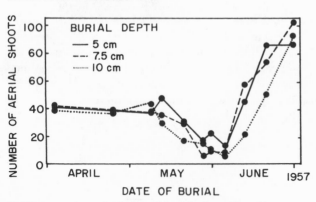

C. Effect on regrowth of time of burial of growing plants

FIGURE 4–11. Relationship among food resources, burial, and regrowth in perennial sowthistle.

Source: Modified from Hakansson, 1969. Reproduced courtesy of S. Hakansson.

11A, there is a small gradual decline in dry matter of the reproductive root piece (1a) during the winter and early spring, followed by a large rapid decline in mid-spring. The rapid decline coincides with initiation of growth of aerial shoots. The late May to early June period is when the reproductive root is least able to withstand burial, as shown both by rhizome weight in November of the same year (Figure 4–11B) and growth of aerial shoots during the following growing season (Figure 4–11C). The time during the spring when regrowth is initiated varies for different species. The sensitive period for vegetative parts varies accordingly. However, the rapid decline of stored foods associated with growth of new shoots, followed by the elaboration of new regeneration parts and buildup of food reserves in them, is the general pattern for carbohydrate utilization and buildup in perennating parts of all species. Further, that period when reserves are their lowest is when such parts are most easily destroyed.

Interactions of Factors

Several of the studies on temperature and moisture effects indicate an interaction between these two effects. Figure 4–12 demonstrates this relationship for yellow nutsedge. At 4°C, essentially no tubers retained their viability in air-dry soil. At 22°C, there was 20% to 40% survival, although viability was much lower in air-dry soil than where some moisture was present. Recall from Figure 4–7 that 4°C is well above the critical minimum for such tubers.

The duration of exposure of rhizomes or tubers to either temperature extremes or desiccation also influences loss in viability. From Figure 4–12, it can be seen that desiccation of yellow nutsedge tubers for 3 weeks at 4°C had little effect under the 70% relative humidity level, whereas viability was markedly reduced under this regime if exposed for 6 or 12 weeks. McWhorter (1972) found surface exposure of johnsongrass rhizomes for 3 days at 45°C was lethal to all buds, whereas their viability was relatively unaffected if exposed for only 2 days at this temperature.

The size of the tuber or rhizome may also affect longevity, although the evidence is indirect. Yellow nutsedge tubers averaging 120 mg in size produced 67% more shoots when buried at 20.3 cm than did tubers averaging 50 mg (Stoller and Wax, 1973). Similarly, emergence from johnsongrass rhizomes was greater from segments 152 mm long than from those 76 mm long when buried 22.9 cm.

Clearly, both the production and retention of viability of vegetative reproductive parts are influenced greatly by several factors. Some factors may be usable in developing management approaches to minimize problems from such weeds.

1 AIR-DRY SOIL
2 STEPWISE PROGRESSION TO 30% RELATIVE HUMIDITY
3 STEPWISE PROGRESSION TO 50% RELATIVE HUMIDITY
4 STEPWISE PROGRESSION TO 70% RELATIVE HUMIDITY
5 90% RELATIVE HUMIDITY THROUGHOUT

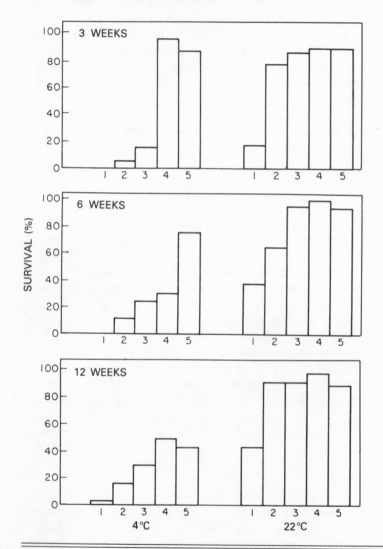

FIGURE 4–12. Percentage survival of yellow nutsedge tubers under various desiccation levels, temperatures, and duration of desiccation.

Source: Thomas, 1969. Reproduced with permission of Blackwell Scientific Publications, Ltd.

SEXUAL VS. VEGETATIVE REPRODUCTION

Plants that depend solely or nearly so on vegetative reproduction do so in spite of obvious drawbacks to this form of reproduction compared with reproduction by seed. The most obvious drawbacks are greater susceptibility to elimination by cultivation, less effective dispersal, and greater genetic uniformity, with attendant lessened plasticity in response to climatic variations or to disease and insect pests. A species solely dependent upon vegetative reproduction will be eliminated from a given area once all vegetative parts are destroyed. Such eradication can be accomplished for even the most persistent species in only two or three years of intensive tillage (Phillips, 1961; and Derscheid et al., 1961). As discussed in the previous chapter, many years tillage may be required to eliminate the seedbank in the soil. Although the importance of seed to survival and spread varies for perennial weeds, as shown in Table 4–3, the fact remains that most such weeds produce at least some seed. Therefore, it is helpful to understand something of the relationship between these two strategies for reproduction.

At the outset, we need to recognize a very basic difference between sexual and vegetative reproduction. In the strictest sense, vegetative reproduction may more appropriately be termed *regrowth* since it results from the development of existing meristems in root or stem tissue. Such regrowth leads to a new plant quite like that from which it developed. In contrast, sexual reproduction begins with a single new cell and leads to the development of a new individual unique in some respects from its parent(s). Thus, sexual reproduction involves recombination of the genetic

TABLE 4-3

Relative importance of seed production in survival and spread of selected perennial weeds.

Species	Vegetative Reproduction Part	Seed Production
Austrian fieldcress	Rhizomes	Unimportant
Canada thistle	Creeping rootstock	Fairly important
Dandelion	Adventitious buds on taproot	Very important
Field bindweed	Creeping rootstock	Very important
Hoary cress	Creeping rootstock	Important
Johnsongrass	Rhizomes	Very important
Kikuyu grass	Stolons and rhizomes	Rarely produced
Purple nutsedge	Tubers	Mostly infertile
Quackgrass	Rhizomes	Fairly important
Wild garlic	Bulbs and bulblets	Unimportant

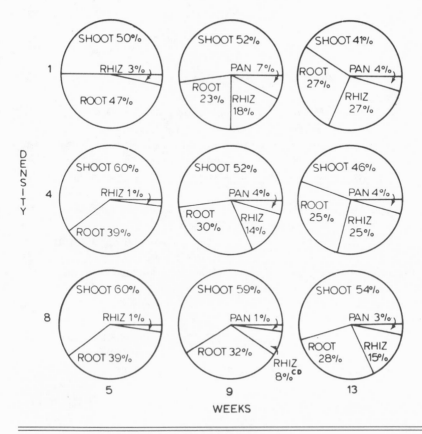

FIGURE 4–13. Influence of plant density and plant age on partitioning of dry weight in johnsongrass plants.

Source: Williams and Ingber, 1977. Reproduced with permission of the Weed Science Society of America.

material, whereas vegetative regrowth involves merely repeating the existing genetic material. Nevertheless, vegetative regeneration is clearly an important means of increasing the *numbers* of plants with which we must deal in weed–crop ecology. In this sense, it acts as a reproductive process and has been treated as such. The basic difference from true reproduction should be kept in mind, however.

Allocation of Resources

An important question is the relative priority of each process on the plant's resources. That is, does the production of seed, once the flowering process has begun, have priority on photosynthate over the production of vegetative reproduction units? The answer has important implications for preventive approaches to weeds. For example, if a species gave priority to seed production over production of perennating parts, we might look for ways of promoting seed production as a way of limiting vegetative reproductive growth and thus competition.

The limited studies have yielded variable answers. In johnsongrass, as shown in Figure 4–13, more of the dry weight was allocated to rhizomes than to panicles (seed production). However, under the stress of increased density, rhizome production suffered relatively more. At 13 weeks, as the density increased from 1 to 8 plants per pot (32 to 256 plants per square meter, respectively), the percent of dry weight in panicles dropped only from 4% to 3%, whereas the dry weight in rhizomes dropped from 27% to 15%. In purple nutsedge (Williams et al., 1977), the opposite effect was observed. As the density increased from 32 to 800 plants per square meter for plants 9 weeks old, the percentage dry weight in tubers increased from 4% to 15%, respectively, compared with a decrease from 15% to 8% in inflorescences.

Of course, dry matter by itself may not adequately measure the value to the species of resources allocated to each type of reproduction. Because of the large difference in size, a gram of dry matter committed to seed production may yield many more potential new plants than a gram committed to rhizomes. This situation is illustrated in Table 4–4 by the numbers of rhizome nodes and seeds produced by johnsongrass. Except for the very earliest planting, the number of reproduction units per plant was from 30 to 150 times greater for seed than for rhizome nodes.

TABLE 4-4

Numbers of seed and of rhizome nodes per plant in johnsongrass 12 weeks after planting.

Date Planted	Number of Rhizome Nodes per Plant	Number of Seeds per Plant
March 1	7	0
April 1	71	3,909
May 1	140	20,870
June 1	145	19,767
July 1	156	11,416
August 1	101	13,282
September 1	8	250
October 1	—	—

Source: Data from Keeley and Thullen, 1979.

Competing Processes

Much of the data discussed suggest that seed and vegetative reproduction are alternative and competing processes. However, interpreting data within a species is often complicated by the fact that each process is commonly produced at somewhat different times in the plant's development and, thus, is subjected to different environments. Further, it is difficult to fully evaluate the success of each process in producing new plants because of dormancy and environmental influences on germination. It is the number of new individuals generated by each type that is the ultimate measure of its efficiency in utilization of resources.

A comparison between two species of *Agropyron,* one that relies mainly on seed and the other on rhizomes, is especially revealing (Harper, 1977). The seed of the two species are closely similar in weight and appearance. When grown as an isolated plant, quackgrass *(Agropyron repens)* was observed to produce 30 seeds and 215 rhizome buds, for a total of 245 reproductive units. *Agropyron caninum* produced only seeds, with a total of 258. In other words, the total number of regenerating units was quite similar. Thus, it appears that clonal reproduction and seed production are alternative processes.

Relationship of Reproduction to Competitiveness

The production of seed and of any vegetative reproductive part is a resource utilization process. Resources allocated to the production of seed clearly detract from the competitiveness of the plant producing them. Resources allocated to vegetative reproduction may or may not contribute to the competitiveness of the plant producing them.

In general terms, resources allocated to produce vegetative regeneration units that grow and become established the year in which they are produced do contribute to competitiveness. For example, the main reason why rhizomatous-producing weeds, such as johnsongrass and quackgrass, are so competitive is that their regeneration units frequently grow the year they are produced. Resources allocated to production of units that grow only in subsequent years represent a sacrifice of competitiveness. Wild garlic bulbs produced one year usually do not germinate until the following year, which is one reason this weed is not a strong competitor with such crops as winter wheat, in which it is found. Rather, it is a problem weed because its bulblets may lower wheat quality. Possibly, the extent of contribution to competitiveness that the resource utilization process makes can be exploited in management to reduce the survival and competitiveness of species possessing such capabilities. Chapter 15 considers this possibility.

CONCEPTS AND CONCLUSIONS

1. Confinement of perennating, or vegetative reproduction, parts near or physically attached to the parent plant maximizes the opportunities for the clone to utilize growth factors in a given area. Restricted dispersal is a major reason for the strong competitiveness of many perennial weeds.
2. The greater competitiveness from restricted dispersal is obtained at a sacrifice of protection against elimination by cultivation and the natural environment.
3. Until a plant originating from a perennating part separated from the parent plant begins to produce such parts on its own, removing the top growth is lethal. During this time, the perennial plant is no different than an annual in this respect.
4. The period after emergence when a perennial weed may be treated like an annual is commonly relatively short.
5. The production of perennating, or vegetative regeneration, parts is sensitive to competition for light.
6. The production of perennating parts is reduced by elevated nitrogen levels in the soil and by low temperatures.
7. The relative longevity of perennating parts in soil is less than that of most seeds.
8. Longevity of perennating parts varies directly with burial depth, due likely to protection against desiccation and low temperature.
9. The ability of perennating parts to support sprouting and growth is directly related to their level of food reserves.
10. The level of food reserves is rapidly reduced during sprouting and early growth. Thus, there is commonly a period of days immediately following the flush of sprouting in the spring when a perennial is most easily destroyed by tillage.

REFERENCES

Agricultural Research Service, USDA. 1970. Selected weeds of the United States, Agricultural handbook no. 366.

Aleixo, M.D., and I.F. Valio. II. 1976. Effect of light, temperature, and endogenous growth regulators on the growth of *Cyperus rotundus* tubers. Zeitschrift fur Pflanzenphysiologie 80 (4):336–37.

Anderson, L.E., A.P. Appleby, and J.W. Weseloh. 1960. Characteristics of johnsongrass rhizomes. Weeds 8 (3):402–06.

Anderson, W.P. 1977. Weed science: Principles. St. Paul: West Publishing.

Beasley, C.A. 1970. Development of axillary buds from johnsongrass rhizomes. Weed Sci. 18 (2):218–22.

Derscheid, L.A., K.E. Wallace, and R.L. Nash. 1960. Leafy spurge control with cultivation, cropping, and chemicals. Weeds 8 (1):115–27.

————, R.L. Nash, and G.A. Wicks. 1961. Thistle control with cultivation, cropping, and chemicals. Weeds 9 (1):90–102.

————, J.F. Stritzke, and W.G. Wright. 1970. Field bindweed control with cultivation, cropping, and chemicals. Weed Sci. 18 (5):590–96.

Dexter, S.T. 1936. Response of quackgrass to defoliation and fertilization. Plant Physiol. 11:843–51.

————. 1937. The drought resistance of quackgrass under various degrees of fertilization with nitrogen. Agron. J. 29:568–76.

————. 1942. Seasonal variations in drought resistance of exposed rhizomes of quackgrass. Agron. J. 34:1125–36.

Garg, D.K., L.E. Bendixen, and S.R. Anderson. 1967. Rhizome differentiation in yellow nutsedge. Weeds 15 (2):124–28.

Hakansson, S. 1969. Experiments with *Sonchus arvensis* L., I. Development and growth, and the response to burial and defoliation in different developmental stages. Lantbrukshogskolans Annaler 35:989–1030.

Harper, J.L. 1977. Population biology of plants. New York: Academic Press.

Harradine, A.R. 1980. The biology of African feathergrass *(Pennisetum macrourum)* in Tasmania, II. Rhizome biology. Weed Res. 20 (3):171–75.

Hill, T.A. 1977. The biology of weeds. London: Edward Arnold.

Hodgson, J.M. 1958. Canada thistle control with cultivation, cropping, and chemical sprays. Weeds 6 (1):1–11.

Holm, L.G., et al. 1977. The world's worst weeds. Honolulu: University Press of Hawaii.

Jansen, L.L. 1971. Morphology and photo response in yellow nutsedge. Weed Sci. 19 (3):210–19.

Jeffrey, L.S., and L.R. Robison. 1971. Growth characteristics of common milkweed. Weed Sci. 19 (3):193–96.

Johnson, A.A., and S.T. Dexter. 1939. The response of quackgrass to variations in height of cutting and rates of application of N. Agron. J. 31:67–76.

Johnson, B.G., and K.P. Buchholtz. 1962. The natural dormancy of vegetative buds on the rhizomes of quackgrass. Weeds 10 (1):53–57.

Keeley, P.E., and R.J. Thullen. 1975. Influence of yellow nutsedge competition on furrow-irrigated cotton. Weed Sci. 23 (3):171–75.

————. 1978. Light requirements of yellow nutsedge *(Cyperus esculentus)* and light interception by crops. Weed Sci. 26 (1):10–16.

————. 1979. Influence of planting date on the growth of johnsongrass from seed. Weed Sci. 27 (5):554–58.

McCarty, M.K., and D.L. Linscott. 1962. Response of ironweed to mowing and 2,4–D. Weeds 10 (3):240–43.

McIntyre, G.E. 1971. Apical dominance in the rhizome of *Agropyron repens* in isolated rhizomes. Can. J. Bot. 49:99–109.

McWhorter, C.G. 1961. Morphology and development of johnsongrass plants from seeds and rhizomes. Weeds 9 (4):558–62.

————. 1972. Factors affecting johnsongrass rhizome production and germination. Weed Sci. 20 (1):41–45.

Meyers, E.J., and D.H. Caso. 1976. The effect of nitrogen supply on the growth of *Sorghum halepense*. Malezas 5 (2):3–12.

Monaco, T.J., and E.L. Cumbo. 1972. Growth and development of curly dock and broadleaf dock. Weed Sci. 20 (1):64–67.

Morrow, L.A. 1979. Studies on the reproductive biology of leafy spurge *(Euphorbia esula)*. Weed Sci. 27 (1):106–09.

Mshiu, E.P. 1978. Studies on *Digitaria scalarum*, Technical crop production, master's thesis. Reading, England: University of Reading.

Myers, G.A., C.A. Beasley, and L.A. Derscheid. 1964. Anatomical studies of *Euphorbia esula* L. Weed Sci. 12 (4):291–95.

Ogden, J. 1974. The reproductive strategy of higher plants, II. The reproductive strategy of *Tussilago farfara* L. J. Ecol. 62:291–324.

Palmer, J.H., and G.R. Sagar. 1963. *Agropyron repens* L. Beauv. J. Ecol. 51:783–94.

Patterson, D.T. 1982. Shading response of purple and yellow nutsedge *(Cyperus rotundus* and *C. esculentus)*. Weed Sci. 30:25–30.

Phillips, W.M. 1961. Control of field bindweed by cultural and chemical methods, USDA technical bulletin no. 1249. Washington, D.C.

Russ, O.G., and L.E. Anderson. 1960. Field bindweed control by combinations of cropping, cultivation, and 2,4–D. Weeds 8 (3):397–401.

Sagar, G.R., and A.M. Mortimer. 1976. An approach to the study of the population dynamics of plants with special reference to weeds. Appl. Biol. 1:1–47.

Seyforth, W., W. Kreil, and O. Knobe. 1978. Investigations into the reserve carbohydrate balance in *Agropyron repens* at various levels of N fertilization of grassland. Soils Fert. 42:5722.

Stoller, E.W. 1977. Differential cold tolerance of quackgrass and johnsongrass rhizomes. Weed Sci. 25 (4):348–51.

————, and L.M. Wax. 1973. Yellow nutsedge shoot emergence and tuber longevity. Weed Sci. 21 (1):76–81.

Thomas, P.E.L. 1969. Effects of desiccation and temperature on survival of *C. esculentus* and *Cynodon dactylon* rhizomes. Weed Res. 9:1–8.

Tumbleson, M.E., and T. Kommedahl. 1961. Reproductive potential of *Cyperus esculentis* by tubers. Weeds 9 (4):646–53.

Williams, R.D., and B.F. Ingber. 1977. The effect of intraspecific competition on the growth and development of johnsongrass under greenhouse conditions. Weed Sci. 25 (4):293–97.

Williams, R.D., P.C. Quimby, Jr., and K.E. Frick. 1977. Intraspecific competition of purple nutsedge *(Cyperus rotundus)* under greenhouse conditions. Weed Sci. 25 (6):477–81.

Wilson, R.G., Jr. 1979. Germination and seedling development of Canada thistle *(Cersium arvense)*. Weed Sci. 27 (2):146–51.

Yeo, R.R. 1964. Life history of common cattail. Weeds 12 (4):284–88.

RESUMPTION OF GROWTH

5

Resumption of growth of seed or vegetative parts and their production, covered in Chapters 3 and 4, are the two phases in a weed's life history of primary concern to weed management. When growth resumes in relationship to the crop's life cycle determines the severity of competition or whether there is competition at all. The numbers are influenced by the number of propagules added to the soil bank in previous years. As discussed in Chapters 3 and 4, both the numbers of propagules produced and their longevity are influenced by a number of factors. We are now ready to consider factors that influence resumption of growth.

Germination can be defined as the resumption of growth of a seed or a vegetative part. Germination of seeds involves a precise sequence of events: (1) imbibition of water, (2) marked increase in respiration, (3) mobilization of food reserves, and (4) digestion of reserved foods. For many crop seeds, this sequence begins promptly after planting and proceeds in an orderly fashion to the emergence of the young seedling. The time required is modified only by soil and temperature conditions. The situation with many weed seeds and vegetative parts is quite different. The process either does not start promptly upon their introduction into the soil or it is stopped along the way. That is to say, the seed or vegetative part has a period of metabolic quiescence—usually termed *dormancy*—after it is produced. When in this state, the seed or the vegetative part does not resume growth, even though all environmental conditions seem to be favorable.

DORMANCY

Dormancy, so common in weeds, needs to be briefly examined, especially relative to environmental influences, before proceding to a discussion of germination.

119

Similarities are found in the relationships between the environment and onset of dormancy in seed and vegetative parts. Therefore, the following discussion of such principles for seeds is assumed to be applicable to vegetative parts also. The perspective of dormancy here is that of a pause in the normal sequence of events leading to germination and emergence. By itself, it is not a factor in competition. However, it is an important factor in persistence and survival of species. In this regard, dormancy plays a very significant function indeed in the life of the weed by protecting the embryo or meristem during dissemination and during periods unfavorable for germination and successful establishment of a new plant. It is outside the purposes of this text to examine the biochemical processes involved or the embryonic development per se. Refer to Chapters 3, 4, and 5 in *Dormancy and Development Arrest* (Clutter, 1978) for a detailed discussion of biochemical reactions in the regulation of dormancy and to any good text on plant anatomy for a discussion of embryology.

Our interest here is in dormancy as it affects longevity and resumption of growth. As discussed in Chapter 3, seeds may survive many years in soil. This survival is the direct result of dormancy. *Dormancy* has many definitions. A useful one for weed–crop ecology is that state in which growth is not resumed even though the environment supports germination and seedling growth of other apparently identical, but nondormant, tissues of the same species or plant. Among other things, this definition recognizes that dormancy is a relative matter and can best be evaluated by comparison with very closely related tissues.

The following developmental timetable of a seed places dormancy in perspective with the other processes:

Stage	Characteristics
Water Loss	
Cleavage and histo-differentiation	Cell division and differentiation of all major tissues, but little growth
Growth	Rapid expansion and division of cells
Maturation	Cessation of cell division and expansion; synthesis and storage of food reserves
Dormancy	Developmental arrest
Water Uptake	
Germination	Resumption of cell division and expansion

The first three stages, with a few exceptions, occur while the developing seed is physically attached to the parent. The final stage, germination, normally occurs after the seed is separated from the parent. The dormant condition may be acquired while the seed is still physically attached to the parent or after it has been released. Thus, the dormant condition may be a result of genetic messages and biochemical reactions between the maternal tissue and the embryo or meristem. Or, the condition may be brought on by the environment to which the reproductive part is exposed.

Types of Dormancy

There are three broad types of dormancy: (1) innate, (2) induced, and (3) enforced. *Innate dormancy*, sometimes referred to as primary dormancy, is that present in the seed or vegetative part when released from the parent. *Induced dormancy*, sometimes referred to as secondary dormancy, is a result of conditions to which the seed or vegetative part is exposed after release from the parent. Once such dormancy is induced, germination or regrowth usually does not commence immediately when the condition is removed. *Enforced dormancy* is that imposed by conditions unfavorable for resumed growth, most commonly a shortage of water or unsuitable temperature. Stated simply: "Some seeds are born dormant, some acquire dormancy, and some have dormancy thrust upon them" (Harper, 1977).

Innate dormancy.   Innate dormancy may be imposed and maintained by several mechanisms. Among them are: immaturity of the embryo, seed coats impermeable to water, seed coats that inhibit gaseous exchange, mechanical resistance of the seed coat to embryo growth, and growth substance imbalance within the embryo. All of these mechanisms are genetically controlled, with the degree of expression, of course, influenced by growing conditions. The most consistent modifier appears to be maturity. Thus, with many weeds, dormancy increases as seeds mature. In one study with wild oat, for example, germination of mature seed was only 8% compared to 50% germination for immature seed (Richardson, 1979). Since maturity is subject to control with management, there may be opportunities to use this fact to reduce the longevity of weed seed in the seedbank. Treatment of the parent plant as a possible approach to reducing the seedbank is considered in Chapter 15.

Seed polymorphism, the production of different kinds of seeds by the same plant, is a characteristic of many weeds that further complicates efforts to deal with innate dormancy. With respect to dormancy, plants of many weed species produce both dormant and nondormant seed. Dormancy may differ among seeds that look alike. For example, dark seeds from the same plant of common purslane varied from 0% to 100% in germination (Egley, 1974). Or, dormant and nondormant seeds may be quite different in appearance. In cocklebur, for example, two seeds are produced in each capsule. Commonly, but not always, one seed occupies the upper position and the other the lower position in the capsule. The upper one is usually dormant and the lower one nondormant.

Induced dormancy.   Seeds of some species, following a period of exposure to unfavorable conditions, do not germinate readily when provided proper conditions. Most commonly, a light requirement is induced. For example, buckhorn plantain, corn spurry, and field poppy seeds that did not require light to germinate before burial would not germinate without light after burial for 50 weeks (Wesson and Wareing, 1969b). A variety of treatments in the laboratory can induce secondary dormancy. A general summary of such treatments is that secondary dormancy can be induced in imbibed seeds by exposure to high temperatures coupled with restriction in the supply of oxygen (Villiers, 1972). Induced dormancy in itself has implications for resumption of growth and for weed management. The more important aspect, however, may be its interaction with innate dormancy. As we know, the vast majority of weeds produce seeds with at least some innate dormancy. Burial may induce a secondary dormancy that greatly extends the longevity of the seed in soil. Because agriculture, even of perennial crops and with reduced tillage, involves tillage that provides burial, the implications for resumption of growth and weed management are substantial.

Enforced dormancy.   Many seeds fail to germinate simply because there is insufficient moisture for the imbibition needed to initiate the process. In temperate regions, low temperature prevents germination. Under these circumstances, dormancy is enforced. That is, seeds remain dormant only because conditions necessary to support growth are absent. As soon as proper moisture and temperature are provided, germination occurs.

Propagule–Environment Interactions in Dormancy

The seed, or propagule, commonly carries information about dormancy: All three major components—embryo, reserves, and seed coat—may have a role. The environment interacts with this inherent information and influences the seed to alter those messages or influences its biochemical processes to change directions or initiate new directions. Level 1 of Figure 5–1 schematically summarizes the relationship between the seed and the environment in dormancy and shows how complex it may be.

All factors in the physical environment may have an effect. Photoperiod (light) would appear to be a primary factor in innate dormancy. Temperature also has an effect, apparently largely as a modifier of the photoperiod effect. Similarly,

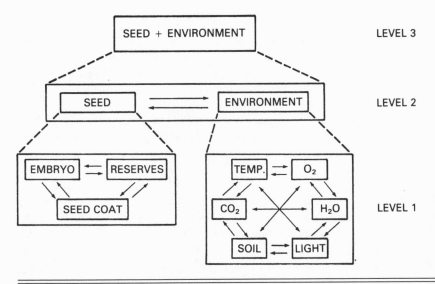

FIGURE 5–1. Levels of organization of a seed–environment system. Each component of the seed and of the environment, plus interactions among them (Level 1), determines seed dormancy.
Source: Simpson, 1978. Reproduced courtesy of Academic Press, Inc.

mineral deficiency and lack of moisture may induce the initial stages of dormancy in buds. For induced dormancy of seed, carbon dioxide and moisture appear to have the greatest impact. Moisture is involved in the development of so-called hard-seed, widespread in members of the Leguminosae family. In this case, induced dormancy involves the hilum acting as a hydrostatic control valve. The *hilum* is a scar on the surface of the seed left after its detachment from the stalk. Under dry conditions, the hilum opens and allows water to escape. Under humid conditions, it closes, thus preventing water uptake. In effect then, the embryo dries progressively to a level equal to the driest environment it has experienced. As long as the integrity of the seed coat is present and the hilum is functioning, such seeds do not imbibe water and thus remain in the "hard" condition.

Carbon dioxide.   Carbon dioxide (CO_2) deserves special comment because it may be the most controllable of the environmental factors, in the sense that plant residues, which are a potential source of CO_2 enrichment, can be incorporated at the discretion of the farmer. It has been shown (Kidd, 1914; Kidd and West, 1917; and Hart and Berrie, 1966) that elevated levels of CO_2 induce dormancy in seeds of some species. Further, the induction of dormancy by CO_2 was related to both temperature and oxygen levels. At 3°C, 2% CO_2 caused about a 90% reduction in germination, whereas 36% CO_2 was required for the same germination reduction at 20°C. Studies of CO_2 in the soil profile (deJong and Schappert, 1972) and in soil with large amounts of green plant materials added (Kidd, 1914) showed levels in the range that might cause dormancy (2% to 20%). It can be speculated that incorporation of weed seeds with large quantities of weed and crop residues may result in CO_2 levels, at the vicinity of the seed, sufficiently high to induce dormancy.

Onset of dormancy related to plant hormones.   Naturally occurring plant hormones appear to be intimately involved with entry into and release from dormancy in both buds and seeds. Abscisic acid would appear to be the dormancy-inducing hormone involved. Production of abscisic acid is apparently triggered by a stimulus from mature leaves under short days. This type of induced dormancy may be viewed as a seasonal dormancy in that it occurs in a fairly predictable fashion following the induction of the stimulus by the right photoperiod. In seeds, production of abscisic acid seems to be related to the water loss that occurs as the seed passes from histo-differentiation to growth to maturation. Here, too, photo-period appears to be involved (Gutterman, 1978). Thus, our concern for the influence of the environment likely comes down to the effect upon the synthesis, transport, and activity of the regulating plant hormones. The precise mechanism involved is yet to be determined.

To summarize, seed structure, environment, and metabolism are all involved in dormancy and probably in an interactive fashion, as shown in Figure 5–1. The fact that the environment affects the onset of dormancy suggests that there may be ways of manipulating the environment to either bring on or prevent dormancy. Where CO_2–induced dormancy is involved, proper timing of the incorporation of the weed seed and the associated plant residues may be a useful approach. Where innate dormancy is involved, such manipulation must likely focus on ways of blocking formation of abscisic acid and possible other growth-inhibiting substances or on increasing the levels of growth-promoting substances. Dormancy, indeed, is fortuitous to the weed involved since it spreads resumption of growth over a period of time; in some cases, even over a period of several years. Thus, one unfavorable growing season does not eliminate the species. Developing a clear understanding of the mechanisms involved is particularly important to weed management because it may be easier to avoid the onset of dormancy than to release the propagule from dormancy once it is established.

ECOLOGICAL RELATIONSHIPS IN RESUMPTION OF GROWTH

The same factors that bring about dormancy are involved in germination, or the resumption of growth. In other words, the seed—environment relationships given in Figure 5–1 for dormancy are also involved in germination. Although there are many similarities in the effects of environment on their resumption of growth, obvious differences also exist between seeds and vegetative regenerating parts. The most notable difference may be the possession of dominance in many vegetative reproduction parts that of course is not a factor with seeds. Also, there are differences in crop associations in the difficulty of control and in the basic approaches to preventing losses from them. Thus, resumption of growth is considered separately for seeds and vegetative parts.

RESUMPTION OF GROWTH: SEED

Season-Anticipating Characteristic of Seed

Seeds of many weeds germinate at a time when conditions can be expected to be favorable for establishment of the new plant and completion of its life cycle. That is, the seed seems to have the ability to predict the right season of the year in which to germinate. This *season-anticipating characteristic* is demonstrated by the fact that seeds of many annual weeds in temperate regions germinate only in the spring and summer when there is sufficient time to mature and produce seed. Germination occurs only at these specific times, even though there most certainly are times in the late summer and early fall when the seed is exposed to the same moisture, temperature, and light conditions as in the spring and early summer. Of course, this situation is fortunate for weeds. If they germinated in the late summer and early fall, they would most likely be killed by frost before producing seed, and the species would soon disappear.

As we have already learned, in many species, dormancy prevents germination for a time after the seed is produced. Our concern now is with those factors that trigger an end to dormancy and with the fact that this change occurs when conditions are favorable for establishment. Further, an end to dormancy does not occur during a brief period of favorable conditions but rather occurs over time. If this were not so, a brief period of favorable conditions, such as a warm period in midwinter, could produce a flush of germination with the seedlings being destroyed by the return of low temperatures. It is this season-anticipating ability that provides the seed a maximum chance for successful germination, seedling establishment, maturation, and seed production. Recall the discussion of safe sites from Chapter 2 where it was pointed out the environment is heterogenous from the perspective of the weed seed. Because the environment is so heterogenous, we expect the seed to respond to many different signals from the environment. Relative to this matter, Koller (1978) makes the comment: "Species which occupy the same habitat rarely have a common denominator environmental control of their germination . . . since different species are able to share the same habitat only by occupying different micro-environmental niches in it." This statement adds to our

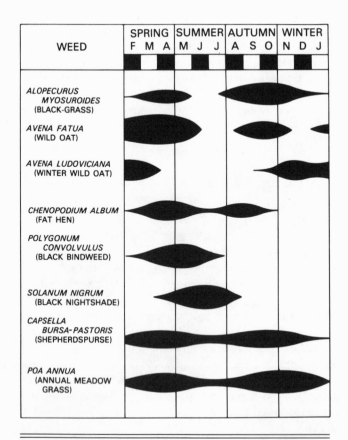

FIGURE 5–2. Period of maximum germination of seeds of eight weeds.

Source: Hill, 1977. Reproduced with permission of Blackwell Scientific Publications, Ltd.

understanding of why we commonly have a mixture of weed species. It also helps to explain why all species of weeds do not germinate at the same time and why individuals of a single species do not. The seed's perception of the environment and the different triggering factors among species are important to our examination of the individual factors affecting germination. The discussion of individual factors, by necessity, emphasizes general patterns.

Periodicity. Not only do seeds of many weeds germinate only when conditions for survival are favorable, but many also have a flush of germination at a given time in the growing season, termed *periodicity*. The germination flush for eight weeds is shown in Figure 5–2. Two generalizations regarding periodicity are supported by

Figure 5–2. One is that species may have more than one flush of germination, as is the case of wild oat. The second is that the discreteness of periodicity varies with species. For example, periodicity for black nightshade is restricted to the late spring and summer periods, whereas annual bluegrass *(Poa annua)* germinates throughout the year, even though it has a peak in spring and fall. Periodicity, particularly where it is discrete, offers possibilities for preventive approaches.

Effect of growth-regulating substances.   Research has conclusively established that seeds contain growth-regulating substances that influence germination. Although the chemistry involved is outside the scope of this text, there is evidence to suggest that such substances influencing germination involve three broad kinds: (1) those that are promoting in their effect (gibberellins or gibberellin-like substances), (2) those that are inhibiting in their effect (quite possibly abscisic acid), and (3) those that are antagonistic to the endogenous inhibitors (possibly cytokinins). All have been found in weed seeds. Further, it has been found that strains of wild oat vary in the levels of cytokinins and gibberellins contained in their seeds (Taylor and Simpson, 1980). Thus, the mounting evidence suggests that germination is dependent upon the balance between promoting and inhibiting growth substances.

The quantity produced of each growth regulator is subject to influence by environmental factors to be discussed in the next section. It should be noted here that the interaction between growth regulators and environmental factors can be expected to modify the period and extent of weed seed germination. Further, there is evidence that leaching (washing) can remove these substances and thus either inhibit or promote germination. For example, as shown in Table 5–1, washing lambsquarters seeds increased their germination, whereas leaching of fumitory *(Fumaria officinalis)* achenes reduced germination, as shown in Figure 5–3. It is significant for weed management that the inhibiting and promoting effects are

TABLE 5-1

Germination of common lambsquarters following different times of washing in running tap water.

Duration of Washing (hours)	Germination (%)
0	27.8
8	39.0
70	49.0

Source: Chu et al., 1978. Reproduced with permission of the Weed Science Society of America.

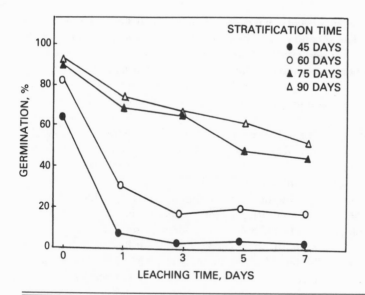

FIGURE 5–3. Effect of leaching achenes of fumitory (*Fumaria officinalis* L.).
Source: Jeffrey and Nalewaja, 1970. Reproduced with permission of the Weed Science Society of America.

influenced by such factors as leaching, which may be controllable under some circumstances.

Environmental Effects on Resumption of Growth

Perception and characterization of the environment by the seed obviously depends upon relatively few factors—mainly temperature, light, and water—but the many possible combinations and sequences among these factors provide many potential signals. Our interest here is in signals from the environment rather than in the processes involved. The present discussion, therefore, focuses primarily on effects of environmental factors on germination with only as much discussion of the processes involved as may be needed to make the effect clear. The environmental effects to be covered include depth of burial in soil, canopy/light, temperature, soil type and condition, soil chemicals, and the several factors interacting with one another.

Depth of burial.   Of all the environmental effects on germination, that of depth of burial is most consistent. First, emergence for many weed seeds is inversely related to depth of seed in the soil from about 1 cm down. For some, emergence is best for seeds on top of the soil, but most emerge better when incorporated in the very shallow surface layer. The relationship shown in Figure 5–4 is representative of the effect of burial depth for many weed seeds. Temperature, of course, influenced emergence, but it did not alter the effect of burial depth. The results depicted allow three broad conclusions about depth: (1) Best emergence occurs from seeds buried shallowly; (2) species differ in their response to burial depth; and (3) some emergence is possible beyond the ideal depth. Although the depth at

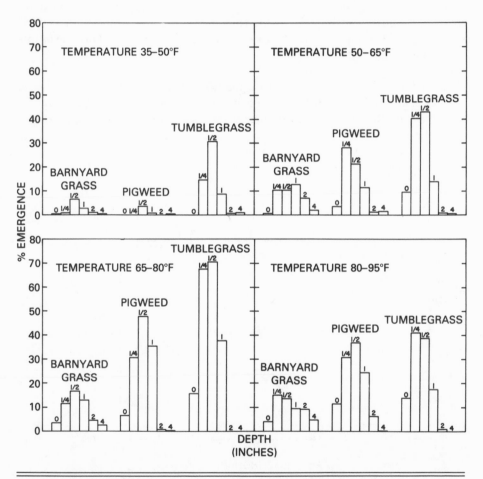

FIGURE 5–4. Effect of burial depth and temperature regimes on emergence of some weeds from seed.

Source: Wiese and Davis, 1967. Reproduced with permission of the Weed Science Society of America.

which the break occurs varies among species and for environmental conditions, the sharp drop-off below this depth is typical of most seeds.

A second aspect to depth of burial is also quite consistent with a wide variety of species, soil conditions, and other environmental effects: Emergence is delayed in a direct relationship with depth of burial. Possible explanations for the effect of burial depth are discussed after considering other individual factors.

At this point, the question remains of whether it is emergence or germination that is affected by burial depth. While the data are insufficient for an unequivocal answer, the preponderance of evidence indicates that depth has little effect on germination *if the conditions for germination have been met*. As we see later, these conditions, which influence metabolic processes, include adequate moisture, right temperature, and for some, light. Thus, burial depth is symptomatic of these factors rather than itself the factor. Its effects, though, are real and may be usable in dealing with weeds.

Canopy/light. We have long known that germination of seeds of many weed species is affected by light. Figure 5–5 shows how pronounced the light requirement may be. Maximum germination after 30 days in a germinator occurred only when the pusley seeds received 12 hours of light each day. Ten hours of light produced more than a three-fold increase in germination compared with 8 hours. Practically no germination occurred without at least 4 hours of light.

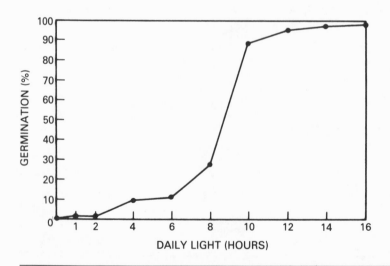

FIGURE 5–5. Effect of light on germination of Florida pusley *(Richardia scabra)*.
Source: Data from Biswas et al., 1975.

TABLE 5-2

Partial list of weed seeds that require light for best germination.

Birdseye speedwell	Corn spurry	Lambsquarters	Sorrel
Black knapweed	Crunchweed	Manyseeded	St. Johnswort
Brazil callalily	Curly dock	goosefoot	Thymeleaf
Bristly foxtail	Fall panicum	Mouse-ear	sandwort
Broadleaf dock	Field pennycress	chickweed spp.	Triple-awned
Buckhorn	Field pepperweed	Nightflowering	grass spp.
plantain	Fingergrass spp.	catchfly	Tumble mustard
Carline thistle	Florida pusley	Oxeye daisy	Virginia
Common	Giant foxtail	Pennsylvania	pepperweed
chickweed	Hairy beggartick	smartweed	Wild carrot
Common	Hawkbit	Perennial	Wild marigold
cinquefoil	Healall	sowthistle	Wild marjoram
Common	Hemp	Prostrate	Wild mustard
purslane	Hedge mustard	knotweed	Wild parsnip
Common ragweed	Hoary plantain	Redroot pigweed	Wormseed
Common yarrow	Johnsongrass	Rock cress	mustard
Corn marigold	Kochia	Smallflower	Yellow bedstraw
Corn poppy	Ladysthumb	galinsoga	Yellow rocket

Table 5–2 lists some weeds that are known to require light for germination. The list includes a broad cross section of plant families.

For many years, this effect was assumed to be simply that of the presence or absence of light. Only within the last half of this century have data accumulated to show that there are three qualitative aspects of light that can affect germination: (1) intensity, (2) spectral composition, and (3) duration. Since all three may vary considerably under natural conditions, it is not surprising that results from studies of light are somewhat variable. The interaction of light with other factors to be discussed later further complicates the picture. Our purpose is to identify and understand the effects of light for those environmental factors over which we may exercise some measure of control. Thus, although intensity and duration can affect germination, it is the effect of spectral composition that is of particular importance. This is so because spectral composition is largely determined by the extent of leaf filtering by the canopy that in turn, can be manipulated. Although intensity is also influenced by the canopy, spectral composition may have a relatively greater effect, as we see in the next section.

Light filtered by leaves. Table 5–3 shows the relative importance of leaf shade. The intensity of light, measured by a light meter, reaching the dishes containing the seed was the same under banana leaf and neutral shade. Germina-

TABLE 5-3

Effect of light and of neutral or leaf shade on seed germination of selected species.

Species*	Percent Germination (each of two dishes)			
	Light	Dark	Banana-Leaf Shade	Neutral-Paper Shade
Achyranthes aspera	97	91	91	95
Ageratum conyzoides	99	0	0	56
Amaranthus caudatus	100	93	6	98
Aristida adscensionis	40	5	20	17
Bidens pilosa	97	81	0	99
Chloris pycnothrix	91	3	52	78
Conyza bonariensis	44	38	25	47
Cynoglossum lanceolatum	97	0	0	16
Ethulia "sp. A"	50	1	0	27
Galinsoga parviflora	93	3	0	80
Launaea cornuta	78	15	20	70
Richardia brazilienis	29	14	0	92
Schkuhria pinnata	62	15	15	33
Setaria verticillata	49	23	29	61
Sonchus oleraceus	86	51	6	86
Tagetes minuta	94	57	2	74
Vernonia hindei	44	33	1	10
Vernonia lasiopus	42	16	3	26

* Because most are not common in this country, only the scientific name is given.
Source: Data from Fenner, 1980c.

tion of 16 of the 18 species was inhibited—6 completely—by leaf shade. Neutral shade inhibited germination of 10 species, but in all but one species *(Aristida adscensionis)*, the inhibition was less than under leaf shade. Note that there are more instances where the effect is a matter of degree than where it is complete.

In other work (Gorski et al., 1977), it was found that leaf canopy inhibition of germination was greater among wild than among cultivated herbaceous species and greater in those species common to open habitats than in those of cultivated areas. Does this suggest that those species common to cultivated areas in Table 5-3 may lose such sensitivity in time?

Dormancy acquired by shading. An important question is whether or not seeds whose germination is inhibited by light filtered through a canopy of leaves acquire a dormancy that inhibits germination after removal of the canopy, at least for a time. This question is important both from the standpoint of survival of the species and for approaches for preventing crop losses from them. Apparently, there are conflicting answers. Silvertown (1980) found no evidence that seeds of 17 species in which dormancy was induced by leaf shade had acquired a light requirement for germination. On the other hand, Fenner (1980a) found that hairy beggarticks *(Bidens pilosa)* seed inhibited from germinating by leaf shade required light for germination. Further, this light requirement was acquired in only 1 hour of shade.

Under the analogous situation of burial in soil, many seeds apparently acquire a dormant condition. Wesson and Wareing (1969a) suspected light-absent dormancy was responsible for the flush of weed seedlings that they observed following cultivation of a field that had been in pasture for 6 years and before that was in cultivated crops. The area had 12.5 seedlings per square meter before disturbance and 300 seedlings per square meter after. Tests were made to determine whether light was the factor responsible. Holes 75 cm by 75 cm wide by 5 cm, 15 cm, and 30 cm deep were dug in the field. The holes were dug at night and the openings either covered or left open. Figure 5–6 shows the results. As can be seen, no germination occurred where light was excluded. Where light was provided, numerous seeds germinated. There were more seedlings at the 5 cm depth than at the 15 cm or 30 cm depth, which Wesson and Wareing attribute to the larger initial population of seeds at the shallower depth.

Sufficient information has now accumulated to indicate that species differ in their light sensitivity following burial. Although the majority likely need light to germinate after burial, Stoller and Wax (1974) found that ivy leaf morning-glory *(Ipomoea hederacea)* and cocklebur did not. The effect of burial on those seeds sensitive to light helps explain why such species are able to survive even though their seeds may not possess innate dormancy.

Furthermore, there is evidence that the burial effect may extend to species not considered to be light sensitive. As mentioned earlier, Wesson and Wareing, in additional work (1969b), found that following 50 weeks of burial, three species not originally sensitive to light needed light to germinate. In addition, common chickweed, which was inhibited by light before burial, needed light after being buried for 50 weeks. These results suggest that the mechanism for acquiring dormancy is different with burial than with exposure to light filtered through a leaf canopy.

Germination affected by phytochrome. It is now known that the responsiveness of seed germination to light is tied to a pigment in the seed called *phytochrome*. Phytochrome exists in the seed in two forms. One form promotes germination and the other does not. The quantities of each present at a given time is determined by light, more precisely by the red to far-red ratio of the light.

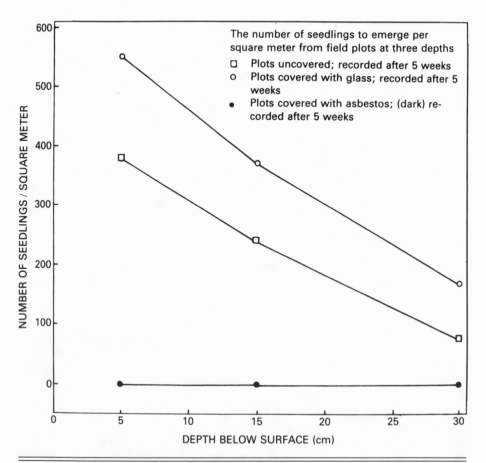

FIGURE 5–6. Light requirement of buried weed seeds. Numbers of seedlings per square meter were counted after 5 weeks at the bottom of holes 5 cm, 15 cm, or 30 cm deep whose openings were treated as follows: (1) uncovered, (2) covered with glass, (3) covered with asbestos (dark), and (4) asbestos cover replaced with a glass cover after 5 weeks and counted 3 weeks later.
Source: Wesson and Wareing, 1969a. From the Journal of Experimental Botany.

Light in the red (650 nm)[1] portion of the spectrum pushes the phytochrome towards the active form. That in the far-red (730 nm) pushes it towards the inactive form. This photoreaction is of the form:

---

[1]A nanometer (nm) is a unit for measuring wavelength. One nanometer is 1/1000 of a micron.

$$\text{Inactive form } (P_r) \quad \xrightarrow{\text{Red (650) nm}} \quad \text{Active form } (P_{fr})$$

$$\xleftarrow{\text{Far-red (730) nm}}$$

Note: Diagram from Taylorson and Borthwick, 1969. Reproduced with permission of Weed Science Society of America.

In the dark, the inactive form predominates. Unfiltered light, which contains a preponderance of red (650 nm range), would shift it to the active form. Since chlorophyll absorption is strong for light in the 650 nm range and weak for that beyond 700 nm, a leaf canopy shifts the red/far-red relationship in the transmitted light towards the far-red. This shift in turn causes an increase in inactive phytochrome, thus inhibiting germination. The red/far-red relationships may vary greatly under different microsites, as shown in Table 5–4. There is more than a three-fold range of ratios for the different types of shade.

A statement by Toole and his workers (1955) in their review of light effects provides a fitting summarization: "The germination process, which depends on respiration, is controlled at different points by the several factors. The photoreaction, while possibly present in all seeds, is not obligatory for germination for all seeds. It controls the levels of two compounds which are also under control by other reactions subject to influence by temperature." This statement serves to emphasize the complexity of the light relationship in germination. Nonetheless, it is clear that light is needed by enough species and in sufficient quantities that there may be opportunities in the use of crop cover and in the timing and depth of tillage to

TABLE 5-4

Red/far-red relationships in different microsites.

Type of Leaf Canopy	Ratio of Red/Far-Red
Shaded bare ground	0.85
Moderate shade, edge of tussock	0.80
Deep shade, middle of tussock	0.67
Bromegrass (Bromus erectus) (2 layers)	0.20
Linden (Tilia europaea) leaves (2 layers)	0.25
Tobacco (Nicotiana Tabaccum) leaves (2 layers)	0.28

Source: Data from Silvertown, 1980.

minimize emergence with the crop and over time the amount of viable seeds in the soil. Chapter 15 explores these opportunities in greater depth.

Temperature. It is common knowledge that temperature affects germination. Over the years, much work has been done with crop seeds, primarily in terms of identifying the best soil temperature for germination and seedling establishment. In view of the effect of temperature on physiological processes, we would expect temperature to have a modifying effect on germination rather than a triggering effect. That is to say, we might expect germination to occur with most species over a fairly wide temperature range. This, indeed, is the case.

Data for Florida pusley in Figure 5–7 are quite representative of the temperature effect on germination. As can be seen, germination approaching 50% or better occurred over a temperature range from 20°C to 35°C, with some germination occurring even at 40°C. Of course, species differ in the range of temperatures for best germination, but the general relationship is bell shaped, as

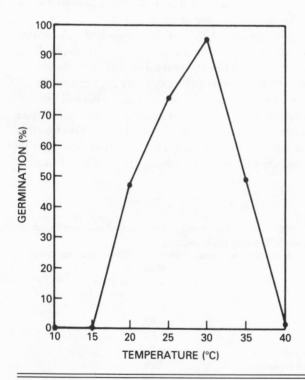

FIGURE 5–7. Effect of temperature on germination of weed seed.
Source: Data from Biswas et al., 1975.

TABLE 5-5

Days required for one-half of total weed emergence
from seeds planted 1/2 in. deep.

Weed	Temperature Ranges (°F)			
	35-50	50-65	65-80	80-95
Redroot pigweed	24	21	6	3
Tumblegrass	21	21	7	3
Barnyardgrass	31	25	8	5

Source: Wiese and Davis, 1967. Reproduced with permission of the
Weed Science Society of America.

TABLE 5-6

Effect of alternating temperatures on the germination
of seeds of wormseed mustard.

Treatment	Percent Germination at 5 Days
20°C constant, water	0
30°C constant, water	0
20°C-30°C, water	67

Source: Adapted from Steinbauer and Grigsby, 1957.

for Florida pusley. Thus, wild oat germinates over a range from 10°C to 30°C, with
the maximum at about 20°C (Friesen and Shebeski, 1961); tall morning-glory
(Ipomoea purpurea) over a range from 15°C to 35°C, with the maximum at 25°C to
30°C (Cole and Coats, 1973); and common mullein over a range from 15°C to 40°C,
with the maximum at 30°C (Semenza et al., 1978).

Temperature also affects the rate of germination. The responses of redroot
pigweed, tumblegrass *(Schedonnardus paniculatus)*, and barnyardgrass, shown
in Table 5–5, are representative of the pronounced effect on rate. Emergence was
6 to 8 times as rapid under the highest as under the lowest regimes. The message
for us in weed—crop ecology is that there may be ways of managing our cultivation
practices so as to avoid providing problem weeds with the temperature range
needed for seed germination. These ways are explored in Chapter 15.

Alternating temperatures.   Laboratory and field studies show that many weed
seeds germinate better under alternating rather than under constant temperatures.
The germination at 20°C to 30°C in Table 5–6 indicates how striking this effect

TABLE 5-7

Exposure of seeds of soapwort *(Saponaria officinalis)* to low temperature for best germination.

Temperature	Percent Germination
15°C constant,	0
20°C constant	0
30°C constant	0
20°C 16 hours, 30°C 8 hours	12
5°C 1 week, then 20°C–30°C	97

* Based on 4 × 100 seeds on two blotters in petri dish with water and darkness. Final counts at 21 days.

Source: Data from Steinbauer and Grigsby, 1957.

may be. Of the 85 weed species involved in these same studies, about 80% showed better germination under alternating rather than under constant temperatures.

Koller (1972) speculates that the effect of alternate temperatures might explain the observed effect of depth of burial on germination. As we saw earlier, many weed seeds emerge best from shallow depths. Because of the damping effect on temperature by the soil itself, temperature alterations are greater closer to the surface than farther down in the soil. Thus, better germination under alternating temperatures, he speculates, may be a matter of the seed's perception of the environment, in this case indicating that the seed is close enough to the surface for the seedling to emerge and become established. Irrespective of the reason, the fact that many weed seeds do germinate better under alternating temperatures and from shallow depths offers possibilities for managing our production practices to control germination of such weeds.

Need for low temperatures. Another temperature effect common to many weeds is that their seeds require temperatures at or below freezing before germination can occur. Further, an accumulation of several days at such temperatures is often necessary to satisfy the low temperature requirement of the seed. Results with soapwort *(Saponaria officinalis)*, shown in Table 5–7, are representative of this phenomenon that is characteristic for many temperate zone weeds.

The low temperature requirement has a clear-cut value for survival of such species in temperate climates. It precludes germination of seeds in the late summer or early fall when the seedling might soon be killed by freezing temperatures. Thus, it is a season-anticipating characteristic on the part of the seed. The physiological/biochemical processes that operate to explain the effect are still unclear. At this point, we can ask if there are ways to keep the seed from receiving the necessary accumulation of near-freezing days.

Water.   As discussed earlier, imbibition of water is the first step in the germination process. It is needed continuously thereafter. Thus, water obviously has a critical effect on germination. The important question for us in terms of weed–crop ecology is: What can be done about the environmental factors that determine the dynamics of water relations from the perspective of germinating weed seeds? Included among the environmental factors are physical properties of the soil, soil compaction, soluble material, the rate of supply and loss of water from the soil, and the seed contact. In this regard, we need to keep in mind that weeds evolved under uncertain soil moisture conditions. Thus, we expect them to be somewhat more tolerant of moisture extremes than crop plants, whose development and production have occurred because of our efforts to assure adequate moisture for germination and establishment.

Soil.   The soil may have an effect on germination. This effect appears to be mainly upon emergence rather than upon germination itself. Reduction in emergence is the result of: (1) obstruction to penetration by the coleoptile/hypocotyl under compacted soil conditions or (2) the inability of the plant shoot to penetrate a surface crust when it forms (Thill et al., 1979; and Wiese and Davis, 1967). Indirectly, of course, the soil can influence a number of factors that in turn affect germination and emergence. For example, both water-holding capacity and temperature are markedly affected by soil properties. In addition, as pointed out in the section on depth of burial, the soil acts as a damper on temperature extremes. For the most part, soil may be viewed as having a modifying effect on germination and seedling emergence.

Nitrate.   For some time, a weak nitrate solution used as a moistening agent has been known to improve germination of many crop seeds under laboratory conditions. Steinbauer and Grigsby (1957) also found that about half of 85 different weed species tested germinated better in dilute nitrate solution than in water alone. It follows that nitrate might have some effect on germination under field conditions. Limited work suggests that it does. Schimpf and Palmblad (1980) found a slight indication that nitrate in the soil stimulated germination of fresh yellow foxtail seed. Fawcett and Slife (1978) found that lambsquarters seed harvested from plots that received up to 336 kilograms of nitrogen per hectare in the form of ammonium nitrate germinated 34% compared with 3% from unfertilized plots. In this regard, they found a close correlation between rates of nitrogen applied and the concentration of nitrate in the lambsquarters seed. They did not see any effect of nitrate in the soil on number of weeds that emerged in the field.

Interactions of factors.   It is difficult to visualize field conditions under which only one of the factors discussed above would be involved as an influence on germination. That is to say, it is not possible to hold them at some constant level.

TABLE 5-8

Interactive effects of alternating temperature, nitrate, and light on germination of seeds of wormseed mustard.

Treatment	Percent Germination at 5 Days
20°C constant, water[2]	0
20°C constant, 0.2% KNO_3[2]	0
30°C constant, water[2]	6
30°C constant, 0.2% KNO_3[2]	7
20°-30°C, water[2]	67
20°-30°C, 0.2% KNO_3[2]	98
20°-30°C, water, light[3]	94
20°-30°C, water, dark[4]	53
20°-30°C, 0.2% KNO_3, light[3]	95
20°-30°C, 0.2% KNO_3, dark[4]	86

[1] Based on 4 × 100 seeds on two blotters in petri dishes.

[2] Darkness except during transfers and counts.

[3] 100 fc illumination from white fluorescent bulb.

[4] Complete darkness by wrapping petri dishes in aluminum foil, final counts only.

Source: Steinbauer and Grigsby, 1957.

Temperatures change with time of day and season, but so do light quality, intensity, and duration. Moisture level influences soil temperature, and so forth. Thus, interactions are the rule rather than the exception under field conditions, and the effects, therefore, are of interest to weed–crop ecology. The interrelationships between and among temperature, light, and nitrate (KNO_3) shown in Table 5–8 not only show that interactions do occur, but also that the effects are of a modifying rather than discrete nature. For example, alternating temperatures improved germination markedly over constant temperatures. Nitrate further improved germination, and light added an additional increment. Vincent and Roberts (1977), in fact, found that studies involving only one factor, especially those conducted in the laboratory, may have relatively limited application to field conditions. This conclusion is based on their finding several first- and second-order interactions among light, alternating temperatures, nitrate, and chilling. In fact, the greatest effect occurred when all three factors were involved.

RESUMPTION OF GROWTH: VEGETATIVE PARTS

Periodicity

As we saw with seeds, perennating parts also commonly exhibit periodicity. In yellow nutsedge, for example, it was found that emergence usually occurs from early May to the end of June in Illinois (Stoller and Wax, 1973). In quackgrass, regrowth usually occurs in early spring and again in late summer and early fall (Johnson and Buchholtz, 1962). This observed periodicity is no doubt related to the interactions of temperature, light, moisture, growth regulators, and any inherent dormancy. Regardless of the explanation, the existence of periodicity needs to be taken into account in any approach to control or manage such weeds. It is important to know also that periodicity is a relative matter. That is, no sharp line demarks the initiation and termination of regrowth. Rather, there is a time when relatively more growth occurs than at other times.

Effect of Correlative Inhibition

Apical dominance effect.   The inhibiting effect of one bud on another, termed *correlative inhibition*, is widespread among vegetative regenerating parts of weeds. Johnson and Buchholtz (1962) found that about 95% of the axillary buds on quackgrass rhizomes did not germinate unless the rhizome was fragmented. In this instance, there is an inhibiting effect of the apical meristem, called the *apical dominance effect*, on the buds at the nodes along the rhizome. The apical meristem effect has also been demonstrated in purple nutsedge (Smith and Fick, 1937), in ironweed (Davis and McCarty, 1966a), in bermudagrass (Moreira and Rosa, 1976), and in johnsongrass (Hull, 1970; and Beasley, 1970).

The inhibiting effect of the apical meristem, although not usually that of complete inhibition of other buds, is nevertheless very pronounced. The magnitude of this effect in johnsongrass, which is fairly representative of the magnitude in bermudagrass and quackgrass, is shown in Table 5–9. The presence of the apical meristem allows only 5% to 7% germination of the axillary buds. Removing the apical meristem allowed a three- to five-fold increase in germination of the axillary buds.

This phenomenon has been extensively studied in quackgrass. Results of this work have greatly expanded our understanding of the environmental effect, leading to these conclusions: (1) Separating the rhizome from the parent increases the apical dominance effect (McIntyre, 1969); (2) dividing the rhizome into single-node sections reduces, but does not completely eliminate, the dominance effect (McIntyre, 1972; Hull, 1970; and Moreira and Rosa, 1976); and (3) apical

TABLE 5-9

Influence of the apical meristem on the sequence of bud germination of three-node johnsongrass rhizome pieces.

	Bud Position		
	Apical	Middle	Basal
	(% Germination*)		
Apical meristem present (74 pieces)	87.8	5.4	6.8
Apical meristem absent (67 pieces)	55.2	28.4	16.4

* The first bud to produce a shoot is regarded as the one germinating.

Source: Hull, 1970. Reproduced with permission of the Weed Science Society of America.

dominance is reduced by high nitrogen fertilization of the parent plant (Robinson, 1976; McIntyre, 1965, 1971, and 1972; and Leakey et al., 1978c). Furthermore, nitrate in the germinating medium either reduces or offsets the apical dominance effect.

Shoot dominance effect. The extensive work with quackgrass also shows a correlative inhibition effect among shoots. This effect is for one or a few shoots to inhibit or completely prevent the growth of other buds on a rhizome fragment. In Figure 5–8, the shoot originating from the number 3 node has restricted growth of buds at the 1, 2, and 4 nodes and almost completely prevented growth at the 5, 6, and 7 nodes.

Light, temperature, nitrogen, and growth regulators have been examined for their possible effects on shoot dominance. Light appears to have two distinct effects (Leakey et al., 1978b). One effect inhibits all buds for a short time (4 weeks) on some fragments. Far-red light appears to increase this incidence. The second effect releases shoot dominance in some fragments. Temperature effects are different for the two extremes (Leakey et al., 1978a). Permanent dominance apparently is not established when temperatures are maintained at about 3°C. At 33°C, very little shoot dominance occurs. In the range from 13°C to 26°C, shoot dominance does occur. Nitrate in the soil may influence the dominance effect. This effect has been demonstrated in some studies in the laboratory (Leakey et al., 1978a), although there are other studies in which it has not (Chancellor, 1974). It appears that the nitrogen content of the rhizome has a greater influence than nitrogen content exogenous to the rhizome.

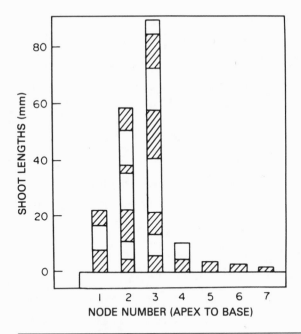

FIGURE 5–8. Shoot dominance effect in quackgrass among shoots on a rhizome fragment. Horizontal lines on bars represent lengths after 3, 5, 7, 10, 12, 14, 17, and 20 days, respectively.

Source: Chancellor, 1974. Reproduced with permission of Blackwell Scientific Publications, Ltd.

Correlative inhibition theories.   A detailed consideration of the mechanisms involved in correlative inhibition is not given here. Some understanding of such mechanisms is important, however, for possible use of the observed effects to prevent losses from weeds. We need to recognize at the outset that both apical and shoot dominance serve to protect some buds against destruction from an environmental catastrophe such as cultivation. Two theories exist to explain the observed result.

The *nutritive control theory* holds that the observed results are an expression of competition, especially for nitrogen (McIntyre, 1965 and 1969). Indeed, it has been shown that there is a gradient of nitrogen in rhizomes in the direction of the apical meristem. Further, it is known that nitrogen enhances utilization of carbohydrate reserves. Thus, growth resumption by the apical bud or nearby buds under this theory is explained by nitrogen-enhanced mobilization of food materials in this area of the rhizome. Once growth of this bud or buds becomes established, there is a flow of food materials to the developing shoot or shoots.

The *growth regulator theory* holds that inhibition is the result of growth regulators that affect translocation of nutrients and inhibition of axillary buds. Many studies show that growth regulators have such a modifying effect in yellow nutsedge (Tumbleson and Kommedahl, 1961; Garg et al., 1967; and Aleixo and Valio, 1976), in ironweed (Davis and McCarty, 1966a), in quackgrass (Leakey et al., 1978a and 1978b), and in johnsongrass (Beasley, 1970). On the basis of available evidence, both theories are likely to be involved, although the exact mechanism is yet to be determined. Not understanding the mechanism further compounds our problems of dealing with such weed species. Nevertheless, the overwhelming evidence showing many effects of factors that can be manipulated is encouraging relative to the potential these factors offer for preventing losses from such species over time.

Age Spectrum

We have thus far considered resumption of growth without regard to the age spectrum of perennating parts. Further, as we have seen, a rhythmic relationship is evident, at least in temperate regions, between season of the year and regeneration of growth from perennating parts. However, a moment's pause to reflect that growth is an on-going process in perennial weeds tells us that rhizomes or rootstocks of different ages are present at any given time. It is this entire population of rhizomes, rootstocks, tubers, and the like on a given land area at a particular point in time that must be dealt with in minimizing competition for our desired plants.

Once new growth begins in the spring, the relationship between new and old perennating parts in many species is likely to be like that shown for quackgrass in Figure 5–9. That is, the sprouting on old parts steadily depletes their viability. This effect is offset by the development of new parts. The result is a shift in the age spectrum as the season progresses. The total in an established stand remains fairly constant except for a period in early June, when the total goes up because new rhizomes are being produced more rapidly than old ones are being depleted. The important point for weed management is that the population of reproductive parts contains parts of different physiological ages. As a result, they are expected to vary in their response to control attempts.

Growth Regulators

The area of growth regulator effects on resumption of growth of perennating parts is quite limited. That work which has been done suggests that endogenous growth regulators affect germination.

Aleixo and Valio (1976) found that the leaching of 70-day-old purple nutsedge tubers markedly decreased growth of the buds compared with those tubers that were not leached. This effect lessened with age of the tubers until at 150 days of

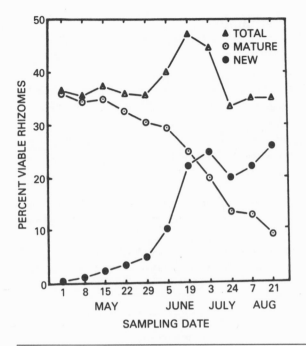

FIGURE 5–9. Shifts in the age spectrum of quackgrass rhizomes during the growing season.
Source: Johnson and Buchholtz, 1962. Reproduced with permission of the Weed Science Society of America.

age, there was no difference in growth between leached and nonleached tubers. The authors suggest that this result is due to the leaching out of growth-promoting gibberellins; the tissues become less leachable with age. Under chromatographic analysis, they identified three types of growth-regulating substances, including gibberellin-like substances, cytokinin-like substances, and an indolic substance. They also found that drying the tubers for up to 96 hours destroyed the gibberellin activity, did not affect the indole activity, and increased the cytokinin activity.

Two studies on yellow nutsedge yielded conflicting results. Tumbleson and Kommedahl (1961) found that leaching the tubers under tap water increased germination about 10 times, thus implicating water-soluble growth inhibitors. Tames and Vieitz (1970), working with the same species, obtained the opposite results. Clearly, additional work is needed before any generalized conclusions can be drawn as to the precise effects of growth-regulating substances on resumption of growth. However, abscisic acid appears to be the primary hormone that causes bud dormancy and apparently is day-length sensitive (Salisbury and Ross, 1978). As more is learned, this area, too, may offer opportunities for manipulation in managing perennial weeds.

Environmental Effects on Resumption of Growth

As in the preceding section on seeds, factors affecting germination and emergence from perennating parts are first examined individually and then collectively to provide as much insight as possible about the factors involved. It must be emphasized, however, that under field conditions, no one factor is apt to be acting independently of at least one or more other factors. As with seeds, the physiological and biochemical processes involved in explaining the observed results are not presented except when they are needed to clarify the effect of a factor.

Depth of burial.   An inverse relationship exists between depth of burial and emergence for most perennating parts, as can be seen for two species in Figures 5–10 and 5–11. For both types of perennating parts—tubers and rhizomes—emergence dropped off rather sharply with increases in depth. Planting depth also influences the rate of emergence. For example, in Figure 5–10, we see that 33

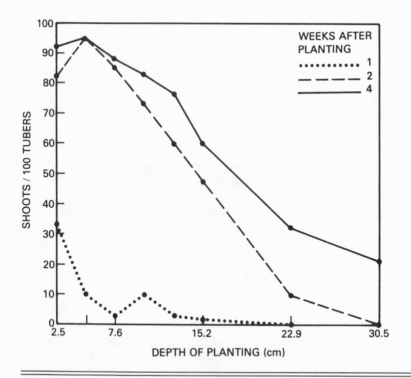

FIGURE 5–10. Effect of burial depth on emergence from yellow nutsedge tubers.
Source: Data from Tumbleson and Kommedahl, 1961.

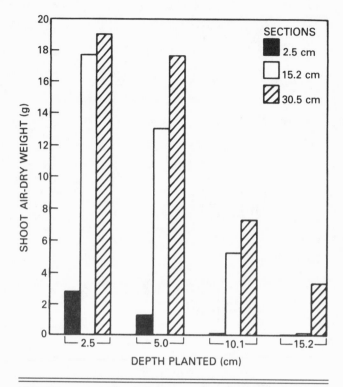

FIGURE 5–11. Effect of size of rhizome section on re-growth of quackgrass from different depths of burial in soil.
Source: Data from Vengris, 1962.

nutsedge shoots had emerged by the end of 1 week from tubers planted 2.5 cm deep, whereas it took 4 weeks for 32 shoots to emerge from 22.9 cm. Further, in quackgrass (Figure 5–11), the size of the rhizome section directly influenced the number of shoots, with emergence from the 15.2 cm (6 in.) depth for 30.5 cm (12 in.) segments being somewhat greater than emergence from 2.5 cm (1 in.) for 2.5 cm (1 in.) segments.

The above study of burial depth with yellow nutsedge was done in the greenhouse, where winter survival was not a factor. In the field, it has been shown for yellow nutsedge (Figure 5–12) that winterkill at shallower depths may cause emergence to increase with depth of burial down to at least 10.2 cm. In this study, less than 4% of the tubers down to 7.6 cm survived the low soil temperatures experienced in the winter. The quackgrass rhizomes in Figure 5–11 were held over winter under conditions intended to simulate exposure in the field. As can be seen, they are quite tolerant of low temperatures.

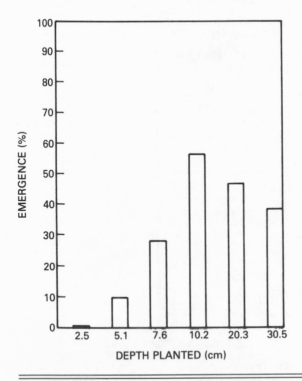

FIGURE 5–12. Effect of burial depth on overwinter survival of yellow nutsedge tubers.
Source: Data from Stoller and Wax, 1973.

In relative terms, it appears that emergence from perennating parts occurs from greater depths than from seed. Indeed, some perennials successfully emerge from perennating parts several meters deep. Offsetting this advantage of perennating parts is the relatively greater resistance to loss of viability at shallow depth on the part of seeds. The net result for preventive control is that depth of burial offers fewer opportunities for effectively dealing with perennating parts than it does with seed. This conclusion will be expanded upon in Chapter 15.

Temperature. The limited work to measure temperature effects indicates that regrowth can occur over a fairly wide range of temperatures, with a relatively narrow optimum range. The temperature effect is shown for two different species in Figure 5–13. The optimum ranges for the two species no doubt determine their distribution. Quackgrass (Figure 5–13B), which is a common weed in the northern temperate regions, has a lower temperature optimum than ironweed *(Vernonia*

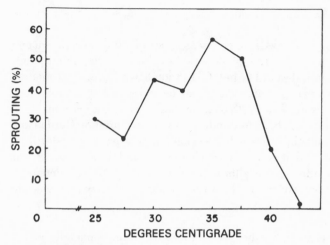

A. Ironweed sprouting

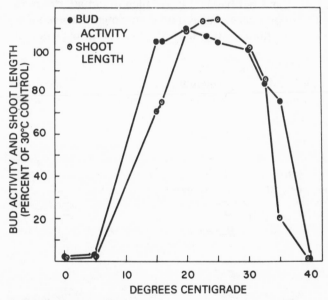

B. Quackgrass sprouting

FIGURE 5–13. Fairly wide temperature range for regrowth of rhizome buds, with relatively narrow optimum range.

Source: Part A from Davis and McCarty, 1966b; Part B from Meyer and Buchholtz, 1963. Reproduced with permission of the Weed Science Society of America.

baldwini) (Figure 5–13A), which is more common somewhat south of quackgrass in northern latitudes.

It appears that buds, as do seeds, have a season-anticipating mechanism and that this mechanism is determined by photoperiod exposure of the parent plant. With respect to temperature, it would be helpful to know to what degree alternating temperatures affect regrowth since this variable can be influenced by time of tillage and depth of burial in the soil. Work with oxalis *(Oxalis cernua)*, a perennial with scaly bulbs, showed regrowth to be better under temperature variation (Jordan and Day, 1967). Also, the fact that regrowth from perennating parts is better from shallow depths in the soil—that is, in places where winterkill does not occur—is at least circumstantial evidence that alternating temperatures may be important since temperature variations are greater closer to the surface than deeper down in the profile.

Light.   Light may be a factor in the resumption of growth, especially in the pattern of such growth. Table 5–10 provides some evidence for this effect. Buds on tubers exposed to white, blue, and red (visible) light failed to initiate rhizomes, although roots and leaves were produced. Far-red light promoted rhizome initiation, as well as roots and leaves. This and other work suggest that the phytochrome system is involved.

Koukkari and Hillman (1966) found that phytochrome is present in vegetative reproductive parts of horticultural and ornamental plants and that it concentrates in such areas of growth as buds and cambial regions. Further, they also showed

TABLE 5-10

Effect of light of different wavelengths on the growth pattern of tuber buds of purple nutsedge.

| Treatments | Pattern of Growth | | |
	Root	Leaf	Rhizome
Darkness	+	−	+
While light	+	+	−
Blue light	+	+	−
Red light	+	+	−
Far-red light	+	+	+

* Results after one week of incubation.

+ = present.

− = not present.

Source: Data from Aleixo and Valio, 1976.

that the total amount of phytochrome can be influenced by exposure to red light. Duke and Williams (1977) found measurable levels of phytochrome in johnson-grass rhizomes, and the amount depended upon location on the rhizome. In general, the phytochrome level decreased basipetally from the apex to the eighth node. More needs to be learned about the effect of light on vegetative regrowth to know if it may offer an opportunity for preventive approaches through tillage and other production practices.

Nitrogen.   In early work, nitrogen fertilizer was found to markedly increase sprouting of buds of quackgrass rhizomes growing in such soil (Dexter, 1937). Further studies showed that soil nitrogen level was associated with concentration of nitrogen in the rhizomes. In addition, rhizomes with a high concentration of nitrogen sprouted more than did those with a low concentration (Dexter, 1942). More recently, nitrogen has also been found to encourage sprouting of lateral buds of johnsongrass. Sprouting was 73.9% for high nitrogen treatment versus 33% at the lowest level of nitrogen (Myers and Caso, 1976). It is not clear whether the effect observed is that of nitrogen or of no nitrogen. That is, is there a type of dormancy associated with no nitrogen, or is sprouting being promoted by available nitrogen under the high nitrogen levels? Irrespective of the mechanism involved, it seems clear that the nitrogen level in the soil in which the perennating part is produced influences the resumption of growth from that part. This information should be usable in developing preventive approaches for such weeds.

Size.   Work on nutsedge, quackgrass, and johnsongrass shows that the size of a vegetative reproductive part is an influence on germination and emergence. For both johnsongrass and quackgrass, the percent of buds that sprouted (germinated) decreased as the length of rhizome increased. This relationship for johnsongrass is shown in Figure 5–14.

A similar pattern was found for quackgrass (Vengris, 1962), although the decline with length was steeper. With quackgrass, 80% of the buds on 2.5 cm (1 in.) rhizome sections produced shoots. This percentage dropped to 31% for 5.2 cm (6 in.) rhizomes. The effect of rhizome length on germination of buds is significant for management and control since it is something that can obviously be affected by the type and amount of tillage. The explanation for this observed effect is likely to lie in the fact that as the length of rhizomes is reduced, the dominance relationship is reduced.

Work with nutsedge tubers, shown in Table 5–11, shows that size of tuber does not affect germination as such (Table 5–11a) but does affect emergence (Table 5–11b). The larger tubers are more successful in producing shoots that emerge. Chapter 4 pointed out that tubers produced by plants in shade are smaller

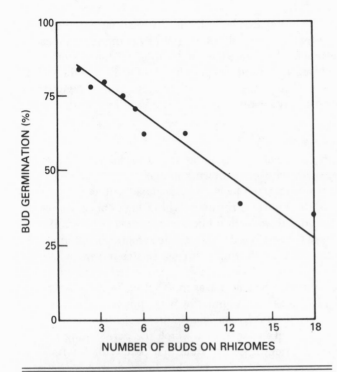

FIGURE 5–14. Inverse relationship of johnsongrass bud germination to the number of buds on the rhizome.
Source: McWhorter, 1972. Reproduced with permission of the Weed Science Society of America.

TABLE 5-11

Germination versus emergence of yellow nutsedge tubers as affected by size of tuber.

Tuber Fresh Weight (mg/tuber)	Germination[a] (%)	Tuber Dry Weight (mg/tuber)	Emergence[b] (%)
294	92	120	44.6
201	91	50	29.7
128	83		
61	86		

[a] Adapted from Stoller, Nema, and Bhan, 1972.

[b] Adapted from Stoller and Wax, 1973.

than those on unshaded plants (Patterson, 1982). The combination of shading and deep burial could reduce an infestation by preventing emergence from the small tubers in the population.

CONCEPTS AND CONCLUSIONS

1. Germination of seeds involves a precise sequence of events; this sequence may either be delayed in its initiation or stopped along the way by what is termed dormancy.
2. Dormancy, although not itself a factor in competition, is important in the persistence and survival of weeds.
3. Many seeds, and possibly vegetative regenerating parts, have an apparent season-anticipating characteristic that assures resumption of growth when chances are optimal for survival and completion of their life cycle.
4. Although there are quite wide differences among species, the general pattern is that emergence from seed is inversely related to depth of burial; the top 2.5 cm soil layer contributes the most new seedlings.
5. Many weed seeds require light for germination; the far-red, which passes through leaves, in fact often inhibits germination.
6. Many weed seeds that do not have innate dormancy acquire dormancy when subjected to shading by burial in the soil and thus are protected against rapid loss of viability.
7. Temperature is a modifying rather than a triggering factor in germination. Thus, the curve relating temperature and germination percentage is S-shaped.
8. Germination of seeds of weeds common to temperate regions is improved by exposure to alternating temperatures and by accumulated exposure to temperatures at or below freezing.
9. Emergence for perennating parts is also inversely related to depth of burial, but in general terms, such emergence is from greater depths than the depths for seeds.
10. Growth-regulating substances are most likely important modifiers of resumption of growth of both seeds and perennating parts.
11. High nitrogen levels in soil are conducive to regrowth from perennating parts produced by weeds grown under such conditions.
12. With rhizomes, an inverse relationship exists between the length of the rhizome and the number of buds that sprout.
13. With perennating parts, it is common for one bud to have an inhibiting effect on regrowth of other buds; the apical bud commonly possesses this inhibiting effect.

REFERENCES

Aamisepp, A. 1966. Herbicide effects on plants from seeds from treated plants. Vaxtodling 22:1–147.

Aleixo, M.D., and I.F. Valio, II. 1976. Effect of light, temperature, and endogenous growth regulators on the growth of *Cyperus rotundus* tubers. Zeitschrift fur Pflangenphipiologic 80 (4):336–47.

Beasley, C.A. 1970. Development of johnsongrass rhizomes. Weed Sci. 18 (2):218–22.

Biswas, R.K., et al. 1975. Germination behavior of Florida pusley seeds. I. Effects of storage, light, temperature, and planting depths on germination. Weed Sci. 23 (5):400–03.

Chancellor, R.J. 1974. The development of dominance amongst shoots arising from fragments of *Agropyron repens* rhizomes. Weed Res. 14:29–38.

Chu, C.C., R.D. Sweet, and J.L. Ozbun. 1978. Some germination characteristics in common lambsquarters *(Chenopodium album)*. Weed Sci. 26 (3):255–58.

Clutter, M.E., ed. 1978. Dormancy and development arrest: Experimental analysis in plants and animals. New York: Academic Press.

Cole, A.W., and G.E. Coats. 1973. Tall morning-glory germination response to herbicides and temperature. Weed Sci. 21 (5):443–46.

Davis, F.S., and M.K. McCarty. 1966a. Effect of several factors on the expression of dormancy in Western ironweed. Weeds 14 (1):62–69.

———. 1966b. Respiration, RQ, and activities of three enzymes during the transition from the dormant to the active state in Western ironweed. Weeds 14 (1):69–73.

deJong, E., and H.J.V. Schappert. 1972. Calculation of soil respiration and activity from CO_2 profiles in the soil. Soil Sci. 113:328–33.

Dexter, S.T. 1937. The drought resistance of quackgrass under various degrees of fertilization with nitrogen. Agron. J. 29:568–76.

———. 1942. Seasonal variations in drought resistance of exposed rhizomes of quackgrass. Agron. J. 34:1125–36.

Duke, S.O., and R.D. Williams. 1977. Phytochrome distribution in johnsongrass rhizomes. Weed Sci. 25 (3):229–32.

Egley, G.J. 1974. Dormancy variations in common purslane seeds. Weed Sci. 22 (6):535–40.

Fawcett, R.S., and F.W. Slife. 1978. Effects of field applications of nitrate on weed seed germination and dormancy. Weed Sci. 26 (6):594–96.

Fenner, M. 1980a. The inhibition of germination of *Bidens pilosa* seeds by leaf canopy shade in some natural vegetation types. New Phyto. 84 (1):95–101.

———. 1980b. Germination tests on 32 East African weed species. Weed Res. 20 (3):135–38.

Friesen, G., and L.H. Shebeski. 1961. The influence of temperature on the germination of wild oat seed. Weeds 9 (4):634–38.

Garg, D.K., L.E. Bendixen, and S.R. Anderson. 1967. Rhizome differentiation in yellow nutsedge. Weeds 15 (2):124–28.

Gorski, T., K. Gorska, and J. Nowicki. 1977. Germination of seeds of various species under leaf canopy. Flora, Morphologie, Geobotanik, Oekophysiologie 166:249–59.

Gutterman, Y. 1978. Germinability of seeds as a function of the maternal environment. Acta Horticulturae 83:41–55.

Harper, J.L. 1977. Population biology of plants. New York: Academic Press.

Hart, J.W., and A.M.M. Berrie. 1966. The germination of *Avena fatua* under different gaseous environments. Physiol. Plant 19:1020–25.

Hill, T.A. 1977. The biology of weeds. London: Edward Arnold.

Hull, R.J. 1970. Germination control of johnsongrass rhizome buds. Weed Sci. 18 (1):118–21.

Jeffrey, L.S., and J.D. Nalewaja. 1970. Studies of achene dormancy in fumitory. Weed Sci. 18 (3):345–48.

Johnson, A.A., and S.T. Dexter. 1939. The response of quackgrass to variations in height of cutting and rates of application of N. Agron. J. 31:67–76.

Johnson, B.G., and K.P. Buchholtz. 1962. The natural dormancy of vegetative buds on the rhizomes of quackgrass. Weeds 10 (1):53–57.

Jordan, L.S., and B.E. Day. 1967. Effect of temperature on growth of *Oxalis cernua* Thumb. Weeds 15 (3):285.

Kidd, F. 1914. The controlling influence of carbon dioxide in the maturation, dormancy, and germination of seeds, Part II. Proc. R. Soc. London, Ser. 13.87:609–25.

―――, and C. West. 1917. The controlling influence of carbon dioxide. Ann. Bot. 31:457–87.

Koller, D. 1972. Environmental control of seed germination. In T.T. Kozlowski, ed., Seed biology, vol. II, pp. 1–101. New York: Academic Press.

Koukkari, W.L., and W.S. Hillman. 1966. Phytochrome levels assayed by in vivo spectrophotometry in modified underground stems and storage roots. Physiol. Plant 19:1073–78.

Leakey, R.R.B., R.T. Chancellor, and D. Vince-Prue. 1978a. Regeneration from rhizome fragments of *Agropyron repens*, 3. Effects of N and temperature on the development of dominance amongst shoots on multinode fragments. Ann. Bot. 42:197–204.

―――. 1978b. Regeneration from rhizome fragments of *Agropyron repens* (L.) Beauv., IV. Effects of light on bud dormancy and development of dominance amongst shoots on multinode fragments. Ann. Bot. 42:205–12.

―――. 1978c. Regeneration from rhizome fragments of Agropyron repens., I. The seasonality of shoot growth and rhizome reserves in single-node fragments. Ann. Appl. Biol. 87:423–31.

Maun, M.A., and P.B. Cavers. 1970. Influences of soil temperature on reproduction of curly dock. Weed Sci. 18 (2):202–03.

McIntyre, G.I. 1965. Some effects of the nitrogen supply on the growth and development of *Agropyron repens*. Weed Res. 5:1–12.

―――. 1969. Apical dominance in the rhizome of *Agropyron repens*, Evidence of competition for carbohydrate as a factor in the mechanism of inhibition. Can. J. Bot. 47:1189–97.

_____. 1971. Apical dominance in the rhizome of *Agropyron repens* in isolated rhizomes. Can. J. Bot. 49:99–109.

_____. 1972. Studies on bud development in the rhizomes of *Agropyron repens*., II. The effect of nitrogen supply. Can. J. Bot. 50:393–401.

McWhorter, C.G. 1972. Factors affecting johnsongrass rhizome production and germination. Weed Sci. 20 (1):41–45.

Meyer, R.E., and K.P. Buchholtz. 1963. Effect of temperature, carbon dioxide, and oxygen levels on quackgrass rhizome buds. Weeds 11 (1):1–7.

Moreira, I., and M.L. Rosa. 1976. The effect of nodal position on the sprouting of buds on *Cynodon dactylon*. In II Simposio Nacional de Herbalogia, Oeircis, vol. 1, pp. 37–43. Lisbon, Portugal.

Myers, E.J., and O.H. Caso. 1976. The effect of nitrogen supply on the growth of *Sorghum halepense*. Malezas 5 (2):3–12.

Palmer, J.H., and G.R. Sagar. 1963. *Agropyron repens* L. Beauv. J. Ecol. 51:783–94.

Patterson, D.T. 1982. Shading responses of purple and yellow nutsedge *(Cyperus rotundus* and *C. esculentus)*. Weed Sci. 30 (1):25–30.

Richardson, S.G. 1979. Factors influencing the development of primary dormancy in wild oat seeds. Can. J. of Plant Sci. 59 (3)777–84.

Robinson, E.L. 1976. Yield and height of cotton as affected by weed density and nitrogen level. Weed Sci. 24 (1):40–42.

Salisbury, F.B., and C.W. Ross. 1978. Plant physiology, 2nd ed. Belmont, Calif.: Wadsworth.

Schimpf, D.J., and I.G. Palmblad. 1980. Germination response of weed seeds to soil nitrate and ammonium with and without simulated overwintering. Weed Sci. 28 (2):190–93.

Semenza, R.J., J.A. Young, and R.A. Evans. 1978. Influence of light and temperature on the germination and seedbed ecology of common mullein *(Verbascum thapsus)*. Weed Sci. 26 (5):577–81.

Silvertown, J. 1980. Leaf-canopy-induced seed dormancy in a grassland flora. New Phyto. 85 (1):109–18.

Simpson, G.M. 1978. Metabolic rate of dormancy in seeds—A case history of the wild oat. In H.E. Clutter, ed., Dormancy and development arrest: Experimental analysis in plants and animals. New York: Academic Press.

Smith, E.V. and G.L. Fick. 1937. Nutgrass eradication studies: 1. Relation of the life history of nutgrass *(Cyperus rotundus* L.), to possible methods of control. J. Am. Soc. Agron. 29:1007–13.

Steinbauer, G.P., and B. Grigsby. 1957. Interaction of temperature, light, and moistening agent in the germination of weed seeds. Weeds 5 (3):175–82.

Stoller, E.W., D.P. Neva, and V.M. Bhan. 1972. Yellow nutsedge tuber germination and seedling development. Weed Sci. 20 (1):93–97.

Stoller, E.W., and L.M. Wax. 1973. Yellow nutsedge shoot emergence and tuber longevity. Weed Sci. 21 (1):76–81.

_____. 1974. Dormancy changes and fate of some annual weed seeds in the soil. Weed Sci. 22 (2):151–55.

Tames, R.S., and E. Vieitz. 1970. Estudios sobre la brotadura de tubereulos de

Cyperus sculentus Tem. Var. Aureus Richt, I. Accion de factores fisicos y quimicos. Anales Edafologia Agrobiology 29:775–81.

Taylor, J.S., and G.M. Simpson. 1980. Endogenous hormones in after-ripening wild oat seed. Can. J. Bot. 58 (9):1016–24.

Taylorson, R.B., and H.A. Borthwick. 1969. Light filtration by foliar canopies: Significance for light-controlled weed seed germination. Weed Sci. 17 (1):48–51.

Thill, D.C., R.D. Schirman, and A.P. Appleby. 1979. Influence of soil moisture, temperature, and compaction on the germination and emergence of downy brome *(Bromus tectorum)*. Weed Sci. 27 (6):625–30.

Toole, E.H., et al. 1955. Interaction of temperatures and light in germination of seeds. Plant Physiol. 30:473–78.

Tumbleson, M.E., and T. Kommedahl. 1961. Reproductive potential of Cyperus esculentus by tubers. Weeds 9 (4):646–53.

Vengris, J. 1962. The effect of rhizome length and depth of planting on the mechanical and chemical control of quackgrass. Weeds 10 (1):71–74.

Villiers, T.A. 1972. Seed dormancy. In T.T. Kozlowski, ed., Seed biology, vol. II, pp. 219–81. New York: Academic Press.

Vincent, E.M., and E.H. Roberts. 1977. The interaction of light, nitrate, and alternating temperatures in promoting germination of dormant seeds of common weed species. Seed Sci. and Tech. 5 (2):659–70.

Walbot, V. 1978. Control mechanisms for plant embryogeny. In M.E. Clutter, ed., Dormancy and developmental arrest: Experimental analysis in plants and animals. New York: Academic Press.

Wesson, G., and P.F. Wareing. 1969a. The role of light in the germination of naturally occurring populations of buried weed seeds. J. Exp. Bot. 20:402–13.

_____. 1969b. The induction of light sensitivity in weed seeds by burial. J. Exp. Bot. 20:414–25.

Wiese, A.F., and R.G. Davis. 1967. Weed emergence from two soils at various moistures, temperatures, and depths. Weeds 15 (2):118–21.

COMPETITIVENESS OF WEEDS

6

A general understanding of losses caused by weeds is important background to an understanding of the complicated nature of competition and ultimately to successful approaches for preventing or minimizing such losses. Answers to such questions as, When must weeds be controlled to avoid losses in crop yield? and How many weeds can a crop tolerate without suffering losses in yield? have been, and continue to be, central to weed research. Thus, it is not surprising that a sizable literature has accumulated on weed–crop competition. A review of such literature to mid-1978 by Zimdahl (1980) includes 586 citations. Refer to this publication for results of studies concerning specific weeds in specific crops. The concepts and general trends and their relationships to established ecological concepts and principles, where such can be established, are covered here.

DIRECT AND INDIRECT LOSSES FROM WEEDS

In general terms, losses may be subdivided into two categories: direct and indirect. *Direct losses* are those that reduce the quantity or cash return of the crop produced. Included are reductions in yield, both that produced and that harvested, and contamination resulting in a dockage for the crop when it is sold. *Indirect losses* are those that represent a cost to society at large or to the crop producer and property owner but in themselves do not represent a reduction in cash return. Included are the harboring of insects, diseases, and pests of other crops; creation of safety hazards, such as limited visibility at highway intersections; creation of health hazards, such as those posed by ragweed pollen for hay fever sufferers and by poison ivy for those sensitive to its toxin; reduction in property values; the increased cost of right-of-way maintenance; and the increased cost of crop production since many of the practices involved in producing crops are primarily for weed control or weed prevention.

Reductions in Crop Yield

The losses of main concern to weed–crop ecology are those related to yield. Thus, direct losses are our concern as we turn to a consideration of competition. Weeds may reduce crop yields in two ways: (1) by reducing the amount of harvestable product (grain, stover, forage, and so on) produced by the crop, and (2) by reducing the amount of crop actually harvested.

Reduction in harvestable crop. As we shall see, the extent of reduction in crop yield caused by weeds varies greatly depending upon the crop, the weed, and the growing conditions. A severe infestation present for the entire growing season may result in complete loss of some crops. Because weeds cut yields, means for controlling them have been an integral part of agriculture for all of recorded history. Great strides have been made in weed control, especially since the 1940s. The impetus for control, of course, has been the availability of selective new herbicides. The net effect has been to very much reduce crop losses from weeds. Even so, it is estimated (Chandler, 1980) that weeds still reduce yields of all crops by about 12% in the United States.

Reductions in harvested crop. Weeds can cause sizable machine losses when grain crops are combined. The losses can be a result of: (1) the additional bulk provided by weeds interfering with threshing and separating of grain, and (2) weeds interfering with actual cutting and movement of the grain into the combine. Some representative losses of this nature are shown in Table 6–1. Average losses

TABLE 6-1

Soybean harvest losses caused by redroot pigweed and giant foxtail.

	Percent Loss		
Weed	Header Losses*	Threshing and Separating Losses	Total Losses
Redroot pigweed	5.35	0.73	6.08
Giant foxtail	1.55	0.81	2.36

* Includes losses from (a) beans free of pods or in pods free of stalks, (b) beans in pods remaining attached to the stubble, (c) beans remaining in pods attached to stalks that were not cut, and (d) beans remaining in pods attached to stalks that were cut but not delivered into the harvester.

Source: Data from Nave and Wax, 1971.

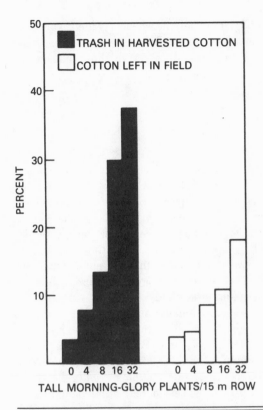

FIGURE 6–1. Reduction in the quality of mechanically harvested cotton and increase in the amount missed by the picker caused by weeds.
Source: Data from Crowley and Buchanan, 1978.

were doubled by redroot pigweed and increased about 1 1/2 times by giant foxtail. The major part of the loss occurred at the header. Weeds, particularly redroot pigweed, resulted in more beans remaining in pods left on the stubble and more beans on stalks cut but not delivered into the combine. Threshing and separating losses were about the same for both weeds and approximately 3 times the losses for weed-free soybeans.

Weeds may also reduce harvested yield and lower the quality of fiber crops such as cotton. Figure 6–1 shows that trash in mechanically harvested cotton and cotton left in the field increased as the number of tall morning-glory plants in the cotton row increased. As few as 4 weeds in a 15-meter row more than doubled the amount of trash.

Some weeds, when present in the harvested crop, reduce the price received by the producer. For example, in Missouri, if the number of wild garlic bulblets is 2 or more per 1000 grams of wheat (about 65 per bushel) the wheat is graded "garlicky" and docked in price. Harvest losses and dockage are direct losses from weeds and should be kept in mind as possible additional losses to those caused by competition.

COMMUNITY YIELD

At the outset, it is important to consider the applicability of the ecological principles of limiting factors to weed–crop competition. Chapter 2 explained that there is a limit to how many individuals can occupy a given area. Does this have implications for the total yield of the crop plus weeds that can be produced on a given area? The answer is important to weed management. If the combined, community, yield exceeds the yield of the weed-free crop, adding the competed-for factor is an alternative to removing the weed. Of course, this may not be practical. If the combined yield does not exceed the yield of the weed-free crop, then the weed must be removed to obtain maximum crop yield.

Combinations of crops have been used occasionally with field and horticultural crops for many years. The practice is quite common with forages. The results of extensive studies of community yield of such mixtures provide principles to help answer the question of weed–crop community yield. Trenbath (1976) summarized and interpreted results of many of these studies. Information on yield related to a single growth factor is discussed first to provide a basis for better understanding the discussion of density and community yield relationships that follows. Growth factors are discussed in detail in Chapter 7. At this point, we need only recognize that competition frequently occurs for light, water, and nutrients in mixtures of species. Q may be any one of these.

Uptake of Growth Factors by Mixtures of Species

By definition, weeds are interfering associates with desired plants. Thus, the proportionate uptake of available resources, or *growth factors*, determines the extent of weed competition. In fact, as we see later, a reduction in crop yield by weeds is a result of the weeds obtaining a disproportionate share of the available resources. Here, a review of the theory involved in competitive uptake by a mixture of species helps to clarify why the community yield usually does not exceed unity.

Figure 6–2 shows the relationship between biomass and uptake of the competed-for factor Q. In this figure, it is assumed that A uses Q more efficiently than does B. When grown together, therefore, per plant uptake by A (resulting in Y_A yield) increases over the uptake when grown alone (resulting in Y_{AA} yield)

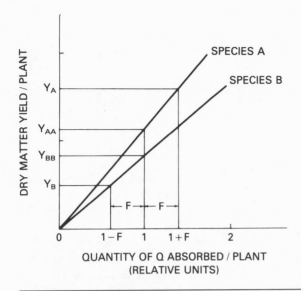

FIGURE 6–2. Model of the biomass yields of the two components in a 1:1 intercrop competing for a growth factor Q in limited supply.
Source: Trenbath, 1976. Reproduced from Multiple cropping, ASA Special Publication no. 27, 1976, by permission of the American Society of Agronomy, Crop Science Society of America, and Soil Science Society of America.

because there are fewer A plants competing. The per plant uptake by B (resulting in Y_B yield) decreases over the uptake when grown alone (resulting in Y_{BB} yield) because B is competing with the more efficient user. The difference in uptake is F. Thus, the per plant yields in the intercrop are

$$Y_A = Y_{AA} (1 + F)$$
$$Y_B = Y_{BB} (1 - F)$$

The *relative yield total* (RYT)[1] in this 1:1 intercrop can be calculated by an appropriate formula (Trenbath, 1976) that reduces to

$$RYT = 1/2 (1 + F + 1 - F) = 1$$

Thus, in this model, the RYT is unity. That is, the combined per plant yield of the two grown together does not exceed that of the two grown separately.

---

[1]RYT = the sum of the relative yields of two species grown together where the relative yield of each is calculated by dividing its yield in mixture by its yield in pure stand.

Density Relationships

Our interest in a weed–crop situation is in the yield for a given land area. Trenbath has shown that the relative yield total is equivalent to a land equivalent ratio of 1.0 where the total density is constant. *Land equivalent ratio* (LER) is a mathematical way of expressing productivity in terms of a land unit. Thus, an LER greater than 1.0 indicates that an intercrop produces more on a given land area than either crop alone.

When LER is measured without total density held constant, the value can be expected to vary, shown by examination of Figure 6–3. If the D1 density is well below the optimum density for each of two species, a 1:1 mixture of the two gives a total yield of $2 \times Y_2$ since the yields of each will be Y_2, assuming equal competitive ability. Thus, the area that produced Y_1 in the sole crop produces much more in the intercrop. Even if the species differ in competitive ability, the total yield will be greater than unity. However, under D3 density, which is assumed to be close to the optimum for each species, the total yield of the intercrop $(2 \times Y_4)$ from the graph can be seen to be very close to the yield of the sole crop (Y_3). Thus, the area yield of the intercrop is quite comparable to that of the sole crop.

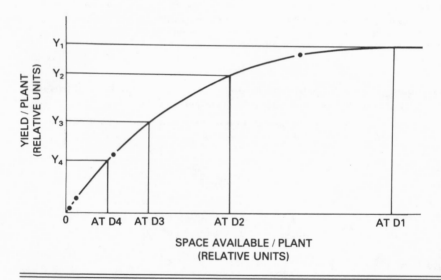

FIGURE 6–3. Typical response of per plant biomass to density. Each density in the sequence D1 to D4 is twice the previous density. D3 is assumed to be optimum for the species.

Source: Trenbath, 1976. Reproduced from Multiple cropping, ASA Special Publication no. 27, 1976, by permission of the American Society of Agronomy, Crop Science Society of America, and Soil Science Society of America.

From this discussion of model and mathematical treatment of density–yield relationships, it can be concluded that if the density is optimum, combined yield will not exceed unity where there is competition for a growth factor in deficient supply. Data from a large number of actual crop mixtures, shown in Figure 6–4, support this conclusion. The preponderance of the LERs are close to 1.0. In other words, the usual situation is that species in a mixture compete for the resources available.

Annidation.   The complementary use of resources is called *annidation*. There are many instances where mixtures outyield the individual species grown alone. The combination of grasses and legumes, widely used in forage production, is one

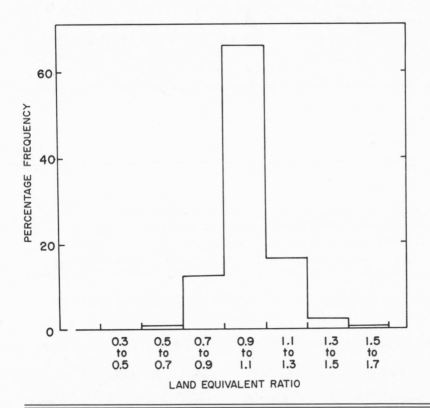

FIGURE 6–4. Land equivalent ratios calculated for either 2 species of legumes or 2 species of nonlegumes from experiments where intercrops and sole crops were grown at the same density.

Source: Modified from Trenbath, 1976. Reproduced from Multiple cropping, ASA Special Publication no. 27, 1976, by permission of the American Society of Agronomy, Crop Science Society of America, and Soil Science Society of America.

example. The Inca indians in South America apparently intercropped their corn and beans, a method still being used in that area. In Missouri, young walnut plantations are sometimes intercropped with forages. In these and other instances, increased total production occurs in the absence or avoidance of competition. That is, the use of resources is complementary not competitive.

The general principles of annidation were discussed in Chapter 2. Annidation may occur for space, nutrients, and time (Trenbath, 1976). Annidation in space may involve both the leaf canopy and root structures. Thus, species with different light requirements and light tolerances growing together are not competing but, rather, are making more effective use of the total light available than either species does alone.

Harper (1977) describes an experiment with *Avena* species that dramatically illustrates the annidation in space with respect to roots. In a study in which *Avena strigosa, Avena fatua, Avena sativa,* and *Avena ludoviciana* were grown in pure stands and in mixtures, RYT values much larger than 1.0 were found when *A. fatua* and *A. strigosa* were grown together on deep soil. On shallow soil, the RYT values approached 1.0. Later studies of rooting depth showed that in the deep soils, the roots of *A. strigosa* developed mainly in the upper layers of the soil profile, whereas the *A. fatua* contributed most to roots deeper in the profile.

An example of annidation in time, which is of increasing interest in the southern part of the Corn Belt and in the Cotton Belt, is the interplanting of soybeans in wheat prior to wheat harvest. Competition for resources is avoided since the soybean plants do not reach a size to be competitive with the wheat while the wheat still needs such resources.

There are many examples of annidation in time in weed–crop relationships. One example, found in the central United States, is infestation of wild garlic in the early fall following corn and soybeans, with at least partial completion of the weeds' life cycle prior to planting the crop the next spring.

Annidation with respect to nutrients is exemplified by grass–legume mixtures. Competition for nitrogen is avoided because the legume has the ability to fix its own. The presence of the legume black medic *(Medicago lupulina)* in pastures is an example of such weed–crop annidation.

Effect of changing weed numbers on combined density.   The separate and combined yields of weeds and crops have been measured in many weed studies. For the most part, these measurements were taken in studies designed to evaluate only the effects of the weeds on the crop. The evaluation is commonly done either by: (1) adding increasing increments of weeds or (2) thinning a dense weed stand to desired levels of decreasing weed density per unit area. The study from which data for Figure 6–1 were obtained was of the first type. Similarly, herbicide effectiveness is commonly measured in studies where weights or numbers of weeds and crops are recorded for different herbicides and rates.

In all such studies, the combined density changes for the various treatments.

The changes may be very large. For example, in Figure 6–1, the combined density of cotton and of tall morning-glory at 32 plants per 15 meters of row is about double that of cotton by itself. Figure 6–3 and its discussion showed that total yield may be greatly influenced by such large changes in combined density. Therefore, caution must be followed in interpreting community yields of weed–crop research. Such studies tell us the effect of weeds on crop yield but do not explain the effect. Thus, they are of little use in identifying the *nature* of competition since density is confounded with competition for growth factors.

Soybeans.   Measurements of community yield in weed research have produced a preponderance of results approaching unity. The results with soybeans deserve special comment. Frequently, combined yields of weeds plus soybeans exceed unity (Moulani et al., 1964; and Knake and Slife, 1969), although sometimes they do not (Knake and Slife, 1962). Even though the relationship is not consistent, combined yields exceeding unity have been observed frequently enough with soybeans and with some other weed–crop situations to warrant an attempted explanation.

In view of what is known about community yield of two crops growing together, it seems quite likely that the occasional greater community yield of soybeans plus weeds, as well as similar occurrences for other weed–crop mixtures, is due to annidation for space. That is, the crop stand may be below its optimum density. As discussed in the preceding section, if the stand is below the optimum density, the total yield is expected to exceed unity. This situation is not improbable with soybeans since they were planted in wide rows in most of the studies cited. Also, if a legume is present, competition may not occur for nitrogen because the legume can fix its own. Thus, occasional greater combined yield of crops plus weeds than of the crop alone may not necessarily detract from the conclusion that a maximum, or plateau, in combined yield of crops plus weeds can be expected for a given area.

As we turn to a consideration of competition between weeds and crops, we should keep firmly in mind that annidation may also be involved in such situations. Further, although weed density is important in determining crop yield loss, if density is not held constant, care must be exercised in using results to understand competition.

CROP YIELD LOSS

The extent of crop yield loss is closely tied to the number of competing weeds and their weight. That is, there is some number or weight above which loss or damage occurs and below which it does not. These are not the only factors involved since, as we shall see, *when* the weed is present in relation to the life cycle of the crop also influences importantly the degree of competition. Nonetheless, numbers and weight are the basic elements of competition, with the time of presence of the weed serving in what might be termed a modifying role. That is, a sparse weed stand cannot cut crop yield, no matter how long it is present. As we shall see, a dense weed stand cannot remain long without reducing the crop yield.

Effect of Weed Numbers

The fact that crop losses increase as weed numbers increase is common knowledge. What is surprising is how few weeds may cut yields. For example, as few as 1 kochia plant per 3 meters (10 feet) of row cut sugarbeet yields 26% (Weatherspoon and Schweizer, 1971); 1 wild mustard plant per 30 centimeters (1 foot) of row cut soybean yields 30% (Berglund and Nalewaja, 1969); and 1 barnyardgrass plant per 0.1 square meter (1 square foot) cut rice yields 57% (Smith, 1968). These examples, plus results from a large number of other studies, show that relatively few weeds may reduce crop yields.

Because of the modifying effects of time of weed presence and of physical aspects of the environment, precise density–crop yield relationships cannot be projected for field conditions. The general relationship is the solid line in Figure 6–5. This relationship is sigmoidal, not linear, and simply means that one weed on

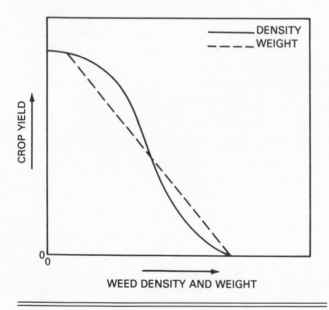

FIGURE 6–5. General relationship between weed density and crop yield and weed weight and crop yield.

the sparse-density end has a greater effect on yield than one weed on the high-density end. This effect is due to plasticity in plant form on the part of both the weed and the crop plant. As the number of weeds on a given area increases, the size of each plant decreases, as expressed in numbers of branches or tillers, numbers of leaves and size, and size of root system.

To the producer, the important point on the density–yield curve is where the yield begins to fall rapidly. That is, How many weeds will the crop tolerate? This point is commonly called the *threshold value*. Efforts to eliminate weeds represent a cost to producers, so they must decide how much they can afford to spend for control or prevention on the basis of what they can expect to gain in yield. The slope drops sharply once the point is reached where density begins to cut yields. In spite of voluminous data that identify threshold value, it is impossible to predict in advance precisely where this value will occur. Thus, without additional information, more specifically without an understanding of what it is the crop and weed are competing for, the fact remains that producers' safest goal must be complete weed removal.

Effect of Weed Weight

As was true for numbers, relatively small weights of weeds can reduce crop yields. For example, as shown in Table 6–2, it was observed in Iowa that 1 kilogram per

TABLE 6-2

Reduction in soybean yields for given weights of three weeds.

Weed Species	Year	Weed Yield (kg/ha)	Soybean Yield (kg/ha) Weed-free	Weedy	Reductions Due to Weeds (kg/ha)	(kg/kg weeds)
Yellow foxtail	1961	4936	2288	1460	828	0.17
	1962	2486	2618	2221	397	0.16
Green foxtail	1963	3304	2571	1454	1117	0.34
Average for foxtail		3584	2490	1710	780	0.22
	1961	1422	2430	1932	498	0.35
Velvetleaf	1962	1792	2140	1481	659	0.37
	1963	1568	2571	1548	1023	0.65
Average for velvetleaf		1590	2383	1642	741	0.47

Source: Staniforth, 1965. Reproduced with permission of the Weed Science Society of America.

hectare reduced soybean yields 0.16 to 0.65 kilos per hectare, depending upon the weed and year. Kilogram for kilogram, velvetleaf was about twice as damaging as the foxtails. Also, kilogram for kilogram, both the foxtail and velvetleaf were about twice as damaging to soybean yields in 1963 as in the previous two years. These differences between species and years emphasize the complexities of competition. At the same time, the relative constancy for weight effects in a given species and under a given set of growing conditions suggests that it may be possible to develop mathematical constants for the weight–yield relationship.

The preceding discussion of density showed that numbers are a relatively poor measure of competition. Weed weight is a better measure since it more correctly measures the quantities of growth factors captured by the weed and thus unavailable to the crop. The suggested weed weight line for a given weed species is shown as the dotted line in Figure 6–5. Although the slope of the line varies depending upon the particular weed and crop being studied, the relationship is essentially linear. Actually, the line is not perfectly straight under most field conditions because as discussed later, the quantity of biomass produced for each unit of growth factor varies. That is, one unit of water may lead to more biomass during cool, humid weather than during hot, dry weather. Similarly, efficiency of use of nutrients and light is not constant. Such differences affect relative competition. Nevertheless, the weight line most likely approaches a straight line from the onset of competition from a given weed in a given experiment to the point of maximum weed weight associated with maximum weed density. There is a short time at the outset of the growth cycle when crop yield is not related to weed weight simply because resources for both crop and weeds are sufficient.

Effect of Period Weeds Are Present

To develop the most effective weed management program, answers are needed for two questions: (1) How soon must weeds be removed from the crop? and (2) When will weeds no longer cut yields if left in? Answering these two questions has been the central theme in much of weed research.

Period weeds tolerated.   Logic tells us that there is a time very early in the crop's growing period when the presence of small weeds will not cut crop yield. The duration of this tolerant period tells us when weeds must be removed to avoid crop yield losses. Most agronomic annual row-crops germinate quickly and have seedlings that grow rapidly. Plant breeding programs indeed have tended to select for these attributes. Thus, competition from weeds is usually not expressed in reduced stands of the crop.

Some species of grasses and legumes used as forages are not this aggressive. Birdsfoot trefoil is one legume that establishes slowly. With these crops, weeds may establish well in advance and have a very pronounced effect upon the stand of the crop, as shown in Table 6–3. Thus, for crops that establish slowly, competition from weeds may occur at the very outset of growth.

The more usual situation is for competition to affect growth, rather than stand, and be reflected in reduced crop yield. Results from a large number of studies, summarized in Table 6–4 (column A), show that most crops can tolerate the presence of weeds for a relatively short time only, depending upon the weed and the crop. For example, mixed annual weeds left longer than 3 weeks in corn resulted in a measurable reduction in crop yield. As can be seen, crops vary greatly in the period of weed presence tolerated, from as little as 3 weeks to as much as 22 weeks. Also, for any given crop, the period tolerated depends upon the weed. Without exception, however, crops tolerated weeds for a time early in the growing season. The practical importance of this fact to the producer is that weeds must be controlled or prevented during the early part of the crop's growing period if losses in yield are to be avoided.

As important as this knowledge is to the producer, it is of little use in understanding competition. That is, it identifies the effect, but not the cause, of weed presence on crop yield. By itself, it does not provide the information needed to make comparisons among years and locations for the same crop and for different crops. For direct comparisons to be made among experiments involving the period of crop tolerance, the specific competitive effects need to be identified. The lack of specific knowledge on competitive effects is a major reason for the profusion of empirical studies, such as those reported in Table 6–4, that in strict terms, provide information applicable only to the individual experiment from which the data came. For example, there is no satisfactory way to explain why corn tolerated weeds for a shorter time than did soybeans. As we move in the direction of weed management and away from control, we need to obtain information on what is being competed for and when. Further, such information may allow us to predict with

TABLE 6-3

Stand of birdsfoot trefoil as affected by weeds.

Weeding Treatment	Trefoil Plants (/1.4 m^2)
No weed removal	7.3
All weeds removed	35.6
Only broadleafs removed[1]	1.7
Only grasses removed[2]	20.7

[1] Waterhemp, pigweeds, lambsquarters, Pennsylvania smartweed, and velvetleaf.

[2] Crabgrasses, foxtails, and fall panicgrass (panicum).

Source: Data from Kerr and Klingman, 1960.

TABLE 6-4

Range of weed–crop relationships with time: (A) duration of weed presence tolerated without yield loss and (B) weed-free period required to prevent crop yield reduction.

Crop	Weed	Location	Weeks after Seeding/Emergence*	
			(A) Period Weed Presence Tolerated	(B) Period Required to Be Weed Free
Bean	Mixed annuals	Washington, USA	8	5
Beet, red	Mixed annuals	England	4	2–4
Cabbage	Mixed annuals	England	3–4	2
Corn	Mixed annuals	Mexico	3	5
Corn	Giant foxtail	Illinois, USA	6	3
Cotton	Mixed annuals	Alabama, USA	8	6
Cotton	Mixed annuals	Mexico	9	4
Lettuce	Mixed annuals	England	3	3
Peanut	Sicklepod Florida beggarweed	Alabama, USA	4	8
Potato	Redroot pigweed, lambsquarters	Lebanon	6	9
Sorghum	Mixed annuals	Nebraska, USA	4	3
Soybeans	Giant foxtail	Illinois, USA	8–9	3
Sugar beets	Barnyardgrass	Washington, USA	12	10
Sugar beets	Kochia	Colorado, USA	4	6
Wheat, winter	Downy brome	Oregon, USA	22	
		Nebraska, USA		2

* Some studies counted weeks from planting and others weeks from crop emergence. Studies reported include only those where one or the other was used for both (A) and (B).

Source: Adapted from Zimdahl, 1980.

some certainty what the weed problems will be as a result of changes in the production system or even in the year following an abnormally dry or abnormally wet year.

The usual procedure for evaluating the effects of weeds also fails to provide discrete information as to the extent of competition. The common measure of effects of weeds on the crop is yield or crop weight obtained at maturity (harvest time). Yields at this time measure both the effects of early competition from the weeds and the crop's ability to compensate for that early competition. Thus, competition and compensation are confounded. To have a discrete measure of competition, crop yield (weight) needs to be measured when weeds are removed.

Weed-free period required.   Selected results of studies to determine the weed-free period required, shown in Table 6–4 (column B), indicate that once well established, most crops effectively compete with weeds. Here, too, the period required is relatively short and, for many crops, is only the first few weeks. As is true for the period tolerated, the weed-free period required varies widely for the different crops and within a single crop. Without information on specific competitive effects, we can only speculate that the explanation is to be found in differences in plant form interacting with growth factors.

Figure 6–6, which shows the two effects of weed duration in a sugar beet

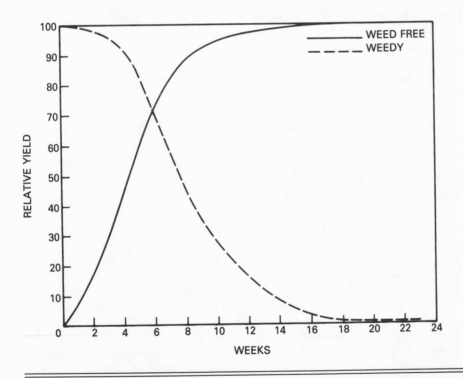

FIGURE 6–6. Effects of weed-free period and weedy period on yields of sugar beets.
Source: Data from Weatherspoon and Schweizer, 1969.

study, is representative of a large number of weed–crop relationships. The figure shows that once competition from weeds begins, crop yields drop sharply from continued weed presence. Similarly, the curve depicting the effect of weed-free period shows that crops quickly become competitive. The shapes (slopes) of the two curves are different, however. The slope showing yields for weed-free duration is skewed to the left compared with that for yields for weed duration, indicating that the required weed-free period is shorter than the presence-tolerated period. In a very general way, the weed-free period measures the relative competitiveness of the crop, while the presence-tolerated period measures the competitiveness of the weed in the crop. As we shall see, most annual weeds are relatively poor competitors compared to most crops, which explains the general relationship between the length of the weed tolerance and weed-free periods. The difference in length of these two periods has important implications for the choice of weed management approaches and is expanded upon in Chapter 15.

Effect of Life Cycle Differences

The relatively shorter life cycle of many annual weeds is a factor in their competitiveness towards crops. This fact is pointed up in Figure 6–7, which compares the time needed to develop maximum leaf area for soybeans and velvetleaf. When planted early (Figure 6–7A), soybeans were continuing to increase in leaf area at 12 weeks, whereas velvetleaf had attained its maximum by that time. In a later planting (Figure 6–7B), velvetleaf reached its maximum at 8 weeks and soybeans at 10 weeks. Further, in the early planting, where velvetleaf is spaced 30 cm in the row, increase in leaf area index was especially rapid from 6 to 8 weeks. Flowering occurred at 8 weeks in the early planting and at 6 weeks in the late planting. These findings simply indicate that most of the growth with velvetleaf is concentrated into a relatively short period compared with soybeans.

Li (1960) suggested that the short life cycle of weeds explained why early competition from weeds cut corn yields. In his studies, he estimated that weeds made 15% to 18% of their total growth during the first 2 to 3 weeks after emergence compared with less than 1% growth for corn during that time. Note, however, that competition for light continues after the weed has stopped increasing in height and leaf area. That is, the weed leaf in place when growth stops will continue to shade the crop leaf. As we have already learned, light quality is changed by passage through a green leaf, and light quality, in addition to quantity, must also be considered in evaluating completely the effects of a canopy. The significance of short life cycles of many weeds for weed management is that efforts to check growth may need to be followed for only a relatively short time.

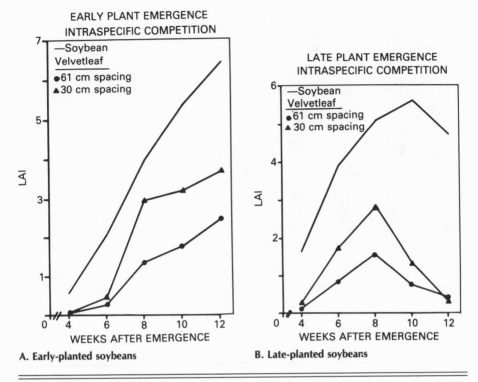

A. Early-planted soybeans

B. Late-planted soybeans

FIGURE 6–7. Faster development than crops of many annual weeds partly accounting for weeds' competitiveness.
Source: Oliver, 1979. Reproduced with permission of the Weed Science Society of America.

Grasses vs. Broadleaf Weeds

Broadleaf weeds tend to cause greater reductions in crop yields than grass or grasslike weeds. Figure 6–8 shows this relationship in peas in terms of numbers of weeds. In terms of reduction in pea yields, 3 mustard plants per 0.1 square meter (1 square foot) were equal in effect to 27 foxtail plants. Staniforth (1965) observed approximately a 2:1 relationship based on weed weights. In his study, soybean yields were reduced 0.47 kilo per hectare for each kilo dry matter of velvetleaf, and 0.22 kilo per hectare for each kilo dry matter of foxtail. McWhorter and Hartwig (1972) found cocklebur to be about twice as damaging to soybean yields as the perennial weed johnsongrass; depending upon the soybean variety, yields were reduced from 27% to 42% by johnsongrass and from 63% to 75% by cocklebur.

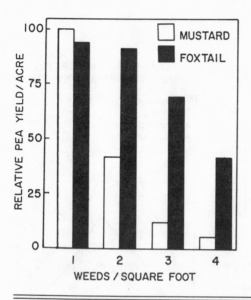

FIGURE 6-8. Relative effect of a grass (foxtail) and a broadleaf (mustard) weed on yield of peas. Weeds were present for the first 10 weeks following pea planting.
Source: Data from Nelson and Nylund, 1962.

Since most weedy grasses are of the C_4 type,[2] the greater effect from broadleaf species is likely explained by their more spreading growth form and more horizontal leaves that make them relatively more competitive for light. The lesser competitiveness of grasses must not be confused with their relative seriousness as weeds or difficulty to control. Of the world's 10 most serious weeds, 8 are grasses or are grasslike (Holm et al., 1977).

Predicting Crop Yield Loss

A way of predicting crop loss for a given weed infestation would help a producer decide if control was warranted. Attempts to develop mathematical equations for predicting yield losses have met with only modest success. Schweizer (1973) was able to predict the effects of kochia on sugar beet yields within 5% of the actual yield by use of a mathematical equation based upon the number of kochia plants

---

[2]The terms C_3 and C_4 are commonly used to denote the CO_2–fixing characteristics of plants although other characteristics are also associated. C_4 plants fix CO_2 into sugars about 50% faster than C_3 plants.

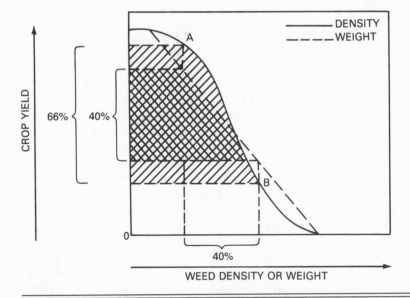

FIGURE 6–9. Hypothetical comparison of weed density (numbers) and weed weight as predictors of crop yield loss. The hatched portion of the yield (x) axis above and below the double-hatched portion is the extent of yield response beyond unity for density compared to weight (66% versus 40%).

per meter of row. However, which of the three polynomial regression equations derived—linear, quadratic, or cubic—best represented the density–yield relationship depended upon the actual density of kochia. No one equation perfectly represented the relationship over the entire density range because of the sigmoidal shape of the curve (Figure 6–5).

Dew (1972) developed an *index of competition* that could be used to estimate losses of yield of barley, wheat, and flax for given densities of wild oat. However, the equation was based on assumptions that restrict usefulness. One assumption was that weed and crop emerge at the same time. Many weeds germinate over an extended period, even if the flush tends to be concentrated in time. A second assumption was that crop and weed had equal access to water, nutrients, and light. As we shall see in Chapter 7, plants may differ greatly in their ability to compete for such growth factors.

The linear relationship between weight and yield suggests that weight has more value in predicting losses from weeds than numbers because a unit change in weight results in approximately a unit change in yield over the entire weight range. A unit change in numbers (density), however, results in either more or less than a unit change in yield, depending upon the actual density being considered. This relationship is shown in Figure 6–9. The place on the density–yield curve where the slope begins to fall sharply is labelled A, and B the place where it begins to flatten out. Extension from these points to the y and x axis and application to the weight line show that there is a unit change in crop yield for each unit change in weed weight (40% yield versus 40% weed weight in this case), but more than a unit change in crop yield for each unit change in weed density (66% yield versus 40% weed density). In this particular example, for the portion of the density–yield curve that identifies the most rapid loss in yield, the density-to-yield relationship is about 1.0:1.65. At the sparse-density end, the relationship is about 1.0:0.3. The wide range of density–yield responses serves as a reminder that although entirely valid as a measure of control efficacy, weed numbers have only limited value to a crop producer in determining if control is warranted.

A *weed-loss survey system* designed for estimating weed losses in soybeans provides an interesting example of a practical way of incorporating several factors involved in competition. The sequence of photographs shown in Figure 6–10 is the basis for estimating yield losses. A percentage yield loss assigned each level of infestation is based upon actual losses recorded in experiments throughout the soybean production region for each infestation. The percentage losses assigned each level of infestation from A to E are, respectively: less than 5%, 5% to 10%, 10% to 20%, 20% to 35%, and greater than 35%. When the photographs are matched with actual field infestations, the loss falls within the level for the photograph. It is interesting that the survey system is apparently fairly accurate, even though it is applied to different weeds, different soils, and different climatic regions. The explanation is found in the fact that the visual appearance of a weed infestation captures several aspects of weeds important to determining competition, including their numbers, their size, the species present, when they became established, and how long they have been present. This survey system serves as an excellent reminder that competition frequently is the net result of several interacting factors.

WEED'S-EYE VIEW OF COMPETITION

Weed–Crop Competition

To this point, we have been looking at the effects of weeds on crops. To understand the relationship between crops and weeds for long-term weed management approaches, we need to examine competition from the weed's standpoint. There is much evidence that weeds, especially annuals, are very intolerant of competition. Knake and Slife (1965) found that foxtail made very little growth in either corn or

A. Weed free, no losses (less than 5%)

B. Slightly weedy, 5% to 10% loss

C. Moderately weedy, 10% to 20% loss

D. Heavy weeds, 20% to 35% loss

E. Disaster, 35% to 100% loss

FIGURE 6–10. Weed-loss survey in soybeans.
Source: Reproduced with permission of Elanco Products Co.

soybeans if the crop was given a 3-week head start. In fact, as shown in Figure 6–11, foxtail seeded into soybeans 3 weeks after the soybeans were planted made practically no growth. Maun (1977), in similar studies involving soybean competition for barnyardgrass, found that even a 1-week head start caused more than a 60% reduction in growth of the weed. Additionally, even though the barnyardgrass managed some growth regardless of how much head start the soybeans had, it was

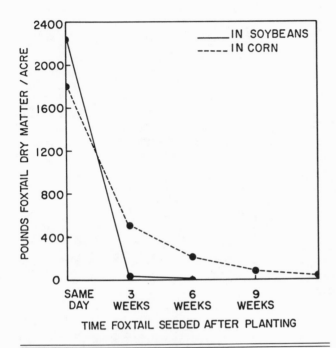

FIGURE 6–11. Effect of competition from corn and soy-beans on growth of giant foxtail.
Source: Data from Knake and Slife, 1965.

not able to produce any seed if the soybeans had as much as a 2-week head start (Figure 6–12). Barnyardgrass weight of the whole plant and of the caryopsis was determined 15 weeks after soybean emergence and compared with the barnyardgrass weight in pots without soybeans. Clearly, the sensitivity of weeds towards competition suggests good opportunities for success in managing production practices to minimize losses from them.

Further, the results certainly strongly imply that light is frequently the factor involved, an implication examined in greater detail in the next chapter. At this point, however, it is worth noting that soybeans were relatively more competitive than corn towards foxtail if the crop had a head start, whereas the opposite was true if the crops and foxtail emerged together (Knake and Slife, 1965). Corn yields were cut about 13%, but soybeans 29% if the foxtail emerged with the crops and remained only 3 weeks. The difference is probably due to light availability to the crop and to the weed under the two different conditions. When foxtail emerges with crops, some of the weeds overtop the beans, whereas the taller-growing corn overtops the foxtail. Thus, foxtail competes for light in soybeans, and yields are cut relatively more than corn yields. On the other hand, the soybean crop provides a

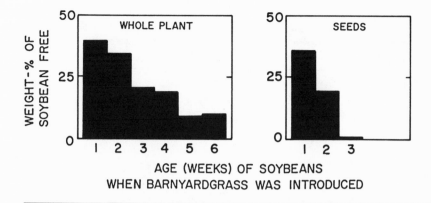

FIGURE 6–12. Effect of competition from soybeans on vegetative growth and seed production of barnyardgrass. Three 1-week-old barnyardgrass plants were transplanted into pots containing a soybean plant of the age shown.
Source: Data from Maun, 1977.

complete canopy more quickly than does corn. Thus, if the soybeans are provided a head start, they let very little light reach the foxtail, while corn continues to let some light filter through to the foxtail for much of the early part of the growing season.

Weed–Weed Competition

Weed-to-weed competition may also have important implications for weed management. Table 6–5 shows redroot pigweed to be much more competitive towards lambsquarters than the reverse. Even when seeded at 10 times the rate of pigweed, lambsquarters had much less growth at 36 days. However, if either weed is given a time advantage over the other, it completely suppresses the later-planted species.

The explanation for the differential competitiveness lies in the germination and growth of the two species in response to temperature. As can be seen in Table 6–6, pigweed germinates much more rapidly than lambsquarters under the higher temperatures but much more slowly under the lower temperatures. Additionally, from Table 6–7 it can be seen that pigweed grows more rapidly under higher temperature, but under the lower temperature regimes, there is little difference between the two species. Pigweed and lambsquarters are common associates in the weed community in horticultural and agronomic row-crop agriculture in many parts of the world. Which species dominates the weed problem can be expected to vary from year to year, depending upon temperature during the early period of their association. Temperature, in turn, could be affected by time of planting. In a relatively dry spring in the Midwest, early planting, when temperatures are

TABLE 6-5

Plant population and shoot dry weights of redroot pigweed (RR) and common lambsquarters (LQ) in a mixed culture in the greenhouse.

Treatment*		Species	Number of Plants ($/m^{-2}$)	Grams Dry Weight of Shoots ($/m^{-2}$)
t_0	t_{20}			
RR	LQ	RR	2307	398
		LQ	0	0
LQ	RR	RR	0	0
		LQ	1985	255
1 RR:1 LQ	0	RR	1862	320
		LQ	457	5
1 RR:10 LQ	0	RR	437	230
		LQ	2240	57

Note: Plants grown for 36 days under average temperatures of 29°C day and 24°C night.

*t_0 = initial sowing; t_{20} = sown 20 days later.

Source: Chu et al., 1978. Reproduced from Crop Science 18 (2):308-10, 1978, by permission of the Crop Science Society of America.

TABLE 6-6

Effect of temperature on the germination of redroot pigweed and common lambsquarters.

Temperature (day/night °C)	Species	Germination Rate Index*
24°/18°	Redroot pigweed	14.8
24°/18°	Lambsquarters	6.6
13°/7°	Redroot pigweed	0.4
13°/7°	Lambsquarters	2.6

* Germination determined daily for 30 days incubation and an index computed as follows

$$\text{Germination rate index} = \sum_{n=1}^{n=30} \frac{\text{number germinated since } n-1}{\eta}$$

where n = days of incubation.

Source: Chu et al., 1978. Reproduced from Crop Science 18 (2):308-10, 1978, by permission of the Crop Science Society of America.

TABLE 6-7

**Effect of temperature on the growth of redroot pigweed and common lambs-
quarters at 11 weeks.**

Temperature (day/night °C)	Species	Shoot Dry Weight (g/plant)	Leaf Area (dm²/plant)
29°/24°	Redroot pigweed	48.5	86.2
	Lambsquarters	11.4	22.0
24°/18°	Redroot pigweed	12.3	31.8
	Lambsquarters	11.8	20.5
18°/13°	Redroot pigweed	6.4	13.7
	Lambsquarters	6.3	10.5

Source: Chu et al., 1978. Reproduced from Crop Science 18 (2):308-10, 1978, by permission of the Crop Science Society of America.

relatively cool, can be expected to favor lambsquarters. Wet weather, necessitating late planting when temperatures are warmer, gives a decided edge to redroot pigweed. This relationship between lambsquarters and redroot pigweed provides another reminder that data on growing conditions are needed for valid comparisons of weed populations among different experiments.

The usual situation with annual weeds in row-crop agriculture is for the makeup of the weed community to change somewhat from year to year. This situation is observed even under monoculture and even though the composition of the seed bank in the soil may be relatively constant from year to year. The relationship between lambsquarters and redroot pigweed in response to environmental conditions may help explain why.

Weeds interacting with other weeds may have long-term effects on the weed community as well. Common milkweed has been increasing steadily over the past many years. A survey of thirteen states in the north-central region of the United States indicated that 26 million acres were infested in 1976 (Evetts, 1977). Every state indicated that this weed had increased in the last five years. The explanation, no doubt, is found in the fact that many annual weeds, both grasses and broadleafs, have been rather well controlled with herbicides in the several years preceding 1976. As seen in Tables 6–8A and 6–8B, common milkweed is very intolerant of competition from both green foxtail and redroot pigweed, two weeds common to row-crop agriculture in this region but effectively controlled with available herbicides. The pronounced reduction in reproduction from roots is especially

TABLE 6-8

Competition of two weeds and sorghum towards common milkweed measured 35 days after planting in the greenhouse.

A. Effects on Shoot Weight

Competing Plant	Shoot Weight for Types of Competition (cg)			
	None	Light	Soil	Full
Green foxtail	41	22	18	11
Redroot pigweed	41	27	25	15
Sorghum	33	23	18	15

B. Effects on Reproduction Percentage

Competing Plant	Percentage Reproduction from Roots			
	None	Light	Soil	Full
Green foxtail	78	9	56	8
Redroot pigweed	81	3	52	11
Sorghum	73	46	56	40

C. Competition Boxes Used for the Studies*

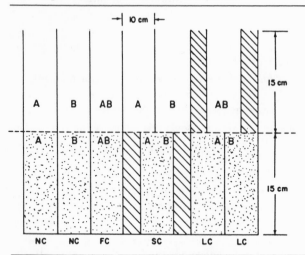

* Diagram of competition boxes with aerial portions above and soil compartments below. No competition (NC) contains two soil and two aerial compartments. Full competition (FC) contains one soil and one aerial compartment. Soil competition (SC) contains one soil and two aerial compartments. Light competition (LC) contains two soil and one aerial compartments. One plant species is represented by (A) and the second by (B).

Source: Adapted from Evetts and Burnside, 1975. Reproduced with permission of the Weed Science Society of America.

dramatic. Sensitivity of milkweed to competition from sorghum supports crop-to-weed competition discussed in the previous section.

Table 6–8C is a diagram of competition boxes used to study no competition (NC), light competition (LC), soil competition (SC), and full competition (FC). Competition was created by the amount of space—aerial space above the dotted horizontal line and soil space below—provided for plants growing in the compartments. For example, in the no-competition treatment, each species, A and B, was grown in individual compartments. In the full-competition treatment, both species were grown in a single compartment.

Many problem weeds are extremely intolerant of competition. As more and more specific data are obtained on the nature and extensiveness of such competition, possibilities for manipulating production practices to give the crop the slight edge it needs should become evident.

Components of Weed Seed Yield Reduction

In view of the importance of the seed to weed survival and to competitive levels, a brief discussion of components of seed yield reduction is desirable. The yield of seed per unit area is determined by: (1) seed size; (2) number of seeds per panicle, per pod, or per plant; and (3) numbers of seed-bearing units, such as tillers, branches, stalks, and so forth. Which of these three factors or combination of the three accounts for the yield of weed seeds per unit area is important in deciding how best to minimize replenishment of the seed bank in the soil. If seed size, for example, is reduced by competition, this fact has implications for survival since as we saw in Chapter 3, small seeds tend to produce seedlings more vulnerable to environmental stress. On the other hand, if it is numbers of seeds that are reduced by competition, a different challenge is presented. In simple terms, under the first example, the most productive emphasis might be on the young seedlings. In the second case, the emphasis might better stress the more mature parent plant in order to reduce as much as possible the number of seeds produced.

Harper (1977) points out that seed size is the least plastic of any plant part. One explanation given is that most plants initiate more seeds than can develop and then, by abortion, reduce that number to a sustainable level. It is important here to recall that plants do have substantial plasticity in growth form. This point is made in Harper's view of an individual plant as being a population, in the sense that while plants vary the number of tillers, stems, leaves, and flowers, the unit that produces the flower or rhizome bud is quite constant in form. The allocation of resources between vegetative and reproductive parts is a related aspect of interest in seed production. In a general way, therefore, the relatively greater constancy of seed size than of seed numbers provides justification for a weed management approach that emphasizes the maturing parent rather than the young seedling.

CONCEPTS AND CONCLUSIONS

1. The tendency is for the combined dry matter production on a given area to be constant irrespective of weed–crop composition; therefore, weeds usually must either be prevented or controlled if crop yield loss is to be avoided.
2. Weeds may cut crop yields by reducing harvestable yield and/or by reducing yield harvested.
3. Weeds must be prevented from growing with the crop during the first few weeks or must be removed after only a few weeks cohabitation to avoid loss of crop yield.
4. Weeds that emerge after about one-third of the crop life cycle of annual crops usually do not reduce harvestable crop yield.
5. The effect of weed numbers on crop yield tends to be sigmoidal in shape, and that of weed weight, linear.
6. Broadleaf weeds tend to cause greater losses in crop yields than grassy weeds.
7. Annual weeds tend to cause greater losses in annual crops, and perennial weeds, greater losses in perennial crops.
8. Most weeds, especially annuals, are very intolerant of competition.
9. Crops, and varieties within crops, differ in their competitiveness toward weeds.

REFERENCES

Berglund, D.R., and J.D. Nalewaja. 1969. Wild mustard competition in soybeans. In Proc. NCWCC., p. 83. Sioux Falls, S. Dak.

Chandler, J.M. 1980. Assessing losses caused by weeds. In Proc. of E.C. Stakman Commemorative Symposium, miscellaneous publication no. 7, pp. 234–40. Agricultural Experiment Station, University of Minnesota, St. Paul, Minn.

Chu, C.C., et al. 1978. Effects of temperature and competition on the establishment and growth of redroot pigweed and common lambsquarters. Crop Sci. 18 (2): 308–10.

Crowley, R.H., and G.A. Buchanan. 1978. Competition of four morning-glory *(Ipomoea* spp.) species with cotton *(Gossypium birsutum)*. Weed Sci. 26 (5):484–88.

Dew, D.A. 1972. An index of competition for estimating crop loss due to weeds. Can. J. Plant Sci. 52:921–27.

Evetts, L.L. 1977. Common milkweed—the problem. In Proc. NCWCC, pp. 96–99. St. Louis, Mo.

————, and O.C. Burnside, 1975. Effect of early competition on growth of milkweed. Weed Sci. 23 (1):1–3.

Harper, J.L. 1977. Population biology of plants. New York: Academic Press.

Holm, L.G., et al. 1977. The world's worst weeds. Honolulu: University Press of Hawaii.

Kerr, H.D., and D.L. Klingman. 1960. Weed control in establishing birdsfoot trefoil. Weeds 8 (2):157–67.

Knake, E.L., and F.W. Slife. 1962. Competition of *Setaria faberii* with corn and beans. Weeds 10 (1):26–29.

_____. 1965. Giant foxtail seeded at various times in corn and soybeans. Weeds 13 (4):331–34.

_____. 1969. Effect of time of giant foxtail removal from corn and soybeans. Weed Sci. 17 (3):281–83.

Li, M.Y. 1960. An evaluation of the critical period and the effects of weed competition on oats and corn, Ph.D. dissertation. Rutgers University, New Brunswick, N.J.

Maun, M.A. 1977. Suppressing effect of soybeans on barnyardgrass. Can. J. Plant Sci. 57 (2):485–90.

McWhorter, C.G., and E.E. Hartwig. 1972. Competition of johnsongrass and cocklebur with six soybean varieties. Weed Sci. 20 (1):56–59.

Moulani, M.K., E.L. Knake, and F.W. Slife. 1964. Competition of smooth pigweed with corn and soybeans. Weeds 12 (2):126–28.

Nave, W.R., and L.M. Wax. 1971. Effect of weeds on soybean yield and harvesting efficiency. Weed Sci. 19 (5):533–35.

Nelson, D.C., and R.E. Nylund. 1962. Competition between peas grown for processing and weeds. Weeds 10 (3):224–29.

Odum, E.P. 1971. Fundamentals of ecology, 3rd ed. Philadelphia: Saunders.

Oliver, L.R. 1979. Influence of soybean *(Glycine max)* planting date on velvetleaf *(Abutilon theophrasti)* competition. Weed Sci. 27 (2):183–88.

Schweizer, E.E. 1973. Formula for predicting sugar beet root losses based on kochia densities. Weed Sci. 21 (6):565–67.

Smith, R.J., Jr. 1968. Weed competition in rice. Weed Sci. 16 (2):252–54.

Staniforth, D.W. 1965. Competitive effects of three foxtail species on soybeans. Weeds 13 (3):191–93.

Trenbath, R.R. 1976. Plant interactions in mixed crop communities. In Multiple cropping, ASA special publication no. 27, pp. 129–69. Madison: American Society of Agronomy.

Weatherspoon, D.M., and E.E. Schweizer. 1969. Competition between kochia and sugar beets. Weed Sci. 17 (4):464–67.

_____. 1971. Competition between sugar beets and five densities of kochia. Weed Sci. 19 (2):125–28.

Zimdahl, R.L. 1980. Weed–crop competition: A review. Corvallis: International Plant Protection Center, Oregon State University.

NATURE OF WEED COMPETITION 7

COMPETITION PARAMETERS

"Competition occurs when each of two or more organisms seeks the measure it wants of any particular factor or things and when the immediate supply of the factor or things is below the combined demand of the organisms." This definition of competition by Donald (1963) represents a condensation of earlier definitions and still fits well the weed–crop competition relationships involved in weed–crop ecology. In particular, it recognizes that both the crop and the weed are involved— not just the weed—in a competitive relationship.

By restricting the definition to competition for some factor that is in limited supply, the definition distinguishes competition from interference; thus, allelopathy, which is discussed in detail in Chapter 8, is not considered to be a factor in competition since it adds "something" to the environment. This definition also helps to provide a proper perspective relative to space. Except in unusual circumstances, such as might exist with root crops, competition is not for space but rather for the things that space contains—that is, for one or more of the five growth factors: nutrients, water, light, carbon dioxide, and oxygen.

Inspection of much of the literature on weed research indicates that the concept of competition is often misused relative to weed–crop relationships. Competition is frequently used to identify the period when weeds are present with the crop, even though there may be no evidence that "each . . . seeks the measure of . . . things below the combined demand. . . ." Such usage of the term competition can be misleading relative to the ecological interrelationships at work in agroecosystems. In effect, it tends to focus only on the weed's effects on the crop, although as we have already learned, there are important effects of the crop upon the weed. As we shall see later, we can draw upon the crop's effects on the weed in building management systems to minimize effects from weeds. Thus, the term *competition* as used in this book is restricted to interactions in which some factor is in insufficient supply to meet the needs of both the weed and the crop. This usage implies removal of something from the environment, thus excluding allelopathy.

Plants require the growth factors light, water, nutrients, carbon dioxide, and oxygen for growth. In line with the definition of competition, the critical issue is whether there is an overlap of the depletion zones for one or more of these growth factors. Clearly, this is a complicated matter. If the entire crop growing season is taken into account, there are likely to be few instances under field conditions where competition is for only one factor, even though individual factors may be separately involved at certain times and under specific circumstances. The reason is that the relationship between the competing plants, and with the environment, is a dynamic one—not static. As discussed in Chapter 2, weeds are active participants in the ecological game. Thus, competition for one factor can be expected to alter the growth form of competing plants, thereby changing their ability to sample the environment for other growth factors. Further, these effects are complicated by density relationships that change with time and by the impact of temperature.

Although not itself a growth factor, air temperature may have a pronounced effect on competition through its effect on plant growth rate and plant growth form. Soil temperatures may also affect the availability of nutrients, especially nitrogen. Of particular significance for weed–crop competition is the more rapid recovery of some weeds from cold temperatures. For example, it was found that velvetleaf and spurred anoda recovered in growth more completely than did cotton after all three were exposed for 3 days to cold temperatures (17°C day/13°C night) (Patterson and Flint, 1979). We can speculate that other weeds may also recover more rapidly from chilling than other crops besides cotton. This speculation is based on weeds' evolvement under stress conditions and consequent production of general-purpose genotypes, discussed in Chapter 3. Because occasional periods of below-normal temperatures are not uncommon during the early growing season for annual crops, it can be seen that this modifying effect of temperature on competition may be fairly widespread.

Even though there are only a few resources, growth factors, that plants compete for, many interacting forces serve to make competition a complex phenomenon. The dynamics and complexities of weed–crop competition are illustrated in Figure 7–1. Characteristics of both weeds and crops are involved with weather, soil treatment, and other pests acting as modifiers. Even though competition is indeed complex, examination of influences on uptake of individual growth factors yields concepts and principles that can be applied in weed management. To do this, growth factors need to be examined both independently and in terms of their interactions. First, we consider competition that occurs aboveground and, second, that which occurs belowground. Only the concepts and principles involved in competition are considered. For a review of the literature on competition between particular weeds in specific crops, refer to the review of weed competition by Zimdahl (1980).

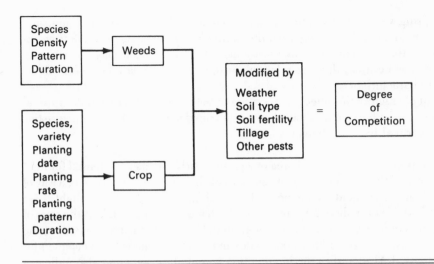

FIGURE 7–1. Interacting forces in weed–crop competition.
Source: After Bleasdale, 1960.

ABOVEGROUND COMPETITION

Plants obtain light and carbon dioxide through their aboveground parts, primarily the leaves. From the discussion of limiting factors in Chapter 2, it is inappropriate to view one growth factor as being any more important to growth than another. However, from a competition standpoint, light is much more frequently involved than is carbon dioxide, if in fact the latter occurs at all under field conditions. This is not to suggest that carbon dioxide may not restrict growth under certain conditions, only that competition for it is not likely to occur.

Competition for Light

The photosynthesis process in plants is driven by light. In this process, light energy is transformed into chemical energy in the green leaf. Thus, it is the leaf, not the plant as such, that is the site of potential competition for light. This point is especially significant relative to competition since light cannot be transferred or stored within the plant. If light is kept from one leaf, that leaf cannot get light from another that is in the light. The end result of this fact is demonstrated by the death of lower leaves and branches on a tall tree in a dense forest. Anytime one leaf is shaded by another, the shaded leaf suffers competition for light.

Anything that affects the absorption of light by the leaf can affect competition for light. In the field, both variations in light itself and variations in the plant may affect absorption. Light may vary in intensity (morning versus midday), duration (early spring versus midsummer), quality (clear versus cloudy), direction, and angle of incidence, depending upon the particular circumstances at the time, as well as the time of year. Although these aspects of light itself may theoretically enter into competition, they are relatively insignificant compared with the effects of plant characteristics.

Plant characteristics affect competition in both the horizontal and the vertical dimensions. The horizontal dimension is influenced mainly by leaf characteristics and the vertical by plant height.

Effect of leaf area.   The leaf area of a plant clearly affects its potential for light absorption and thus its competitiveness for light. In view of its importance, a way of relating leaf area to land area is needed for evaluating competition for light. Leaf area index (LAI) provides such a measure. As discussed earlier, LAI is the ratio of surface area of leaves to a given area of ground. The larger the index number, the more leaf area for a given land area. Index numbers as high as 8 are common for many plants. LAI identifies the interception potential for light and also indicates the amount of light available to successively lower levels within a canopy. Figure 2–7 graphically depicts these effects in a mixed grass–clover sward. As can be seen, light intensity drops steadily with the increase in accumulated LAI associated with progressively lower levels in the canopy. It falls rapidly to zero as the combined LAI approaches 2.0. This extinction of light occurs at a height of 20 cm. Reductions in LAI within a canopy as a result of interception are usually exponential.

Effect of leaf angle and arrangement.   The plant can also influence light interception through its determination of the angle of inclination of the leaves towards the sun, as well as by its pattern of leaf arrangement. As shown in Figure 7–2, leaf inclination can have a pronounced effect on light interception. The relatively horizontal leaves of clover intercept much more light than the upright grass leaves at any LAI level. Thus, weeds that have leaves more or less horizontal to the ground, such as velvetleaf, are relatively more competitive for light than weeds that have leaves more or less upright, such as giant foxtail. Similarly, weeds with opposite leaves, such as common milkweed, may be less competitive for light than those with alternate leaves, such as kochia, that form a mosaic whorl. Therefore, although LAI identifies the potential for light interception, it fails to take into account aspects of the light itself and plant characteristics that may affect competition.

Effects within the canopy.   Leaves absorb those wavelengths that are most effectively utilized in photosynthesis. Thus, the light that reaches progressively lower levels in the canopy is not only of lower intensity but also of inferior quality. The significance of this fact emphasizes further the effect of competition for light on lower levels within the community canopy and for the lower-story species. The

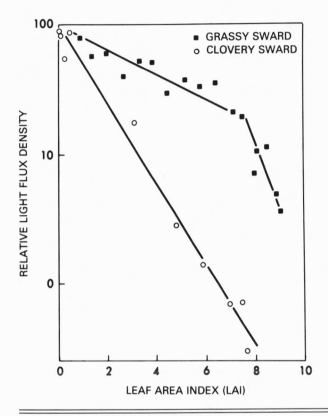

FIGURE 7–2. Effect of leaf inclination on light interception.
Source: Trenbath, 1976. Reproduced from Multiple cropping, ASA
Special Publication no. 27, 1976, by permission of the American Society
of Agronomy, Crop Science Society of America, and Soil Science
Society of America.

significance for weed–crop relationships is that a very slight height advantage of
the crop over the weeds can result in a strong competitive edge for the crop or vice
versa.

The potential impact of a height difference was strikingly demonstrated in a
study (Black, 1958) in which small and large seeds of subterranean clover were
planted together. Plants from the small seeds, although not genetically different
from the large-seed plants, were sufficiently less vigorous, and therefore shorter, at
the outset that they obtained only 2% of the incident light after 82 days.

Effects on the whole plant.   Although the leaf is the site of competition, it is
the effect of competition for light on the whole plant that is of concern to us in the
weed–crop context. That is, the combined reduction in production of photosyn-

thate by all leaves on a plant tells us how much loss that plant has suffered from competition for light. On a whole plant basis, the leaves in the upper story are of primary importance in photosynthesis. It follows that this level in the canopy is where the extent of competition between a crop and weeds is largely determined.

The effect of canopy level is clearly evident in Figure 7–3. As can be seen, even at midday, those leaves in the bottom one-third of the canopy are net users rather than net producers of energy. Those in the top one-third are the main source of net production.

Leaf and height characteristics together determine the relative competitiveness of a species for light. In identifying those characteristics that enable a crop to be competitive for light, Trenbath (1976) cited the following: (1) rapid expansion of a tall canopy, (2) leaves horizontal under overcast conditions and plagiotropic under sunny conditions, (3) large leaves to minimize penumbra effects, (4) leaves with the C_4 photosynthesis pathway and low transmissivity, (5) leaves forming a mosaic leaf arrangement, (6) a climbing habit, (7) a high allocation of dry matter to building a tall stem, and (8) rapid stem extension in response to shading. Similarly, these several characteristics serve to identify the relative competitive ability of a weed for light.

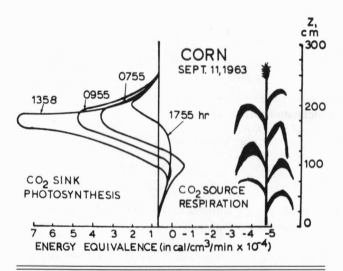

FIGURE 7–3. Effect of level in a corn canopy on photosynthesis and respiration. Positive values indicate net photosynthesis, whereas negative values indicate net respiration. At no time during the day are leaves in the lower one-third of the canopy net producers of photosynthate.

Source: Lemon and Wright, 1969. Reproduced from Agron. J., vol. 61, 1969, pp. 405–11, by permission of the American Society of Agronomy.

Effects within a weed—crop community.   Light effects on an individual plant basis translate into sizable effects in a weed—crop community in the field. This fact was demonstrated early on in the modern weed research era. For example, light intensities reaching vegetable crops in which weeds overtop the crops may be reduced as much as 85% (Shadbolt and Holm, 1956). Similarly, light intensity at the soil surface decreased from 6458 lumens per square meter (600 footcandles per square foot) with 1 foxtail every 70 cm (24 in.) in the row in corn to about 2152 lumens per square meter (200 footcandles per square foot) for 1 foxtail every 2.5 cm (1 in.) in the row (Knake and Slife, 1962). There can be no doubt that competition for light is a major source of weed competition with crops. Nonetheless, data are lacking to identify the discrete relationship—that is, the unit crop yield reduction per unit of light lost through competition.

Competition for light by a crop may have a pronounced inhibiting effect on a weed. For example, soybeans in 50 cm rows had only 28% as much dry weed weight 16 weeks after planting as soybeans in 100 cm rows (Felton, 1976). Since the soybeans were irrigated throughout the season, it is assumed competition for light accounts for the pronounced difference in weed yield. Referring back to Figure 6–11, we see that a 3-week head start by the crop markedly reduces dry matter production of giant foxtail. In soybeans, practically no growth occurred with this head start. Fertilizer was provided and sufficient rainfall occurred to minimize the likelihood that either of these factors could have accounted for the reduction in foxtail. Actual measurement showed that only 2.5% to 3.0% of the incident light reached the ground under the soybean canopy once it was established. It has been shown that at least 50% reduction in light is needed for crops to effectively suppress weeds (Sweet, 1976). More than 60% reduction was readily obtained by sweet corn, potatoes, and tomatoes. Crop variety, or *cultivar*, has also been shown to affect competitive ability for light (Sweet, 1976 and 1979; Smith, 1974; Burnside, 1972; McWhorter and Hartwig, 1972; and Staniforth, 1961). Clearly, field results indicate that characteristics imparting competitive ability for light can be built into varieties and production programs to enhance a crop's competitive ability for light. Possibilities for using such characteristics in weed management are examined in greater depth in Chapter 15.

Competition for Carbon Dioxide

Carbon dioxide (CO_2) and water are the basic raw materials involved in the photosynthetic capture of light and its transfer into chemical energy. CO_2 is obtained from the atmosphere. Studies have shown that the concentration is reduced within vegetation. Further, it has been shown that CO_2 supplementation increases the rate of photosynthesis under enclosed conditions. Thus, competition for CO_2 seems possible. However, as Trenbath (1976) points out, competition is not likely to occur in the field because turbulence within the canopy is so great that it causes rapid mixing between the interior and exterior atmospheres. Further, a reduced level of CO_2 is hard to visualize without an attendant reduced light intensity, which, since it is nontransferable within the plant, might be expected to be the limiting factor.

CO_2 fixation: C_3 vs. C_4 pathway.   Although competition for CO_2 may not be an important direct factor in competition between crops and weeds, the C_3 versus C_4 pathway for CO_2 fixation may have an indirect effect. Because C_3 leaves become saturated with light at relatively lower intensities than do C_4 leaves, plants of the C_3 type may be more apt to succeed under shade. On the other hand, C_4 plants use water more efficiently than C_3 plants, which may make them more competitive for other growth factors. Some evidence exists that shading may disrupt the C_4 function in species with this capability (Paul and Patterson, 1980). If so, the C_4 pathway might be either an asset or a liability under competition conditions, depending upon the relative heights of the competing species.

The C_3 versus C_4 pathway may influence the relative competitiveness of species over time if the concentration of CO_2 in the atmosphere continues to increase. The burning of fossil fuels and conversion of forests to agricultural production have caused an increase in CO_2 content from the longtime constant of about 300 ppm. The level may double by the year 2025. It has been speculated that such CO_2 enrichment will make C_3 weeds more competitive with C_4 crops (such as corn) and C_4 weeds more competitive with C_3 crops (such as soybeans) (Patterson and Flint, 1980).

BELOWGROUND COMPETITION

Roots take up nutrients, water, and oxygen. The rate of uptake may be influenced by other factors, such as temperature, inherent soil properties, and root growth form, but competition can develop only for the three growth factors. Unlike light, which is nontransferable within the plant, each of these three factors obtained from the soil is mobile—although to different degrees—both within the soil and within the plant itself. Indeed, in a sense, a plant can create a supply of one of the soil-obtained growth factors by creating a concentration gradient along which nutrients move towards the root. This concept is described diagrammatically in Figure 7–4. As can be seen in the figure, evaporation is the driving force for establishing a water gradient that in turn, serves as the carrier for readily soluble nutrients and oxygen for which gradients are then established.

In considering the nature of competition for the soil-supplied factors, we need to remember that the surface area of roots may be many times that of tops. Thus, the

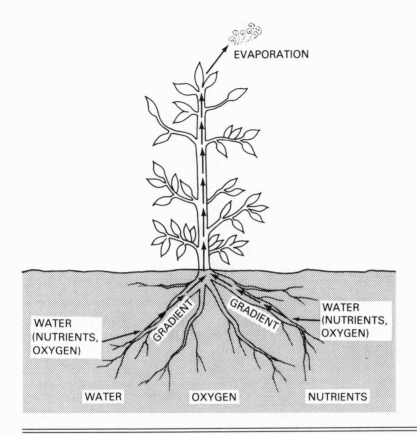

FIGURE 7–4. Gradient for movement of soil-supplied growth factors created by water evaporation.

soil can soon become crowded, even though competition cannot occur until there is an actual overlap between two plants of the depletion zones for one or more of these growth factors.

Competition for Water

As depicted in Figure 7–4, water moves from the soil to the root, then into the plant, where 1% to 3% is used in the process of photosynthesis. The remaining 97% to 99% of the water entering the plant on average is lost through evaporation. Evaporation, thus, is a principle driving force in the establishment of the water gradient. Both time and distance are important aspects in competition for water. Moisture may begin to move towards a root from several centimeters away in a matter of days. Trenbath (1976) refers to movement from 12 cm away in 6 days under laboratory conditions with a calculated depletion zone extending outward to 25 cm.

These dimensions are significant for weed–crop situations. There is a time immediately after emergence when the limited extent of the root systems makes competition improbable. However, in view of the rather intimate space relationships often encountered between weeds and crops in the field, overlap of depletion zones for water, if in limited supply, could occur in a relatively short time.

Root volume. The degree of competition for water between a crop and a weed is determined primarily by the relative root volume occupied by each. Moisture extraction profiles provide a good indicator of root volume. Species differ in both the depth and breadth of moisture extraction. Profiles of individual plants of several different species are shown in Figure 7–5. As can be seen, there is more than a two-fold difference between kochia 1.9 m^2 (20 ft^2 in cross section) and cocklebur 4.1 m^2 (44 ft^2 in cross section), suggesting that the density of weed infestation necessary to cause a given degree of competition for moisture varies from weed to weed.

Figure 7–5 provides a perception of both the lateral and vertical distribution as factors in determining the moisture extraction capacities. Depending upon the types of root systems of the crop and the weed and the supply or distribution of water in the soil profile, either extensive lateral or extensive vertical distribution can impart a competitive advantage for one species over the other. For example, a kochia plant in the crop row is probably more competitive for water than a plant in between crop rows because its lateral root distribution is relatively narrow. By contrast, cocklebur, because of its extensive lateral root distribution, might be competitive even if growing only in between rows. Russian thistle *(Salsola kali* L. var. *Tenuifolia Tausch)* might be relatively more competitive for moisture in deep soils than other weeds because of its deeper vertical root distribution.

The above emphasis on evaporation and root volume does not mean that there are no other important aspects. Differences among species in their inherent efficiency of water use are well known. Also, as already mentioned, C$_4$ plants are relatively more efficient in water utilization than C$_3$ plants. Studies involving weeds in crops have shown that some weeds may be able to produce more dry matter per unit of water than other weeds and than some crops. Nevertheless, because of the 97% to 99% pass-through of water, differences in water use efficiency tend to be overshadowed by the root volume–evaporation effect.

Relative competitive ability of weeds and crops. Species differ in response to competition for water. This situation is shown for ten species in Figure 7–6. The species were grown together in the greenhouse. The growth (dry matter produced) of each under the three moisture regimes indicates that the species responded differently. The soil for the wet level was maintained at about field capacity; soil for the medium level was brought to about one-half field capacity when plants began to wilt; and for the dry level, plants were allowed to wilt severely, then watered to

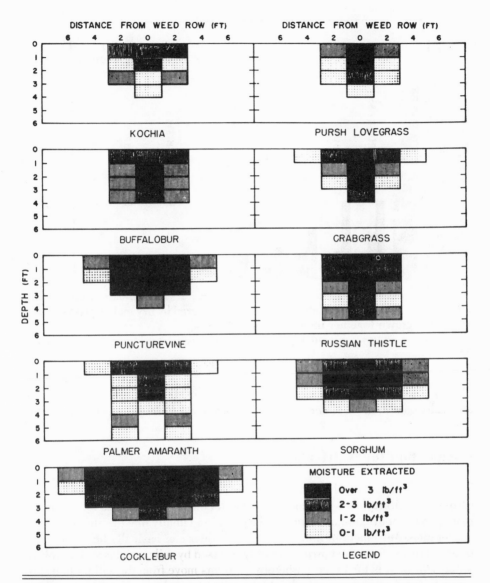

FIGURE 7–5. Root moisture extraction profiles for selected weeds and sorghum.
Plants were in rows marked by 0 on the graphs.
Source: Davis et al., 1967. Reprinted from Agron. J., vol. 59, 1967, p. 556, by permission of the American
Society of Agronomy.

slightly above wilting. In general, the species that produced the most growth under
wet conditions—corn, barnyardgrass, and cocklebur—were hurt most by competition under dry conditions. Those species that produced relatively little under wet
conditions—kochia, Russian thistle, buffalobur *(Solanum rostratum)*, and tum-

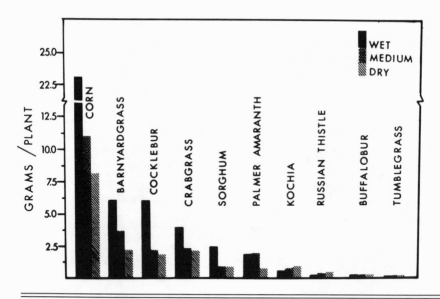

FIGURE 7–6. Competitive ability for water as measured by dry matter production of 10 species grown together under 3 moisture levels.
Source: Wiese and Vandiver, 1970. Reproduced with permission of the Weed Science Society of America.

blegrass—were not hurt by dry conditions. In fact, the first two produced more under dry conditions. Palmer amaranth *(Amaranthus Palmeri)* was intermediate.

Competition for Nutrients

Two phenomena are involved in competition for nutrients in soil: (1) mass flow and (2) diffusion. *Mass flow* is the movement of water through the soil to a root, from the root up to the aboveground portion of the plant, and finally into the atmosphere by evaporation. Movement of nutrients with the water can basically be viewed as a passive process for those nutrients readily released by soil particles and soluble in water. *Diffusion* is the process whereby nutrients move from the soil particles, or ionize if in a chemical compound, into the soil water and then disperse throughout the soil water. Diffusion into the soil water is determined by the tightness with which the nutrient is held on the soil particle or by ionization and solubility if in a chemical compound. Nutrients strongly absorbed on soil particles move mainly by diffusion, which is a relatively slow process.

Nitrogen.   The nitrate ion is not held strongly on soil particles and is, therefore, highly mobile. Its depletion zone is the same as that for water providing the nitrogen is utilized as it arrives at the root. Thus, as with water, relative competitiveness of weeds and crops for nitrogen is largely determined by the soil volume occupied by the roots of each. Because it moves freely with soil water, nitrogen is frequently a competed-for nutrient. Typical nitrogen deficiency symptoms, such as firing of lower leaves in corn, are common for crops with heavy weed infestations.

Even though nitrogen competition can be mainly determined by relative root volumes and spatial distribution of the weed and the crop, the differences among species in their rate of utilization may also be a factor. Weeds usually take up fertilizer more rapidly than crops (Alkamper, 1976). The relative ability of corn and redroot pigweed to compete for nitrogen shows a striking advantage for the pigweed. Vengris et al. (1955) observed that corn plants growing with pigweed contained only 58% as much nitrogen as weed-free corn plants.

Crop varieties also vary in their relative competitiveness for nitrogen, as shown in Figure 7–7. In competition with yellow foxtail, the early corn hybrids as a group were relatively more competitive for nitrogen than the late hybrids. Under 157 kilograms of nitrogen per hectare (140 pounds per acre), weeds reduced yield of

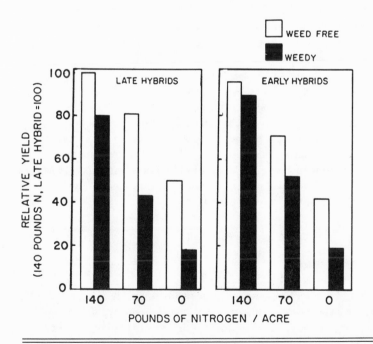

FIGURE 7–7. Relative competitiveness for nitrogen of late and early maturing corn hybrids.
Source: Data from Staniforth, 1961.

late-maturing varieties 20%, but early maturing varieties only 6%. A possible explanation is considered in the discussion of interactions later in the chapter. Here, we need only be aware that such differences may be usable in designing competitive production systems.

As we have seen, competition for nitrogen can either be the result of relatively passive aspects associated with crop–weed density or the result of relatively active aspects associated with nitrogen utilization.

Phosphorus, potassium, and other cations. Phosphorus (P), Potassium (K), and other cations are nutrients that are relatively immobile in the soil, but for different reasons. Because of their positive charge, K and other cations (positively charged ions) are held on the negatively charged clay particles. P is commonly applied in the phosphate form, which is negatively charged; however, it readily forms insoluble salts with calcium, iron, and other cations in the soil. Thus, the movement of such salts is dependent upon diffusion. Because diffusion is a relatively slow process, the depletion zones are small and develop slowly. Trenbath (1976), in his review, cites 0.7 cm as the extent of a depletion zone from a root for P after one week. Very recent work suggests that mycorrhizae could extend this depletion zone somewhat (Chiariello et al., 1982). *Mycorrhizae* are fungal growths that attach to roots of many plant species and are a factor in nutrient uptake, among other things. Chieriello et al. showed that the common connection between neighboring plants provided by mycorrhizae could be a route for phosphorus movement. In effect, mycorrhizal connections might extend the root's depletion zones. There is also evidence that the plant root itself actively affects uptake of P and K as the result of the cation exchange capacity of the root; thus, this capacity becomes a factor in competition for these nutrients. Irrespective of the process involved, movement for these nutrients is slow and for comparatively short distances. This fact suggests that competition for such nutrients is much less likely than competition for nitrogen and water. Competition for such nutrients is most apt to occur after the crop and weeds are well established, when chances for extensive root development and overlapping are at a maximum.

Competition for Oxygen

There is no evidence of competition for oxygen even though it is theoretically possible. That is, there are conditions under which insufficient oxygen limits plant growth. For example, oxygen is a limiting factor for the growth of plants in very wet soils. However, there is no research to show that competition occurs between plants under such conditions. Under most conditions, oxygen in the soil and available to roots is adequate for respiration of roots.

Characteristics Imparting Competitiveness for Soil Factors

As he did for competition for light, Trenbath (1976) also identified characteristics that could impart competitiveness for soil factors to a plant. These characteristics are: (1) early and fast root penetration of the soil, (2) high root density, (3) high root/shoot ratio, (4) high root length/root weight, (5) high proportion of root system actively growing, (6) long root hairs, and (7) high uptake potential for the nutrient. The uptake of a nutrient beyond its efficient utilization may give a competitive advantage to the plant possessing that capability. It may also explain the competitiveness of some weeds since research has shown that some weeds may accumulate a nutrient well beyond their apparent need. Chambers and Holm (1965), for example, found that pigweed had a total P content 7 times that of snap bean. Such uptake on the part of a weed may be especially significant in view of the fact that successful competition for one factor may well lead to successful competition for others.

INTERACTIONS OF GROWTH FACTORS IN COMPETITION

As we have seen, plants are active partners in ecosystem development. Associated with this characteristic is their plasticity of growth form in response to conditions imposed by the environment. Thus, it is to be expected that competition for one growth factor affects competition for others. This relationship may be represented schematically as follows:

Competition for Light

↓

Reduced Production of Photosynthate

↓

Lower Root/Shoot Ratio

↓

Reduced Uptake of Soil Factors

↓

Reduced Root/Shoot Ratio

↓

Competition for Light

The schematic diagram may be entered at any point, thereby establishing the probable next phase of competition. For example, if a soil factor is in short supply early in a weed–crop situation, the loser is started on the road to reduced shoot growth and competition for light. If competition for light occurs, the loser is started on the road to competition for a soil factor. The schematic representation of interactions provides a simple way of perceiving an answer to the question: Which comes first, competition for light or competition for soil factors? Competition for light comes first if soil conditions are adequate, but first for soil factors if their supply is short enough to slow LAI development and light levels are high.

Interactions of Light and Nitrogen

Let us first consider interactions between light and nitrogen (N). As shown in Figure 7–8, competition for light reduces roots more than leaves. Root/leaf ratio is about 1:2 for control and 1:4 for low-light plants, suggesting that ability to obtain N (and other soil factors) is also reduced. Because weeds, especially annuals,

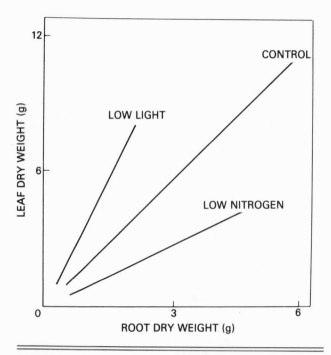

FIGURE 7–8. General effect of below-optimal supply of light and nitrogen on root and leaf weight of bean (*Phaseolus vulgaris*).

Source: Brouwer and deWit, 1969. Reproduced from Root growth with permission of Plenum Press.

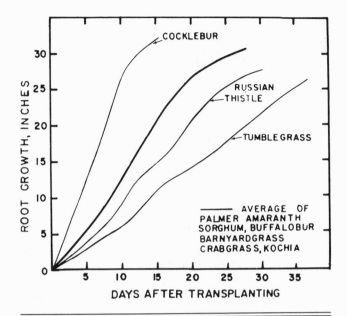

FIGURE 7–9. Differences in rate of root elongation for plants.
Source: Wiese, 1968. Reproduced with permission of the Weed Science Society of America.

evolved under conditions of nutrient stress, we expect them to grow relatively better than the crop when N is in short supply. Conversely, we might expect the crop to be the more aggressive in utilizing added N. The latter situation, in fact, frequently does not occur. Rather, the weed appears to be the more effective in both rate and quantity of uptake of added nutrients. The explanation likely lies in the comparative time necessary to complete their respective life cycles. As was pointed out in Chapter 6 (Li, 1960), most annual weeds do so in less time than the crops with which they are competing. In order to do so, they must, in effect, grow at a faster rate. The relationship to N uptake may be a result of: (1) more rapid elaboration of the root system and/or (2) the ability to utilize the N arriving at their roots more quickly, thereby allowing more N to flow to their roots.

Plants do differ in rate of root elongation, as can be seen in Figure 7–9. Palmer amaranth, cocklebur, barnyardgrass and crabgrass had extended their roots farther in 15 days than sorghum had in 20 days. There is also evidence that uptake of nutrients occurs over a shorter period in weeds. In quackgrass, Bandeen and Buchholtz (1967) found that by maturity in mid-July, quackgrass growing with corn had taken up 55%, 45%, and 68% of the total N, P, and K taken up by the weed for the entire season. Although comparable data were not obtained for the

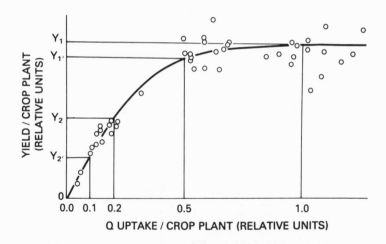

FIGURE 7–10. Effects of competition on the quantity of soil-supplied growth factor Q needed to give maximum yield. The uptake of growth factor needed to give maximum yield is taken as 1 unit. Y_1 and Y_2 are yields of weed-free crop plants for 1.0 and 0.2 units of Q. Y_1' and Y_2' are comparable crop yields where weeds are present at an equal density. The small circles are data obtained from research that served as the basis for the plotted curve.

Source: Trenbath, 1976. Reproduced from Multiple cropping, ASA Special Publication no. 27, 1976, by permission of the American Society of Agronomy, Crop Science Society of America, and Soil Science Society of America.

corn, the quantities obviously would be much less since corn, at this time, would still have the large majority of its dry matter production ahead of it.

Figure 7–8 also shows that shoot growth is restricted more than root growth by low N. The shoot/root ratio is about 2:1 for control plants and 4:1 for low-light plants. This relationship is further influenced by moisture supply. Since N moves passively with water to the root, it follows that competition for N is not apt to occur unless there is sufficient soil moisture for mass flow. Without mass flow, N would be left to move by diffusion, which is a slow process, thus minimizing the opportunity for differential (competitive) uptake.

A practical question suggested by the above discussion is the merit of adding the competed-for factor to offset reduction in crop yield. For example, is it practical to add nitrogen (or other soil factor) to offset potential yield depression from a heavy weed infestation? The answer can be deduced by inspection of Figure 7–10. Where maximum crop yield (Y_1) is obtained by 1.0 unit of the growth factor Q, infestation of an equal number of weeds reduces the yield to Y_1' since the unit of growth factor must be shared (0.5 for crop, 0.5 for weed). For maximum yield to be maintained, the amount of growth factor would have to be doubled so that the crop and weed could each have 1.0 unit of the growth factor. Thus, although it is theoretically possible to meet the needs of both the weed and the crop, it is not practical. This picture is further complicated by interactions among growth factors. Doubling the amount of N, for example, could be expected to change the total amount of water needed for maximum crop yield. Also, aboveground growth form and size would be changed, thus influencing competition for light.

Figure 7–10 can also be used to illustrate a principle important in weed–crop relationships: Weedy crops respond more to the addition of a growth factor. For a weed-free crop at the 0.2 Q level, addition of 0.8 units of Q approximately doubles the yield (Y_2 versus Y_1). If weedy, crop yield is more than tripled (Y'_2 versus Y'_1) by the addition of 0.8 units of Q.

Interactions of Carbon Dioxide and Other Growth Factors

Although, as already noted, competition for CO_2 is rare under field conditions, differences in CO_2 assimilation may lead to competition for other growth factors. Oliver and Schreiber (1974) found that pigweed net carbon exchange was at least 10 milligrams per square decimeter higher than birdsfoot trefoil during early stages of canopy development. More efficient CO_2 use helped it to grow more rapidly, thereby increasing its chances of competing for light.

Interactions of Growth Regulators and Growth Factors

A final factor that may interact in a variety of ways with competition for growth factors is the site of production and action of endogenous plant growth regulators. As can be seen in Table 7–1, both where the growth regulators are produced in plants and where they exert their effects vary, depending upon the substance. For example, both abscisic acid and cytokinins are produced in roots, but abscisic acid promotes leaf abscission, whereas cytokinins reduce leaf senescence (and thus abscission). Auxins are produced mainly in shoots. It follows that competition for a given growth factor could differentially affect either production or action of growth substances or both, depending upon the plant part most affected by the competition. It seems likely that all competition effects are at least partially explained by the interacting influence of plant growth substances.

Furthermore, the action of growth-regulating substances may provide the explanation for some of the crop yield reductions not readily explained by competition as such. For example, competition seems inadequate as an explanation for losses sometimes caused by weed presence during only the first 2 or 3

TABLE 7-1

Summary of information on endogenous plant growth substances.

	Auxins	Cytokinins
Chemical nature	Indol–3yl–acetic acid (IAA) and related compounds after conversion to IAA.	6–substituted amino-purines and their ribosides and ribotides, e.g., Zeatin.
Production and occurrence	Produced mainly in meristematic and growing regions of shoots; senescent tissue has also been suggested. Found in most tissues.	Root apices appear to be a major source; found also in seeds, immature fruits, and shoots.
Transport	Move readily from shoots to roots in phloem and more slowly by cell-to-cell polar transport, basipetally in shoots and acropetally in roots.	Move in xylem from roots to shoots and weakly by cell-to-cell basipetal polar transport in shoots.
Main effects	*Promote:* elongation of stems and coleoptiles, photo- and geotropic curvature, adventitious rooting and lateral root initiation, xylem differentiation, fruit growth, cambium activity, and leaf epinasty. *Inhibit:* root elongation, leaf senescence, and fruit abscission. Maintain apical dominance of axillary buds.	*Promote:* cell division, leaf and cotyledon expansion, seed germination, coleoptile elongation, stolon and shoot initiation, translocation of assimilates and inorganic phosphorus, and transpiration. *Inhibit:* leaf senescence. Release some seeds from dormancy and axillary buds from apical dominance.
Factors affecting production, movement, and action	Production is inhibited by zinc and phosphorus deficiencies and increased by gibberellins and cytokinins. Destruction is promoted by light, ethylene, and several phenolic compounds. Polar transport is stimulated by cytokinins or gibberellins and inhibited by abscisic acid or ethylene; and slow in older tissues. Action is modified by cell type, stage of development, and other hormones.	Little information available. Production in roots and movement to the shoots inhibited by flooding, drought, and high temperatures. Production in seeds increased by chilling and ethylene. Some production possible from the breakdown of RNA during senescence. Effects modified by other hormones.

Source: From Russell, 1977. Reproduced from Plant root systems: Their function and interaction with the soil by permission of McGraw-Hill Book Company (UK), Limited.

Gibberellins	Ethylene	Abscisic Acid
A gibbane skeleton carboxylated at position 10 of the central ring. Twenty-three such compounds had been isolated from higher plants by 1973.	Olefine gas, C_2H_4 (also called ethene).	A dextrorotatory sesquiterpene.
Root apices believed to be a major source; found also in seeds, young stems, and leaves.	Produced by all parts of plants, particularly by ripening fruit, apical growing zones, and senescing tissue.	The root cap is one site of synthesis; found also in seeds, fruit, tubers, leaves, and buds.
Move from roots to shoots in xylem and from leaves in phloem and by cell-to-cell basipetal polar transport in shoots.	Little evidence available but can move from roots to shoots.	Moves in the stele from leaves, cotyledons, and roots and by cell-to-cell basipetal polar transport in shoots.
Promote: stem elongation (especially in dwarf plants) by increasing cell elongation and division, flowering in some long-day plants, seed germination, leaf expansion, abscission, and fruit growth. *Inhibit:* leaf senescence, adventitious rooting, and fruit ripening. Release buds from apical dominance and winter dormancy and root elongation from inhibition by light. Involved in photo- and geotropic curvature of stems.	*Promotes:* senescence, germination, adventitious rooting, leaf epinasty, abscission, fruit ripening and stem elongation in some water plants. *Inhibits:* stem and root elongation, cell division, stelar differentiation, geotropic bending of stems and roots and hypocotyl hook opening in legumes. Releases axillary buds from apical dominance.	*Promotes:* abscission, bud dormancy, tuber formation, adventitious rooting, leaf senescence and stomatal closure. *Inhibits:* seed germination, axillary bud growth, transpiration, stem and root elongation, ion transport and flower initiation. Involved in geotropic curvature of roots.
Production in roots and movement to shoots inhibited by flooding. Production in shoots inhibited by short days. Seed production stimulated by chilling, light, and abscisic acid. Auxin and ethylene sometimes required for full activity. Abscisic acid normally inhibits activity.	Production increased by fruit ripening, senescence of leaves and flowers, mechanical wounding, flooding, drought, and other hormones. Production affected by light and inhibited by anaerobiosis. Little known about ethylene breakdown and factors affecting transport. Action modified by auxin and other hormones and antagonized by carbon dioxide.	Production increased by drought, flooding, nutrient deficiency, saline conditions, ripening, and senescence. Light and short days have little effect. Little known about breakdown and factors affecting transport. Inhibitory effects reversed in part at least by cytokinins, gibberellins, and auxin.

weeks after crop emergence. Losses occasionally occur in several crops, including corn, cotton, flax, rice, soybeans, several vegetables, and spring wheat, from such brief exposure to weeds (Zimdahl, 1980). In that short time, however, it is difficult to visualize that weed growth would be sufficient to interfere with light, water, or nutrient availability to the crop in such a way that the crop would not completely recover.

On the other hand, it is conceivable that interference with light availability in that time could affect production, transport, or action of one or more growth regulators. This interference could have a lasting effect on those plants so affected. Thus, although macroeffects of competition for water, nutrients, and light continue to be of primary importance in explaining crop losses from weeds, we must be mindful of the secondary role of interactions between availability of growth factors and growth-regulating substances.

COMBINED IMPACT OF PEST COMPETITION

Before leaving competition, we need to consider the potential combined impact on the crop of competition from a weed and from an insect, disease, or both. It is not uncommon for a crop to be subjected to stress from at least two classes of pest. In fact, this situation may be the usual one. Very little information is available to document the combined effect of weeds, insects, and diseases on crop yield and the relative contribution of each. A key question from the weed–crop ecology perspective is: Are such effects synergistic or merely additive? If the relationships are synergistic, a crude generalized conclusion would be that relatively less competition could be tolerated from a weed than if the effects were only additive.

A hypothetical weed–insect–crop situation illustrates this conclusion. An anticipated 95% control of a given weed and a given insect would be adequate if their effects were additive (5% loss from each) and the cost of 100% control of each was greater than the 10% yield saved. On the other hand, if the presence of the weed and insect together had a synergistic effect, causing the 5% population of each to inflict a 10% loss, the resulting 20% loss might indeed justify attempts to further reduce the pest infestation. The only known examination of these relationships is that by Higgins et al. (1981). They found that the effects of velvetleaf competition and green clover worm on soybeans were largely additive except under high density.

In summary, the complexities of weed competition with crops can best be understood and dealt with by keeping in mind that the leaf is the site of competition for light and the root the site of competition for soil factors. Any practice in crop management—selection of crop or variety, date of planting, crop stand, fertilizer management, and so forth—designed to selectively enhance the crop canopy and root volume occupied will assist the crop in its competitive struggle with weeds.

Competition for light is probably the most widespread competed-for growth factor. Competition for water and nitrogen is also common, while competition for nonmobile mineral nutrients, CO_2 and oxygen is quite uncommon if, in fact, competition for the latter two occur at all under field conditions.

CONCEPTS AND CONCLUSIONS

1. The leaf is the site of competition for light.
2. Light can neither be transferred nor stored within the plant; therefore, plant height is paramount in determining competition for light.
3. Light is likely to be the most frequently competed-for growth factor.
4. Most weeds, especially annuals, are very intolerant of shade.
5. Competition for CO_2 is not likely to occur under field conditions.
6. The root is the site of competition for water and mineral nutrients.
7. Competition for a soil factor cannot occur until the root depletion zones of neighboring plants overlap.
8. Relative competitiveness of weeds and crops for soil factors is largely determined by the soil volume occupied by the roots of each.
9. Weeds and crops differ greatly in the moisture extraction profiles of their roots.
10. Competition between weeds and crops occurs frequently for water and N, but rarely for K and P.
11. N moves mainly as the result of mass flow with soil water to the plant root; movement may be quite rapid, with the resulting depletion zone being roughly comparable to that for water.
12. K, P, and some other minerals move mainly as the result of diffusion, which is a slow process.
13. Competition is seldom restricted to a single growth factor because of the interrelationships between competition and plant growth form and rate.
14. Weeds commonly take up added nutrients (fertilizer) more rapidly and in larger quantities than do crops.
15. Attempts to provide enough of a competed-for growth factor to meet the needs of both the crop and the weeds are impractical.
16. A relatively scarce supply of a growth factor encourages earlier onset of competition for that factor.

REFERENCES

Alkamper, J. 1976. Influences of weed infestation on effect of fertilizer dressings. Pflanzenschutz-Nachrichten 29:191–235.

Bandeen, J.D., and K.P. Buchholtz. 1967. Competitive effects of quackgrass upon corn as modified by fertilization. Weeds 15 (3):220–24.

Black, J.N. 1958. Competition between plants of different initial seed sizes in swards of subterranean clover (*Trifolium subterraneum* L.). Aust. J. Agric. Res. 9:299–318.

Bleasdale, J.K.A. 1960. Studies on plant competition. In J.L. Harper, ed., The biology of weeds, pp. 133–42. Oxford: Blackwell Scientific.

Brouwer, R., and C.T. deWit. 1969. A simulation model of plant growth with special attention to root growth and its consequences. In W.J. Whittington, ed., Root growth, pp. 224–44. London: Butterworths.

Burnside, O.C. 1972. Tolerance of soybean cultivars to weed competition and herbicides. Weed Sci. 29 (4):294–97.

Chambers, E.E., and L.G. Holm. 1965. Phosphorus uptake as influenced by associated plants. Weeds 13 (4):312–14.

Chiariello, N., J.C. Hickman, and H.A. Mooney. 1982. Endomycorrhizal role for interspecific transfer of phosphorus in a community of annual plants. Science 217 (4563):941–43.

Davis, R.G., W.C. Johnson, and F.O. Wood. 1967. Weed root profiles. Agron. J. 59 (6):555–56.

Donald, C.M. 1963. Competition among crop and pasture plants. Adv. Agron. 15:1–118.

Feltner, K.C., H.R. Hurst, and L.E. Anderson. 1969. Yellow foxtail competition in sorghum. Weed Sci. 17 (2):211–13.

Felton, W.L. 1976. The influence of row spacing and plant population on the effect of weed competition in soybeans (*Glycine max*). Australian Journal of Experimental Agriculture and Animal Husbandry 16:926–31.

Higgins, R.A., D.W. Staniforth, and L.P. Pedigo. 1981. Interdisciplinary weed and insect stress research on soybeans in Iowa. Presented at 1981 Meeting of NCWCC, Des Moines, Iowa, unpublished.

Knake, E.L., and F.W. Slife. 1962. Competition of (*Setaria faberii*) with corn and beans. Weeds 10 (1):26–29.

―――――. 1965. Giant foxtail seeded at various times in corn and soybeans. Weeds 13 (4):331–34.

Lemon, E.R., and J.L. Wright. 1969. Photosynthesis under field conditions, XA. Assessing sources and sinks of carbon dioxide in a corn crop using a momentum balance approach. Agron. J. 61:405–11.

Li, M.Y. 1960. An evaluation of the critical period and the effects of weed competition on oats and corn, Ph.D. dissertation. Rutgers University, New Brunswick, N.J.

McWhorter, C.G., and E.E. Hartwig. 1972. Competition of johnsongrass and cocklebur with six soybean varieties. Weed Sci. 20 (1):56–59.

Oliver, L.R., and M.M. Schreiber. 1974. Competition for CO_2 in a heteroculture. Weed Sci. 22 (2):125–30.

Patterson, D.T., and E.P. Flint. 1979. Effects of chilling on cotton (*Gossypium hirsutum*), velvetleaf (*Abutilon theophrasti*), and spurred anoda (*Anoda cristata*). Weed Sci. 27:473–79.

―――――. 1980. Potential effects of global CO_2 enrichment on the growth and competitiveness of C_3 and C_4 weed and crop plants. Weed Sci. 28 (1):71–75.

Paul, R.N., and D.T. Patterson. 1980. Effects of shading on the anatomy and ultrastructure of the leaf mesophyll and vascular bundles of itchgrass *(Rottboellia exaltata)*. Weed Sci. 28 (2):216–24.

Russell, R.S. 1977. Plant root systems: Their function and interaction with the soil. Maidenhead, Berkshire, England: McGraw-Hill.

Shadbolt, C.A., and L.G. Holm. 1956. Some quantitative aspects of weed competition in vegetable crops. Weeds 4 (2):111–23.

Smith, R.J., Jr. 1974. Competition of barnyardgrass with rice cultivars. Weed Sci. 22 (5):423–26.

Staniforth, D.W. 1961. Responses of corn hybrids to yellow foxtail competition. Weeds 9 (1):132–36.

Sweet, R.D. 1976. When it comes to competing with weeds, some are more equal than others. Crops and Soils 28 (6):7–9.

———. 1979. Influence of variety and spacing of potatoes on yield and weed suppression. In Proc. NEWSS, vol. 33, p. 110. Boston, Mass.

Trenbath, R.R. 1976. Plant interactions in mixed crop communities. In Multiple cropping, ASA special publication no. 27, pp. 129–69. Madison, Wis.: American Society of Agronomy.

Vengris, J., W.G. Colby, and M. Drake. 1955. Plant nutrient competition between weeds and corn. Agron. J. 47:213–16.

Wiese, A.F. 1968. Rate of weed root elongation. Weed Sci. 16 (1):11–13.

———, and C.W. Vandiver. 1970. Soil moisture effects on competitive ability of weeds. Weed Sci. 18 (4):518–19.

Zimdahl, R.L. 1980. Weed–crop competition: A review. Corvallis: International Plant Protection Center, Oregon State University.

ALLELOPATHY IN WEED MANAGEMENT 8

ALLELOPATHY

Plants produce many metabolites that have no known utility in plant growth and development. Thus, the concept that plants produce chemicals toxic to themselves and to other plants and differ in their response to these chemicals is not illogical.

Based on their known chemistry, such chemicals can be expected to be harmful if present in sufficient concentration and proximity to a neighboring seed or growing plant. Further, harmful effects of one plant on another that cannot easily be explained by depletion of needed resources have long been observed. Among the examples are problems with orchard establishment on old orchard land, with reforestation, and with certain crop rotations and monoculture. A sizable literature has accumulated on *allelopathy*, the term used to identify the toxic effects of chemicals produced by one plant on another. In a recent update of such research, more than four hundred references are cited (Rice, 1979).

Nonetheless, the concept of allelopathy is still a matter of controversy. The observations and results of research are largely descriptive rather than analytical and therefore provide only circumstantial evidence for it, leaving room for explanations other than allelopathy for the observed results. Ideally, proof of a specific allelopathic effect requires: (1) isolation of the suspected allelochemical, (2) demonstration that the isolated chemical causes the observed effect, (3) identification of the chemical, and (4) synthesis of the chemical and verification that its activity is the same as that of the natural chemical. For reasons discussed later, the research called for is extremely complex. Thus, only a very few true allelochemicals are known today. In fact, the allelochemical known as juglone, produced by walnuts, is probably the only one to have passed through the four steps required for proof.

Our concern is not so much with the proof as with the influence in weed–crop relationships. The evidence for allelopathic effects is indeed overwhelming, even though few proofs are available. Thus, it is essential we examine what is known in terms of weed–crop relationships.

Historical Background

Knowledge about allelopathy has developed slowly. In reviewing its history, Rice (1974) traces its beginnings to DeCandolle in the early 1800s, who was among the first to suggest that some plants excrete substances injurious to other plants. This suggestion was based on the observation that some crop plants grow poorly in association with certain weeds or other crops and in soil following other crops. It was nearly fifty years before the possibility again emerged with a report by Stickney and Hay in 1881 of the harmful effects of walnut trees on the growth of other plants beneath them. Then, more than forty years passed until, in 1925, Massey reported studies of the walnut effect in some detail.

The results of Massey's study, shown in Figure 8–1, indicated that a deleterious root relationship existed between walnut and tomato plants. Tomato plants beyond the walnut roots were healthy, whereas those within the area of the walnut roots wilted and died. Over the next forty years the number of reports of similar effects expanded steadily. Most reports involved crop plants and fruit trees, but at least one involved weeds. In 1950, Keever observed that horseweed (*Conyza canadensis*) disappeared quickly from abandoned fields. In followup studies, it was found that decaying roots of this weed inhibit growth of seedlings of the same species. From about 1965 on, there has been a growing interest in possible allelopathic relationships between weeds and crops. Evidence has mounted that indeed both crop and weed plants introduce chemicals into the environment that are toxic to themselves and plants of other species.

Definition

Rice (1974) defines *allelopathy* as any direct or indirect, harmful effect by one plant on another through the production of chemical compounds that escape into the environment. One feature that distinguishes allelopathy from competition is that something is being added to the environment, as opposed to something being removed from it. There are two types of allelopathy: (1) true and (2) functional. *True allelopathy* is the release into the environment of compounds that are toxic in the form in which they are produced by the plant. *Functional allelopathy* is the

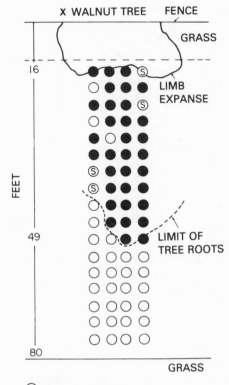

O REMAINED HEALTHY
Ⓢ DIED SOON AFTER TRANSPLANTING
● WILTED AND DIED BY 8 WEEKS

FIGURE 8–1. Allelopathic effects of a black walnut tree on tomato plants 8 weeks after transplanting.
Source: Rice, 1974. Reproduced courtesy of Academic Press, Inc.

release into the environment of substances that are toxic as the result of transformation by microorganisms. Both types may be important for weed–crop relationships.

Chemical nature of plant compounds. In general terms, *allelochemicals*, the toxic chemicals in allelopathy, are categorized as secondary plant compounds. *Secondary plant compounds* are those compounds that have no physiological function essential for the maintenance of life. Figure 8–2 shows the major groups of organic compounds implicated as allelochemicals and their relationship to primary plant metabolism. It is important to note that acetic acid (acetate) and amino acids are the basic components from which the secondary components are

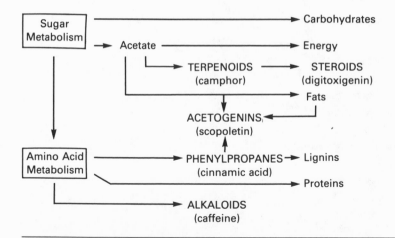

FIGURE 8–2. Metabolic relationships of the major groups of secondary compounds (shown in large type) to primary metabolism. An example of an allelochemical is shown in parenthesis above each group of secondary compounds.
Source: After Whittaker and Feeny, 1971. From Science, vol. 171, pp. 757–70, Figure 1, 26 February, 1971. Copyright 1971 by the American Association for the Advancement of Science.

derived. While no detailed discussion of the chemistry is given here, it should also be noted that the several classes of such chemicals represent a wide spectrum indeed. Within the classes, there may be many individual chemicals. Thus, it is not surprising that the isolation of compounds responsible for allelopathic effects is difficult.

Such isolation—and verification of effect—is, of course, important to full understanding of their role in weed–crop and weed–weed relationships and to their use in weed management. As helpful as such information might be, the lack of it need not preclude research to identify possible species relationships in weed communities. Also, as our knowledge expands of the occurrence of such chemicals and of the factors affecting their production, possibilities for using them in weed management can also be increased. Such possibilities are considered in Chapter 15.

Problems in Studying Allelopathy

Allelopathy is a particularly difficult phenomenon to study. It is difficult, for example, to separate the effects of allelopathy from those of competition because growth and yield may be influenced by each. For example, adverse effects of plant residues on seed germination and plant growth could be the result of the tie-up of large amounts of nutrients by the microorganisms involved, of the release of allelochemicals, or both. Thus, care must be taken to exclude competition as a factor, which is not easy because it, too, often involves a complex of factors, as discussed in Chapters 6 and 7.

Further, except under desert conditions where the effect may occur through the atmosphere, the effects of allelopathy are manifested in the soil environment. The soil environment inherently provides myriad physical, chemical, and biological processes that may interact with allelochemicals and thus interfere with their study.

Finally, isolation of suspected allelochemicals has commonly required chemical extraction of fresh or dried tissue. Thus, altered, rather than naturally occurring, compounds are collected. Under these circumstances, it is difficult to know if the collected compound has the same effect and activity as the native compound.

SIGNIFICANCE OF ALLELOPATHY FOR WEED–CROP ECOLOGY

Allelopathy is significant for weed–crop ecology in three respects: (1) as another factor affecting changes in weed composition, (2) as another source of weed interference with crop growth and yield, and (3) as a possible tool in reducing crop losses from weeds. All three roles are considered here.

As efforts expand to document the reason for changes in weed composition, we must be alert to the possibility that allelopathy may be involved. Similarly, as we move towards a better understanding of competition, it is essential that any allelopathic relationships be fully accounted for. In particular, allelopathy must be kept in mind to help explain results not easily explained by other environmental circumstances. This is not to say that allelopathy should automatically be identified as a contributing factor when all other factors seem to have been ruled out. Rather, it is a matter of recognizing that allelopathy should not be overlooked when the results appear to be anomalous.

Allelopathic Effects on Weed Composition

Effect on plant succession. As discussed in Chapter 2, there is a natural succession of plants in nature. In effect, plants change the environment, thus leading to a predictable succession, with the early colonizers being those species that rely upon large numbers of seeds and the later entrants those species that rely on their competitive ability. Rice and his co-workers (1974) observed instances where succession seemed contradictory of these established ecological concepts.

The inconsistency centered on the annual grass triple-awned grass *(Aristida oligantha)* in the succession shown in Table 2–3. In particular, why does such a noncompetitive species like triple-awned grass take over so quickly from the relatively robust species of the pioneer stage, and why does the annual grass and perennial bunch grass stage last so long? As we see, triple-awned grass begins to enter within 3 years after the onset of succession and is still present after 10 years.

From about the mid-1960s on, Rice and his co-workers conducted a number of different studies designed to determine if toxins produced by plants in the succession stages could be a factor in the observed anomaly. Studies were designed to evaluate the effects of addition of plant parts to soil, the effects of growing plants, and the effects of leachate from plant parts. The results of many of these studies are summarized in Table 8–1. Stage 1 species are toxic (+) towards themselves and less toxic (−)—if toxic at all—toward triple-awned grass. The exception seems to be crabgrass, which is toxic both to stage 1 species and to triple-awned grass from stage 2 species. It is presumed that the presence of crabgrass prevents triple-awned grass from entering early during stage 1. Because crabgrass seedlings are quite sensitive to the presence of other pioneer species, it is one of the first to be lost, thus allowing triple-awned grass to enter. Further, many pioneer species produce allelochemicals toxic to themselves that serve to shorten their persistence.

The persistence of triple-awned grass and the associated delay in takeover by the true prairie species is attributed to nitrogen relationships. It has been found

TABLE 8-1

Toxicity of selected pioneer weed species (stage 1) towards themselves and towards triple-awned grass (a stage 2 species) in tall grass prairie old-field succession.

Stage 1 Species	Toxicity	
	Stage 1 Species	Triple-Awned Grass
Johnsongrass	+	Slight
Wild sunflower	+	−
Crabgrass	+	+
Western ragweed	+	−
Prostrate spurge	+	Slight
Flowering spurge	+	−

+ Indicates a toxic effect.

− Indicates a nontoxic effect.

Source: Data from Rice, 1974.

that nitrogen fixation by bacteria and by bluegreen algae, as well as nodulation of legumes, may be inhibited by many species of the pioneer stage and by triple-awned grass of the second stage. It has also been shown that the nitrogen requirements of species increases as succession progresses. Thus, succession from stage 2 is delayed because the nitrogen supply is inadequate for the associated species to compete successfully with triple-awned grass and its lower requirements.

Allelopathic substances have been implicated as influencing plant succession in central and southern Japan (Kobayashi et al., 1980). A goldenrod *(Solidago altissima)* and fleabanes *(Erigeron* spp.), which are dominants of stage 2, produce allelochemicals highly toxic to the perennial grass eulalia *(Miscanthus sinensis)* of stage 3 and to common ragweed *(Ambrosia artemisiifolia)* of stage 1. The allelochemicals were identified as C_{10}–polyacetylenes.

These studies of the role of allelochemicals in succession have important implications for weed–crop ecology. They imply that the differential production of allelochemicals by crops and weeds and differential responses to them may well be involved in the shifts in weed composition associated with changes in production practices.

Effect on patterns of perennial distribution.   Because of the characteristic of perennial species to concentrate offshoots around a parent—known as the *patch effect*—it can be reasoned that allelopathy could be especially beneficial to such species. The very fact that dense colonies of some perennials frequently occur essentially as pure stands in itself implicates allelopathy. Allelopathy has been shown to affect plant community composition in abandoned fields (Rice, 1974) and in native grassland (Muller, 1957), but there is relatively little evidence of it as a factor in the composition of weeds in land under cultivation. Work by Steenhagen and Zimdahl (1979) indicates the presence of such weed-to-weed inhibition in the perennial weed leafy spurge. Their work involved both field observations and soil evaluations in the greenhouse. The field observation utilized an infested area that had been undisturbed for 4 years. Species diversity was measured across the area and on the surrounding area. They found that quackgrass and common ragweed, although present on the perimeter, did not occur in the high-density areas of leafy spurge; but some other weeds, such as kochia and crabgrass, did. Work in the greenhouse indicated that the effect was probably not due to competition. They point out, however, that the active agent has yet to be isolated and shown to exert its effect through the soil. Even so, it is highly probable that allelopathy in perennial weeds is frequently a factor determining the makeup of weed communities.

Effect on weed seed longevity.   The effect of allelochemicals on the longevity of weed seeds deserves special consideration in a weed–crop ecology context because of its potential impact on the success of attempts to alter the ecological environment to favor the crop. Hence, if weed seeds contain antimicrobial agents, or if such agents are produced as the result of decomposition of plant material, this characteristic must be dealt with in attempts to reduce interference from weeds over time. Rice (1974) goes so far as to suggest that antifungal properties of weed seeds may be the major reason for the observed longevity of some weed seeds in soils. Ecologically, this role of allelopathy may be its most significant.

The presence of antimicrobial agents in seed was demonstrated by Lane (1965) working with wild sunflower. He found that thorough leaching of seed did not alter the state of dormancy, but the seeds molded and decayed rapidly. If the seeds were exposed to low temperatures for several weeks without leaching, they did not mold and germinated well.

In other studies, Nickell (1960) tabulated all species of vascular plants reported to inhibit any or all of the following: gram-positive bacteria, gram-negative bacteria, fungi, microbacteria, protozoa, phage, virus, and yeast. He found that 50 species in 23 families had seeds that possessed antimicrobial activities. Many of the species were weeds, including the widespread species common ragweed, curly dock, and pennycress.

It has also been found (Patrick and Koch, 1958) that antifungal compounds are produced during decomposition of timothy, corn, rye, and tobacco plant material. If the residues are in the vicinity of weed seeds, presumably, the antifungal compounds produced might help prevent decay of the weed seed. Thus, it would seem that any attempt to explain, and influence, longevity of weed seeds in soil should consider the possibility that allelochemicals are involved.

Allelopathic Effects on Weed Interference with Crops

Allelopathy may be a factor in weed interference with crops in two respects: (1) in inhibiting germination and seedling establishment and (2) in inhibiting growth of the crop. The effect on germination may be the easiest to identify, but effects on growth may be the most common under field conditions.

Effect on crop seed germination.   Kommedahl and his co-workers (1959) showed that a stand of five crops was reduced by a heavy infestation of quackgrass in the soil previous to planting the crops. The results shown in Table 8–2 indicate alfalfa and barley to be particularly sensitive. In these studies, the heavy infestation of quackgrass was incorporated in the soil, but active growth of quackgrass was prevented. Missed rhizomes were weeded out when the quack-grass shoots emerged. Thus, the effect could be due either to the presence of an active agent released from the living rhizomes before or when they were incorporated (true allelochemicals), or to the production of a toxic substance during decomposition of the rhizomes by microorganisms (functional allelochemicals), or to both.

TABLE 8-2

Effect of previously infested quackgrass soil on the stand of 5 crops 3 months after sowing.

Crop	Percent Reduction of Stand on Infested Soil
Alfalfa	56
Flax	81
Barley	52
Oats	76
Wheat	66

Source: Data from Kommedahl et al., 1959.

TABLE 8-3

Inhibition of crop seed germination by water extracts of weed seeds.

Weed Species	Crop Germination*				
	Percent Germination at 23 Hours		Hours for 50% Germination		
	Alfalfa	Turnip	Pepper	Timothy	Tomato
Water control	82	64	117	68	44
Velvetleaf	5	25	>250	>250	106
Redroot pigweed	29	54	153	87	56
Common ragweed	31	12	132	92	61
Yellow rocket	5	16	>250	>250	103
Indian mustard	5	32	>250	>250	59
Lambsquarters	50	42	164	106	63
Crabgrass	76	41	152	72	54
Barnyardgrass	41	43	151	84	58
Pennsylvania smartweed	29	52	128	70	52
Common purslane	46	47	194	90	59
Yellow foxtail	20	43	182	92	57

* Alfalfa variety California Ranger, turnip variety Purple Top, pepper variety California Wonder, tomato variety Roma.
Source: Data from Gressel and Holm, 1964.

Work by Gressel and Holm (1964) showed that many weed seeds contain true allelochemical inhibitors to crop seed germination. In their studies, weed seeds were ground, extracted with water, and the extract tested for effects on germination. Thus, possible reaction of microorganisms was excluded. Table 8–3 shows first that many weed seeds prepared in this way yield substances toxic to germination of a variety of crops when compared with the water control. Second, the data of hours for 50% germination show that the effect is more of delay than of prevention of germination.

Water extracts of peppergrass, crabgrass, and evening primrose *(Oenothera biennis)* plants have been reported to inhibit germination of grown vetch (Bieber and Hoveland, 1968). In addition, it was found that extracts of peppergrass inhibited germination of fescue and several forage legumes. Creel and his co-workers (1968) found that water extracts of sicklepod *(Cassia obtusifolia)* inhibited cotton germination in the greenhouse.

Thus, there is considerable evidence that weeds may inhibit germination of crop seeds. All weed parts and both true and functional allelopathy are implicated. The significance for field conditions of the observed effect with weed seeds is not clear. It is possible for weed seeds to be near enough to crop seeds for leaching of a toxic agent to occur at precisely the right time to inhibit germination of the crop seeds, and it likely happens. Nonetheless, the chances for this combination of proximity and timing would seem to make this situation less likely than for decomposition of residues to yield a toxic agent or agents. After all, the residues represent a much larger biomass.

Effect on crop growth.   There is much evidence that allelochemicals from weeds inhibit crop growth. Among the earliest reported was that of soil previously infested with quackgrass inhibiting the growth of alfalfa, flax, barley, oats, and wheat (Kommedahl et al., 1959). Subsequent work has established that the effect is probably the result of decomposition (functional allelopathy) of the rhizomes (Ohman and Kommedahl, 1964; Harvey and Linscott, 1978; and Toai and Linscott, 1979).

Many weeds have been implicated as being allelopathic towards the crops with which they are growing. Separating allelopathy from competition is difficult in such situations. The following examples demonstrate different approaches for separating allelopathy from other interference of weeds with crops.

Allelopathy of giant foxtail towards corn was shown using a staircase arrangement of pots in the greenhouse (Bell and Koeppe, 1972). A diagrammatic representation of one line of the apparatus is shown in Figure 8–3. Test lines contained pots of corn alternating with pots of giant foxtail. Control lines contained only pots of corn. Solution was supplied to the uppermost pot from the quartz sand growing medium to a funnel and into the next pot in the series. The culture solution, after filtering through each pot in the series, was then pumped from a collecting reservoir back to the supply reservoir.

By using Hoagland's nutrient solution full strength and monitoring for conductivity and pH, uniform growing conditions were maintained in the test and control lines. Figures 8–4 and 8–5 show the effects on corn of different kinds of exposure to giant foxtail. From Figure 8–4, we see that foxtail seedlings had no harmful

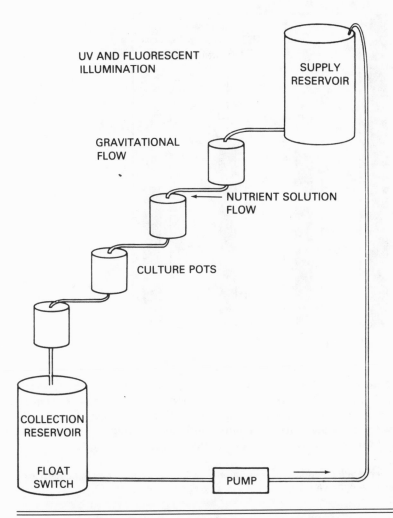

FIGURE 8–3. Diagrammatic representation of one line of a staircase apparatus for ascertaining allelopathic effects.
Source: Bell and Koeppe, 1972. Reproduced Agron. J., vol. 64, 1972, pp. 321–25, by permission of the American Society of Agronomy.

effects on the corn, but mature, live foxtail plants markedly reduced corn height (white bars), fresh weight (black bars), and dry weight (hatched bars). Since nutrients, water, and light were not limiting factors, it is assumed that a toxin to corn was released from the mature giant foxtail roots.

This method provides a direct way of identifying allelopathic effects but does not address the matter of relative biomass to that encountered in the field. As can

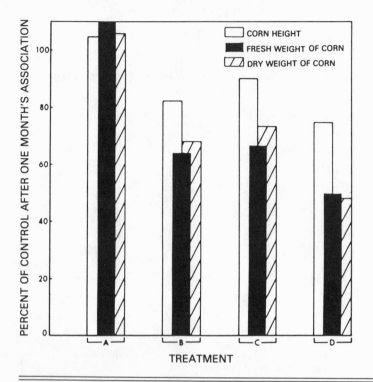

FIGURE 8–4. Allelopathic effects of giant foxtail on corn measured by the staircase apparatus shown in Figure 8–3. Treatments included corn seedlings (A) started together with giant foxtail seedlings; (B) growing with mature, live giant foxtail; (C) growing with dead giant foxtail plants; and (D) growing in contact with macerated giant foxtail leaf and root material incorporated into the sand culture pots.

Source: Bell and Koeppe, 1972. Reproduced from Agron. J., vol. 64, 1972, pp. 321–25 by permission of the American Society of Agronomy.

be seen, mature dead plants and incorporated foxtail residue also inhibited the corn. The incorporated residue was more inhibitory than either the living or dead whole plant. It was not determined if this effect was due to microbial transformation or simply to greater release from the macerated and incorporated material. Results from evaluation of time of exposure, shown in Figure 8–5, provide at least circumstantial evidence for microbiological activity. Maximum effects from incorporation (Figure 8–5B) showed up somewhat later than effects from the intact living plant (Figure 8–5A). Maximum reduction in fresh weight (black bars) and dry weight (hatched bars) shown for the incorporated material occurred at the last date, 31 days, whereas at 23 days, nearly maximum reduction had occurred with the living, mature foxtail. If only physical release were involved, we might expect

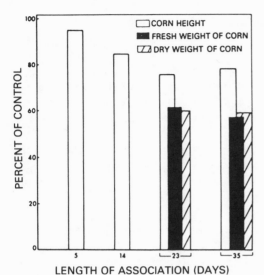

A. Effect of living, mature foxtail on corn

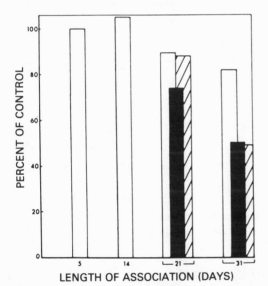

B. Effect of incorporated foxtail plant material on corn

FIGURE 8–5. Time needed for maximum allelopathic effects from living, mature foxtail plants vs. macerated and incorporated foxtail plants.

Source: Bell and Koeppe, 1972. Reproduced from Agron. J., vol. 64, 1972, pp. 321–25 by permission of the American Society of Agronomy.

maceration of incorporated plant material to cause earlier expression of effects. It may be assumed that time is required for the microorganism population to reach a fully effective level, whereas no such time element is involved with exudation from the living plant. In addition to showing that living foxtail roots release a toxin into the soil, this research also shows that both true and functional allelopathy may be involved in explaining the full allelopathic effects of foxtail on corn. It seems likely that both types are commonly involved in other instances of allelopathy of weeds towards crops.

Allelopathic effects of yellow nutsedge on growth of corn and soybeans were studied using indirect methods to relate effects to quantities of weed biomass representative of those encountered in the field (Drost and Doll, 1980). Various quantities of ground nutsedge tubers and foliage were either extracted with water or incorporated into potting media and tested for effects on the crops. It can be seen from Table 8–4 that 0.5% weight of tubers per weight of sand either incorporated or extracted with water reduced root growth of soybeans in pots in the greenhouse. This weight of tubers is representative of the quantity present in the upper 15 cm of soil in Wisconsin. Thus, the reduction for the water extract of tubers suggests the potential inhibition that might occur from yellow nutsedge growing with soybeans. That is, it can be postulated that toxin in the tubers is released into the soil–soybean root environment under moist soil conditions.

In this same study, it was also found, as shown in Figure 8–6, that exposure of the crop seeds to nutsedge residues placed at the same level as the seed was relatively more inhibitory to crop growth than placement either below or above the seed. This finding suggests that the depth of incorporation of allelopathic weed residue may influence the degree of allelopathic effects.

Although the greenhouse studies with foxtail and nutsedge provide valuable information, it is the effect encountered in the field that is important in interpreting and dealing with allelopathy. It is unwise to assume that results obtained under

TABLE 8-4

Inhibition of soybean root growth by both yellow nutsedge tuber residue and water extracts of tuber residues.

Quantity of Nutsedge Tuber Residue (%)[1]	Soybean Root Growth (%)[2]	
	Tuber Residue Incorporated	**Water Extracts of Tubers**
None	100	100
0.50	45	73

[1] Weight based on 1500 grams of silica sand.

[2] Based on untreated control.

Source: Data from Drost and Doll, 1980.

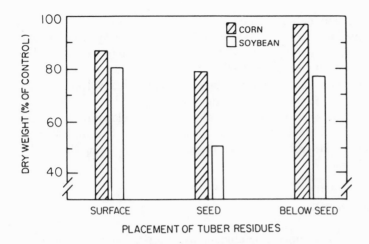

FIGURE 8–6. Allelopathic effects of yellow nutsedge residue towards corn and soybean seed at seed level, below the seed, or at the soil surface.
Source: Drost and Doll, 1980. Reproduced with permission of the Weed Science Society of America.

greenhouse conditions will be the same under field conditions. In fact, results will likely not be the same. One reason is that competition and allelopathy, where it occurs, are both quite apt to be involved in weed–crop situations in the field. As we shall see, stress (competition) appears to have a marked effect on production of allelochemicals. Further, both true and functional allelopathy may well be involved, as we have seen. Therefore, allelopathy must ultimately be evaluated in the field to be certain of its significance in weed–crop relationships. The complexities of such research have already been discussed.

A way of dealing with these complexities has been suggested by Dekker et al. (1982). These workers suggest the design of experiments and analysis of data that *collectively* provide *inferential* measures of allelopathy. By drawing upon what is known about plant and density relationships, some divergence from that expected for competition provides an inference for the presence of allelopathy. Use of replacement experimental designs is basic to this approach. In *replacement designs,* total density is held constant and the proportions of each of two species varied. By measuring several growth parameters and subjecting the data to mathematical and graphical treatments, inference statements can be developed.

This approach was applied to velvetleaf interacting with soybeans. It was found that soybean flowering node numbers, soybean relative yields, relative replacement rate of soybean by velvetleaf, and relative thinning of flowering nodes under high plant density supported the presence of an allelopathic mechanism. Because much of the interpretation is theoretical, application to other weed–crop situations and collection of discrete data are needed. Nevertheless, the approach provides valuable background for evaluating allelopathy under field conditions.

Irrespective of the explanation, it is clear that allelopathy from weeds may be involved in the detrimental effects of weeds on crops. The effect may be expressed both through a reduction in germination and through a reduction in growth. Under field conditions, it is speculated that reduction in growth may be the effect most frequently encountered. Further, microorganisms are commonly involved, both to implement release of the toxic agent and to produce such agents. If the allelochemical is exuded by the weed, removing it should alleviate the allelopathic effect. If, on the other hand, the allelochemical is released from weed residue during decomposition, weed growth will need to be prevented to avoid crop damage.

Potential of Allelopathy for Weed Management

With the mounting evidence supporting allelopathy as a phenomenon in nature, there is growing interest in the possibility of using this characteristic on the part of the crop to minimize interference from weeds. Although the work is still sketchy, enough has been done to suggest this attribute could indeed be a usable tool against weeds.

Suppressing germination and emergence of weeds.   Both allelopathy of the growing crop and of its residue might be utilized to reduce weed stands. There are examples of success with each approach. Lockerman and Putnam (1979) found that one cucumber selection of several studied markedly reduced the stand of barnyardgrass and redroot pigweed. From Table 8–5 we see that the stand of barnyardgrass was reduced about 80% and redroot pigweed about 60% by the accession PI 169391.

Of course, as already learned, such reductions in weed numbers may not be enough to prevent significant reductions in crop growth. In this case, the remaining weeds caused a 25% reduction in fresh weight of the cucumber vines at maturity. This fact and inconsistent weed suppression (Leather and Forrence, 1979) suggest that if this approach is utilized, it is likely to be in conjunction with other methods

TABLE 8-5

Weed numbers in the presence and absence of selected cucumbers in the field.

Cucumber Accession or Cultivar	Barnyardgrass		Redroot Pigweed	
	Days after Planting			
	10	**48**	**10**	**48**
No cucumber	31	38	58	54
Pioneer	26	21	39	40
PI 169391	7	7	23	21

Source: Adapted from Lockerman and Putnam, 1979.

of weed management. Nevertheless, it appears that allelopathy could be incorporated into crop cultivars.

Substantial reductions in weed stands from crop residues have also been demonstrated. Grain sorghum residue reduced stands of smooth crabgrass *(Digitaria Ischaemum)* 98% and of common purslane 94% in one study (DeFrank and Putnam, 1979). Reductions this great could be expected to prevent losses in crop yield.

Suppressing growth of weeds.   The growing crop and its residue may also be used to suppress weed growth. Results of an evaluation of the worldwide collection of oat germ plasm indicate the potential of the former (Fay and Duke, 1977).

In this study, 3000 accessions were screened for scopoletin content. The allelochemical scopoletin is known to be inhibitory towards plant growth. Garry oat was used as a standard for comparison. Twenty-five accessions had more scopoletin than Garry. Four had 3 times as much and 1, number 266281, nearly 4 times as much. Figure 8–7 shows that accession 266281 was more inhibitory toward

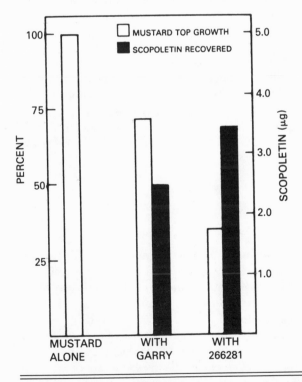

FIGURE 8–7. Varying allelopathic effects of crop germ plasm on weeds.
Source: Fay and Duke, 1977. Reproduced with permission of the Weed Science Society of America.

mustard top growth than was Garry. In fact, mustard exposed to this accession made only about one-third as much growth as mustard alone.

Residue of a rye line selected for its suppressing ability was shown to offer promise for suppressing weed growth in a no-till vegetable production system (Barnes and Putnam, 1982). Up to 95% control of weed biomass was obtained with the rye planted in the fall, killed in the spring, and vegetables planted in the residue. Snap beans were not damaged by the residue.

Thus, we see that allelopathy on the part of the crop offers several possibilities for preventing or reducing crop losses from weeds. These possibilities are examined in Chapter 15.

ALLELOCHEMICALS

There is overwhelming evidence that allelochemicals are a part of the natural environment within which plants grow. Further, we have seen that they are a factor in ecological relationships between weeds and crops. Thus, an understanding of the general nature of such chemicals is important to an appreciation of their significance for weed–crop relationships, as well as to the possible utilization of such knowledge in weed management. This is not the place for an in-depth consideration of their chemistry. Other sources for such information are Whittaker and Feeney (1971) and Rice (1974 and 1979). Here we consider allelochemicals in terms of their significance for weed–crop interrelationships. The items to be covered include what is known about their presence in plant parts, factors affecting quantities produced, entry into the environment, and metabolic processes affected.

Allelochemical Sources

In discussing effects upon plants early in the chapter, reference was made to roots, seeds, and leaves as sources of allelochemicals. Rice (1974) cites literature to show that the chemicals may be produced in other major organs. Leaves may be the most consistent source of such inhibitors. Roots are considered to contain fewer and less potent toxins or smaller amounts. More complete knowledge of their location in the plant is needed in connection with efforts to use the production of such chemicals by growing crops to suppress weeds. To have maximal effect against weeds growing with a crop, the allelochemicals need to be concentrated in the roots, leaves, or stems, rather than in the flowers and fruits. If concentrated in the flowers and fruits, it is unlikely they could be available in time to prevent interference from the weed. In instances where the plant material containing the toxin or from which the toxin is produced is to be incorporated in soil to inhibit germination and growth, location within the plant may be relatively unimportant. Rather, total biomass to be incorporated and concentration of the toxin are the important aspects.

Allelochemical Quantities Produced

Knowledge about quantities produced is of obvious importance to possible use of allelochemicals in weed management. As our knowledge of factors affecting quantities of allelochemicals produced expands, opportunities for manipulating crop production practices to maximize allelopathy should suggest themselves. Rice (1974 and 1979) cites considerable evidence to indicate that a variety of environmental factors do indeed influence the quantity of allelochemicals produced by plants. Some of the environmental factors identified as influencing quantity follow.

First, quantities of some known allelochemicals are influenced by light quality, intensity, and duration. The most significant finding for weed–crop ecology may be that quantities produced are greatest under exposure to ultraviolet light and long-day photoperiods. Thus, understory plants might be expected to produce less quantity because of the filtering out of some of the ultraviolet rays by overstory vegetation. Also, plants during the peak of the growing season could be expected to produce more allelochemicals than those plants earlier or later in the growing season.

Second, quantities are greater under conditions of mineral deficiency. The magnitude of the difference may be severalfold, as shown for nitrogen on sunflower in Table 8–6. Deficient older leaves and stems contained 8 to 10 times as much total chlorogenic acids, a group of compounds known to be toxic.

Third, the amount of allelochemicals produced is greater under drought stress.

Fourth, quantities may be greater under cool than under what are considered normal growing temperatures, although the location within the plant and effects on specific allelochemicals seem to be variable.

Fifth, application of plant growth regulators, such as 2,4–D and maleic hytrazide, and of other allelochemicals apparently may greatly increase the quantities of allelochemicals produced by a plant.

Effect of stress.   As we have seen, there are many indications that environmental conditions that restrict growth tend to increase the production of allelochemicals. It is only a short step from this general effect to the postulation that allelopathy may frequently be an accentuator of competition, even though not itself a part of competition. After all, competition between weeds and crops in itself implies the creation or presence of stress conditions. Thus, if stress from competition increases the quantities of allelochemicals produced, it is conceivable

TABLE 8-6

Concentrations of total chlorogenic acids and scopolin in nitrogen-deficient and control sunflower plants 5 weeks from start of treatment.

Plant Organ and Treatment	μg/g Fresh Weight	
	Total Chlorogenic Acids	Scopolin
Older leaves		
Control	1139	7.2
Deficient	8884	6.4
Younger leaves		
Control	1737	—
Deficient	873	—
Stems		
Control	383	1.8
Deficient	3275	—
Roots		
Control	303	—
Deficient	490	—

— Below amounts determinable by procedure used.

Source: Rice, 1974. Data from Lehman and Rice, 1972.

the allelochemicals will inhibit growth of some species and not others, thereby further reducing the ability of the affected species to compete.

The postulation of the stress effect suggests that growth factors and growing conditions may interact to influence the quantities of allelochemicals produced. Indeed, there is evidence that exposure to more than one stress factor may have a compound effect on quantities of chemicals produced. This evidence is shown in Table 8–7. The combination of stress for nitrogen and moisture resulted in a fifteenfold increase in the chlorogenic acids and a sixteenfold increase in the isochlorogenic acids over the control. This particular combination has special relevance for weed management since both factors may be controllable, at least to a degree, depending upon the geographic location, season, crop, and production system.

It is important to remember that plants producing allelochemicals and those affected by them are a part of an ecosystem. This means that rarely, if ever, will one factor vary without changes in one or more other factors. Light can be expected to interact with temperature and indirectly with soil moisture, and so it goes. This is one more reason allelopathy needs to be ever in mind as a possible factor in explaining weed–crop relationships.

TABLE 8-7

Effects of stress factors on concentrations of total chlorogenic acids and total isochlorogenic acids in sunflower plants.

	μg/g Dry Weight*	
Stress Applied	Total Chlorogenic Acids	Total Isochlorogenic Acids
None, control	43	135
Ultraviolet light	113	203
-Water	258	320
Ultraviolet light; -water	455	512
-Nitrogen	458	1065
-Nitrogen; ultraviolet light	310	375
-Nitrogen; -water	645	2185
-Nitrogen; -water; ultraviolet light	546	979

- indicates reduced quantity; data from del Moral, 1972.

* Weighted mean of leaf, stem, and root tissues.

Source: Rice, 1974.

Allelochemical Modes of Entry into the Environment

The fact that allelochemicals can be identified in plants does not mean they necessarily have an effect in the weed–crop ecosystem. To have an effect, the chemicals must enter the environment of the weed–crop ecosystem and at a time when they can have an effect. That is, if the allelochemical is not released from the plant that produces it, obviously it can have no effect on other plants. If the allelochemical is released to the soil environment at the end of the growing season, only to be dissipated before the next growing season, it may have no effect. There are four ways allelochemicals can enter the environment: (1) volatilization, (2) leaching, (3) exudation, and (4) decomposition. These modes of entry are shown schematically in Figure 8–8.

Volatilization. There are many examples of *volatilization*—that is, release into the atmosphere—as a way of allelochemical entry into the environment under natural conditions (Rice, 1974). In general, this mode of entry is only significant under arid or semiarid conditions.

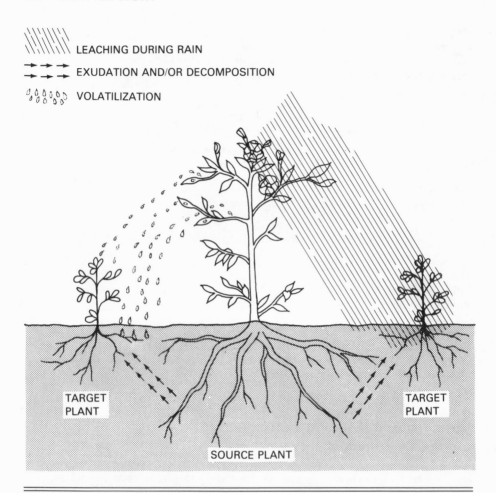

FIGURE 8–8. Schematic representation of ways allelochemicals enter a weed–crop ecosystem.

A phenomenon related to volatilization with possible implications for weed management is the interaction between plants and other living things, especially insects. Many aspects of insect behavior may, at least at times, be related to plant chemistry. Of special interest to us in weed management is the fact that phytophagous (plant-eating) insects use volatile compounds emanating from plants as cues to find their particular host plants. This fact suggests the possibility of interfacing allelopathy and biological control of weeds by insects. This potential would seem to be within reach since it is likely that this type of control already occurs in nature.

Leaching.   Water in rainfall, irrigation water, or dew may pick up or, *leach*, allelochemicals that are subsequently deposited on other plants or on the soil. We can visualize this mode of entry as an important factor in plant ecological relationships because it could serve to extend the time and quantities of exposure over what would occur from the other modes of entry. Here, too, there are many examples of entry into the environment in this way (Rice, 1974). Leaching of plant residues on or in the soil may also move allelochemicals into the soil environment. The work of Drost and Doll (1980) referred to earlier showing leachate from nutsedge leaves and tubers to inhibit corn and soybeans is an example of this mode of entry.

Exudation.   Exudation of allelochemicals from plant roots into the soil environment is implicated as a mode of entry by many studies. The work of Bell and Koeppe (1972) showed that allelopathy is most likely the result of exudation of allelochemicals from giant foxtail roots since watering in the staircase arrangement precludes leaching from aboveground parts. However, it is possible the observed effect is simply the result of allelochemicals being leached from the roots. In this case, although decomposition cannot be ruled out, at least as a contributor, it is unlikely to be the major mechanism, due both to the short-term nature of the study and the fact that the sand medium used may be presumed to be low in microorganisms.

Decomposition.   There is much evidence that toxic substances result from the decomposition of plant residue. The work with quackgrass reported earlier showed decomposition to be the mode of entry (Ohman and Kommedahl, 1964; Harvey and Linscott, 1978; and Toai and Linscott, 1979). It is difficult, however, to determine whether the toxic substance is contained in the residue and simply released upon decomposition or is produced instead by the microorganisms utilizing the residue.

Problems in studying modes of entry.   As we have seen, entry of allelochemicals into the environment is indeed complex. The toxic effects of one plant on another in the soil environment may be the result of leaching from aboveground plant parts, exudation from living roots, release as a result of breakdown of sloughed-off cells, or formation of such toxins by organisms living on the plant material. Separating these mechanisms is difficult at best, especially under field conditions. Further, all mechanisms could conceivably be involved at the same time in the field. However, entry by leaching and decay of litter together are more likely to have a greater effect on weed–crop relationships than entry in other ways (Putnam and Duke, 1978).

A method for collecting allelochemicals directly from roots has been devel-

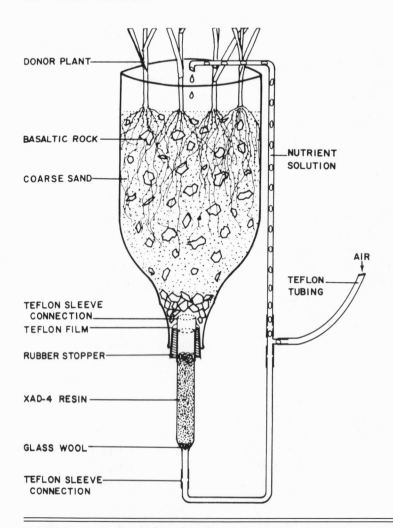

DONOR PLANT

BASALTIC ROCK

COARSE SAND

NUTRIENT
SOLUTION

AIR

TEFLON
TUBING

TEFLON SLEEVE
CONNECTION
TEFLON FILM

RUBBER STOPPER

XAD-4 RESIN

GLASS WOOL

TEFLON SLEEVE
CONNECTION

FIGURE 8–9. Hydrophobic root-trapping system.
Source: Tang and Young, 1982. Reproduced with permission of the American Society of Plant
Physiologists.

oped (Tang and Young, 1982). This method, depicted schematically in Figure 8–
9, allows continuous trapping of extracellular chemicals on a resin column.
Nutrient solution continuously circulated through the roots of donor plants picks
up extracellular organic compounds (exudates) from the sand culture. The
hydrophobic or partially hydrophobic exudates are selectively retained on the
XAD–4 resin column while the inorganic nutrients pass through. The trapped
chemicals can then be eluted (extracted) for identification, quantification, and

measurement of activity. This methodology may prove useful in separating exudation, leaching, and decomposition as modes of allelochemical entry into the soil environment.

Plant Processes Affected by Allelochemicals

As we have learned, allelochemicals can affect both germination and growth of plants. These effects may be manifested through a wide variety of metabolic activities. Specific plant processes identified as being affected include: cell division and elongation, action of inherent growth regulators, mineral uptake, photosynthesis, respiration, stomatal opening, protein synthesis, lipid and organic acid metabolism, hemoglobin synthesis, membrane permeability, and actions of specific enzymes (Retig et al., 1972; Rice, 1974; and Harper and Balke, 1981). The challenge for students of weed–crop ecology is to identify the processes most manipulatable in weed management. In this regard, those processes most directly related to competition seem to offer the best possibilities. Although all of the processes identified are, of course, involved in growth, some, especially cell division and elongation, are more directly involved than others.

INTERRELATIONSHIPS OF ALLELOPATHY IN WEED–CROP ECOLOGY

Figure 8–10 summarizes in schematic fashion what is known about allelochemicals and suggests their ecological significance for weed–crop relationships. As can be seen, the weed and the crop can be affected anytime throughout their life cycles. The reason is the pervasiveness of allelochemicals in plant parts and in the environment, the multiplicity of factors affecting their production, and the many growth processes affected. The end effects on the agroecosystem are in three broad areas: (1) weed persistence, (2) crop yield, and (3) weed composition.

Allelochemicals' role in weed persistence, and thus composition, may be most significant with perennial species. It can be postulated that the production of such chemicals would be of relatively greater value to survival of perennial than of annual weeds. As is known, most annual weeds rely upon numbers (r-strategy) for survival. Thus, their strategy is to maximize the number of different sites they can occupy. Although allelopathy towards other species conceivably might help them become established in those sites, it would not appear to offer any substantial advantage for their primary strategy, which is to produce many seeds. Most perennials, on the other hand, rely upon their competitive ability (K-strategy) for

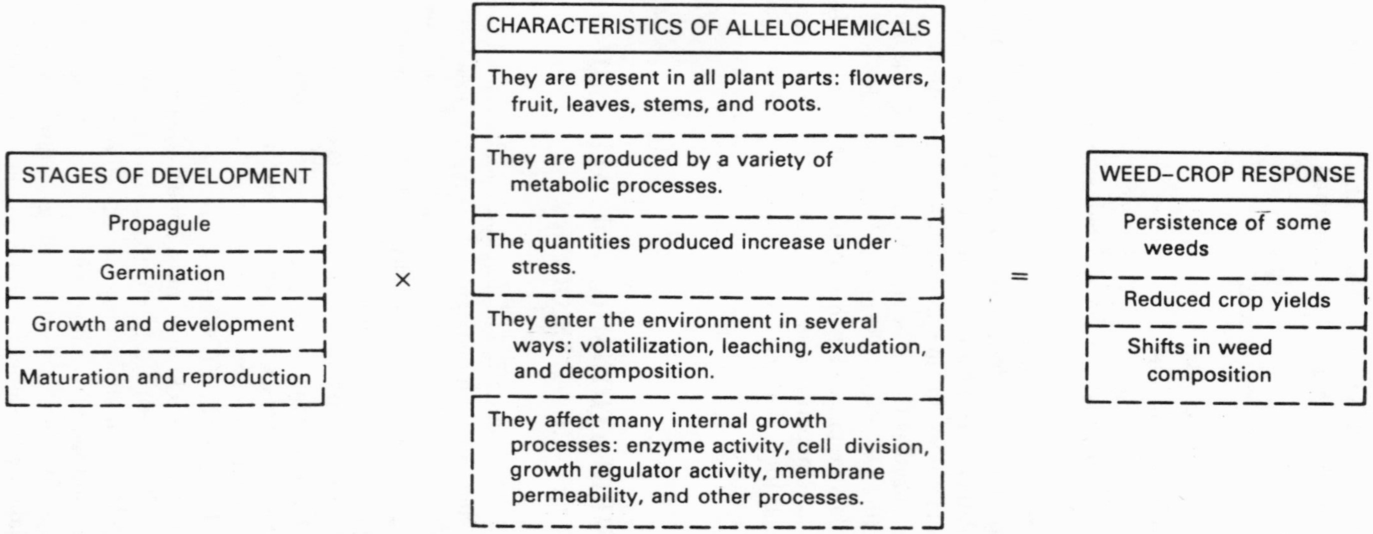

FIGURE 8–10. Schematic representation of allelopathic relationships in weed–crop ecology.

survival. That is, they depend upon characteristics that increase their ability to gain a disproportionate share of the resources in a given area. Production of allelochemicals that exclude other species would clearly aid a perennial in its competitive struggle. Since perennial weeds increase under reduced tillage, it can be further postulated that allelopathy will become relatively more important for all areas of weed–crop response as this practice continues to expand.

The effect on yield may well be the most significant effect for weed management. It has been established that the presence and quantity of allelochemicals is under genetic influence. Further, the amount produced by a given plant and its release into the environment are influenced by factors that can be controlled, at least to some degree, by cultural practices. Thus, the yield response offers the two-pronged approach of crop breeding and production management in utilizing allelopathy for minimizing or reducing interference from weeds.

CONCEPTS AND CONCLUSIONS

1. Allelopathy probably influences the composition of the weed community; the influence may be especially important if perennial weeds are involved.
2. Allelochemicals are secondary plant products that inhibit both germination and growth of plants; in doing so, many metabolic processes may be affected.
3. Allelochemicals may exert their effect through the atmosphere (volatilization) and through the soil (leaching, exudation, and decomposition).
4. Evidence exists that production of allelochemicals is genetically controlled.
5. Allelopathy must be recognized as a potential compounding factor when weeds are competing with crops.
6. Allelochemicals are produced in all plant parts.
7. Many environmental factors influence the quantity of allelochemicals produced in plants; there appears to be a direct relationship between stress on the plant and quantity produced.
8. A large number of chemicals, widely different in their nature, cause allelopathic effects.
9. The fact that the capacity to produce allelochemicals is genetically controlled and the fact that the quantities produced are determined by a number of environmental factors offer encouragement that ways can be developed to use them in weed management.

REFERENCES

Barnes, J.P., and A.R. Putnam. 1982. Weed suppression with rye cover crops in vegetable cropping systems. In Abstract of 1982 Meeting of WSSA, p. 67. Boston, Mass.

Bell, D.T., and D.E. Koeppe. 1972. Noncompetitive effects of giant foxtail on the growth of corn. Agron. J. 64:321–25.

Bieber, G.L., and C.S. Hoveland. 1968. Phytotoxicity of plant materials on seed germination of crownvetch, *Coronilla varia* L. Agron. J. 60:185–88.

Creel, J.M., Jr., C.S. Hoveland and G.A. Buchanan. 1968. Germination, growth, and ecology of sicklepod. Weeds 16 (3):396–400.

DeFrank, J., and A.R. Putnam. 1979. Efficacy of rotational crop residue for weed control. In abstract of 1979 Meeting of WSSA, pp. 84–85. San Francisco, Calif.

Dekker, J.H., W.F. Meggit, and A.R. Putnam. 1982. Experimental methodologies to demonstrate allelopathic plant interactions: The *Abutilon theophrasti-Gycine max* model. J. Chem. Ecol., in press.

Drost, D.C., and J.D. Doll. 1980. The allelopathic effect of yellow nutsedge on corn and soybeans. Weed Sci. 28 (2):229–33.

Fay, P.K., and W.B. Duke. 1977. An assessment of allelopathic potential in *Avena* germ plasm. Weed Sci. 25(3):224–28.

Gressel, J.B., and L.G. Holm. 1964. Chemical inhibition of crop germination by weed seeds and the nature of inhibition by *Abutilon theophrasti*. Weed Res. 4:44–53.

Harper, J.R., and N.E. Balke. 1981. Relationship of salicylic acid absorption to inhibition of potassium absorption in oat roots. In Abstracts of 1981 Meeting of WSSA, p. 89. Las Vegas, Nev.

Harvey, R.G., and J.J. Linscott. 1978. Ethylene production in soil containing quackgrass rhizomes and other plant material. Soil Sci. Soc. Am. J. 42 (5):721–24.

Keever, C. 1950. Causes of succession on old fields of the Piedmont, North Carolina. Ecol. Monogr. 20:229–50.

Kobayashi, A., et al. 1980. $C_{1}0$–polyacetylenes in early stages of secondary succession. J. of Chem. Ecol. 6 (1):119–31.

Kommedahl, T., J.B. Kotheimer, and J.V. Bernardini. 1959. The effects of quackgrass on germination and seedling development of certain crop plants. Weeds 7 (1):1–12.

Lane, F.E. 1965. Dormancy and germination in fruits of the sunflower, Ph.D. dissertation. University of Oklahoma, Norman, Okla.

Leather, G.R., and L.E. Forrence. 1979. Allelopathic potential of thirteen varieties of sunflower (*H. annuns* L.). In Abstract 172 of 1979 Meeting of WSSA, San Francisco, Calif.

Lehman, R.H., and E.L. Rice. 1972. Effect of deficiencies of nitrogen, potassium, and sulfur on chlorogenic acids and scopolin in sunflower. Amer. Midl. Natur. 84:71–80.

Lockerman, R.H., and A.R. Putnam. 1979. Evaluation of allelopathic cucumbers *Cucurbita sativus* as an aid to weed control. Weed Sci. 27 (1):54–57.

Massantini, F., et al. 1977. Evidence for allelopathic control of weeds in lines of soybeans. In Proc. EWRS Symposium, vol. 1, pp. 23–28. Uppsala, Sweden.

Massey, A.B. 1925. Antagonism of the walnuts (*Juglans nigra* L. and *J. cinerea* L.) in certain plant associations. Phytopathology 15:773–84.

Muller, C.H. 1957. The role of chemical inhibition (allelopathy) in vegetational composition. Bul. Torrey Bot. Club 93:332–51.

Nickell, L.G. 1960. Antimicrobial activity of vascular plants. Econ. Bot. 13:281–318.

Ohman, J.H., and T. Kommedahl. 1964. Plant extracts, residues, and soil minerals in relation to competition of quackgrass with oats and alfalfa. Weeds 12 (3):222–31.

Patrick, Z.A., and L.W. Koch. 1958. Inhibition of respiration, germination and growth by substances arising during the decomposition of certain plant residues in the soil. Can. J. Bot. 36:621–47.

Retig, B., L.G. Holm, and B.E. Struckmeyer. 1972. Effects of weeds on the anatomy of roots of cabbage and tomato. Weed Sci. 20 (1):33–36.

Rice, E.L. 1974. Allelopathy. New York: Academic Press.

———. 1979. Allelopathy—An update. Bot. Rev. 45:15–109.

Steenhagen, D.A., and R.L. Zimdahl. 1979. Allelopathy of leafy spurge *(Euphorbia esula)*. Weed Sci. 27 (1):1–3.

Tang, C., and C. Young. 1982. Collection and identification of allelopathic compound from the indisturbed root system of bigalta limpgrass *(Hemarthria altissima)*. Plant Physiol. 69:155–60.

Toai, T.V., and D.L. Linscott. 1979. Phytotoxic effect of decaying quackgrass *(Agropyron repens)* residues. Weed Sci. 27 (6):595–98.

Whittaker, R.H., and P.P. Feeney. 1971. Allelochemicals: Chemical interactions between species. Sci. 171 (3973):757–70.

BIOTIC AGENTS IN WEED MANAGEMENT

9

Weeds have their enemies. Chapter 3 discussed the fact that a significant portion of the weed seeds produced are destroyed by predators before ever reaching the soil, and many more are destroyed by predators and microorganisms in the soil. The growing weed is also preyed upon. These effects of natural enemies, biotic agents, may go relatively unnoticed unless of a dramatic nature, such as the elimination of American elm in much of the eastern United States by the Dutch elm disease during the second half of this century. It seems reasonable to expect that some weeds have similarly been eliminated by natural enemies and, therefore, logical to believe that natural enemies might be used in weed control. In fact, attempts to use such natural enemies in controlling troublesome weeds go back to at least the beginning of this century.

Before considering biological control, we should again remind ourselves that we are dealing with an ecological system. Insects, plant pathogens, and other crop pests, along with weeds, humans, the environment, and the crop are all part of this system. As discussed in Chapter 2, a change in any part of this system causes changes in the other parts. Thus, as we change our practices for dealing with weeds, we must be alert to the changes that will occur with the other pests. Similarly, we must take into account the potential harmful effects on biotic weed control agents of control treatments, especially pesticides, used against other crop pests. It has been found, for example, that fungicides used in vegetable crops may reduce control of yellow nutsedge with the rust *Puccinia canaliculata* (Phatak et al., 1983).

The purpose of this discussion of biotic agents is to identify the place for such agents in weed management and to develop an understanding of factors affecting their successful use. To do this, it is necessary to draw upon work that was designed to control a particular weed since this is the nature of most available information. The concepts appropriate to weed management are identified from the research reported on control.

A knowledge of weeds' natural enemies gained in the process should help conserve and augment infestations of such natural enemies. Selected examples of successful control with biotic agents are used to identify and develop the concepts, but no attempt is made to review all available literature. Refer to the proceedings of the *IV International Symposium on Weeds* (Freeman, ed., 1976) for information on control of specific weeds.

SUCCESSFUL CONTROL OF WEEDS WITH BIOTIC AGENTS

Insects

Among the potential biotic agents, insects have received by far the most attention. Goeden et al. (1974), in a review of the status of research on biological control of weeds through 1973, found that of the 78 weeds under study, 73 were the target of insects. Thus, it is not surprising that a majority of the successes in biological control have been with insects. This fact should not be construed as indicative of the relative potential of insects since there is reason to believe, as discussed later, that pathogens may offer at least as great a potential.

Prickly pear cactus in Australia.   Control of the prickly pear cactus *(Opuntia inermis* and *O. stricta)* in Australia was the first large-scale success in biological control of a weed. These cacti were introduced as ornamentals in the 1800s from America, where they are native. They escaped, and by 1925, about 24 million hectares of good grazing land were infested; 12 million hectares so much so that the land was useless. In addition, the infestation was spreading to new areas at the rate of about 400,000 hectares per year.

The government established a Commonwealth Prickly Pear Board in 1920. One of the board's first decisions was to send an entomologist to America to search for natural enemies. About 150 insects were identified as selective feeders on the cacti. Of these, 50 were sent to Australia for further study and rearing. Twelve were released and had begun to exert some pressure on the weed when the cactus moth *(Cactoblastis cactorum* Berg) was discovered to be especially effective. Larvae of this moth were collected in Argentina in 1925. Some 3,000 eggs were placed on prickly pear leaves and shipped to Australia where they were increased during the remainder of 1925 and the resulting eggs released in the field early in 1926.

Four to 6 years later (1930–1932), large areas had been freed of the pest. Following this, the insect population dropped and prickly pear regrowth occurred. The moth then increased, and by 1935, about 95% of the infested hectares in Queensland and 75% of the infested hectares in New South Wales had been freed of the weed. The density of some infestations and effective control with the cactus moth are shown in Figures 9–1A, 9–1B, and 9–1C. Control is actually accomplished by the larvae tunnelling through the plant—even the roots—in their feeding.

St. Johnswort in western United States. Control of St. Johnswort *(Hypericum perforatum)* was the first success with biological control in the United States. St. Johnswort or Klamath weed, is a perennial introduced from Europe. It became a serious problem on rangeland in western United States and Canada. By 1930, some 28,000 hectares were infested with this weed in Humboldt County, California, alone.

Control of the weed by a beetle *(Chrysolina quadrigemina)* is shown in Figure 9–2. This example illustrates the importance of synchronization of life cycles between the control agent and the target weed. The beetle adults emerge from pupae in the spring and feed on new foliage of the St. Johnswort. Both the insect and the weed go through a resting stage from mid-spring until fall. Initiation of weed growth with fall grazing is accompanied by returned feeding activity, mating, and egg-laying by the beetles. In the spring, eggs complete hatching and larvae feed on the trailing growth until the shoots appear. In this case, both the beetle and the larvae contribute to ultimate destruction of the weed. About 3 years was required from release of 8,600 to 12,300 beetles per hectare until the population built to the point where effective control of St. Johnswort was obtained.

Musk thistle in pasture in the United States. An additional example of insect control is cited to show what can be done by focusing on seed production. Musk thistle *(Carduus* spp.) was introduced into the United States from Europe in the early 1900s. It has since become a serious weed in pasture throughout the United States. Biological control programs were initiated in 1969 with the introduction of two European weevils *(Rhinocyllus conicus* and *Trichosirocalus horridus)*. *R. conicus* lays its eggs on the backs of thistle heads where larvae feed on developing seeds within the receptacle or tunnel into the stems, causing the flower heads to turn brown and die (Figure 9–3).

Weevil feeding reduces production of seed in the infested head, but is partially offset by greater production in the uninfested heads (Figure 9–4). Thus, production per plant was not reduced until the level of infestation reached 10 per head,

A. Cactus-infested range before establishment of *Cactoblastis*

B. Virtual elimination of cactus following release of *Cactoblastis*

C. Rhodes grass (*Chloris* spp.) pasture one year after burning dead cactus in 9–1B

FIGURE 9–1. Biological control of prickly pear cactus by the cactus moth *(Cactoblastis cactorum)* in Queensland, Australia.
Source: Dodd, 1940. Reproduced with permission of Department of Lands, Queensland, Australia.

A. Photograph taken in 1946, with foreground showing weeds in heavy flower while rest of field has just been killed by beetles

B. Portion of same location in 1949 when heavy cover of grass had developed

C. Photograph taken in 1966 showing degree of control that has persisted since 1949 (similar results reported throughout state)

FIGURE 9–2. Control of St. Johnswort or Klamath weed by *Chrysolina quadrigemina* at Blocksburg, California.

Source: C.B. Huffaker, 1957. Reproduced courtesy of C.B. Huffaker, University of California.

B. Larvae tunnel into bracts and into receptacles to feed on developing seeds.

A. Weevils lay eggs on bracts of developing flowers.

C. Larvae may tunnel into stem.

D. Tunnelling causes flower heads to turn brown and die.

FIGURE 9–3. Control of musk thistle seed production with *Rhinocyllus conicus*.
Source: Roof et al., 1982. Reproduced courtesy of University of Missouri–Columbia, Extension Division.

even though production per head was reduced by 7 per head. Because even a few escapes may produce many seeds, we might conclude that a large infestation would need to be maintained for several years to cause significant reduction in the thistle population. Indeed, Surles and Kok (1976) indicated "first substantial control occurring after 6 years" from the 1969–70 releases. Progeny from the 1969–70

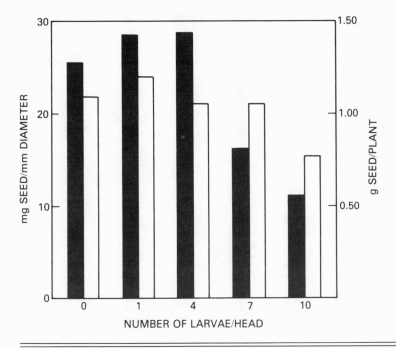

FIGURE 9–4. Effect of weevil numbers on seed production of musk thistle.
Source: Data from Surles and Kok, 1976.

releases were reported as yielding "substantial control" after 4 years. Thus, some period of time is needed for an introduced species to become adapted to a new site. These results also reflect the characteristic of many weeds to produce more seeds than needed to fully occupy an area if all of them germinated (carrying capacity, Chapter 2).

In other work (McCarty and Lamp, 1982), time of flowering was also shown to be a factor in the extent of larval feeding. As can be seen in Figure 9–5, weevil pupation chambers per head (an indirect measure of weevil numbers) decreased as the season progressed. By July 17, the infestation level was down to only 0.2 chambers per head. The associated percent of well-developed seed increased from 10% on June 26 to 50% on July 17. Although not shown in the figure, seed production for the four flowering dates combined was 78%. Still left is production of a relatively large number of seeds, but the researchers indicate that proportionately more infestation will occur on late-blooming heads as weevil populations grow in subsequent years. It appears that a second weevil *(R. horridus)*, which feeds on the rosette crown, may be needed for fully satisfactory control (Enlow, 1982).

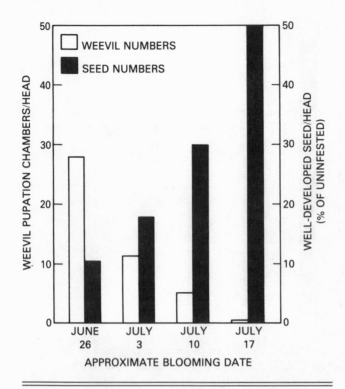

FIGURE 9–5. Effect of time of thistle flowering on extent of weevil infestation and associated seed production.
Source: Data from McCarty and Lamp, 1982.

Plant Pathogens

Although work with plant pathogens is much more recent than that with insects, some striking results point up the potential for their use. The examples are of fungi, but bacteria and viruses may ultimately find a place.

Skeleton weed in Australia. Skeleton weed *(Chondrilla juncea)* is a deep-rooted perennial that was introduced from Europe to Australia and to the United States. The weed is being controlled in Australia with a rust *(Puccinia chondrillina)* as the major biotic agent, although others are also involved. The rust, also imported from Europe, has similarly been introduced into the western United States for control.

The rust has been common in the field in all areas of Australia since 1972. Figure 9–6 shows changes in rosettes (weed density) that have occurred. As was true of weevils for the control of musk thistle, several years of infection (3 or more)

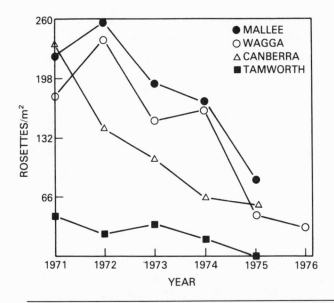

FIGURE 9–6. Reductions in skeleton weed in continuous pastures in southeast Australia by an introduced rust plus a midge.
Source: Data from Cullen, 1976.

were needed before substantial reduction occurred in the skeleton weed population. Recent work by Lee et al. (1981) provides information about the developing effectiveness of this rust with time. Where the rust had been released for less than a year, the size of the skeleton weed was reduced, but reproductive capacity was not impaired. Two years after release, the rust populations developed to the point where infection of stems and the flower calyx was severe. Such plants produced fewer flowers and seed; furthermore, the seeds had lower viability. This effect on reproduction reduces the potential for spread and reinfestation, thus accounting for gradual control of a given population.

Jointvetch in rice in the United States. In Arkansas, control of northern jointvetch *(Aeschynomene virginca)* by northern jointvetch anthracnose *(Colletotrichum gloeosporiodes* f. sp. *aeschynomene)* represents a major change in biological control for two reasons. First, jointvetch (apparently) is a weed native to the United States, whereas previous examples involved control of introduced weeds by pests from their native sites. Second, control was obtained by applying quantities of pathogenic spores sufficient to prevent competition from the weed rather than by introducing the pathogen and waiting for it to build to control levels. Treatment was a suspension of spores of northern jointvetch anthracnose at 188 billion spores per hectare (76 billion per acre) in 94 liters (10 gallons) of water. In this respect, the application is like that of a herbicide. Nearly complete kill of the jointvetch has been obtained in rice by this augmentation of the natural infestations, as shown in Figure 9–7.

Smartweed seed production.   Work with skeleton weed suggested that pathogens might be effective against seed production. The potential in such specific use of pathogens is demonstrated in work by Jordan (1981) with Pennsylvania smartweed. He reported the destruction of host reproductive tissues by a smut (*Ustilago urticulosa* Nees.) that infects the developing flowers and seeds of the smartweed.

Other Biotic Agents

As experience is gained with biological control and as we develop a preventive mindset towards weeds, it is conceivable that additional biotic agents will find a place in weed management in crop production. Some that have been used or studied in a limited way include nematodes, large animals (geese, goats, and other grazing animals), and weak or noncompetitive plant species.

Nematodes.   Work in the USSR, supplemented by work in the United States, suggests that nematodes have potential for selective weed control. This work involved the effects of the nematode (*Paranguina picrides* Kirjanova and Ivanova) against Russian knapweed *(Acroptilon repens)* (Watson, 1976). Russian knapweed is a problem in cultivated hay and pasture crops in western Canada and in western and central United States, in addition to being a problem in crops in its apparent native range in southeastern USSR. In his review of the Russian work, Watson indicates that the nematode causes galls to form at the site of penetration of the knapweed. Second-stage larvae in the soil enter emerging knapweed shoots in the spring, feed and mature within the gall, complete two generations from eggs, then become dormant and overwinter in the gall. The cycle is reinitiated in the spring. Further, the Russian work demonstrated up to 100% infection of knapweed, with 20% destroyed and 30% severely damaged. Their report of greatly reduced seed production has implications for the use of nematodes in weed management in general.

Large animals.   Large animals are selective in their choice of plants to feed upon. This fact has been utilized to manage weed growth in special situations. One example is the use of geese to remove weeds in strawberries and in cotton. The geese prefer weed seedlings, especially grasses, to established strawberry and cotton plants as their feed and have been successfully used to prevent weed interference with the crop. Because their use is so specialized, large animals are not considered further here.

A. Untreated

B. Treated with a suspension of spores of
Colletotrichum gloeosporioides f. sp.
aeschynomene

FIGURE 9–7. Control of northern jointvetch in rice with an anthracnose disease.
Source: Reproduced courtesy of USDA, Agricultural Research Service, Stuttgart, Arkansas.

Weak or noncompetitive plant species. The last example of biological
approaches to be considered is *plant replacement*—that is, the planned establishment of weak or noncompetitive plant species to prevent encroachment of weeds.
Common reed *(Phragmites communis)* is being used in this way in land reclama-
tion projects in the Netherlands (Van Zoa, 1976). The common reed prevents
establishment of weeds that could be a problem for later use of the land for

agriculture. An extension of this concept might be the planting of species easily controlled by herbicides or other control tactics to keep out weeds much more difficult to contend with.

Nonagricultural Weed Control with Biotic Agents

Weeds often pose a problem in recreational waters and in waterways. In fact, weed infestation may become so great that swimming and boating are discouraged. Similarly, weeds may so clog waterways that water flow and navigation are severely impeded. Biotic agents have been successfully used against such problems. The grass carp *(Ctenopharyngodon idella)*, a nonselective herbivorous fish from China, has been stocked in 80 lakes in Arkansas since 1968 to control aquatic weeds (Beach et al., 1976). The fish may consume several times its own weight in vegetation daily. This approach is being extended to other states and to other countries. The mottled waterhyacinth weevil *(Neochetina eichhorniae)* was introduced into Florida in 1972 to control waterhyacinth *(Eichhornia crassipes)* in waterways (Perkins, 1973). This weevil and a mite *(Orthogalumna terebrantis)* apparently introduced with waterhyacinth have successfully reduced the waterhyacinth but, as with introduced biotic agents against agricultural weeds, control develops slowly over a period of years.

CONCEPTS IN SUCCESSFUL USE

Two categories of use of biotic agents for weed control can be identified in the examples of control cited: (1) inoculation and (2) mass exposure. *Inoculation* involves releasing into a weed's environment specimens of a natural enemy and then leaving them on their own to build to control levels. This is the classical approach to biological control. All of the examples of success cited for insects used this approach, as did the use of grass carp.

Mass exposure is the release of a biological agent that controls a weed at the applied concentration. The single application of spores of anthracnose in sufficient numbers to eliminate competition from jointvetch is an example of mass exposure. This method is known as the biological-herbicide approach (Templeton, 1982). The addition to a naturally developing insect population is termed the manipulative method (Andres, 1982). For ease of discussion, the term *bioherbicides* is used in this book for application of any biotic agent designed to provide control the year in which released. Both the classical approach and bioherbicides may involve the use of either *exotic* (introduced) or *indigenous* (native) enemies.

A number of concepts apply to biological control. The discussion that follows identifies and examines these concepts.

1. Plant pathogens may be better adapted to the bioherbicide approach than insects. They are better adapted because of their relative ease of application and storage. In any bioherbicide treatment, large numbers of the biotic agent are needed. To control jointvetch in rice, for example, 2 to 6 million spores of the anthracnose per milliliter were applied at a rate of 94 to 374 liters per hectare. The largest volume is somewhat higher than used for herbicides, but still not so high as to make it impractical. By comparison, in augmenting natural populations of *Bactra verutana*, an insect that feeds on purple nutsedge, 60 adult pairs per 4 square meter were needed to be fully effective under caged conditions. Under field conditions, an infestation level of 3 larvae per shoot was needed (Frick and Chandler, 1978). These statistics translate into 150,000 adult pairs per hectare and possibly 10 million larvae per hectare. Rearing and releasing such numbers of insects clearly pose practical obstacles for large-scale use by mass exposure. For their part, some pathogens can be applied in a spray or in granular form and either post- or preemergence to the weed seedlings (Quimby and Walker, 1982). Further, spores or mycelial formulations offer convenient forms in which to store and formulate the biotic agent.

2. Eradication is rarely, if ever, achieved. Experience in the control of prickly pear cactus by the cactus moth is an example. The cactus moth reduced the prickly pear cactus after 5 to 6 years to the point where there was not enough to support the cactus moth population. Cactus regrowth occurred, quickly followed by reinfestation and buildup on the part of the moth. This type of wave action and reaction on the part of the biotic agent and target weed is typical of classical biological control. It is represented schematically in Figure 9–8. Fluctuation in

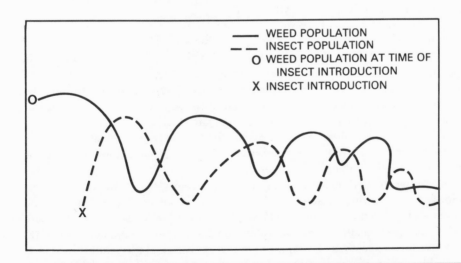

FIGURE 9–8. Wave action relationship over time between weed numbers and numbers of an insect used in weed control.

Source: Muzik, 1970. Reproduced with permission of T.J. Muzik.

numbers of weeds and insects leads to a series of ups and downs in populations until an equilibrium of low numbers of both weed and insect is reached. Although this wave action applies to the relationship between an insect and the target weed, it could just as well apply to pathogens and other biotic agents. The culmination is an ecological balance among the biotic agent, the host, and the environment. If the control is successful, this ecological balance stabilizes at a level of weed infestation below the economic threshold. In areas where the bioherbicide approach is used, the relationship is still wavelike, although the peaks and valleys are much sharper. With anthracnose for jointvetch control, for example, although complete control of the weed may be obtained the year it is treated, reinfestation at a somewhat smaller population level can be expected from the seedbank in the soil the following year, with a steady overall decline in subsequent years. The level ultimately reached depends upon the annual degree of control and the years of treatment.

3. Control with the classical approach is usually achieved only over a period of years. Although dramatic first-year effects may occasionally occur, the more usual situation requires 3 to 10 years for the biotic agent to build to a level to provide effective control. For example, it took about 10 years from the first release of the cactus moth before the infestation of prickly pear cactus was reduced to a satisfactory low level of infestation. With St. Johnswort, about 3 years was required following release of the beetle in sufficient numbers for it to reduce the weed below the economic damage level. Use of rust against skeleton weed required several years before buildup was reflected in significant reduction of the weed. It should be recalled in this regard, from Kok's work on weevils to control musk thistle, that biotic agents most likely improve in their overall efficiency with time as they become adapted to their new environment.

4. Classical biological control is more apt to be successful against introduced weeds than against native weeds. Several reasons underlie this statement. Biotic agents introduced from the native habitat can be expected to be free from constraints of predators and pathogens that might interfere with their effectiveness in the native habitat. Also, from the standpoint of the target weed, control may be achieved before the weed has time to adjust to the presence of the biotic agent, assuming it has lost whatever tolerance it may have had for the biotic agent in its native habitat. The bioherbicide approach stands a better chance of succeeding against native weeds, but is still constrained by the same factors affecting the inoculum approach, albeit to a lesser degree.

5. Native bioherbicides may be more satisfactory than introduced bioherbicides. The following reasons for this concept are adapted from Quimby and Walker's discussion of pathogens (1982): (1) Native biotic agents may be more readily obtained because overseas exploration and quarantine are not needed; (2) the native biotic agent may be expected to revert to original levels, thus lessening the problem of spread and adaptation to nontarget hosts; (3) native biotic agents can be expected to be better adapted to the climate and environment of the area; and (4) public concern may be less with native than with introduced biotic agents.

6. Success with biological control can be expected to be better against a single weed species than against a mixed population of weeds. The classical approach, almost of necessity, is restricted to single species. The problems in using a multitude of pests necessary to control a mixture of weeds simply are too great for this approach to offer much potential. The use of a single biotic agent with a broad spectrum of species upon which it is active can be expected to very much increase the chances of its attacking nontarget plants. Furthermore, control of one or a few weeds in a larger mixture of weeds can be expected to allow the uncontrolled species to pose as large a problem in competition as that posed by the entire mixture. The bioherbicide approach offers some possibility for controlling mixtures of weeds. A combination of pathogens has been tried for control of winged waterprimrose *(Jussiaea decurrens)* and jointvetch in rice (Boyette et al., 1979). However, the use of bioherbicides faces the same problems as the classical approach. The difference is a matter of degree.

7. Perennial and biennial weeds are a more likely target than annuals. This statement is especially true for the classical approach. Under the classical approach, the continuity that the biotic agent needs in a host is best provided by a perennial in order for the agent to build to effective control levels. Annual weeds vary greatly in numbers of individuals from year to year and are present for only part of the year. Furthermore, annual weeds may have fewer natural enemies from which to select effective biotic agents by virtue of their evolutionary heritage. As early colonizers in ecological succession, many annual weeds were continuously establishing on new sites, thus lessening the opportunities for natural enemies to become established. Finally, sexual reproduction common to annual species assures greater heterogeneity with the associated greater potential to evolve resistance than is found in species, such as many perennials, that reproduce asexually (Burdon and Marshall, 1981). These arguments do not mean that biological control does not have a place in the control of annual weeds. In particular, the bioherbicide approach may be usable because buildup—and thus continuous availability of the host—is not required.

8. Biological control, at least with the classical approach, has its greatest potential on the less intensively tilled land. The 3 or more years required for the biotic agent to build to a control level, during which some losses are occurring, cannot be tolerated in the more intensive grain and row-crop farming systems. The early successes with biological control were all on extensive grazing land.

9. The more closely the target weed is related to the crop, the less likely the crop will be safe from activity by the biotic agent. This fact is one of the reasons why more progress has not been made in controlling weedy grasses with biotic agents. Most weedy grasses are genetically related to our major grain crops—that is, rice, wheat, corn, and the like. Other genetic and ecological aspects are involved also. Widely distributed plant species have been shown to have more insect associates than rare species (Lawton and Schroder, 1976). It follows that the chances of finding an effective biotic agent may be better with widely distributed species. However, proportionately more of the insects associated with widely

distributed plants feed on several plant species rather than on only one plant. This relationship makes it less likely to find the necessary host specificity for practical use of the biotic agent. There is also evidence that the feeding type—chewing, mining, sucking, seed- and flower-feeding, and gall-forming—is also related to evolutionary background. That is, gall-forming and mining, which require more specialization on the part of the insect than the other three types are more common among widely distributed plants. Particularly significant for weed prevention was the finding, shown in Table 9–1, that there were many insects in the Cynareae tribe that feed on the seed, fruit, and flowers of weeds. This fact is elaborated on later. At this point, we simply want to recognize that there is evidence that selective feeders on seed, fruit, and flowers may be widespread.

10. For biological control to be successful, the life cycle of the target weed must be synchronized with that of the biotic agent. The effective control of St. Johnswort with the Chrysolina beetle is a good example of this concept. The period of rapid growth of St. Johnswort in the spring and fall coincides with high activity (feeding) by beetle adults. The following spring, eggs complete hatching and the larvae feed on the shallow rootstocks until shoots appear. Additionally, best success with biotic agents can be expected where their peaks of activity coincide with those times when the target weed is most vulnerable. Thus, insects that actively feed at the time in the life cycle of a perennial weed when it is producing food for storage can be expected to be especially effective.

11. Pathogens as bioherbicides offer the best opportunity for commercialization. Two pathogens have been marketed. Abbott Laboratories markets the fungus *Phytophthora palmivora* under the trade name Devine® for the control of strangler vine *(Morrenia odorata)*, a weed parasitic on citrus. The Upjohn Company markets the jointvetch anthracnose under the trade name Collego®. The problems of rearing, storing, and applying insects as bioherbicides make them less likely candidates for commercialization. Commercialization is important to widespread use and rapid adoption, especially with the bioherbicide approach. It is the best way for adequate quantities to be made available to prospective users, especially if they are widely scattered.

TABLE 9-1

Comparison of feeding types of selected genera within the Cynareae tribe.

Chewing (n/%)	Mining (n/%)	Gall-Forming (n/%)	Seed-, Fruit-, and Flower-Feeding (n/%)	Sucking (n/%)
261 (30%)	184 (21%)	18 (2%)	310 (36%)	91 (11%)

Source: Data from Lawton and Schroder, 1976.

ROLE OF BIOLOGICAL CONTROL IN
WEED MANAGEMENT

A potential hazard exists in overemphasis of the bioherbicide approach. This approach offers some clear-cut advantages over the classical approach discussed in the previous section and can be summed up by the analogy that in methods of application and activity, bioherbicides are quite comparable to chemical herbicides. As with herbicides, however, elimination of a weed by a biotic agent can be expected to be followed by replacement with another weed unless we do something about the conditions that caused us to have the weed in the first place—a niche for it. Any approach, whether with herbicides, biotic agents, or tillage, that looks only to *control* a weed without regard to the conditions that accounted for its presence is destined to be only a short-term solution for the agroecosystem, or indeed, the individual farm, on which it is used.

We should also keep in mind that there are conflicting interests in weeds that are likely to always pose a problem for biological control, especially with the classical approach. Once a biotic agent is established, for example, it cannot easily be kept from spreading to all areas infested with the target weed. That is, it is no respecter of land use or ownership. The agent could remove the target weed from grazing land where the weed has value for forage, or from game preserves, parks, or forests where it might be an important source of food or protection for game.

What then may be the role of biotic agents in systems of crop production? It would seem they will continue to play a part in the control of specific weeds on relatively low-value land. Their role on relatively high-value land in intensive agriculture may well be as an adjunct to the other approaches. Thus, they need to take their place alongside tillage and cropping practices, herbicides, and allelopathy as one of the tools available for effective weed management.

In this context, it should be emphasized that biotic agents, if used, become a part of the agroecosystem, which is dynamic. As already mentioned, removal of a weed leaves room for another to enter. Further, the interrelationships of weeds with insects and diseases will be affected; secondary infection with other biotic agents may frequently be involved in bringing about the final effect. Fertility and other factors affecting overall vigor of the crop may also influence results with biological control. The importance of these ecological relationships for biological control is in pointing up the merits of planning their use in terms of the entire production system, not simply in terms of control of a particular weed. As our knowledge and experience with them grows, and as we shift our weed control thinking towards management, roles for biotic agents should increase. Some of the broad usages are discussed here. Usage in management systems is considered in Chapter 15.

Preventing Weed Seed Production

One role for biotic agents may be in preventing seed production of weed specimens that escape the other weed management practices. As mentioned previously, preventing seed production (renewal of the seedbank in the soil) must be accomplished for a long-term effort to reduce weed problems to be fully successful. In Chapter 15, we examine the several practices that might be embraced in attaining this goal. Here, we simply need to recognize that a farmer or other land owner will probably not be able to justify more than a modest cost for practices designed to cut weed seed production.

The reason is that weed seed production in itself does not represent a yield loss for a particular crop in a particular year. But that crop, in effect, must pay the cost of a treatment to reduce weed seed. Thus, we need a relatively inexpensive treatment, but one that does not necessarily have to destroy the weed since competition may not be involved. Biotic agents may fit these requirements, especially if it is acceptable for the biotic effect to develop over a period of years and to be less than 100% effective. Both qualifications indeed may be acceptable.

Preventing Weed Buildup

Biotic agents may also have a place in checking weed species that have not yet reached a competitive threshold level. An example might be their use against perennial weeds that are increasing under reduced-tillage farming systems. More is said about tillage level and weed relationships in Chapter 14. Note, however, that the general tendency is for perennial species to increase as amount of tillage decreases. For example, we are experiencing an increase in common milkweed in Missouri, at least in part because of reduced tillage. Even so, although present in wheat, soybeans and other crops, common milkweed is probably not an important cause of reduced crop yields. Biotic agents might provide a way of keeping the weed from becoming an economic problem. Common milkweed is mentioned only to illustrate the circumstances where biotic agents might play a role. There is no reason to believe biotic agents will be used against milkweed since work is not underway to identify and develop them. However, we will continue to have shifts in weed composition in response to changes in crop practices that will provide the circumstance of a subcompetitive population level during the early years of the shift. This level would seem to be a fruitful target for biological weed management.

Special Weed Situations

Biotic agents may also be of significant value when it is difficult to deal with weeds by other means. For example, weeds that encroach late in the season in row crops when cultivation is not possible and when the crop canopy may prevent adequate contact with herbicides can be difficult to control. Biotic agents may provide the most effective way of obtaining control under such conditions.

Weed Depressant

Finally, biotic agents may have a particular role as weed depressants on weeds in fence rows, ditch banks, and other right of ways that serve as reservoirs for reinfestation of adjacent tilled land. Under such circumstances, some weed growth can be tolerated for the time it may take a biotic agent to reach the population level necessary to eliminate the weed as a source of reinfestation. In these situations, of course, plant control would not be essential. Rather, control of seed production and spread by vegetative parts is all that would be needed.

Weed Management vs. Weed Control

It is conceivable that biotic agents will achieve a level of usage in *weed management* well beyond their potential in *weed control*. Realizing their potential in weed management will require careful articulation of the objectives and the selection of appropriate evaluation measures. With uses in management, *numbers*, used as a measure in control approaches, have little value. For example, numbers of weeds destroyed or prevented from developing by a biotic agent, although a measure of the agent's activity, do not in themselves tell us the effect on a given weed population over time. Yet, it is the latter information that will determine whether or not such a management effort should be initiated. Using biotic agents to keep a weed below a economic loss level calls for an understanding of the nature of competition involved in order to identify the best ways to measure it. In a larger sense, uses of biotic agents in weed management require a way of measuring and assigning the costs and returns not provided by measures of control approaches. Developing satisfactory measures must be addressed for biotic agent technology to advance.

CONCEPTS AND CONCLUSIONS

1. Biological control is taking place continuously in the plant world.
2. Biotic agents can be selective not only against specific weeds, but also against specific plant parts.
3. Biotic agents may have greater potential value in weed management than in weed control.
4. Success with biotic agents in weed management calls for a full understanding of ecological relationships between the weed and the biotic agent and of both as a part of a larger ecosystem.
5. Evaluating effectiveness of biotic agents in weed management requires different measures than those used in weed control.

REFERENCES

Andres, L.A. 1982. Integrating weed biological control agents into a pest-management program. Weed Sci. 30 (Supplement 1):25–30.

Beach, M.L., R.L. Lazor, and A.P. Burkhalter. 1976. Some aspects of the environmental impact of the white amur (*Ctenopharyngodon ideles* Val.) in Florida, and its use for aquatic weed control. In T.E. Freeman, ed., Proc. of 4th International Symposium on Biological Control of Weeds, pp. 269–89. Gainesville: Center for Environmental Programs, Institute of Food and Agricultural Sciences, University of Florida.

Boyette, C.D., G.E. Templeton, and R.J. Smith, Jr. 1979. Control of winged waterprimrose (*Jussiaea decurrens*) and northern jointvetch (*Aeschynomine virginica*) with fungal pathogens. Weed Sci. 27(5):497–501.

Burdon, J.J. and D.R. Marshall. 1981. Biological control and the reproductive mode of weeds. J. of App. Ecol. 18:649–58.

Cullen, J.M. 1976. Evaluating the success of the programme for the biological control of *Chondrilla juncea* L. In T.E. Freeman, ed., Proc. of 4th International Symposium on Biological Control of Weeds, pp. 117–21. Gainesville: Center for Environmental Programs, Institute of Food and Agricultural Sciences, University of Florida.

Dodd, A.P. 1940. The biological campaign against prickly pear. Brisbane, Australia: Commonwealth Prickly Pear Board.

Enlow, R.E. 1982. The biography of an insect assassin. Agr. Res. 31 (4):4–6.

Freeman, T.E., ed. 1976. Proceedings of 4th International Symposium on Biological Control of Weeds. Gainesville: Center for Environmental Programs, Institute of Food and Agricultural Sciences, University of Florida.

Frick, K.E., and J.M. Chandler. 1978. Augmenting the moth (*Bactra verutana*) in field plots for early season suppression of purple nutsedge (*Cyperus rotundus*). Weed Sci. 26(6):703–10.

Goeden, R.D., et al. 1974. Present status of projects on the biological control of weeds with insects and plant pathogens in the United States and Canada. Weed Sci. 22 (5):490–95.

Huffaker, C.B. 1957. Fundamentals of biological control of weeds. Hilgardia 27:101–57.

Jordan, J.L. 1981. *Ustilago verticulosa:* Biological control of Pennsylvania smart-weed, (*Polygonum pensylvanicum* L.). In Abstract 199 of 1981 Meeting of WSSA, Las Vegas, Nev.

Lawton, J.H., and D. Schroder. 1976. Some observations on the structure of phytophagous insect communities: The implications for biological control. In T.E. Freeman, ed., Proc. of 4th International Symposium on Biological Control of Weeds, pp. 57–73. Gainesville: Center for Environmental Programs, Institute of Food and Agricultural Sciences, University of Florida.

Lee, G.A., T.M. Cheney, and D.C. Thill. 1981. The influence of *Puccinia chondrilla* Bub. and Syd. on the flowering, seed production, and seed viability of rush skeleton weed (*Chondrilla juncea* L.). In Abstract 198 of 1981 Meeting of WSSA, Las Vegas, Nev.

McCarty, M.K., and W.O. Lamp. 1982. Effect of a weevil *(Rhinocyllus conicus)* on musk thistle *(Carduus thoermeri)* seed production. Weed Sci. 30 (2):136–40.

Perkins, B.D. 1973. Release in the United States of *Neochetina sichhorniae* Warner, an enemy of waterhyacinth. In Proc. of Southern Weed Science Society, vol. 26, p. 268. New Orleans, La.

Phatak, S.C., D.R. Summer, H.D. Wells, and N.C. Glaze. 1983. Biological control of yellow nutsedge with the indigenous rust fungus *(Puccinia canaliculata)*. Sci. 219:1446–1447.

Quimby, P.C., Jr., and H.L. Walker. 1982. Pathogens as mechanisms for weed management. Weed Sci. 30 (Supplement 1):30–34.

Roof, M.E., B. Puttler, and L.E. Anderson. 1982. Controlling musk thistle with an introduced weevil. Columbia: Science and Technology Guide Number 4867, University of Missouri, Columbia, Extension Division.

Surles, W.W., and L.J. Kok. 1976. Response of *Carduus nutans* L. to infestation by *Rhinocyllus conicus* Froel. (Coleoptera: cureulionidae) and mechanical damage. In T.E. Freeman, ed., Proc. of 4th International Symposium on Biological Control of Weeds, pp. 105–07. Gainesville: Center for Environmental Programs, Institute of Food and Agricultural Sciences, University of Florida.

Sweetman, H.L. 1958. The principles of biological control. Dubuque, Iowa: Brown.

Templeton, G.E. 1982. Biological herbicides: Discovery, development, deployment. Weed Sci. 30 (4):430–33.

Van Zon, J.C.J. 1976. Status of biotic agents, other than insects or pathogens, as biocontrols. In T.E. Freeman, ed., Proc. of 4th International Symposium on Biological Control of Weeds, pp. 245–50. Gainesville: Center for Environmental Programs, Institute of Food and Agricultural Sciences, University of Florida.

Watson, A.K. 1976. The biological control of Russian knapweed with a nematode. In T.E. Freeman, ed., Proc. of 4th International Symposium on Biological Control of Weeds, pp. 221–23. Gainesville: Center for Environmental Programs, Institute of Food and Agricultural Sciences, University of Florida.

HERBICIDE USE

10

Chemicals have long been used to control weeds. Some of those associated with the expanding application of chemistry during the later part of the nineteenth century introduced selective control to agriculture. However, it was the auxin-type herbicides MCPA and 2,4–D, discovered almost simultaneously in the 1940s in Great Britain and the United States, that ushered in the modern era of chemical weed control. In the United States, adoption of 2,4–D occurred rapidly from a few thousand acres in 1946 to several million acres by the end of the decade. Whereas most of the chemicals used prior to 2,4–D were inorganic, all of those introduced since are organic.

There are several reasons why modern herbicides expanded so rapidly to reach the position of widespread usage they now enjoy. One important reason is that they can be applied at relatively low rates and in low volumes of water. Many of the pre–2,4–D herbicides called for the handling of considerable bulk, which was costly for transportation and cumbersome to apply. Not infrequently, the older-type herbicides were applied in large volumes of water. By contrast, early research with 2,4–D showed control to be as good when it was applied in 50 to 100 liters of water per hectare as when it was applied in higher volumes, provided it was evenly distributed on the weed or on the soil.

Selectivity because of differences in internal reactions of weeds and crops was another reason for the rapid expansion of herbicide use. Selectivity of the older-type herbicides was based primarily on physical differences of contact and penetration between the weed and the crop that frequently provided relatively little margin for error. With modern herbicides, on the other hand, selectivity may be due mainly to differences in the biochemistry of sensitive and tolerant species. Such biological selectivity may provide a very wide range of tolerance. For

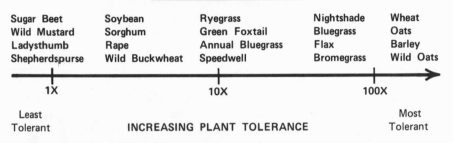

FIGURE 10–1. Variance of plant species in their biological tolerance of modern herbicides.
Source: Courtesy E.I. du Pont de Nemours & Company.

example, as shown in Figure 10–1, there is more than a hundredfold difference in tolerance between wild mustard and wheat to the herbicide chlorsulfuron applied postemergence. Such large differences in tolerance provide the necessary wide margin for complete weed kill with little, if any, crop injury.

A third major reason for the rapid expansion of herbicide usage since the discovery of 2,4–D is the incentive offered private industry to carry out the necessary development and marketing of these chemicals. With all the many advantages of the newer herbicides and the spectacular results that can be achieved, their widespread usage could never have occurred without the massive effort on the part of the chemical industry to develop effective formulations and manufacturing processes and to assure their availability through effective distribution networks.

Successful use of 2,4–D to literally save a crop of corn being overrun by giant ragweed set the tone for the use of these organic herbicides in the ensuing years. Several hundred hectares of Ohio riverbottom land in Henderson County, Kentucky, were being overrun by giant ragweed in July of 1947. Rains had prevented early cultivation, and as a result, the crop and the weeds had become too large to be cultivated. Application of 2,4–D at the rate of 0.6 kilograms per hectare resulted in complete kill of the giant ragweed. Although some injury symptoms occurred on the corn, a crop was harvested, whereas there otherwise would have been a total loss.

USE OF HERBICIDES IN WEED CONTROL

Our primary emphasis on herbicides continues to be short term. That is, the common approach is to only consider the efficacy of a particular herbicide in

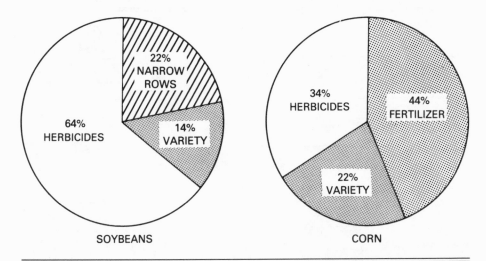

FIGURE 10–2. Contribution of technology adoption to increases in corn and soybean yields, Corn Belt region, 1964 to 1979.
Source: Data from Schroder et al., 1981 and 1982.

controlling weeds in a given crop in the current year, with relatively little attention being given to a long-term approach. This usage has been responsible for sizable increases in production of food. For example, as seen in Figure 10–2, herbicides were a major contributor to increases in yield of corn and soybeans for five Corn Belt states (Illinois, Indiana, Iowa, Ohio, and Missouri) between 1964 and 1979 (Schroder et al., 1981 and 1982). In this period, soybean yields increased 437 kilograms per hectare in response to technology. Herbicides accounted for nearly two-thirds of this increase. Herbicides are credited with one-third of the 1771 kilogram per hectare increase in corn yield for the same period.

In the years since 1947, ways of utilizing herbicides for weed control in crops have expanded rapidly. In 1948, Wolf and Anderson reported successful selective control of weeds in corn with 2,4–D applied to the soil after planting but before corn emergence. Many refinements and modifications of post- and preemergence application followed. As shown in Figure 10–3, herbicides may now be applied literally at any time relative to the stage of development of both the weed and the crop. For example, herbicides may be applied prior to planting the crop and either prior to emergence of weeds or to growing weeds. With the expansion of reduced tillage of crops, applying herbicides to kill growing weeds and planting directly into the killed sod have become commonplace. Also, development of horizontal and wick applicators allows nonselective chemicals to be used selectively to remove weeds overtopping crops. Each application has its unique place in weed control. However, for all of the applications, the focus is on the current season.

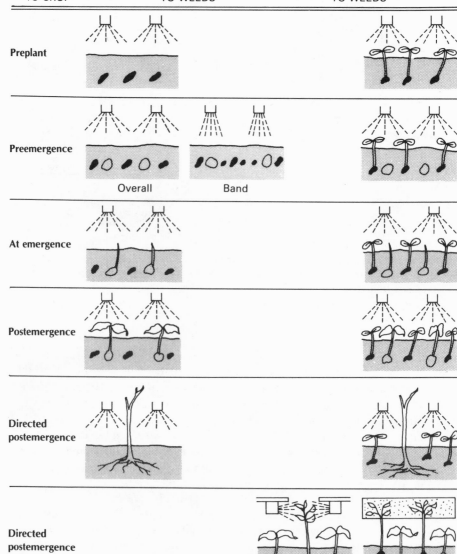

WITH RESPECT TO CROP	PREEMERGENCE TO WEEDS	POSTEMERGENCE TO WEEDS
Preplant		
Preemergence	Overall Band	
At emergence		
Postemergence		
Directed postemergence		
Directed postemergence	Horizontal Wick	

 WEED CROP

FIGURE 10–3. Stages of growth of weed and crop plants when herbicides may be applied for selective weed control.

Source: After Fryer and Evans, 1968. Reproduced with permission of Blackwell Scientific Publications, Ltd.

Discussion of specific control of weeds in crops can be found in several references, including Anderson (1977), Klingman et al. (1975), and Crafts (1975).

USE OF HERBICIDES IN WEED MANAGEMENT

As valuable as the contributions of herbicides have been in weed control, even greater contributions are possible in a weed management context—that is, if they are used as part of a system designed to minimize losses from weeds in the entire production enterprise over time. As we will see in Chapter 15, usage in a weed management context may also improve control with herbicides.

Further, herbicides can be a valuable tool in making a preventive weed management program work. They offer a relatively simple, inexpensive way of preventing renewal of the seedbank in the soil by escapes from weed control efforts. Such escapes, although they may not reduce crop yields, may well produce enough seed to restock the soil, as already discussed. This usage has never been exploited, although it was discovered early in the modern era that many of the new organic herbicides could have pronounced effects on the quantity and viability of seeds produced on treated plants.

Indeed, it is safe to say that not having an effective way of dealing with escapes has been the missing link in a total weed management program. Machines cannot practically be used because the crop at this advanced stage would be damaged. Also, in many cases, the weed may be the same height or shorter than the crop, precluding mechanical removal of the weed's seedheads. Giant foxtail in corn is an example. Hand removal, although it could be effective, is simply too costly, at least in most U.S. agriculture.

Herbicides have three broad purposes in weed management, as shown diagrammatically in Figure 10–4: (1) to prevent emergence of weeds with the crop, (2) to minimize competition from weeds growing with the crop, and (3) to reduce the number of viable weed propagules in the soil. From the standpoint of the herbicide application itself, there is no real difference between role 1 and role 2 and their corresponding applications (Figure 10–3). The difference is in perspective and purpose. As already mentioned, applications shown in Figure 10–3 have control for that season as their focus. The comparable applications in weed management imply a broader purpose. Thus, using herbicides to prevent weed emergence with a crop (role 1) leaves room, conceptually, for cropping and tillage practices, allelopathy, and other approaches to be used in conjunction with the herbicides.

Similarly, using herbicides to minimize competition from weeds growing with a crop (role 2) may be in conjunction with the other approaches. Additionally, the emphasis is on *competition*. This is as it should be since it is the degree of competition prevented, not the degree of control obtained, that determines whether or not the treatment is satisfactory. The practical significance of this

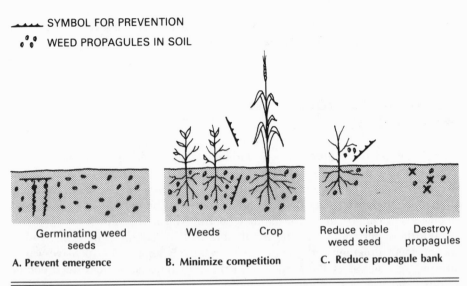

SYMBOL FOR PREVENTION

WEED PROPAGULES IN SOIL

Germinating weed seeds	Weeds Crop	Reduce viable weed seed Destroy propagules
A. Prevent emergence	B. Minimize competition	C. Reduce propagule bank

FIGURE 10–4. Schematic representation of three potential roles for herbicides in a comprehensive weed management program.

perspective is that it allows for usage that may suppress but not eliminate the weeds. Suppression may increase in importance under conservation tillage systems, especially as attempts are made to maximize plant cover on the land. The use of herbicides to reduce propagules in the soil (role 3) is not embraced by weed control as such in Figure 10–3.

Although the concept of weed management has been known to weed scientists for many years, the evidence is that only now is this concept attracting the attention necessary to in fact make it become a reality. For example, Meggitt (1978) stated: "For integrated weed management, we need to know what types of changes we're getting in ecology from our current systems and how we can back up and integrate cultural, chemical, and biological controls. What we're after is a total system that will eliminate some of the weed problems or prevent further shifts in weed ecology." Baldwin and Santelmann (1980) stated: "Weed scientists must discern the conditions under which weeds would be most susceptible to management tactics to enable them to predict the responses of weeds to various control procedures and cropping practices. They must conduct research on developing methods of predicting weed infestations prior to seeding of the crop." Thus, as we examine in detail the use of herbicides, we need to keep in mind that their greatest contributions may still be ahead as they are used as part of a total system of weed management.

We need to remember also that with most crop–herbicide situations, selectivity is relative rather than absolute. That is, the difference is often relatively narrow between the dosage of herbicide required to obtain satisfactory weed control and that which will damage the crop.

The place of chemicals for each purpose in weed management will be examined in detail. Because there are wide differences in factors influencing results, applications to the soil (Chapter 12) are considered separately from applications to growing plants (Chapter 13).

CONCEPTS AND CONCLUSIONS

1. The primary emphasis on herbicides continues to be short term.
2. Herbicides may be used in three ways in weed management: to prevent weed emergence with crops, to minimize competition from weeds growing with crops, and to reduce the number of viable propagules in soil.

REFERENCES

Anderson, W.P. 1977. Weed science: Principles. St. Paul, Minn.: West Publishing.

Baldwin, F.L., and P.W. Santelmann. 1980. Weed science in integrated pest management. Biosci. 30 (10):675–78.

Crafts, A.S. 1975. Modern weed control. Berkeley: University of California Press.

Fryer, T.D., and S.A. Evans. 1968. Weed control handbook, principles, vol. 1. Oxford, England: Blackwell Scientific.

Klingman, G.C., F.M. Ashton, and L.J. Noordhoff. 1975. Weed science: Principles and practices. New York: Wiley.

Meggitt, W.F. 1978. Integrated weed management—Ecology shifts challenge weed scientists. Agri-News, June, p. 4.

Schroder, D., J.D. Headley, and R.M. Finley. 1981. The contribution of pesticides and other technologies to soybean production in the Corn Belt region, 1964 to 1979, agricultural economics paper no. 1981–33. Columbia: University of Missouri.

———. 1982. The contribution of pesticides and other technologies to corn production in the Corn Belt region, 1964 to 1969, agricultural economics paper no. 1982–8. Columbia: University of Missouri.

Wolf, D.E., and J.C. Anderson. 1948. Preemergence control of weeds in corn with 2,4–D. Agron. J. 40:453–58.

HERBICIDE ENTRY, TRANSPORT, AND GENERAL EFFECTS

11

In the previous chapter, we discussed the place of herbicides in weed management. Here, we want to examine herbicide entry, transport, and their general effects in somewhat greater detail. The purpose is to develop a broad knowledge of the relationship between these aspects and plant growth as influenced by environmental conditions. This information is an aid to understanding herbicidal selectivity and factors affecting results with herbicides that are discussed in Chapters 12 and 13. Further, this background is helpful for our consideration of weed shifts in response to herbicides in Chapter 14 and the discussion in Chapter 15 of the place of herbicides in a comprehensive weed management program.

This chapter needs to be approached with such a broad, forward-looking perspective in order to visualize how what is discussed relates to the success of a weed management program under the environment of new and different production practices. For example, how might conservation tillage systems with the associated reduction in tillage and possible increases in cover crops and in plant residues influence our approaches to weed management?

Response of a plant to a herbicide involves four broad components: (1) the stage of development of the plant, (2) the genetic makeup of the plant, (3) the environment, and (4) the chemical. To understand the influence of these components on plant reaction, it is first necessary to understand something about the anatomy of a plant as it determines entry of the herbicide and movement within the plant once it enters.

For growing plants, two parts are main points of entry: the leaf and the root. A third point of entry important mainly in grass seedlings is the coleoptile node. This is not to say that herbicides cannot enter the stem and flowers, but simply recognizes that these parts represent a much smaller surface area and period of exposure for herbicide entry than do leaves and roots. Also, although dormant and nongerminating seeds may be penetrated by herbicides, such uptake is relatively unimportant as a point of entry in explaining results obtained with herbicides applied to the soil for selective control of weeds.

In general terms, but not exclusively so, leaf uptake is the primary point of entry in aerial applications and root uptake is the primary point of entry in soil applications. Shoot uptake may also be important, however, especially in grasses. Aerial applications and soil applications pose different opportunities for the environment to influence effects on the plant. As we will see, both directly and indirectly, aerial applications are relatively more affected by temperature, humidity, and rainfall as they influence plant growth. Although soil applications may also be affected by these factors, the effect is more apt to be a delayed one.

For their part, the soil applications are affected by a variety of soil attributes, including organic matter content, clay content, and the soil microflora and microfauna. No matter how uniformly the herbicide may be applied to the soil surface or how uniformly it is mixed with the top two or so inches, the fact remains that individual herbicide molecules are not contiguous but are separated. Where uptake from the soil is through the coleoptile node, the relatively fewer plant parts, compared with roots, decrease the chance for contacting the passive herbicide in the soil. This disadvantage is offset by the movement of the coleoptile node through the zone in which herbicides may be located.

Hartley (1960) has developed information on the protected space between herbicide particles on or in the soil. With a surface spray of 0.08 cubic meter per hectare, the particles will be about 1.3 mm apart if perfectly spread on a flat surface. If the spray application is perfectly mixed to a depth of 1 cm, the calculated randomly oriented distances between neighboring herbicide centers are between 12 and 31 mm. Thus, soil applications offer some opportunity for the germinating and developing weed seedlings to escape the herbicide, at least for a time. This circumstance in part explains the fact that soil applications are usually considerably higher in rate than are aerial applications.

PLANT TISSUE SYSTEMS

The body of *vascular plants*—that is, those containing xylem and phloem—can be viewed as consisting of three systems of tissues: (1) dermal, (2) vascular, and (3) fundamental or ground. The *dermal system* provides the outer wrapping of the plant and is represented in the young plant by the epidermis. Later, with additional (secondary) growth, the epidermis may be replaced by another dermal system. The *vascular system* includes the two main conducting tissues, the phloem and the xylem. This system provides for the movement of water, minerals, photosynthate, and other chemical constituents within the plant. The *fundamental system,* or *ground system,* includes the remaining tissues, such as apical meristems and reproductive cells, that determine the overall form and function of the plant.

Even though these systems are discrete and fairly readily identifiable, as can be seen diagrammatically in Figure 11–1, the systems are nonetheless dependent upon one another. Furthermore, there is a continuity of the living matter (protoplasm) of the many, many cells that constitute tissues of these three systems.

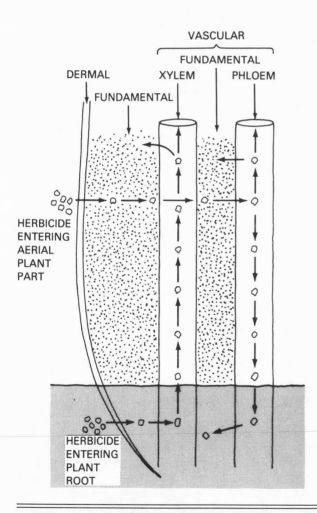

FIGURE 11–1. Simplified diagram showing the proximal relationships among the three tissue systems of vascular plants and the entry and movement of herbicides.

Herbicides must commonly interact with all three systems of Figure 11–1 in manifesting their effects upon plants. There are two broad categories of herbicides based upon the nature of their killing action: (1) *contact herbicides*—that is, those that kill by acute toxicity—and (2) *systemic herbicides*—those that interfere with the weed's physiological and metabolic processes.

In theory, contact herbicides need only penetrate the dermal to exert their effects of weakening and disorganizing the cellular membranes of the fundamental system and, thus, to destroy the plant. But it is likely that even these herbicides are moved, albeit for only very short distances, in the vascular system of the leaf, stem, or root. To better understand the entry and movement of herbicides within plants, it may be helpful to view the plant body as one in which the fundamental tissue is a sea within which the vascular system is imbedded. Viewed in this way, the fundamental tissue provides the linkage for herbicides between the dermal and vascular systems and within the plant provides the linkage between the xylem and phloem components of the vascular system.

Herbicides must reach the living protoplasm to exert their effect. As already mentioned, contact herbicides kill by contact with the living cells. Thus, entry is the main obstacle to their exerting their expected influence on the weed. Normally, it is necessary for systemic herbicides, the other broad category of herbicides, to reach the vascular system and be moved throughout the plant to the sites of action.

The relationships between some basic plant processes and herbicide entry and movement are shown in Figure 11–2. The left side of the figure pertains to photosynthesis and movement in phloem. The right side pertains to water and transport in the xylem. The ⊥ indicates points of potential interference with entry and transport. An essential point to be made by the figure is that movement in the phloem (symplast), with products of photosynthesis, may be either upward or downward to other parts of the plant. Movement in the xylem (apoplast) is only upward.

Transport Systems

Most texts treat transport in terms of two separate systems. *Apoplast* is the term for the transport system that is composed of the xylem, the nonliving cell walls of fundamental tissue, and the intercellular spaces. The term *symplast* is used for the transport system that consists of the phloem and other living (protoplasm) matter of the fundamental tissue. Although adequate for dealing with herbicide transport in mature tissue, these definitions suggest an unrealistic degree of independence between the two systems, do not adequately embrace the interrelationships of entry with movement, and leave in question the movement of herbicides in immature tissue that may contain no nonliving cells. As we shall see when we examine the xylem in greater detail, although the xylem is composed of nonliving cells in the mature tissue, it originates from cambium, which is living cell tissue. Transition

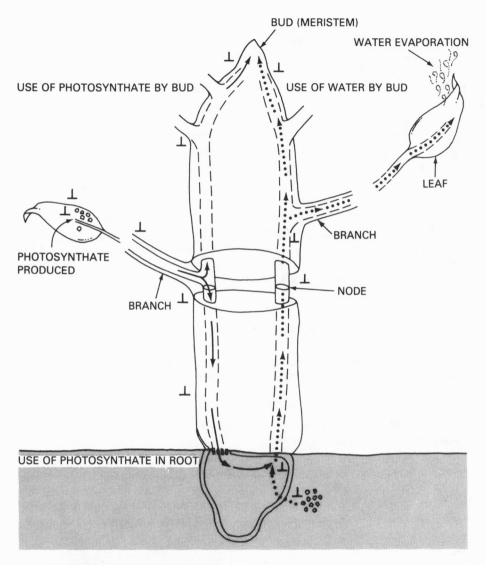

FIGURE 11–2. Schematic diagram relating metabolic processes and herbicide entry and movement in plants.

from living to nonliving occurs at a very early age in the development process. Nevertheless, as already discussed, some herbicides are taken up and exert their effect during this early stage of development. *Polar transport*—that is, transport within the fundamental tissue—is sometimes identified as a third transport pathway for herbicides. Apparently, plant auxins may indeed move in this tissue system. However, it seems unlikely that this system of transport can account for herbicide movement of more than a few millimeters at most, in that it relies upon diffusion, which is a relatively slow process. Thus, transport is considered here in terms of movement in the xylem and in the phloem. Even so, we must remember that these are interrelated parts of the vascular system with ties also to the fundamental tissue. Most commonly, as depicted in Figure 11–1, herbicides interact with all tissues at some time during their time in the plant.

In order to fully understand the relationship between the plant structure and herbicide entry and action, the anatomy of plants needs to be examined in greater detail. The dermal tissue system is examined in the section where we look at the leaf as a point of herbicide entry. At this point, let us examine in somewhat greater detail the fundamental and vascular tissue systems.

Fundamental Tissue System

From the herbicide's standpoint during the entry phase, the fundamental system is an obstacle to reaching the vascular system, which is the ultimate goal of the entry phase. The fundamental tissue system, as the system from which the various parts—roots, stems, leaves, and flowers—originate, must necessarily be composed of a wide variety of cells. As already pointed out, there is a continuity of the protoplasm of the living cells in the three tissue systems of plants. However, the fundamental tissue system, as well as the other tissue systems, is interlaced with intercellular spaces. These spaces may be open, or they may be filled with material excreted from the living cells surrounding them. If not filled with excreted material, they may be occupied by water or by gasses, depending upon the state of hydration of the entire system. Viewed in this way, the fundamental system provides a vehicle for movement of a herbicide through either living cells or open spaces.

Vascular System

Xylem.   The *xylem* is the principle conducting vehicle for water and mineral nutrients. It consists of several different types of cells, living and nonliving. The most characteristic are the tracheary parts, but fibers and living parenchyma cells are ultimately found in the xylem.

The *tracheary elements* are of primary concern in herbicide movement since they are responsible for the movement of water within the plant. There are two basic types of tracheary elements: the tracheids and the vessels. In both, as the cells mature, the secondary wall becomes lignified and contains no protoplast. The difference between the two is that the *vessels* are perforated in certain areas of contact with other vessel members. The perforations are normally on the ends, thus resulting in a long, continuous tube. The *tracheids,* on the other hand, are not perforated but do have pits in the common walls between two such walls. Thus, sap moving through these cells can do so freely from one to another in the vessels, but in the tracheids must pass through the walls, primarily the thin membranes over the pits. Vessels and tracheids of the xylem are shown in Figure 11–3A.

Phloem. The *phloem* is the food-conducting (photosynthate-conducting) tissue of vascular plants. It, like the xylem, consists of several different kinds of cells possessing different functions. The most important, from the standpoint of herbicide movement, are the sieve elements. They are of two kinds: *sieve cells* that are relatively unspecialized and the more specialized *sieve tubes*. Sieve cells are characteristic of the lower vascular plants and *gymnosperms*—that is, naked seed plants, such as conifers. Sieve tubes are characteristic of most *angiosperms*—that is, covered seed plants, such as corn. The difference between sieve cells and sieve tubes is in the degree of differentiation of the sieve areas and in their distribution on the cell walls. *Sieve areas* are areas in the cell walls with pores or holes in them through which the elements of adjacent cells are interconnected by extrusions of protoplast whose nucleus is not retained. The size of the pores may range from a fraction of a micron to 15 or more microns in some dicotyledons. A sieve cell has relatively nonspecific areas for the pores. Sieve tubes, on the other hand, have the sieve area in a more or less specified location termed *sieve plate*. Since the sieve plates occur mainly on end walls, the sieve tube members become stacked one upon another to form a conducting tube.

The phloem tube commonly includes *companion cells*. Although companion cells arise from the same meristematic cell as the sieve cells or sieve tubes, they differ from the sieve elements. They retain their nucleus and do not develop sieve areas. Rather, movement between such cells and between them and the sieve element occurs through depressed areas or *pit fields*. Gymnosperms and vascular cryptogams (which reproduce by spores) do not contain companion cells, but do contain cells termed *albuminous cells* that are closely associated with their sieve cells.

The phloem also commonly contains a number of parenchyma cells besides the companion and albuminous cells. As in the xylem, these may be arranged in rings around the phloem or in rays passing through them. *Parenchyma cells* serve as a place for storage of starch, fat, and other organic foods and for the accumulation of tannins and resins. Phloem may also contain fibers as a source of storage for starch. The elements in phloem are shown in Figure 11–3B. Figure 11–3C shows the

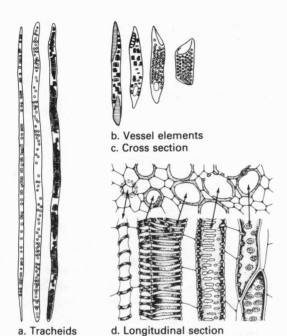

b. Vessel elements
c. Cross section

a. Tracheids   d. Longitudinal section

A. Elements usually found in xylem: (a and b) tracheids and vessel elements shown isolated from the tissue, (c) in cross section, and (d) in longitudinal section

phloem parenchyma cell

sieve plate

slime bodies

sieve-tube member

phloem parenchyma cell

companion cell

companion cell

a. Longitudinal section

b. Face view of a sieve plate

B. Elements usually found in phloem: (a) longitudinal view of a mature sieve-tube member and companion cell, (b) face view of a sieve plate (black areas are actually holes in the walls)

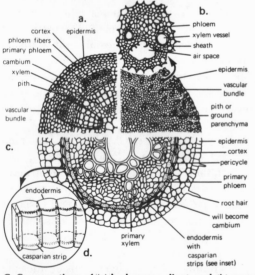

a.
cortex
phloem fibers
primary phloem
cambium
xylem
pith
epidermis

vascular bundle

b.
phloem
xylem vessel
sheath
air space

epidermis

vascular bundle

pith or ground parenchyma

c.

endodermis

casparian strip   d.

primary xylem

epidermis
cortex
pericycle
primary phloem
root hair
will become cambium
endodermis with casparian strips (see inset)

C. Cross sections of (a) herbaceous dicot and (b) monocot stems and of (c) a young root ; the three-dimensional drawing of the endodermal cells (d) showing position of casparian strips in the walls

FIGURE 11–3. Elements commonly found in vascular tissue and the close physical relationship among them.

Source: Salisbury and Ross, 1978. Reprinted by permission of Wadsworth Publishing Company, Belmont, Calif. © 1978 by Wadsworth, Inc.

close spatial relationship between the xylem and the phloem in both roots and stems.

LEAF AS POINT OF HERBICIDE ENTRY

Figure 11–4 is a schematic diagram of a leaf showing the structural characteristics to be discussed in connection with herbicide entry. We begin our examination of this structure from the outside (cuticle) into the leaf vein. The *cuticle* is a discrete, nonliving layer on the outer wall of the epidermal cells. It may be thought of as a continuous noncellular sheet. The process of herbicide entry into the leaf is one of penetrating this nonliving exterior layer in order to reach the living, dermal (epidermal cell), layer that provides access to the fundamental and vascular (vein) systems. The cuticle contains cutin, waxes, pectin, and cellulose, all compounds with varying degrees of polarity. Lipophilic waxes and lipoidal material that predominate on the outside of the cuticle pose the first barrier to herbicide entry, termed the *lipoidal phase*. In general, nonpolar herbicides move fairly readily through this lipoidal area, while polar compounds, such as water-soluble herbicides, do not.

However, we know that polar herbicides do gain entry through the leaves. The leaf cuticle presents two functioning phases: the lipoidal phase just discussed and the *aqueous phase*. It is now known that the cuticle is not an uninterrupted sheet as once thought. Rather, when examined under an electron microscope, it shows

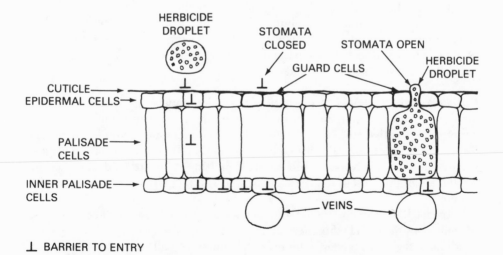

FIGURE 11–4. Cross section of the upper portion of a leaf showing barriers to entry of a herbicide to the vascular system (vein). Entry through the open stomata offers easier access to the vein than through the cuticle.

layering and often has microfibrils (plasmodesmata) extending into it from the underlying epidermal cells. Thus, it is comparable in structure to a sponge with quite possibly an interconnecting network of pores. When filled with water, this network provides an aqueous route for polar herbicides to pass through the cuticle.

Factors Affecting Entry and Passage Rate

Penetration and its rate depend upon both absorption by and thickness of the cuticular layer. For the herbicide spray droplet to move from the leaf surface to the interior of the leaf requires that a gradient be established. Both the concentration of the herbicide solution on the leaf surface and its rate of acceptance (translocation or metabolism) by the epidermal cell clearly influence the steepness of this gradient.

Several other factors may affect the gradient. It may be affected by purely physical aspects of the environment in which the spray droplet finds itself; it may be washed off by rain; or it may dry out, leaving the herbicide in crystalline form rather than in solution. The surface topography of the leaf itself may prevent effective contact between the leaf and the cuticle, thus preventing establishment of the gradient. For example, the gently undulating surface of nutsedge leaves allows greater contact of spray droplets than do the sharp surface features of bermudagrass and redroot pigweed. These physical factors affect entry (gradient) of the herbicide whether polar or nonpolar in character. The appendix to this chapter, Figures 11–1 through 11–6, shows leaf surface characteristics of various weeds.

Since, as we shall see later, the herbicide is a passenger with photosynthate, the state of photosynthesis affects acceptance of the herbicide and, thus, the gradient. If photosynthesis is minimal or not taking place, the herbicide may accumulate in the epidermal or palisade cells and prevent a gradient from being established. Any aspect of the environment that reduces overall rate of metabolism could thus reduce herbicide uptake.

Cuticle. The thickness of the cuticle itself determines the distance the herbicide must travel. Many factors in the environment influence thickness of the cuticle. Factors that tend to cause the cuticle to be thin are shade, low temperature, and wet soil. Reduced tillage, plant residues, and cover crops may create just such conditions. Conversely, full sunlight and low moisture tend to cause the production of thicker cuticle. Also, both acid and alkaline soil result in heavier cuticle.

Age itself is an important determinant of cuticle thickness. As the plant ages, not only does the cuticle thickness increase, but in some species and under some conditions, there is a tendency for even the epidermal cells immediately beneath the cuticular layer to cutinize. A quick inspection of factors affecting thickness of the cuticle indicates that thickness may vary for leaves within the same plant.

TABLE 11-1

Effect of temperature on deposition of cuticle and its components, wax and cutin, in tobacco (*Nicotiana glauea*) leaves.

Day Temperature (°C)	Weight of Cuticle (gm)	Wax (%)	Cutin (%)
10	0.0105	23	77
17	0.018	38	62
23	0.0132	50	50
30	0.0145	51	49

Source: Adapted from Skoss, 1955.

Those within the canopy may be subject to rather heavy shade and may be of a different physiological age than outer leaves.

The composition of the cuticle, as well as its quantity, is also apparently affected by environmental factors, as indicated in Table 11-1. The percentage cutin is 77% under 10°C days, dropping to 50% as the daytime temperature increases to 23°C or higher. There is a corresponding change in wax percentage. These differences could affect absorption of a herbicide by the cuticle. Thus, we see that the environment can affect both the quantity and quality of cuticle present on the leaf surface. Therefore, as the point of entry for aerial applications, leaf surface can account for some of the variation in results encountered with herbicides.

Stomata.   Both the upper and lower surfaces of most leaves contain openings in the epidermis and cuticle called *stomata* through which an interchange of gasses occurs between the atmosphere and the subepidermal cells. Note the differences in size and location of stomata for different weeds in the appendix to Chapter 11. These openings are spaces between two special epidermal cells known as *guard cells*. Changes in the size and shape of these guard cells determine the size of the opening. As can be seen in Figure 11-4, open stomata provide direct access of the herbicide to the living tissue and, thus, to the symplast transport system. *Palisade cells* provide a barrier to direct herbicide entry to the symplast system through the cuticle.

Turgor is the driving force for opening and closing of the stomata. An increase causes the stomata to open and a decrease causes them to close. If the stomata are closed, the cuticular barrier is continuous. When the stomata are open, penetration by herbicide sprays can be expected to be very rapid as compared with the relatively slow uptake through the cuticle.

Since many factors affect stomatal opening and stomata are present only on the lower surface of leaves of many species, stomatal entry is likely to be relatively unimportant as a point of entry for herbicides. Conditions that favor stomatal uptake also favor cuticular uptake of the aqueous phase. Because of the much larger surface area of the nonstomatal cuticle, entry through it is relatively more important. Thus, stomatal entry may be too minor to determine success or failure in control of the targeted weed species but may nevertheless, at least partially, explain the occurrence or absence of injury to the nontargeted crop.

Leaf hairs.   Other leaf integuments or characteristics may influence the leaf as a point of entry of a herbicide. One is *pubescence*, or leaf hairs. These structures originate from the epidermal cells and may vary from single-celled organs to variously branched multicellular plates (Chapter 11 Appendix). Such structures clearly can affect the degree of contact between a herbicidal spray and the cuticle. A thick stand of epidermal hairs could prevent contact between the herbicide and cuticle. On the other hand, a thin stand might help to retain the spray droplets on the leaf's surface. There is some evidence also that individual hairs may serve as a point of entry for herbicides. Because species differ in the presence and amount of epidermal hairs, these structures may, therefore, be the source for some differences in effects of herbicides on plants.

Leaf shape and size.   Leaf shape and size may influence entry because they determine area available for retention of the spray droplet. These differences, of course, are genetically based, but the leaf area in particular is quite plastic. That is, its size is influenced by light intensity, quality, and duration; by water stress during development; and by nutrition.

Fate of Applied Herbicide

With respect to the leaf as a point of entry, five events may occur with an applied herbicide: (1) It may be lost into the atmosphere by volatilization; (2) it may be washed off by rain; (3) it may remain on the cuticle because of evaporating down to a crystalline or viscous liquid; (4) it may enter the cuticle but remain there in lipoidal solution; and (5) it may pass through the cuticle and enter either the apoplast or symplast transport system, or both. Obviously, unless point 5 occurs, the applied herbicide will not affect the plant. If the objective is to destroy the foliage (leaves), it can best be accomplished if in point 5, the herbicide enters only the aqueous phase of the apoplast system since this entry assures its concentrating in the leaf. Conversely, if translocation into all parts of the aboveground portion as well as into the roots is desired, the herbicide must enter the symplast system.

ROOT AS POINT OF HERBICIDE ENTRY

Factors Affecting Entry and Passage Rates

A schematic representation of a root in Figure 11–5A identifies the tissues, and something of their developmental ontogeny, important in herbicide entry. The emphasis implied in the figure is on the root during early development. This emphasis helps visualize the chronological development of two elements paramount in results with herbicides applied to the soil: the *casparian strip*—a waxy band in the cell walls of the root endodermis—and the xylem. Unlike the leaf, the root likely does not have a cuticle; or if it does, it is neither as thick nor as persistent as in the leaf. The penetration of the root through the soil, with the associated abrasive action, would tend to remove or disrupt any such layer. Furthermore, the root contains relatively more "free space" in the fundamental tissue than does the leaf. The reason is that cells in the cortex of the root commonly separate at their adjoining walls, thus adding this space to the space provided by the "poor fit" at the corners or edges of cells (Figure 11–5B). In effect, this means that a herbicide in the soil, if dissolved in or dispersed in the soil solution, conceivably could be in contact with the semipermeable cell membranes of all living cells in the dermal and cortex regions, as well as rather quickly and easily reaching the vicinity of the endodermal cells that bar access to the vascular system.

Thus, the root provides a barrier to entry analogous to that provided by open stomata in the leaves. In the case of the root, however, the exposure can be visualized as continuous along the outer surface of the endodermis, as opposed to comparable exposure in the leaf only where stomata interrupt the leaf surface. Evidence supporting comparatively easy penetration of the epidermis and cortex is found in the fact that most herbicides initially are taken up rather rapidly upon reaching the soil root interface. This fact can be explained by the filling of the intercellular spaces. Once this space is filled, uptake can be expected to slow down because of the need either to cross the casparian strip or cross the cell membrane shown in Figure 11–5B. As we will see in Chapter 12, however, relatively easier access of herbicides through the roots is apt to be more than offset by phenomena that can relieve the root from exposure to a herbicide (root growth beyond the herbicide zone, leaching of the herbicide, adsorption of the herbicide on soil particles, and decomposition of the herbicide).

The objective for soil-applied selective herbicides is to reach the xylem or phloem of the weed root to access sites of action throughout the plant. The two routes and combination of routes by which this objective can occur are shown in Figure 11–5B as apoplast and symplast entry. Inspection of Figure 11–4, Chapter 11 Appendix, and Figure 11–5 suggests that there are fewer barriers to entry through the root than there are to entry through the shoot. In effect, the root presents only two barriers: (1) that posed by the semipermeable membrane of the

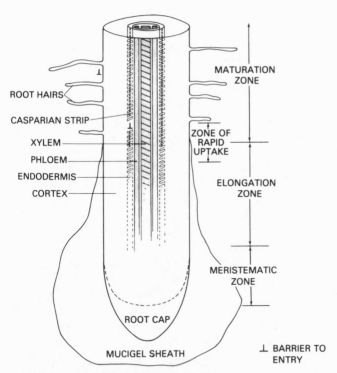

A. Three-dimensional diagram of a young root showing
ontogeny and the relationship to entry.

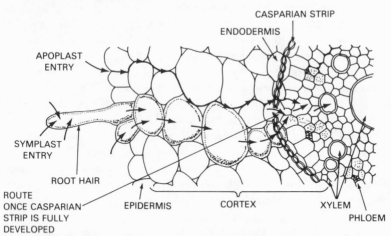

B. Transection of a root showing the two routes for entry: apoplast (xylem) and
symplast (phloem). Position of casparian strip between the root exterior and the
vascular vessels is also shown.

FIGURE 11–5. Root as a point of uptake for herbicides.

Source: Part A after Russell, 1977. Reproduced by permission of McGraw-Hill Book Company (UK), Ltd.
Part B modified from Esau, 1965.

living root cell and (2) that posed by the casparian strip in the walls of the endodermal cells.

Xylem maturity. The xylem is the tissue that provides movement of water from the soil to the aboveground parts. As shown by the grading-in of the stipling of the xylem in Figure 11–5A, xylem attains its mature status towards the juncture of the elongation zone with the maturation zone. This maturation point is a relatively short distance from the root tip—in the neighborhood of 50 mm—depending on the species and growing conditions. The zone of rapid uptake of water identified in the figure includes part of the maturation zone and part of the elongation zone. This is not to say that uptake does not occur in older tissue, only that uptake is most rapid in the young tissue. Similarly, it appears that this area is also the primary site of entry for herbicides. Thus, the age of the root as it determines maturity of the xylem has an important effect on herbicide entry.

Casparian strip. The casparian strip plays a key, and in a sense a controlling, role in herbicide entry of roots. This strip, shown in Figures 11–5A and 11–5B, is formed in the maturation zone during the early development of the endodermal cells and is an integral part of the primary wall. Chemically, it apparently consists of suberin, lignen, or a combination of both that is highly hydrophobic. Once it is fully established, the strip forces chemicals to enter via the living protoplasm in order to access the vascular tissues. Thus, this barrier provides one basis for selectivity in that it conceivably prevents access to the plants of those chemicals that cannot penetrate the cell membrane.

There is a time before the casparian strip is fully established when chemicals presumably do gain entry to the xylem by way of the intercellular and the wall spaces. Depending upon the chemical and physical nature of the herbicide, the herbicide may be restricted to entry by the apoplast, by the symplast, or by both routes.

Active and passive uptake. It is known from studies of mineral nutrient absorption by plants (roots) that such uptake may be both passive and active. *Passive uptake* may be most easily visualized as free movement with water from the soil solution into the root and upward in the xylem. *Active uptake* is uptake that depends upon expenditure of energy on the part of the plant. It is most easily visualized where the uptake occurs against a *concentration gradient*. That is, the concentration in the xylem is greater than that of the mineral nutrient at the soil–root interface. Work on uptake of herbicides indicates that both passive and active uptake are involved also and vary from herbicide to herbicide. Knowledge of the mechanism involved with candidate herbicides will help decide which herbicides would be best for the intended use and condition.

Dicots vs. monocots. The distinct difference between dicotyledonous and

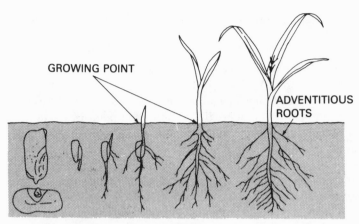

GROWING POINT

ADVENTITIOUS ROOTS

A. Seedling development of a grass plant (monocot)

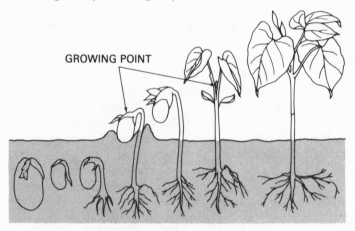

GROWING POINT

B. Seedling development of an epigeal emerging dicot

FIGURE 11–6. Differences in the location of growing points and roots relative to the soil surface of monocots and dicots as a basis for selective control of weeds with herbicides.

monocotyledonous plants in the source of their root systems may well have a bearing on the comparative importance of herbicide uptake from the soil. In dicots, the root system develops from the radical of the embryo upon its elongation and branching. In monocots, the first root derived from the root meristem of the embryo usually dies at an early age. The permanent root system then develops from stem tissue as adventitious roots. Thus, roots in monocots are closer proximally to the apical meristem of the shoot than are those in dicots.

Figure 11–6 contrasts the different anatomical structures of dicots and monocots during germination and early seedling development. The early development of adventitious roots by monocots also means that they may well have roots closer to the soil surface than do dicots, at least during their early stage of development. Both the penetration of roots by soil and their numbers are influenced by physical factors of the soil itself, such as its density, organic matter content, and water content. All of these factors may be increased by reduced tillage. To the extent that dicots and monocots respond differently to these factors, another variable is introduced to their response to soil-applied herbicides.

COLEOPTILE AS POINT OF HERBICIDE ENTRY

The *coleoptile* is an atomical structure unique to the grasses. For interpretative purposes, it can be visualized as a specialized leaf that forms a cone-shaped tube surrounding the apical meristem or growing point. It has a hole at the apex through which the first foliage leaves emerge. It has stomata that, given the high humidity both internal and external to it, can be presumed to be open. Thus, the coleoptile could conceivably provide relatively easy access of a herbicide to the growing point inside. During early development of the grass seedling, this growing point may be at any place from essentially the level of the seed in the soil to the soil surface when the leaves actually emerge through the soil. In dicotyledons, by contrast, since the growing point is borne in the axis of the first true leaves that in turn is between the cotyledons, the growing point is aboveground once the cotyledons—or first true leaves—emerge through the soil. It should be noted, however, that some dicots actively take up herbicides through the hypocotyl for a time during germination and early seedling development. Legumes in the hook stage are an example. This period is the stage from the number 3 to the number 5 seedling in Figure 11–6B.

Dawson (1963) showed that uptake of herbicides from the soil could occur through the coleoptile in addition to plant roots. He found that uptake of EPTC by the primary root of barnyardgrass had relatively little effect, whereas uptake by the shoot resulted in severe injury. He concluded that the leaf is the important site of EPTC uptake in the control of barnyardgrass. Much work since then supports this finding by Dawson.

Further, it appears that the region of the so-called coleoptile node is the key, at least in determining the effect of uptake on the plant. The importance of the coleoptile was shown in work reported by Holly (1976) in which the herbicide diallate was evaluated for its effect on wheat and on wild oat when placed at different locations in the soil relative to the seed (Figure 11–7). As can be seen, both wheat (W) and wild oat (A) were very sensitive to the herbicide immediately above their seed. However, wheat was essentially unaffected where the diallate layer was close to the soil surface, whereas wild oat was nearly completely killed by this layer. The difference is explained by the fact that the coleoptile node (growing

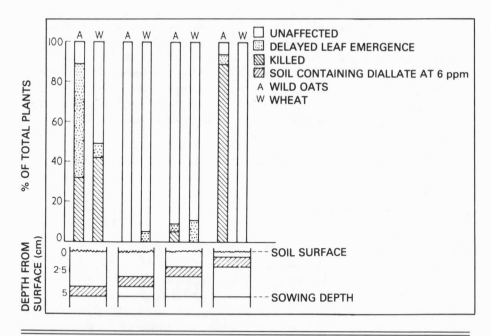

FIGURE 11–7. Differences in the location of the growing point relative to the seed in the soil of monocots as the basis for selective weed control.
Source: Holly, 1976. Reproduced by permission of Academic Press, Inc.

point) in wheat remains close to the seed for a time and below the herbicide layer. In wild oat, however, the coleoptile node moves upward into the treated soil at a very early stage.

HERBICIDE EFFECTS ON BIOCHEMICAL REACTIONS

The acute toxicity of the earlier, contact herbicides on plants was readily apparent and quite easily understood. The effect of the newer, systemic herbicides is much more complex since they are readily translocated and often exert their effect at sites some distance from the point of entry. It is understandable, then, that much is yet to be learned to fully explain the action of most of the systemic herbicides. Even so, enough has been learned to separate their action into two broad categories: Mechanism of action and mode of action. *Mechanism of action* is the biochemical and biophysical response of the plant to a herbicide. *Mode of action* encompasses the total phytotoxic effects of the herbicide, some of which are the result of secondary reactions, including effects on growth and growth form. Knowledge of the two categories of effects determines when the herbicide will be most effective against the weed with least chance of harming the crop and what will be the likely effect of growing conditions on results.

Primary Biochemical Site of Action

Identifying the primary biochemical sites of action of herbicides is difficult, but doing so will help us to understand the relationship between the physical and the biochemical basis for herbicide selectivity. Ashton and Crafts (1981) define the *primary biochemical site of action* as the single metabolic reaction that is affected at a herbicide concentration lower than any other reaction or the first reaction affected at a given low concentration. They consider other reactions that are affected at higher concentrations of the herbicide or at a later time to be secondary in nature. The definition of primary biochemical sites in itself indicates one of the difficulties in identifying primary sites since it may be extremely difficult to determine the precise concentration that affects the metabolic reaction.

Determining the end relationships among metabolic processes also complicates the determination of primary biochemical sites. That is, an effect upon any one basic process—respiration, photosynthesis, or nucleic acid metabolism and protein synthesis—relatively quickly affects the other processes as well. Furthermore, the processes of photosynthesis and nucleic acid metabolism and protein synthesis are located in several tissues, not just in one or a few, thus facilitating interactions among them. In spite of the difficulties, much is now known, and the beginnings of a catalog of effects is taking shape.

Most of the early herbicides were salts and acids that acted as contact killers. Thus, they are called contact herbicides. Such materials were acutely toxic to the plant and its tissues. Their general effect was one of rapidly weakening and disorganizing the cellular membranes, causing the membranes to be more permeable. Oils widely used early in the history of chemical weed control and still being used today also appear to destroy the semipermeable nature of cell membranes. Although herbicides of the modern era also appear to act by changing the function of cellular membranes, their mechanisms are decidedly different from earlier contact herbicides.

Systemic herbicides, descriptive of the majority of the newer herbicides, generally act by interfering with normal functioning of the physiological or metabolic processes. Their action is one of chronic toxicity as opposed to the acute toxicity of a contact herbicide. Thus, the ultimate effect of systemic herbicides may not be reached for several days or even weeks following their application. The phenoxy herbicides—that is, 2,4–D, 2,4,5–T, and MCPA—were the first commercially available systemic herbicides. Early in the research with these herbicides, it was concluded that their sites of action were the rapidly growing meristematic tissues. These herbicides were earlier identified as growth regulators, thus implicating meristematic tissues as the site of action. Subsequent work has supported this earlier work implicating meristematic tissues as the site for physiological response but has shown the basic process affected to be that of nucleic acid metabolism and protein synthesis. Between that early work and the more recent work identifying the primary biochemical site of action, a wide range of effects were reported that Ashton and Crafts (1981) feel are secondary in nature.

This brief account of the development of our understanding of sites of action for the phenoxy herbicides indicates the magnitude of the task of providing such information for all herbicides since there are more than 150 in use, with new ones constantly being added and some existing ones being dropped. An in-depth discussion of biochemical sites of action of individual herbicides is outside the purpose of this text. Refer to Ashton and Crafts (1981) for a detailed review of the mode and mechanism of action of individual herbicides. These researchers identified four primary biochemical reactions for plant responses to herbicides: (1) respiration and mitochondrial electron transport, (2) photosynthesis, (3) nucleic acid metabolism and protein synthesis, and (4) lipid metabolism. The four biochemical reactions are reviewed here to identify their relevancy to understanding biological selectivity.

Respiration and mitochondrial electron transport. Respiration provides plants with energy needed for many functions, such as mineral uptake, protein and lipid synthesis, and transport of photosynthates. Thus, it represents a basic plant process and one that herbicides have been shown to affect. In simple terms, *respiration* is the process by which sugars are broken down into water and carbon dioxide with the release of energy. The process occurs in three steps: (1) the conversion of sugars to the three-carbon pyruvic acid (glycolysis), (2) metabolism of the pyruvic acid to carbon dioxide, and (3) further metabolism in which water is formed. The first of these steps occurs in the cytoplasm within the cell. The second and third take place within organelles called *mitochondria* contained within the cytoplasm itself. It is during this third step that energy released in the overall process of respiration is trapped and stored for use in the energy-dependent functions of the plant. This energy is stored as adenosine triphosphate (ATP), the production of which in turn is the result of *oxidative phosphorylation*—that is, the acceptance of phosphate by oxygen—with associated processes of both electron and energy transfers. Herbicides that affect respiration act at this level, although some may also affect the first step. The effect of the herbicide at the mitochondrial level may be to prevent the formation of adenosine triphosphate or to interfere with electron or energy transfer.

Table 11–2 lists herbicides known to act as uncouplers and inhibitors of oxidative phosphorylation. As can be seen, this process is affected by a broad cross section of herbicides.

TABLE 11-2

Herbicides known to affect aerobic respiration by uncoupling or inhibiting oxidative phosphorylation.

Amiben	Dicamba	Monuron	Simazine
Amitrole	Dinoben	Nitralin	Tricamba
Atrazine	EPTC	Oryzalin	TCA
Barban	Fluometuron	Picloram	2,4-D
CDAA	Ioxynil	Prometryn	2,4-DB
4-CPA	MCPA	Propham	2,4,5-T
2-CPA	MCPB	Propanil	2,3,6-TBA
Dalapon			

Photosynthesis

The conversion of radiant to chemical energy during the process of photosynthesis is another of the basic biochemical reactions affected by herbicides. In simple terms, *photosynthesis* is the combining of water and carbon dioxide in a way that captures energy from the sun in the organic compounds (sugar) produced. The site of this reaction is mainly in organelles found within the cytoplasm of leaves of green plants. The actual process is an extremely complex one involving a large number of chemical reactions. Refer to the review by Moreland (1980) for a detailed discussion of this process and the effects of specific herbicides.

For our purposes here, it is sufficient to recognize that the process involves two broad steps: (1) splitting of water, which requires light, and (2) fixation of carbon dioxide, which can occur in the dark. It is now known that most herbicides that affect photosynthesis do so in the light reaction phase. The light part of the reaction, as is true in respiration, involves the acceptance and transfer of electrons. Herbicides may interfere with both. Further, interference occurs in each of the two pigment systems involved in the light reactions, commonly called *photosystem I* and *photosystem II*.

Herbicides considered to act by interfering with electron transfer (in photosystem II) are shown in Table 11-3. Those in the first column act by removing or inactivating an electron carrier. Perfluidone acts by dissociating electron transport from ATP formation. The 1,2,3-thiadiazolyl-phenylureas apparently inhibit energy flow at a somewhat later phase in ATP formation. Inhibitory uncouplers affect both electron carrier and uncoupling reactions.

Electron acceptance is provided by hydrogen resulting from the splitting of water during the light reaction. The herbicides paraquat and diquat can serve as electron acceptors (in photosystem I) and thus disrupt photosynthesis. The resulting free radicals quickly oxidize to form hydrogen peroxide, oxygen, and the

TABLE 11-3

Herbicides considered to interfere with a specific aspect of electron transfer.

Electron Carrier	Uncoupler	Energy Transfer	Inhibitory Uncouplers
p-Alkylanilides	Perfluidone	1,2,3–thiadiazolyl-phenylureas	Acylanilides
p-Alkylthioanilides			Benzimidazoles
Amino-triazinones			Bromofenoxim
Azido-s-triazines			Dinitroanilines
Bis-carbamates			Dinitrophenols
Clorinated dimethylphenylureas			Halogenated benzonitriles
Chlorinated-s-triazines			Imidazoles
Cyclopropane-carboxamides			
Diphenylethers			N-Phenylcarbamates
Pyridazinones			Pyridinols
Triazinones			Thiadiazoles
Urea-carbamates			
Uracils			

Source: Data from Moreland, 1980..

hydroxyl radical. The hydrogen peroxide and, based on recent research, the more important hydroxyl radical actually account for the toxic effect of these herbicides. But since the effects are triggered by photosynthesis reactions, paraquat and diquat can appropriately be identified as having their fundamental biochemical site of reaction in this process. All told, it has been suggested that more than half of the herbicides interfere in some way with photosynthesis.

The fact that many herbicides interfere with photosynthesis suggests that results from herbicide applications may be affected by both physical and biological aspects of the environment as they determine light available to the treated plant. Indeed, this hypothesis has been found to be true. Herbicides that interfere with photosynthesis are most effective during bright, sunny conditions and with plants growing in full sunlight as opposed to being shaded by an overstoried canopy. The most common symptom is *chlorosis*—that is, lack of green color—which may be veinal, interveinal, marginal, or spotted.

Nucleic Acid Metabolism and Protein Synthesis

Nucleic acid metabolism and protein synthesis are closely linked processes and are responsible for the transfer of genetic information within the plant. In effect, they determine both growth form and function. The end result of interference in these processes is well expressed by the extensive bending and twisting (epinasty) and splitting of stems following application of 2,4–D to sensitive plants. Genetic information transfer involves deoxyribonucleic acid (DNA) and ribonucleic acid (RNA).

Table 11–4 summarizes results of separate studies of herbicidal effects on RNA and protein synthesis. As can be seen, many herbicides affect these processes. In view of the intimate relationship between these processes and plant growth and development, it is to be expected that maturity of the plant affects the degree of the response in sensitive plants.

TABLE 11-4

Herbicides shown to affect RNA and protein synthesis.

RNA Synthesis	Protein Synthesis
Amitrole	Amitrole
Atrazine	Atrazine
Bromacil	Bromacil
CDAA	CDAA
CDEC	CDEC
Chloramben	Chloramben
Chlorpropham	Chlorpropham
2,4–D	2,4–D
Dalapon	Dalapon
Dicamba	DCPA
Dichlobenil	Dicamba
Dinoseb	Dichlobenil
Diuron	Dinoseb
EPTC	Diphenamid
Fenac	Diuron
Isocil	EPTC
Ioxynil	Endothal
Monuron	Fenac
Paraquat	Isocil
Picloram	Ioxynil
Propachlor	Monuron
Propanil	Naptalam
2,4,5–T	Paraquat
Trifluralin	PCP
	Propachlor
	Pyrazon
	2,4,5–T
	Trifluralin

Source: Adapted from Ashton and Crafts, 1981.

TABLE 11-5

Herbicides shown to affect lipid synthesis.

Amitrole	Chlorpropham	EPTC	Picloram
Atrazine	2,4-D	Endothal	Propanil
Barban	Dalapon	Ioxynil	Simzaine
Bromacil	DCPA	Monuron	2,4,5-T
CDAA	Dichlobenil	Naptalam	Trifluralin
CDEC	Dinoseb	Paraquat	
Chloramben	Diphenamid	PCP	

Source: Adapted from Ashton and Crafts, 1981.

Lipid Synthesis and Metabolism

Lipids serve several purposes in plants. They can be reserve food materials, components of cell membranes, and, as part of the cuticle, protectors of the plant. The effect of herbicides on their synthesis has not been extensively studied, but enough has been done to show that this basic biochemical process is also affected. Table 11–5 summarizes some of these results.

WHOLE PLANT RESPONSE TO HERBICIDES

The response of the whole plant to herbicides is a consequence of effects on one or more of the four biochemical processes. The processes themselves are not readily observable, but the resulting changes in the plant following application of herbicides often can be easily seen. These changes are the results of the combined effects on the plant's anatomy, physiology, and biochemistry. Mode of action, discussed in the previous section, is the phrase commonly used to identify these combined effects. By contrast, mechanism of action, also discussed in the previous section, is restricted to the primary biochemical or biophysical interference caused by a herbicide.

A summary diagram showing the relationship between mechanism and mode of action is given in Figure 11–8. The left part of the figure, under the headings Type of action or interference and Primary action, deals with mechanism of action, and the right part, with mode of action. This figure helps to visualize the relationship between primary action and secondary action as the links between mechanism and mode of action.

A brief discussion of mode of action, with accompanying photographs showing typical plant responses, helps us to understand the underlying biochemical

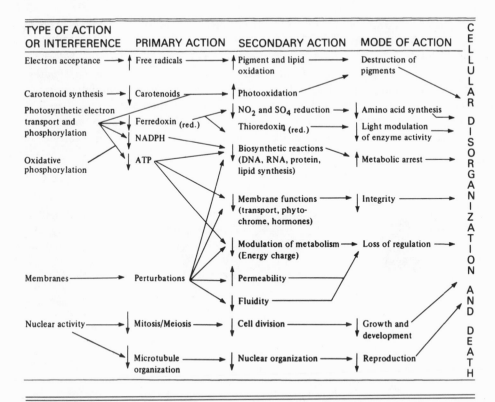

FIGURE 11–8. Summary diagram relating mechanisms of action to the mode of action of herbicides. Increases in activity or concentrations are indicated by arrows pointing up and decreases are shown with arrows pointing down.

Source: Moreland, 1980. Reproduced with permission, from the Ann. Rev. Plant Physiol. 31:597–638. © 1980 by Annual Reviews, Inc.

reaction. Four gross categories of plant responses are reviewed: (1) growth form, (2) chlorophyll formation and function, (3) membrane permeability, and (4) developmental arrest.

Effect on Growth Form

In general terms, growth (size and shape) is a result of cell division, cell enlargement, and cell differentiation. These processes proceed more or less simultaneously and are integrated to assure development of a mature plant of more or less predictable size and shape. Herbicides, largely through their effect on the basic biochemical process of nucleic acid metabolism and protein synthesis, may affect all three components of growth.

Cell division and enlargement. Many herbicides inhibit cell division but do not prevent cell enlargement. Where this inhibition occurs, the resulting root and shoot are shortened and thickened at their tips. This effect may be caused directly by the blocking (poisoning) of mitosis (such as that caused by the carbamates, maleic hydrazide, trifluralin, and other herbicides) or indirectly through interrelationships with the plant's native auxins. In either case, the resulting seedling may have the appearance of those shown in Figure 11–9 that were exposed to trifluralin. The corn and soybean seeds were germinated in pots in the presence of an excessive rate of trifluralin.

A. Soybean seedlings   B. Corn seedlings

FIGURE 11–9. Clublike root tips of soybean and corn seedlings caused by inhibition of cell division followed by abnormal cell enlargement in response to contact with trifluralin. For each species, the seedling on the left is from an untreated pot and the one on the right from a pot in which seeds germinated in the presence of trifluralin.

FIGURE 11–10. Proliferation of cells along the stem of a velvetleaf plant treated with 2,4–D.

Cell proliferation. Stimulation of cells to proliferate is also commonly observed following application of herbicides. Proliferation can occur in the primary meristems or even in mature cells following differentiation. The response of velvetleaf to 2,4–D, shown in Figure 11–10, is representative of such extensive proliferation. If this proliferation occurs with meristematic cells deep within the stem or root, we can visualize that extensive disruption of the flow of water, minerals, and assimilate will also occur.

Cell differentiation. Closely allied with cell proliferation as a symptom is that of effects of herbicides on cell differentiation. Some herbicides can interfere with the differentiation to form the seed or kernel, resulting, for example, in nearly barren cobs in corn, as shown in Figure 11–11.

FIGURE 11–11. Barren cobs caused by interference in cell differentiation in response to dicamba applied near the time corn was tasseling.
Source: Miller et al., 1980. Reproduced with permission.

Tropic reactions.   Plants have an inherent mechanism to respond to gravity and to light. Thus, if a seedling is inverted, the shoot still turns upward and the root portion turns downward. The morphactins, naptalam, and some substituted benzoic acid herbicides interfere with these normal tropic reactions. Figure 11–12 shows disorientation of root and shoot growth in lettuce seedlings caused by a morphactin.

Epinasty.   A characteristic response to many of the auxin-type herbicides, such as 2,4–D, is extreme twisting and bending, commonly called *epinasty*. Extreme epinasty of the type shown in Figure 11–13 may well be the result of the combined effects of reduced cell division, stimulated cell enlargement and proliferation, and interference with tropic response. Since nucleic acid metabolism and protein synthesis are the basic chemical reactions involved, it is understandable that epinastic effects are most pronounced in young, rapidly growing plants.

Effect on Chlorophyll Formation and Function

The result of herbicidal effects on photosynthesis may be expressed both as the prevention of chlorophyll formation and as the interference with its functioning.

FIGURE 11–12. Disorientation effect of herbicides on tropic responses in seedlings. Here lettuce seedlings germinated in the presence of 6 × 10⁻⁵ M n-butyl-9-hydroxyfluorene-(9)-carboxylate (shown on left) exhibit a haphazard response to gravity compared to the precise response in untreated seedlings.
Source: Kahn, 1967. Reproduced with permission of Physiologia plantarum.

Amitrole (Figure 11–14) has the former effect. It does not interfere with chlorophyll in the older leaves but blocks the formation of chlorophyll in the new leaves. Thus, it produces the striking effect of nearly white growth in the youngest leaves. Chlorosis—the bleaching out of the green color in leaves—is a characteristic response to many of the herbicides, including the ureas, s-triazines, uracils, diphenylethers, benzonitriles, and phenylcarbamates. The effect is that leaves of susceptible plants gradually lose their green color in spots or along veins.

Effect on Membrane Permeability

Herbicidal effects on membranes may be manifested in several ways, including leakage of cell contents, a decrease or increase in ion transport, an increase or decrease in water influx, and others. Further, many herbicides can be assumed to have opportunity to alter the discriminating function of the membranes, either as the biochemical site of action or as a secondary effect. Thus, the mode of action

FIGURE 11–13. Epinasty effect of auxin-type herbicides on leaf petioles and stems. Here can be seen epinastic responses of curly dock to 2,4–D.

FIGURE 11–14. Effect of herbicides on chlorophyll formation. Here the youngest leaves are nearly white on a velvetleaf plant treated with amitrole.

effect of disrupting membrane integrity is somewhat of a catchall category. Among the typical early symptoms are a water-soaked, flaccid appearance of leaves caused by herbicidal oils and the wilted appearance of leaves following application of paraquat.

Developmental Arrest

Typically, seeds of many species, both weeds and crops, are not prevented from germinating in the presence of herbicides, but their growth of seedlings is arrested at an early age. This statement is not meant to imply that some herbicides may not prevent germination. However, the much more common response is for the early steps in germination to take place with further development of the seedling arrested. Figure 11–9 shows the arresting effect of trifluralin on the development of corn and soybeans.

CONCEPTS AND CONCLUSIONS

1. Herbicides, especially systemic herbicides, must commonly interact with all three tissue systems—dermal, vascular, and fundamental—to express their effects on plants.
2. The leaf, the root, and, in grasses, the coleoptile are the main points of entry of herbicides into plants.
   a. Leaf cuticle quantity and quality, pubescence, and growth form, all of which are influenced by growing conditions, affect herbicide entry.
   b. The root is a relatively nondiscriminating point of entry for herbicides. Uptake is influenced by such abiotic aspects as clay and organic matter content, rainfall, and evaporation.
   c. The presence or absence of a coleoptile and the location of the growing point within it influence the extent and affect of herbicide uptake from soil.
3. Systemic herbicides must move through the vascular system to reach the site(s) of biochemical reaction(s). Herbicides entering through the leaves must move through the living phloem. Herbicides entering via the root must usually move to the reaction vicinity in the nonliving xylem and then reenter living cells.
4. The four primary biochemical reactions affected by herbicides are: respiration and mitochondrial electron transport, photosynthesis, nucleic acid metabolism and protein synthesis, and lipid metabolism.
5. Although biochemical reactions are not readily seen, gross responses (mode of action) of the plant to them are. These responses are evident in overall growth form, chlorophyll formation and function, membrane permeability, and developmental arrest.
6. Herbicide entry, transport, and effect are each subject to influence by the natural and imposed environment.

REFERENCES

Aldrich, R.J. 1950. Factors affecting the practicability of the preemergence use of 2,4–D on corn, Ph.D. dissertation. Ohio State University, Columbus.

Ashton, F.M., and A.S. Crafts. 1981. Mode of action of herbicides, 2nd ed. New York: Wiley.

Cartwright, P.M. 1976. General growth response of plants. In L.J. Audus, ed., Herbicides: Physiology, biochemistry, ecology, 2nd ed., vol. 2, pp. 55–82. New York: Academic Press.

Dawson, J.H. 1963. Development of barnyardgrass seedlings and their response to EPTC. Weeds 11(1):60–67.

Esau, K. 1965. Plant anatomy. New York: Wiley.

Hartley, G.S. 1960. Physio-chemical aspects of the availability of herbicides in soils. In E.K. Woodford and C.R. Sagar, eds., Herbicides and the soil, pp. 63–78. Oxford, England: Blackwell Scientific.

Holly, K. 1976. Selectivity in relation to formulation and application methods. In L.J. Audus, ed., Herbicides: Physiology, biochemistry, ecology, vol. 2, pp. 249–77. New York: Academic Press.

Kahn, A.A. 1967. Physiology of morphactin: Effect on gravi- and photo-response. Physiologia Pl. 20:306–13.

Miller, G.R., D. Breneman, and R. Behrens. 1980. Herbicide symptoms in corn, North central regional extension publication 94, extension folder 487. St. Paul: Agricultural Extension Service, University of Minnesota.

Moreland, D.E. 1980. Mechanisms of action of herbicides. Ann. Rev. Plant Physiol. 31:597–638.

Russell, R.S. 1977. Plant root systems: Their function and interaction with the soil. London: McGraw-Hill.

Salisbury, F.B., and C.W. Ross. 1978. Plant physiology, 2nd ed. Belmont, Calif.: Wadsworth.

Skoss, J.D. 1955. Structure and composition of plant cuticle in relation to environmental factors and permeability. Bot. Gaz. 117:55–72.

APPENDIX TO CHAPTER 11

Leaf Surface Characteristics of Various Weeds

Source: Courtesy of F.D. Hess and Wiley-Interscience.

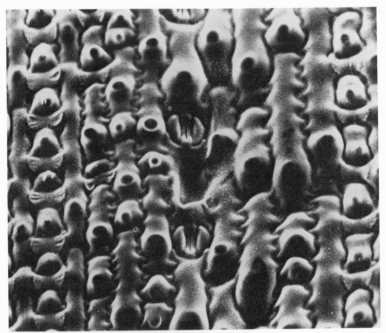

1. Bermudagrass (*Cynodon dactylon* [L.] pers.), 600X

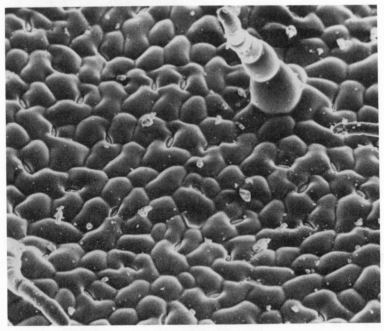

2. Redroot pigweed (*Amaranthus retroflexus* L.), 250 X

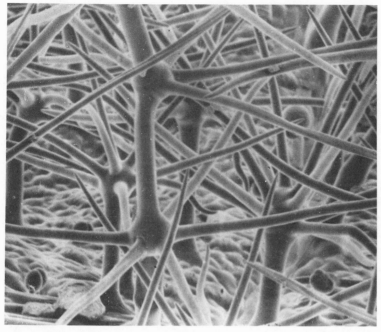

3. Common mullein (*Verbascum thapsus* L.), 250X

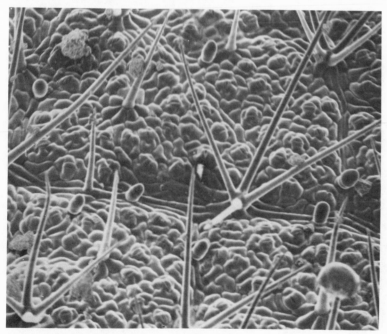

4. Velvetleaf (*Abutilon theophrasti* Medic.), 150X

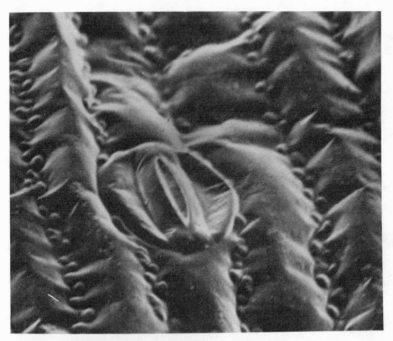

5. Yellow nutsedge (*Cyperus esculentus* L.), 1750X

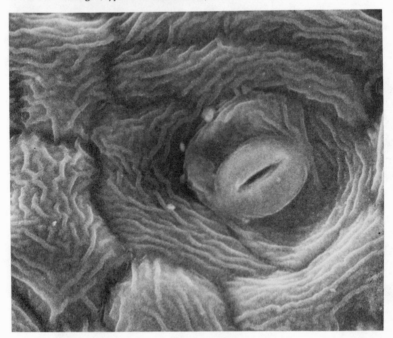

6. Field bindweed (*Convoluulus arvensis* L.), 1250X

PREVENTING WEED EMERGENCE WITH HERBICIDES

12

The application of herbicides to soil to prevent weed emergence is based upon three well-established facts: (1) Most annual weeds originate from seeds in the top 2.5 cm to 5.0 cm; (2) the germination and early seedling development stage is often the most vulnerable period in the weed's life cycle; and (3) if weeds can be kept out for only a few weeks, most crops can successfully compete thereafter. This method of preventing weeds from interfering with crop production offers certain practical advantages as well. One is to provide protection against conditions that may prevent later control, such as rainfall delaying cultivation or postemergence herbicide application until weeds either cannot be effectively controlled or have already inflicted some permanent damage on the crop. Another advantage is to enable herbicide application to be done in one operation with planting. Further, herbicides can be safely used in this way on crops not tolerant when they are up and growing.

HERBICIDE SELECTIVITY

The successful use of herbicides applied to the soil calls for the selective prevention of weed emergence and establishment without damage to the crop. Figure 12–1 shows the two most commonly used methods of soil applications designed, at least in part, to insure adequate selectivity. Application to the soil surface after or at the time of planting the crop was the earliest method used (Figure 12–1A).

A. Application at or after planting of crops. Herbicide applied to soil surface moves downward into the weed seed germination zone with percolating water.

B. Application before planting of crops. Herbicide applied to soil surface is mechanically mixed into the weed seed germination zone.

FIGURE 12–1. Two most commonly used methods of herbicide application to soil for selective control of annual weeds.

For effective control to be obtained, rainfall or irrigation is needed to move the herbicide into the weed seed germination zone. Further, with most herbicides, this transfer must occur before the weed seeds germinate. For these reasons, and to reduce herbicide loss from evaporation and photodecomposition, many herbicides are now routinely incorporated mechanically into the weed seed germination zone prior to planting the crop (Figure 12–1B). Truly spectacular results can be obtained, as shown in Figure 12–2. Atrazine applied preemergence at 2.2 kilograms per hectare, with no cultivation or other weed control, completely prevented emergence of the several annual weeds present in the untreated area. Effective control persisted for the entire growing season.

With any soil application method, selectivity may be based upon physical factors, biological factors, or a combination of both. The reason is that the plant, the soil, the herbicide, and the climate may each influence results obtained. If the herbicide is to be effective against the weed, it must be in contact with the seed or the developing seedling, and it must enter the weed to reach the site of biochemical reaction. At the same time, one or the other or both of these phenomena must be avoided by the crop seed and seedling. In general terms, physical factors are the ones most responsible for avoiding or assuring contact, whereas biological factors are involved in entry and biochemical reactions.

Physical Basis for Selectivity

Selectivity based on physical factors must provide differential contact of the herbicide with the primary root and young shoot of the weed and the crop in the soil. The developing root and shoot are the important points of entry for soil-applied herbicides. Although herbicides may enter the seed, the seed may be relatively unaffected if it is dormant. Further, it appears that with many her-

A. Untreated corn

B. Corn treated with 2.2 kilograms per hectare of atrazine applied preemergence

FIGURE 12–2. Complete and season-long prevention of emergence of annual weeds in corn.

Source: Reproduced courtesy of O. Hale Fletchall, Department of Agronomy, University of Missouri–Columbia.

bicides, imbibition by the seed does not prevent initiation of the germination process. Herbicides otherwise equally toxic to the crop and the weeds may be used selectively by physically exposing the weed's points of entry and not the points of entry of the crop. This technique may be accomplished by physically separating the crop seed and the herbicide and is commonly termed *depth protection*. In general terms, depth protection may be accomplished by mechanical means, through the use of absorptive barriers, and through the use of different herbicides.

Seeding crop below herbicide zone.   The most common method for providing depth protection is by mechanically seeding the crop below the herbicide zone in the soil or below the zone that the herbicide may be expected to reach. Figure 12–3 demonstrates the effectiveness of this approach for selective use of CDAA for annual grass control in cotton. Cotton planted 5 cm (2 in.) deep was reduced in stand only by the heaviest rate—that is, 7.3 kg (16 lb) of CDAA incorporated to a depth of 3.8 cm (1 1/2 in.). Since this rate is about 16 times the amount needed to provide effective grass control, there clearly is a sizable safety margin. Where the

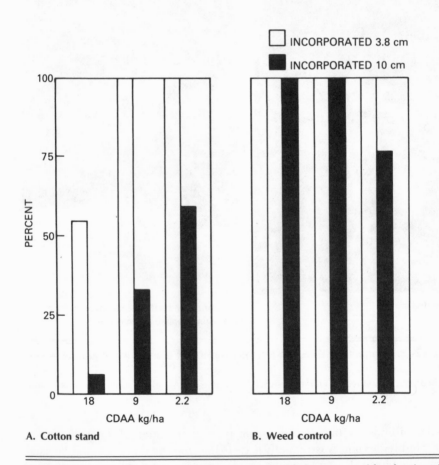

FIGURE 12–3. Seeding the crop below the herbicide layer to avoid reductions in crop stands with herbicides incorporated in the soil. Here cotton was planted 5 cm (2 in.) deep.

Source: Data from Kemper et al., 1963.

cotton was planted 5 cm (2 in.) and CDAA incorporated to a depth of 10 cm (4 in.), the stand was reduced by one-third with a rate of only 0.9 kilogram per hectare (2 pounds per acre). It should be noted also that weed control was less effective with the 1.1 kg and 2.2 kg rates incorporated to a depth of 10 cm than where incorporated only 3.8 cm. With deeper incorporation, relatively less herbicide was concentrated in the surface zone in which most of the weeds germinate.

Other adaptations of this concept of separation have been successfully used. Hauser (1965) was able to effectively control yellow nutsedge in peanuts by placing a band of EPTC, PPTC (S-propyl butylethylthiocarbamate), or PEBC (S-propyl dipropylthiocarbamate) 3.8 cm (1 1/2 in.) below the soil surface with rates that were not unduly harmful to peanuts. Holstun and Wooten (1964) used a combination of subsurface and surface spraying to improve selective control of weeds in cotton with EPTC. They used herbicides tolerated by cotton in a band over the cotton row with adjacent row-shoulder subsurface treatments of EPTC. The band application controlled the annual weeds in the row, and the shoulder applications controlled the nutsedge as well as the annual weeds beyond the row.

Absorptive barriers.   A way of physically separating the herbicide and crop seed is by use of *absorptive barriers*. This technique is shown in Figure 12–4. In this technique, an absorptive (absorbent) layer of activated carbon placed above the crop seed prevents downward movement of the herbicide to the crop seed by absorbing any of the herbicide that reaches it. An adaptation of the absorptive barrier concept is to dip seedlings of transplants into solutions of activated carbon. Under this approach, the herbicide in the soil does not damage the transplants because it is absorbed by the activated carbon on the root surface.

Herbicide differences.   As discussed later, herbicides vary greatly in their mobility in soil. Some move very freely with percolating water. Others are held to

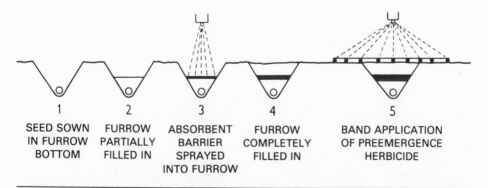

1	2	3	4	5
SEED SOWN IN FURROW BOTTOM	FURROW PARTIALLY FILLED IN	ABSORBENT BARRIER SPRAYED INTO FURROW	FURROW COMPLETELY FILLED IN	BAND APPLICATION OF PREEMERGENCE HERBICIDE

FIGURE 12–4. Reductions in crop stand from residual preemergence herbicides avoided by placing a barrier of activated charcoal above the seed.
Source: Holly, 1976. Reproduced with permission of Academic Press, Inc.

varying degrees on soil particles and move relatively little with percolating water. Thus, the use of a relatively immobile herbicide may provide a physical separation of the herbicide from the germinating crop and weed seed. This technique was demonstrated with 2,4–D formulation in very early research (Aldrich and Willard, 1951). As can be seen in Table 12–1, the butyl ester caused little or no reduction in corn stands, whereas stands were reduced 23% by the triethylamine salt formulation. Sufficient irrigation water was applied immediately after 2,4–D application to wet down to the corn seeds. Laboratory studies showed that the butyl ester moved downward less freely, which explains the field results in Table 12–1.

Although physical separation is an important factor in selectivity with soil-applied herbicides in crops, it seldom provides adequate selectivity by itself. Some degree of physiological tolerance on the part of the crop is also needed. Thus, EPTC, which does not readily move downward in the soil, can be safely used for weed control in soybeans, which have some physiological tolerance, but not in corn, which has no tolerance.

Biological Basis for Selectivity

Differences in morphology and in internal physiology and metabolism of the crop and the weeds may provide the basis for selectivity. Since selectivity is commonly only a matter of degree, it is often desirable to utilize physical selectivity, if possible, in addition to biological selectivity.

Weed–crop morphological differences.   Differences in morphology as a basis for selectivity depend upon biological factors to accomplish a separation between the crop and the weed and point of uptake of the herbicide. In other words, the plant is the source of separation comparable to that provided by physical factors in physical selectivity. The difference in root systems, or more appropriately in their origin within the plant, is one difference in morphology that can be the basis for selectivity. Most dicotyledons have a taproot system that develops from the radicle in the embryo, whereas in most monocotyledons, this primary root

TABLE 12-1

Effect of 2,4-D formulation applied preemergence on stands of corn.

4 Pounds 2,4-D per Acre	Corn Plants per Plot
Butyl ester	45.7
Amine salt	37.4
Untreated	48.8

Source: Data from Aldrich and Willard, 1951.

usually does not survive very long but is replaced by adventitious roots that develop from the coleoptile nodes (Figure 2–10). This characteristic may be utilized with some dicotyledonous crops to provide some measure of protection from a soil-applied herbicide. Where uptake is through the root, development of the radicle and the taproot moves the zone of potential uptake away from the herbicide zone, even if the latter should advance downward. Such separation can be visualized for cotton in the research shown in Figure 12–3 in that shortly after germination of the cotton, its zone of potential herbicide uptake is a few millimeters deeper than the 5 cm (2 in.) at which the cotton seed was planted. For its part, the barnyardgrass initiates its roots in the top 1.2 cm (1/2 in.) of soil and continues to have absorbing roots in this zone because of their development from the coleoptile node.

The coleoptile in grasses is itself an important point of entry for some soil-applied herbicides. The shoot apex is just above the first node of this coleoptile. Grasses differ in where the first node, and thus the growing point, is located in the soil (coleoptile uptake, Chapter 11). The difference in the location of the growing point of wild oat and wheat was the basis of selective control of the weed with diallate shown in Figure 11–7. The actual location of the coleoptilar node in some species appears to be in relation to the seed, and in others, in relation to the soil surface. In barnyardgrass, for example, the node is in the upper 1.2 cm, irrespective of the depth at which the seed is located. In barley, it is within about 1.2 cm of the seed, so depth of planting determines its location relative to the soil surface. This morphological difference may also provide some degree of selectivity.

Weed–crop physiological and metabolic differences. With soil-applied herbicides, selectivity based on physiological and metabolic differences is primarily a matter of what happens after the herbicide enters the plant since most are readily absorbed from the soil. This uptake is apparently less specific than is uptake through the leaves. Although herbicides enter mainly in solution, some, such as trifluralin, also gain entry as a vapor. The fact is that species of plants differ in the quantity of herbicides they can tolerate in the soil environment. A detailed discussion of herbicide physiology and metabolism is beyond the scope of this text. Volumes I and II of *Herbicides: Biochemistry, Physiology, Ecology*, edited by Audus (1976a and 1976b); *Mode of Action of Herbicides* (Ashton and Crafts, 1981); and *Metabolism of Herbicides in Higher Plants* (Hatzios and Penner, 1982) provide thorough treatment of this subject.

For our purposes, we need only recognize that tolerance on the part of one species to a herbicide that kills another is the result of failure of the herbicide to reach and accumulate lethal levels at the sites of action in the tolerant species. This tolerance may be due to differences in translocation, differences in absorption at sites other than the biochemical reaction sites for the herbicides, differences in breakdown of the herbicide within the plant, and differences in the complexing of the herbicide with th· cell constituents.

Translocation of herbicide. Differences between weeds and crops in the ease and extent of movement of herbicides in them provide a basis for selectivity. To reach the sites of action, herbicides must move within the plant, mainly in the xylem. With respect to translocation, it appears that amiben, prometryn, pyrazone, and terbacil are readily transported in the xylem of susceptible weeds to sites of activity in the shoots or leaves; whereas, with amiben and pyrazone at least, they are not readily translocated in wheat and beets, respectively. Tolerance of wheat to amiben is augmented also by the fact that the herbicide joins with constituents within the wheat root cells to form an immobile compound identified as glycosylamiben. This immobile conjugate is not formed in barnyardgrass, which is susceptible to amiben.

Absorption of herbicide. If a herbicide is absorbed at a site other than its site of biochemical reaction, its killing action is prevented. With the phenoxy acid herbicides, it has been found that plants differ in the extent to which they are absorbed on the plant membrane phospholipids. Species with the ability to absorb these herbicides on the membrane phospholipids may thus be protected from injury simply because the herbicide does not reach the sites of biochemical reaction.

Detoxification of herbicide. The ability of tolerant species to detoxify a potential herbicide appears to be the most important single factor contributing to selectivity. The herbicide within the plant represents an alien substance and thus is subject to attack by the enzymes inherent to that species or simply by interactions with chemical constituents of the cell without the aid of enzyme catalysts. Plants contain a large number of chemicals, including enzymes, and differ widely in their biochemical makeup. It is not surprising, therefore, that selectivity frequently is based on the differing ability of the weed and the crop to detoxify the potential herbicide taken up from the soil. Many chemical reactions are involved in herbicide metabolism in plants (Hatzios and Penner, 1982). The most important reactions with respect to selectivity are: (1) oxidation, (2) reduction, (3) hydrolysis, and (4) conjugation.

An example of *oxidation*—that is, the loss of electrons—is provided by 2,4–DB. This chemical is not toxic to plants. However, some plants have the capacity to remove two carbon atoms from the butyric acid side-chain (via beta oxidation), thus creating the highly toxic 2,4–D. Many small-seeded legumes, including alfalfa, are tolerant of 2,4–DB in part because beta oxidation does not occur.

Reduction—that is, the gaining of electrons—of the nitro group of trifluralin by soybean roots probably accounts in part for this crop's tolerance of trifluralin. Susceptible species, such as corn, apparently do not reduce the nitro group.

Differential *hydrolysis*—that is, the addition of water—of s-triazine herbicides provides part of the basis for selectivity of these herbicides. In corn, which is tolerant, hydrolysis of atrazine at the number 2 position on the ring, the basic structure of the herbicide molecule, appears to be mainly responsible for tolerance.

Conjugation—that is, the joining of compounds—is a source of selectivity with many herbicides. In cotton, for example, tolerance to fluorodifen is associated with the joining of the herbicide molecule and glutathione within the cotton plant to form an inactive conjugate.

Antidotes for crop tolerance of herbicide.   Chemicals that have the capacity to make an otherwise sensitive crop tolerant of a herbicide are termed *antidotes* and offer another form of selectivity. This possibility was first reported for the herbicide barban in wheat. Barban is effective for control of several weeds in small grains and other crops but occasionally causes some crop damage. It was found that about 75% of the inhibition of wheat by barban applied to the foliage was prevented by a chemical previously dusted on the wheat seed (Hoffman, 1962). Later, chemicals were found that could protect the crop from herbicides applied to the soil (Burnside et al., 1971), but the quantities needed necessitated seed treatment. Soon thereafter, chemicals were introduced that were sufficiently active and specific that they could be applied to soil (Chang et al., 1973). The protection has been achieved without sacrificing weed control.

Figure 12–5 shows that the degree of protection can be very pronounced. Corn

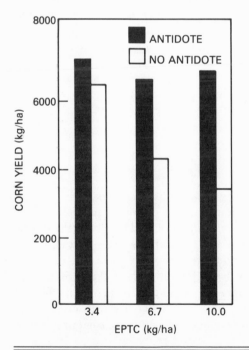

FIGURE 12–5. Protection of otherwise sensitive crops from herbicide injury by use of antidotes. Here corn is protected from EPTC injury by an antidote applied to the corn seed.

Source: Data from Burnside et al., 1971.

treated with an antidote was not damaged by rates of EPTC higher than needed for complete weed control. Without the antidote, corn yields were cut about 10% by the lowest rate and by about 50% by the heaviest rate. This form of selectivity offers a way of extending the use of existing herbicides to the control of some problem weeds, such as the nutsedges, in selected crops where the margin of selectivity is too narrow. Since the protection is a result of chemical reactions within the plant, antidotes provide another type of biological selectivity.

ENVIRONMENTAL FACTORS AFFECTING SUCCESS

Several factors can prevent fully satisfactory weed control with a soil-applied herbicide. The major ones to be examined in some depth here include: (1) adsorption, (2) leaching, (3) evaporation, and (4) decomposition. These are all factors that under certain circumstances can prevent the herbicide from being in contact with the germinating weed seed and developing seedling. Such contact is important in view of the fact that this is the stage when most weeds are most vulnerable to effects from herbicides. Further, if we are to attain the objective of preventing emergence of the weed with the crop, the herbicide must be maximally effective to weeds in this stage of development.

Our major concern here is the influence of each process on results obtained, not the nature of the process itself. A thorough discussion of the processes themselves may be found in Hance (1980) and in Guenzi (1974).

Adsorption

Adsorption is the retention of a dissolved or gaseous substance on or in the surface of the soil particles. As the definition implies, the extent of adsorption is a reflection of surface area. Surface area in turn, is determined largely by the size of the soil particles. The three broad categories of soil particle size—that is, sand, silt, and clay—expose vastly different surface areas. For any given quantity, clay particles (less than 2 μ) have 2,000 times the surface area of silt (2 μ to 50 μ) and 100,000 times the surface area of sand (larger than 50 μ). The practical effect of adsorption on herbicide usage in preventing weed emergence with crops is to require somewhat higher rates on soils high in organic matter and somewhat lower rates on very sandy soils.

Clay and organic colloids.   Most soils contain some clay (inorganic) and organic matter, although quantities may be quite small. Because of its much greater surface, the clay fraction of the inorganic matter is much more important than the other inorganic fractions in adsorption of herbicides in the soil. Further, the clay particles 1 μm or smaller in size are chemically the most reactive. Particles in this size range can be suspended in water and remain suspended for considerable periods of time. These particles are insoluble for the most part and have many of the properties of glue and other plastic materials, which accounts for the name *colloid*, from *kolla*, the Greek word for glue. Organic matter at the right stage in its decomposition also contains particles small enough to be termed colloidal. The particles of inorganic clay and organic matter together provide the soil colloids that are the most important factors in adsorption of herbicides. Figure 12–6 is a diagrammatic representation of the adsorbing phenomenon. The figure shows the particles as having negative charges imparted by unsatisfied oxygen charges (bonds). These unsatisfied charges are points of attachment for positively charged sites of a herbicide molecule.

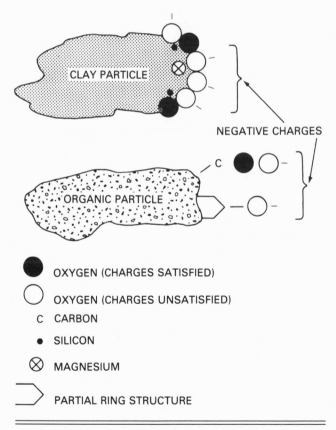

NEGATIVE CHARGES

⬤ OXYGEN (CHARGES SATISFIED)

◯ OXYGEN (CHARGES UNSATISFIED)

C CARBON

• SILICON

⊗ MAGNESIUM

◯/⟩ PARTIAL RING STRUCTURE

FIGURE 12–6. Diagram of clay and organic matter colloidal particles showing the typical negative surface charge that gives the colloid its adsorbing capacity.

Early in the modern herbicide era, it was shown that organic matter and clay adsorbed herbicides and affected their final toxicity. In Table 12–2, we see that there are large differences among the herbicides tested with respect to their adsorption on charcoal. Monuron, CIPC and IPC are nearly completely adsorbed, whereas TCA is only slightly adsorbed. In Table 12–3, we see that adsorption of EPTC is influenced by soil type. Adsorption, in turn, influences toxicity towards oats. We also see that adsorption by dry soil is relatively much larger than by moist soil. In the ensuing years, the degree of adsorption has been shown to be affected by the type of clay, soil pH, temperature, solubility of the herbicide, the herbicide's polarity or lack of it, and its degree of ionization.

Reversibility. We know from the physics of adsorption that simple physical adsorption is reversible. That is, it represents an equilibrium relationship between the concentration of the adsorbed substance in solution and the concentration on the adsorbant. It follows that uptake of an adsorbed herbicide by the weed root or seedling reduces the concentration of the herbicide substance in the soil–water solution, thus allowing some of that adsorbed on the soil particle to go back into solution. It has been found that simple physical adsorption is involved with many herbicides. Since the herbicide in solution is directly available for uptake, it appears that adsorption by itself affects mainly the time required for uptake of a given herbicide rather than the total quantity taken up. Because seedlings of many weeds become progressively less vulnerable to many herbicides as germination and emergence proceed, a delay in uptake due to adsorption by itself may affect

TABLE 12-2

Adsorption of some common herbicides onto charcoal from 10^{-4} solutions with 400 milligrams per liter of charcoal.

Herbicide	Percent Adsorption
Monuron	98
CIPC	98
IPC	96
NPA	82
2,4,5–T	65
2,4–D	49
TBA (principally sodium salt)	32
TCA	13

Source: Leopold et al., 1960. Reproduced with permission of the Weed Science Society of America.

TABLE 12-3

Effect of soil type on the toxicity of EPTC to oats and on the soil adsorption of EPTC vapor.

Soil Type	Organic Matter (%)	Clay (%)	Oats Injury (ED$_{50}$)[1]	Relative Soil Adsorption	
				Soil at Field Capacity	Air-Dry Soil
Egbert series	4.8	79.5	1.55	20	100
Yolo silty clay	2.4	45.0	1.20	14	75
Yolo clay loam	2.4	38.7	0.88	15	70
Yolo sandy clay loam	1.4	22.5	0.44	10	70
Hesperia sandy loam	0.3	16.0	0.24	8	56

[1] The ED$_{50}$ is the concentration in ppm that reduced the fresh weight of oats 50%.

[2] Calculated using adsorption on air-dry Egbert soil as 100, from the original data that were reported in counts per minute of radioactivated EPTC.

Source: Adapted from Ashton and Sheets, 1959. Reproduced with permission of the Weed Science Society of America.

success, but likely only to a minor degree. Exceptions may be: (1) on very sandy soil where all of the applied herbicide may be assumed to be completely available for uptake; (2) on soils very high in organic matter where adsorption is not of the simple physical type but rather involves penetration of the herbicide into the organic particle itself; and (3) where there is a specific absorption within the clay particle, such as that which occurs with the herbicides diquat and paraquat. With diquat and paraquat, the attachment is so strong that doses normally used in agriculture are completely inactivated in the soil.

The effect of clays on glyphosate in the soil also represents a special kind of adsorption. Glyphosate apparently is adsorbed by clays in the presence of iron, aluminum, or other multivalent metals to form insoluble complexes with these soil bases. Although this complex may be partly reversed by the addition of inorganic phosphate, it nonetheless represents a type of adsorption less readily desorbed than where simple adsorption is involved.

Leaching

Leaching is the term applied to the movement of herbicides with water in soil. Such movement can be downward, lateral, or upward. It is most commonly thought of in terms of downward movement because the volume that may move with percolating rainwater or irrigation water is much greater than the volume that moves upward or laterally. Ideally, a herbicide applied to the soil to prevent weed emergence with the crop would be placed in the soil zone from which the weeds originate and remain there until all of the nondormant seeds had germinated. Several factors can prevent this ideal from being realized. First, we need to realize that herbicides that are mainly effective when absorbed by the weed root or young shoot usually need to penetrate the soil some distance to be in contact with these organs. In fact, if the herbicide is mainly effective when absorbed by the root, it commonly needs to be distributed through 5 cm or more of the surface layer of soils to be most effective. On the other hand, with soil-applied herbicides that are mainly absorbed by the coleoptile or shoot, free movement with percolating rainwater can move the herbicide beyond its required soil zone and thereby render the herbicide ineffective. Poor control because of inadequate herbicide movement is much more common as a reason for failure than movement of the herbicide beyond the effective zone.

Effect of adsorption.   Although, as we have seen, adsorption plays only a minor role in total uptake, it plays a major role in leaching. Retention against leaching where adsorption occurs is due to the equilibrium relationship between the herbicide in solution and that adsorbed and absorbed. In the simplest situation of physical adsorption, replacement of the soil solution containing a herbicide with new water results in some movement of the herbicide from the soil particle into the new solution. The movement continues until the same relative proportion of dissolved herbicide to adsorbed herbicide is established—that is, until the equilibration balance for the particular herbicide and soil colloid is attained.

For example, using Monuron or CIPC from Table 12–2, 98% of which was absorbed by activated charcoal, if the solution containing 2% of the applied herbicide is replaced with new water, the same 98:2 relationship will be reestablished. That is, only 2% of the 98% adsorbed releases into the new water. Following this flushing, the charcoal would then have 96.04% of the original application, 98% − (2 × 98%). If this process of flushing is repeated three more times, the resulting percentages on the charcoal will be 94.12%, 92.23%, and 90.39%. If the flushing is assumed to be the result of a rain sufficient to wet or pass completely through the soil zone containing the adsorbed herbicides, even after four such rains, only about 10% of the original application of monuron or CIPC will have moved out of the zone in which it was adsorbed. In most agriculture usage situations, the herbicide accomplishes its intended purpose long before this much percolation has occurred.

Effect of solubility.   Contrary to early belief, solubility is not a major factor in leaching, even though it is true that the portion of the herbicide in solution is the part available to be leached. The reason is found in the relative mass of the soil as opposed to that of the applied herbicide. That is, the amount of applied herbicide is normally extremely small compared to the amount of soil as a potential adsorbing surface and the amount of water as a potential dissolving medium.

This fact can be illustrated by a simple comparison of weights. The weight of the top 15 cm of soil is often estimated to be about 2,242,760 kilograms per hectare. Thus, a 2.2 kilogram per hectare application of herbicide represents about one part of herbicide to one million parts of soil (the potential adsorbent). The space in the plow layer is occupied roughly equally by solid material and by open space, commonly termed *pores*. Thus, there would be roughly 1,500 cubic meters of such open space in the top 15 cm of a hectare of soil. If all of this space was occupied by water, there would be 1,500,000 kg. On a weight-to-weight basis, the water would need only the capacity to dissolve one part of herbicide in about 680,000 parts of water to completely dissolve all of the herbicide in a 2.2 kilogram per hectare application if none of it is adsorbed. Thus, it is adsorption, as influenced by the type of clay and organic colloids present and interacting with the physicochemistry of the herbicide, that largely determines leachability.

The effect of adsorption is well illustrated in Figure 12–7 by the restricted downward movement of the completely soluble amine salt formulation of silvex; 2,4–D; and 2,4,5–T. In this study, 500 cc was enough water to wet dry soil to a depth of about 56 cm (22 in.). Application of 500 cc to wet soil resulted in 450 cc percolating from the bottom of the tubes. Even where 500 cc was added to wet soil, these completely soluble herbicides failed to reach the bottom of the tubes. Retention against downward movement is assumed to be due to adsorption on the soil colloids.

Effect of herbicide formulation. Figure 12–7 also clearly shows that formulation affects herbicide leaching. The ester formulations of 2,4,5–T; 2,4–D; and silvex all penetrated the soil columns less than did the amine formulations. Part of the reason may be differences in solubility since the solubility of the esters is about 16 ppm, whereas the amines are completely soluble. However, solubility by itself is likely to be less important as the explanation than differences in adsorption for the reasons discussed in the previous section.

Differences between the amine salt and ester formulations of silvex; 2,4–D; and 2,4,5–T may also be due to a difference in their amphoteric properties. *Amphoteric* is a term often applied to surfactants and means that they have both a lipophilic and hydrophilic portion on the same molecule. The phenoxyacetic acid herbicides have this property in weak degree. The esters could be expected to have this to a greater extent than the amine salts, thus increasing their adsorption. Irrespective of the explanation, as we saw in Table 12–1, differences in downward movement of 2,4–D formulations can be sufficiently great that amine formulations reduce corn stands significantly, whereas the 2,4–D ester does not.

Impact of leaching. Although the likelihood of leaching causing a readily leached herbicide to be moved out of the zone from which most of the weeds

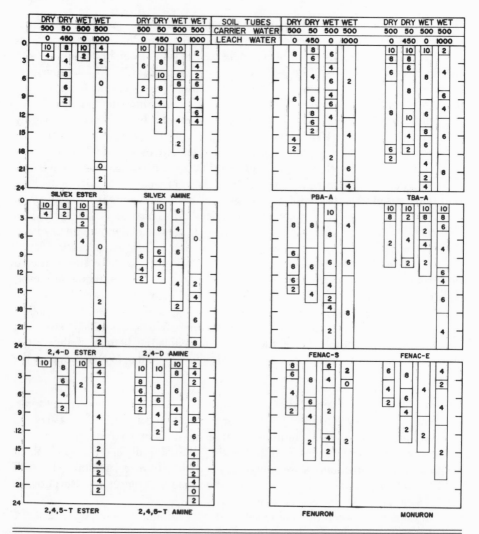

FIGURE 12–7. Differences in herbicides in their downward movement in soil. Soil moisture at time of application also influences the extent of herbicide penetration. The herbicides shown were applied to 7.6 cm (3 in.) soil columns 61 cm (24 in.) deep. Applications were made in the quantities of water shown opposite *Carrier water* and the columns flushed with quantities of water shown opposite *Leach water*. Numbers in bars are injury scores of soybeans grown in soil from the indicated depths; a score of 0 = no injury and 10 = plant dead.

Source: Wiese and Davis, 1964. Reproduced with permission of the Weed Science Society of America.

TABLE 12-4

Effect of depth of planting on reduction in corn stands from 2,4-D amine applied 4 days after planting. A 0.6 in. rain occurred immediately after application that was sufficient to wet at least to the seed level.

| Pounds of 2,4-D per Acre | Corn Plants per Plot* | |
	Planted 1½ in.	Planted 3½ in.
0	65.4	66.1
1	61.2	62.5
2	61.5	58.6
4	56.0	49.9

*Average of 3 replications.
Source: Aldrich, 1950.

originate is minimal, some evidence suggests that this situation may occur. As can be seen in Figure 12–7, for all herbicides except Fenac-E, flushing with 1000 cc of water reduced the amount of herbicides in the surface 2.5 cm (1 in.) to the point that soybeans were only moderately affected, if at all. Indirect evidence supporting this possibility under field conditions is found in earlier work by Aldrich (1950), reported in Table 12–4. Aldrich found that corn stands were reduced more in a planting 9 cm (3 1/2 in.) deep than in one 3.8 cm (1 1/2 in.) deep when rain immediately followed the application, thus suggesting that rain reduced the 2,4–D concentration in soil closer to the surface.

There is also evidence that herbicides may move upward in the soil and in sufficient quantity to be toxic to plants germinating or growing in that area (Figure 12–8). The horizontal bars in the figure show the fresh weight of oats, a species sensitive to dicamba and diphenimid, as a percent of untreated when grown in the greenhouse on soil from each depth. Covering after watering provided for downward but not upward movement of the herbicides. Leaving open after watering allowed evaporation to occur, thus providing for upward movement. The dry-open treatment provided a check against the importance of water as a vehicle for movement. As can be seen, growth of oats was only slightly reduced above or below the herbicide zone in the dry soil, indicating little herbicide movement. Oat growth in the top 2.5 cm (1 in.) of soil was reduced more than 75% by dicamba in the wet-open treatment, showing it is readily moved upward by water evaporation. By

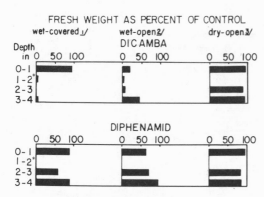

FRESH WEIGHT AS PERCENT OF CONTROL

¹Received 1 surface inch of water and covered
to prevent evaporation
²As treatment 1, but water was allowed to
evaporate freely from the soil surface.
³Soil left air-dry and uncovered.
*Herbicides were applied at this level.

FIGURE 12–8. Toxicity to oats from upward movement of the mobile herbicide dicamba in soil. Enough dicamba, which is weakly adsorbed on colloids if at all, moves to the top 2.5 cm (1 in.) soil layer when provided conditions for evaporation (wet-open) to reduce oat fresh weight more than 75%. Diphenamid, which presumably is adsorbed, does not move away from the point of application enough to cut fresh weight even 50% under any treatment.

Source: Harris, 1964. Reproduced with permission of the Weed Science Society of America.

contrast, oat growth exceeded 50% of untreated for all diphenimid treatments except the applied level, which shows diphenimid is relatively immobile.

Figure 12–9 suggests that both the total amount of percolating water and its intensity influence extent of downward movement. Further, adsorption has a marked modifying effect. Dicamba, which apparently is adsorbed weakly if at all, is removed from the top 7.5 cm (3 in.) with 12.5 cm (5 in.) of water, providing the water is added in small increments. If it is added in 2.5 cm (1 in.) increments, even 25 cm (10 in.) does not remove the dicamba. Just the opposite occurs with diphenamid, which apparently is adsorbed. That is, more downward movement occurs when water is added in large rather than in small increments. The results with diphenamid are understandable from what we learned about adsorption and desorption. Dicamba, on the other hand, is dependent for its movement on being dissolved in water passing through the surface of the soil. In this situation, time

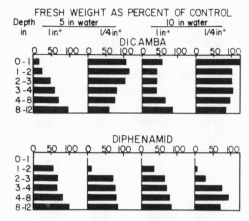

FRESH WEIGHT AS PERCENT OF CONTROL

*Increments of 0.25 and of 1 surface inch
were poured directly onto the column surfaces at 30-minute intervals for the 5 in.
treatment. The 10 in. treatment was exactly
the same as two 5 in. treatments on two
successive days.

FIGURE 12–9. Effects of duration and intensity of leaching on movement of unadsorbed or weakly adsorbed diphenamid and readily adsorbed dicamba in soil. Bars showing growth of the test plant, oats, in soil from the several depths are a measure of herbicide amount at the depth indicated.

Source: Harris, 1964. Reproduced with permission of the Weed Science Society of America.

becomes a factor. Where 12.5 cm (5 in.) of water was applied in 0.6 cm (1/4 in.) increments every 30 minutes, 10 hours was required to make the necessary 20 applications. In effect, therefore, the dicamba on the soil surface under this water treatment was available for pickup in the passing water for 10 hours. Where the 12.5 cm was applied in 2.5 cm increments, the time for pickup was only 2 1/2 hours.

In summary, leaching, which is controlled by adsorption and by the amount and duration of water moving through the herbicide zone, may affect results in a number of ways. It may help move the herbicide into the soil zone critical for best weed control. It may move the herbicide out of this critical zone for weed control, thus detracting from satisfactory prevention of emergence. Or, it may either reduce or increase the hazard of damage to the germinating crop seed and developing seedling.

Evaporation

Evaporation is the third major source of variability in success of herbicides used to prevent weed emergence. For many herbicides, it can be the most important source of loss from the soil during the first few weeks following application. The extent of such loss under certain circumstances can be substantial. Hartley (1960) calculated that EPTC, which is one of the most volatile herbicides, could be lost from a glass surface at a rate of 76 kilograms per hectare per day. Since EPTC and other volatile herbicides are used successfully as soil applications, there must be factors in the soil that prevent rates of evaporative loss such as calculated by Hartley. Adsorption and soil moisture are two such factors that greatly influence evaporative loss.

Effect of adsorption.   Adsorption, especially upon dry soil (Table 12–3), is a major reason even the volatile herbicides are not lost from the surface more quickly. Gaseous substances tend to condense on solids—especially those solids having a collection of molecules with residual attraction, such as clay and organic particles in soil—rather than remain associated with one another. This attraction is especially strong in dry soil because of limited competition with water for which soil particles have a stronger attraction. The soil surface available for adsorption of a gas is very large. Roughly one half of the soil bulk is open space available to gas penetration if not filled with water. It is also segregated into variable-sized clumps that frequently contain clay and organic matter particles with very large surface areas. Recognizing that the soil surface is frequently dry when the herbicide is applied, we can therefore understand why even a very volatile herbicide does not rapidly dissipate into the atmosphere.

The clay and organic matter in the soil effectively hold volatile herbicides, just as they do those in solution. Table 12–5 shows the combined relationships between these soil components and loss of the volatile herbicide EPTC from soil. Loss from the higher organic matter and clay soil (heavy texture) clearly is less than from the lower organic matter and clay soil (light texture). This work was done under laboratory conditions where the EPTC was added to soil wetted to different moisture levels then allowed to dry at room temperature. Since the quantity of soil was relatively small, we might expect that nearly all of the soil particles offered an opportunity for evaporation of the adsorbed EPTC. Thus, evaporation under these conditions might be greater than would be expected under field conditions, where some of the herbicide might be at a depth at which access to the atmosphere via evaporation is restricted.

Figure 12–10 shows losses of the several s-triazine herbicides from a metal surface (Figure 12–10A) and of prometone from five different soils (Figure 12–10B). Simazine (number 1 in A), among the least volatile of the herbicides, did have some loss from the metal. The most volatile of these seven s-triazines, prometone (number 4 in A), by contrast lost only about 10% of the amount

TABLE 12-5

Composition of soils and its effect on the loss of EPTC-S^{35} applied at 10 ppm during the evaporation of various amounts of soil water from wet soil.

Soil	pH	Percent of Organic Matter	Clay	Percent Loss of EPTC during Drying of Soil Containing[2] 33% Water	50% Water	60% Water
Light texture						
Loamy sand from Klamath[1]	7.6	0.9	5	64	78	80
Ritzville very fine sandy loam	6.9	1.7	15	66	76	78
Newberg sandy loam	6.3	1.5	19	74	82	84
Heavy texture						
Chehalis loam	5.8	2.8	24	48	53	67
Loam from Eastern Oregon[1]	7.5	2.1	25	59	64	80
Willamette silty clay loam	6.8	4.0	34	52	61	66
Melbourne clay	5.5	4.9	49	40	43	61
Peat	5.6	83.3	—	14	15	25

[1] Soil series unknown.

[2] Average of triplicate determinations.

Source: Fang et al., 1961. Reproduced with permission of the Weed Science Society of America.

originally applied in 24 hours in all soils except the tifton loamy sand. The latter soil had the lowest combined content of clay and organic matter, again suggesting the importance of these components in reducing evaporative loss. Nearly 80% of the prometone was lost in 2 hours from the metal surface.

Effect of soil moisture. Soil moisture plays a key role in herbicide loss through evaporation. It does so through its effect on retention of the herbicide on soil particles and on movement of the herbicide with water during evaporation. As discussed earlier, adsorption on dry soil can be especially strong. Fang and his co-workers (1961) found no loss of even the most volatile of herbicides—in this case, EPTC—from dry soil after 42 days in the open. This situation, of course, is not usually encountered in the agricultural use of herbicides.

The more usual situation is one in which the soil is moist, at least just below the soil surface, and rains occur at intervals following application. These conditions present a much different situation relative to evaporative loss of herbicide. As we

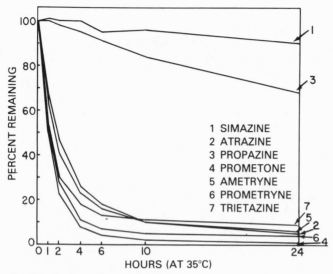

A. s-Triazine losses from metal surface

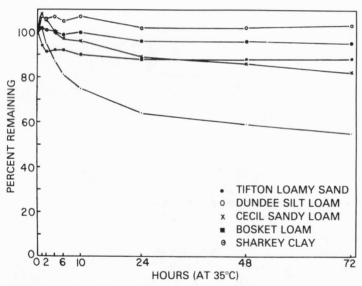

B. Prometone loss from five different soils

FIGURE 12–10. Effect of surface type on herbicide evaporation.

Source: Kearney et al., 1964. Reproduced with permission of the Weed Science Society of America.

have already seen, gases (volatile herbicides) tend to condense on soil particles. However, many clays and organic matter are strongly hydrophilic. That is, they readily displace other substances, such as an adsorbed herbicide, with water. The displaced herbicide, depending upon its volatility, may then evaporate or be carried off with the evaporating water, depending upon the moisture conditions. Referring back to Table 12–5, we see that the amount of moisture in the soil does affect loss of EPTC. If we consider only the soils identified as having heavy texture, the average relative loss is 1.0:1.1:1.4 for the three increasing moisture contents, respectively. Again, these results were obtained under laboratory conditions where all of the soil was provided the opportunity to lose its adsorbed EPTC. Nonetheless, this study indicates that since moisture is commonly available immediately beneath the surface or at the surface following rainfall, soil moisture is commonly a factor in evaporative loss. If sufficient opportunity for evaporative loss occurs during the period immediately following application, preventive weed control could be poor. On the other hand, if an extended dry period is followed by a rainy period, herbicidal effects may appear due to the displacement of the absorbed herbicide by water. In this case, whether or not the treatment is effective depends upon the point of entry for the particular herbicide and stage of growth of the weeds at the time.

Effect of incorporation.   Mechanically mixing the herbicide with the surface few inches of soil is called *incorporation*. Now a common practice with many soil-applied herbicides, incorporation is done to improve control by distributing the herbicide throughout the zone from which a majority of the weeds originate and to reduce loss from volatility.

Figure 12–11 is representative of the improvement in weed control that can be obtained by this practice. Incorporating EPTC reduced the amount needed by about one half, as can be seen by comparing 2.2 kilograms per hectare (2 pounds per acre) incorporated with 4.4 kilograms (4 pounds) not incorporated. The barnyardgrass in this study was actually planted at 1.2 cm (1/2 in.) below the soil surface. Two important points about incorporated treatments can be made from the data obtained.

First, where the herbicide involved is taken up both by the shoot and the root—as is the case with EPTC—best results are obtained if the herbicide is distributed deeply enough for the root system to be exposed. Thus, even though the barnyardgrass was seeded at 1.2 cm, best control with the lowest two rates used was obtained where the EPTC was incorporated to a depth of 2.5 cm (1 in.). With the herbicide incorporated to this depth, the emerging root of the barnyardgrass is exposed to it for the first 1.2 cm of growth made beyond the seed.

Second, control is less effective if the herbicide is distributed throughout at too great a depth unless an excessive rate is used. Poorer control would appear to be simply a result of the dilution effect. Diluting the 454 g (1 lb) application by mixing

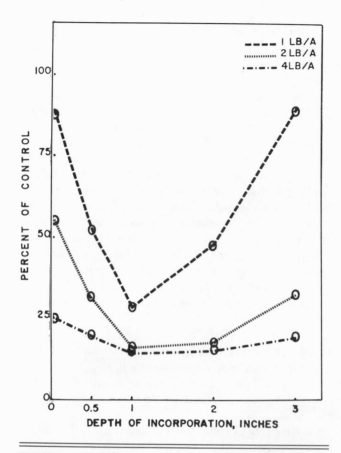

FIGURE 12–11. Soil incorporation as a means to greatly improve weed control with volatile herbicides applied to soil. Here, 2.2 kilograms of EPTC per hectare (2 pounds per acre) incorporated was as effective in controlling barnyardgrass as 4.4 kilograms (4 pounds) not incorporated.

Source: Ashton and Dunster, 1961. Reproduced with permission of the Weed Science Society of America.

it in the top 7.6 cm (3 in.) reduced the amount in the vicinity of the barnyardgrass below that needed for control.

Even though incorporation can substantially reduce herbicide loss by evaporation, evaporation loss may still be substantial. This occurrence is mainly the result of mass flow of water to the surface as a result of evaporation from that soil surface. As long as the surface of the soil is moist, providing for a continuity of the capillaries in the soil within which the water must move, upward movement will occur as evaporation takes place. Because the soil is a relatively poor wick—that is, the capillaries are not continuous vertical tubes but are more a network of open spaces laced with many interruptions—upward movement may be only a few centimeters. In view of the fact that the relatively shallow surface zone of soil is the source of most annual weeds in a given crop, this movement may nonetheless be sufficient to reduce weed control. This source of loss may be significant even for relatively nonvolatile herbicides because the movement in mass flow with water to the surface may result in accumulation of the herbicide at that point until it reaches the evaporative level. The frequency and amount of rainfall determines the degree of such loss.

Effect of temperature.   Temperature acts as a modifier of all types of evaporative loss. In quite general terms, the temperature effect roughly doubles evaporation for each $10°$ to $15°$ rise. This effect is clearly demonstrated in Figure 12–12. Loss of atrazine ranged from about 20% to 40% at 35°C for the five soils (Figure 12–12A) and from about 30% to 60% at 45°C (Figure 12–12B).

Decomposition

Microbial decomposition.   *Decomposition*—that is, the breakdown of the herbicide into nontoxic components—is the fourth major factor that may influence results from soil applications. Given sufficient time, the microflora and microfauna present in the soil have the ability, or can adapt to obtain such ability, to degrade literally any compound introduced to the soil. It has been well established that such microbial degradation plays a key role in the ultimate dissipation of most herbicides in soil. However, the brief time frame (only a few weeks) within which the herbicide needs to be available in the soil makes microbial decomposition a relatively unimportant factor in determining the success of a given soil application for weed control. The exception may be where the same herbicide is used in successive years. It was found early in the history of 2,4–D (Audus, 1949) that degradation in soil was more rapid with successive applications. Subsequent research has shown that degradation of other herbicides is similarly affected. The extent of this effect is shown for EPTC in Figure 12–13. EPTC was broken down more quickly in soil previously treated (solid line) than in previously untreated soil (dashed line). Although not shown in the figure, the half-life where EPTC had been used annually for 8 years was only one half (9 days) that of EPTC in previously untreated soil (18 days). This factor may be especially important in success with soil-applied herbicides under a monoculture crop system.

Nonbiological decomposition.   Nonbiological degradation of herbicides may also occur. Soil, after all, is a complex of surfaces and chemicals with which reactive herbicides may interact. For example, the negative charge on clays makes

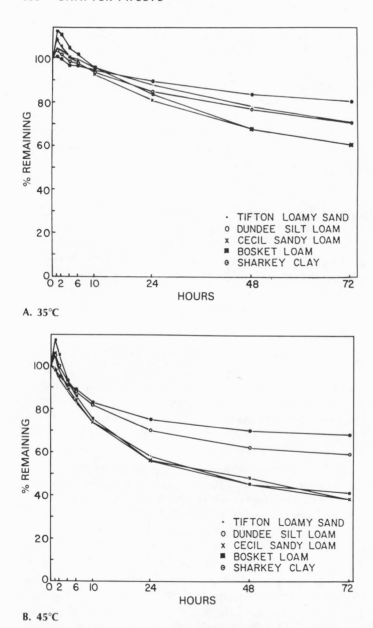

A. 35°C

B. 45°C

FIGURE 12–12. Pronounced effect of temperature on evaporation of herbicides from soil as shown by the loss of atrazine from five soils.

Source: Kearney et al., 1964. Reproduced with permission of the Weed Science Society of America.

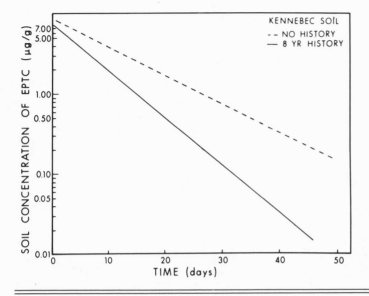

FIGURE 12–13. Effect of previous application on hastening degradation of a soil-applied herbicide.
Source: Obrigawitch et al., 1982. Reproduced with permission of the Weed Science Society of America.

them cationic exchangers. Organic matter itself provides a wide variety of reactive chemicals; numerous reactive metals are typically associated with the clays (magnesium, iron, copper, and so forth); and the clays have acidic and basic sites. Finally, water is nearly always present to act as a solvent, to permit formation of acid and amine salts, and as to serve as a medium for many chemical reactions. Even though reactions involving the soil capabilities have been demonstrated in a number of studies under laboratory conditions, few examples exist where such reactions have been a major factor in the poor results from soil applications except in very unusual conditions for selected herbicides.

Photodegradation decomposition. Photodegradation, on the other hand, may have a pronounced effect on success of soil applications of many herbicides. Light in the range from about 290 nm to 450 nm is a highly effective energizer of several common reactions, such as oxidation, reduction, elimination, hydrolysis, substitution, and isomerization. We now know that many herbicides may have their activity reduced if exposed to light for any length of time on the soil surface.

Figure 12–14 shows that the detoxification effect of sunlight may be very pronounced with even a relatively brief exposure. In this case, trifluralin was completely degraded in 4 hours. Among the other herbicides found to be sensitive to photodegradation are amiben (Sheets, 1963), diuron and monuron (Harris and

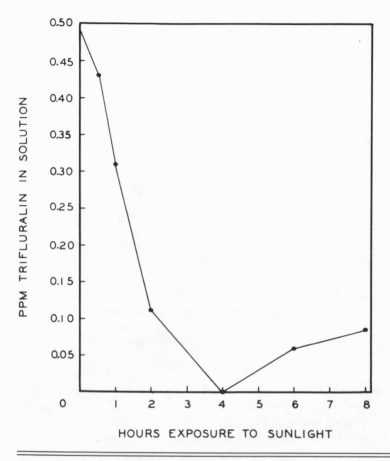

FIGURE 12–14. Rapid detoxification effect of sunlight on herbicides. Here trifluralin activity was measured by sorghum bioassay.

Source: Messersmith et al., 1971. Reproduced with permission of the Weed Science Society of America.

Warren, 1964), the s-triazines (Jordan et al., 1963), and paraquat and diquat (Crosby and Tang, 1969).

Anything that prevents exposure to direct sunlight reduces the loss. Under field conditions, herbicide loss is commonly less than that observed under controlled laboratory or greenhouse conditions. In the field, the soil, at least from the vantage point of the herbicide it contains, does not expose a smooth surface to the sun. Rather, the soil contains clumps of varying size and an uneven topography that protect some parts from direct sunlight. In addition, adsorption, which, as we

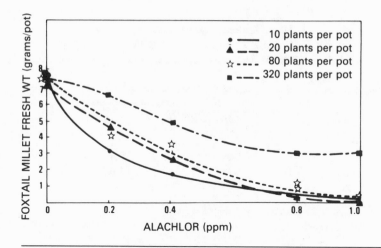

FIGURE 12–15. Influence of seed and seedling density on effectiveness of alachlor applied to soil.

Source: Winkle et al., 1981. Reproduced with permission of the Weed Science Society of America.

have already seen may be substantial for many herbicides, also protects against photodegradation. Under field usage, of course, loss from photodegradation is essentially prevented by incorporating the herbicides for which this may be a problem.

Weed–Crop Density

Since removal of any part of the applied herbicide from the soil reduces that available for weed control, it follows that the number of weed and crop seeds present may influence control. Indeed, this effect has been found with atrazine (Hoffman and Lavy, 1978; and Winkle et al., 1981), diuron (Burrill and Appleby, 1978) and alachlor (Winkle et al., 1981).

The relationship between alachlor rate and foxtail millet (*Setaria italica* L. Beauv.) seeding rate shown in Figure 12–15 indicates that the effect may be quite pronounced. At the densest seeding rate, even the highest rate of alachlor (1.0 ppm) only reduced growth of the test species about 60%; whereas at the lowest density, the same reduction of growth was accomplished with only one-fifth as much alachlor (0.2 ppm). Table 12–6 provides the explanation. As density increases, the amount of alachlor absorbed per plant decreases. Thus, at the high density, less herbicide is available in the plant to exert herbicidal effect.

TABLE 12-6

Absorption of alachlor by foxtail millet as affected by plant density. Plants grown in pots containing 170g of Sharpsburg silty clay loam soil were harvested 21 days after treatment.

Foxtail Millet (plants/pot)	Alachlor Rate (ppmw)	Alachlor Absorbed	
		(ng/seedling)	(µg/g fresh weight)
20	0.4	42	0.7
80	0.4	20	0.4
20	0.8	96	64.0
80	0.8	40	0.7

Note: Data represents average of 2 experiments with 2 replications.

Source: Winkle et al., 1981. Reproduced with permission of the Weed Science Society of America.

HERBICIDE PERSISTENCE IN THE SOIL

The persistence of a herbicide following application to soil is important in three respects. First, it is a factor influencing weed control with a given application and of applications in subsequent years. As discussed in the previous section, some herbicides may not persist long enough to provide the needed weed control. With others, persistence in subsequent years may be reduced to the point that control is inadequate. Second, persistence also is important through its potential effect on contamination of the environment. For example, the longer a herbicide remains on or in the soil, the greater the chance of its being moved to adjacent areas or water supplies in water runoff and percolation and with soil itself in water and wind erosion. Third, persistence is important as a possible source of injury to other crops grown on the field the following year. A notable example is injury to soybeans the year following weed control with atrazine in corn.

Factors Affecting Rate of Loss

The relative persistence of several herbicides in soil is shown in Figure 12–16. Each bar represents the time required for the loss of 75% to 100% of the bioactivity from a normal rate and under normal agricultural conditions. Of course, many factors may cause persistence of a specific application to be quite different from that shown. The four factors previously discussed for their effect on success— adsorption, leaching, evaporation, and decomposition—are primary mechanisms for removal. Uptake by the plants and mechanical removal in runoff and erosion are secondary mechanisms. The several factors that may influence rate of loss under field conditions were reviewed by Hurle and Walker (1980).

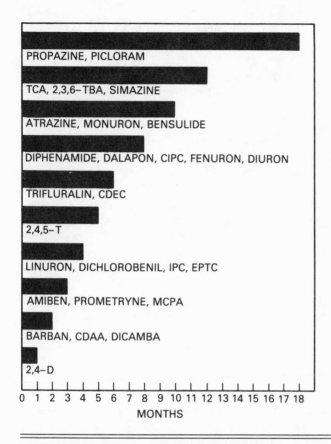

FIGURE 12–16. Relative persistence of herbicides in soil.
Source: Adapted from Kearney et al., 1969.

Rate of application. There are herbicides and circumstances for which the rate of disappearance is influenced by initial amount applied. However, it is concluded that persistence only increases disproportionately if unusually high rates of application are used.

Soil type. Because all primary mechanisms for removal may be influenced by soil type with more than one type involved at the same time, it is difficult to identify specific effects. Organic matter, through its effect on microbial populations and on adsorption, has been shown to be an aspect of soil type that influences persistence. However, the relationship between degradation and adsorption as influenced by organic matter may be antagonistic or complementary, depending upon the herbicide.

Adsorption.   There is no clear-cut, consistent effect of adsorption on persistence. It does not always protect against degradation nor always result in faster loss.

Soil pH.   Soil pH affects persistence. Here again, the effect varies with the herbicide, the pH range involved, and other treatment of the soil.

Soil amendments.   There are instances of an increase in degradation from additions of soil amendments, such as plant residues. Conversely, instances have been recorded where such additions slowed degradation. Effects of additions of mineral nutrients (nitrogen, phosphorus, and potassium) were also variable.

Temperature and moisture.   The effect of temperature approaches a constant because of its effect on the rate of chemical reactions. Similarly, degradation increases with moisture content up to field capacity. The significance of these factors for field use is that herbicide persistence is greater in the cooler northern and dryer regions than in semitropical regions.

Distribution in soil.   Incorporation of herbicides subject to loss through volatilization, photodecomposition, or both—trifluralin and EPTC, for example—markedly increases persistence. Rate of degradation is less in subsoil than in topsoil, and the relationship with depth tends to be linear for some herbicides studied.

Repeat treatment.   As mentioned under factors affecting success, some herbicides are degraded more rapidly in repeat applications. The mechanism is discussed in the next section. At the other extreme, no evidence exists that repeat applications at recommended rates leads to accumulation of toxic levels.

Cropping.   Cropping practices can have various effects on herbicide persistence in soil. As mentioned earlier, the number of weed and crop seeds available to take up an applied herbicide may affect the degree of weed control. It follows that the amount of weed and crop biomass present may influence the removal of an applied herbicide and, thus, its persistence. Indeed, this effect has been shown in some instances, although the amount so removed is probably not very large. Further, the extent of plant cover may well influence both soil temperature and soil moisture. A dense crop cover might reduce both, thus decreasing the rate of decomposition. Thus, the influences of cropping on herbicide persistence may well be counteracting.

Herbicide formulation.   Granular formulations of volatile herbicides are more persistent than emulsions, miscible liquids, or wettable powders. Persistence can also be greater for nonvolatile herbicides formulated as granules. Weather conditions largely determine the importance of formulation effect. Increased persistence of granules is likely to be significant mainly for herbicides such as atrazine that already pose a potential carryover hazard for certain crops such as soybeans.

Pesticide combinations.   There is evidence that herbicide persistence can be extended by applications of fungicides, insecticides, and other herbicides. There is also evidence that degradation of some herbicides can be increased by other pesticides. Where herbicide loss is influenced by other pesticides, it apparently is due to combined effects on microbial activity.

Microbial Decomposition

Irrespective of the mechanism by which a herbicide is removed from a given area, decomposition, or degradation, ultimately determines its fate in the environment at large. Further, microorganisms are able to degrade literally any compound introduced into the soil, but the time required and, as we just saw, the rate of breakdown may vary. Thus, it is useful to have a general understanding of microbial decomposition of herbicides. Microorganisms mainly involved in herbicide decomposition are bacteria, fungi, and actinomycetes capable of using natural carbon compounds (Hiltbold, 1974). The ability to utilize the carbon of an applied herbicide largely determines the shape and slope of the decomposition curve.

Direct metabolism of herbicide.   If microorganisms are able to develop the enzymes necessary to directly metabolize a given herbicide, then availability of the herbicide results in expansion of that microbial population. Under these circumstances, an initial lag period is followed by rapid disappearance of the herbicide. Also, such herbicides commonly break down more rapidly in subsequent applications. Among the herbicides that serve as a direct source of energy are 2,4-D; MCPA; chlorpropham; endothal; TCA; dalapon; chloridazon; and CEPC (2-chloroethyl-N-[3-chlorophenyl] carbamate).

Incidental metabolism of herbicide.   If production of the necessary enzymes is not induced, the microbial decomposition that does occur is dependent upon the size and activity of the existing microbial population and the concentration of the herbicide. In this situation, degradation is coincidental to the growth of microorganisms on some other carbon source. The rate of loss tends to be constant and unaffected by previous application. Some of the herbicides degraded in this way are simazine, linuron, monuron, triallate, and diuron. Additions of the other carbon source might be expected to increase the rate of disappearance of such herbicides by increasing the population of the microorganisms responsible for coincidental metabolism (cometabolism). Indeed, adding microbial nutrient broth, sucrose, plant residues, and manure to soil increased the rate of herbicide disappearance for some herbicides (Hurle and Walker, 1980). For a detailed discussion of microbial processes in soil as factors in herbicide persistence, see the review by Kaufmann and Kearney (1976).

CONCEPTS AND CONCLUSIONS

1. For soil-applied herbicides, selectivity may be based on both physical and biological factors.
2. Selectivity based on physical factors is the result of a separation in space between the crop seed and the herbicide. It may be accomplished by mechanical means, by the use of absorptive barriers, or by the use of herbicide formulation.
3. Selectivity based on biological factors is the result of differences in morphology and in internal physiology and metabolism of the crop and weed. Antidotes are a type of biological selectivity provided by the use of a second chemical that prevents the herbicide from expressing its activity in an otherwise sensitive crop.
4. Adsorption on soil particles, leaching, evaporation, and decomposition can reduce effectiveness of soil-applied herbicides in preventing weed emergence. The first three factors may also be responsible for crop injury from otherwise safe herbicides.
5. Persistence in soil is important as a factor influencing weed control with a given application and of application in subsequent years, as a possible source of carryover injury to crops that follow, and as a potential effect on contamination of the environment.
6. Adsorption, leaching, evaporation, and decomposition are primary mechanisms of herbicide removal from soil. Uptake by plants and physical removal in runoff and in soil erosion are secondary mechanisms of removal.
7. Decomposition by microorganisms may be the result of either utilization of the herbicide as a source of carbon for growth or breakdown coincidental to utilization of some other carbon source. With the former mechanism, decomposition increases with time; with the latter, it remains more or less constant.

REFERENCES

Aldrich, R.J. 1950. Factors affecting the practicability of the preemergence use of 2,4–D on corn, Ph.D. dissertation. Ohio State University, Columbus.
———, and C.J. Willard. 1951. Factors affecting the preemergence use of 2,4–D in corn. Weeds 1 (4):338–45.

Ashton, F.M., and A.S. Crafts. 1981. Mode of action of herbicides, 2nd ed. New York: Wiley.

————, and K. Dunster. 1961. The herbicidal effect of EPTC, CDEC, and CDAA on *Echinochloa crusgali* with various depths of soil incorporation. Weeds 9 (2):312–17.

————, and T.J. Sheets. 1959. The relationship of soil adsorption of EPTC to oats injury in various soil types. Weeds 7 (1):88–90.

Audus, L.J. 1949. Biological detoxification of 2,4–D. Plant Soil 2:31–35.

Audus, L.J., ed. 1976a. Herbicides: Physiology, biochemistry, ecology, 2nd ed., vol. 1. New York: Academic Press.

————. 1976b. Herbicides: Physiology, biochemistry, ecology, 2nd ed. vol. 2. New York: Academic Press.

Burnside, O.C., G.A. Wicks, and C.R. Fenster. 1971. Protecting corn from herbicide injury by seed treatment. Weed Sci. 19(5):565–68.

Burrill, L.C., and A.P. Appleby. 1978. Influence of Italina ryegrass on efficacy of diuron herbicide. Agron. J. 70:505–07.

Chang, F.Y., G.R. Stephenson, and J.D. Bandsen. 1973. Comparative effects of three EPTC antidotes. Weed Sci. 21(4):292–95.

Crosby, D.G., and C.S. Tang. 1969. Photodecomposition of 3-(p-chlorophenyl)-1,1-dimethylurea (monuron). J. Agr. Fd. Chem. 17:1041–44.

Fang, S.C., P. Theisen, and V.H. Freed. 1961. Effects of water evaporation, temperature and, rates of application on the retention of the ethyl-N, N-di-n-propylthiolcarbamate in various soils. Weeds 9 (4):569–74.

Guenzi, W.D., ed. 1974. Pesticides in soil and water. Madison, Wis.: Soil Science Society of America, Inc.

Hance, R.J., ed. 1980. Interactions between herbicides and the soil. New York: Academic Press.

Harris, C.J. 1964. Movement of dicamba and diphenamid in soils. Weeds 12 (2):112–15.

————, and G.F. Warren. 1964. Adsorption and desorption of herbicides by soil. Weeds 12 (2):120–26.

Hartley, G.S. 1960. Physiochemical aspects of the availability of herbicides in soils. In E.K. Woodford and C.R. Sagar, eds., Herbicides and the soil, pp. 63–78. Oxford, England: Blackwell Scientific.

Hatzios, K.K., and D. Penner. 1982. Metabolism of herbicides in higher plants. Minneapolis: Burgess Publishing.

Hauser, E.W. 1965. Preemergence activity of three thiocarbamate herbicides in relation to depth of placement in the soil. Weeds 13 (3):255–57.

Hiltbold, A.E. 1974. Persistence of pesticides in soil. In W.D. Guenzi, ed., Pesticides in soil and water, pp. 203–22. Madison, Wis.: Soil Science Society of America, Inc.

Hoffman, D.W., and T.L. Lavy. 1978. Plant competition for atrazine. Weed Sci. 26(1):94–99.

Hoffman, O.L. 1962. Chemical seed treatments as herbicidal antidotes. Weeds 10(4):322–23.

Holly, K. 1976. Selectivity in relation to formulation and application methods. In L.J. Audus, ed., Herbicides: Physiology, biochemistry, ecology, 2nd ed., vol. 2, pp. 249–77. New York: Academic Press.

Holstun, J.T., and O.B. Wooten. 1964. A promising new concept: Triband application of herbicides. Agr. Chem. 19:24–25, 123–24.

Hurle, K., and A. Walker. 1980. Persistence and its prediction. In R.J. Hance, ed., Interactions between herbicides and the soil, pp. 83–122. New York: Academic Press.

Jordan, L.S., B.E. Day, and W.A. Clerx. 1963. Photodecomposition of triazine. Weeds 12 (3):5–6.

Kaufmann, D.D., and P.C. Kearney. 1976. Microbial transformations in the soil. In L.J. Audus, ed., Herbicides: Physiology, biochemistry, ecology, 2nd ed., vol. 2, pp. 29–64. New York: Academic Press.

Kearney, P.C., R.G. Nash, and A.R. Isensee. 1969. Persistence of pesticide residues in soils. In M.W. Miller and G.G. Berg, eds., Chemicals fallout: Current research on persistent pesticides. Springfield, Ill.: Charles C. Thomas.

Kearney, P.C., T.J. Sheets, and J.W. Smith. 1964. Volatility of seven s-triazines. Weeds 12 (2):83–87.

Kemper, H.M., J.H. Miller, and L.M. Carter. 1963. Preemergence herbicides incorporated in moist soils for control of annual grass in irrigated cotton. Weeds 11 (4):300–07.

Leopold, A.C., P. van Schaik, and M. Neal. 1960. Molecular structure and herbicide adsorption. Weeds 8 (1):48–54.

Messersmith, C.G., O.C. Burnside, and T.L. Lavy. 1971. Biological and non-biological dissipation of trifluralin from soil. Weed Sci. 19 (3):285–90.

Obrigawitch, T., et al. 1982. The influence of temperature, moisture, and prior EPTC application on the degradation of EPTC in soils. Weed Sci. 30 (2):175–84.

Sheets, T.J. 1963. Photochemical alteration and inactivation of amiben. Weeds 11 (3):186–90.

Wiese, A.F., and R.G. Davis. 1964. Herbicide movement in soil with various amounts of water. Weeds 12 (2):101–03.

Winkle, M.E., J.R.C. Leavitt, and O.C. Burnside. 1981. Effects of weed density on herbicide absorption and bioactivity. Weed Sci. 29 (4):405–09.

MINIMIZING COMPETITION AND REDUCING PROPAGULES WITH HERBICIDES

13

As with soil application, applying herbicides to growing weeds in crops has some clear-cut advantages. One obvious advantage is that the weed problem is known both in terms of species and their numbers. There is a growing list of herbicides that can be used to selectively remove either grass or broadleaf weeds from most crops; some can selectively remove both from some crops. Therefore, the choice of herbicide and, in fact, the decision to apply it can be governed by the specific weed problem present. By contrast, soil applications must be based on the assumption that specific weeds that can be controlled with a given herbicide will be present and in sufficient numbers to warrant control. Climatic conditions, time of planting, and other factors may indeed affect both the numbers and kinds of weeds present, as we have already seen.

A second advantage with treatment of the growing crop–weed complex is that smaller dosages are usually needed than with soil application. This result is largely due to the diluting effect of soil on soil—applied herbicides.

A third advantage is less direct but highly important nevertheless, especially to a long-term weed management effort: Herbicide treatment of the growing weed–crop complex can provide a more feasible way to reduce weed seed production. Rates even lower than those needed for postemergence control may be adequate for preventing weed seed production. Further, with proper timing, it may be possible to combine treatments to minimize competition and treatment to prevent seed production. With soil treatment, in addition to the need for higher rates, unless weed emergence is completely prevented, a second treatment will be needed to prevent seed production by the weed escapes.

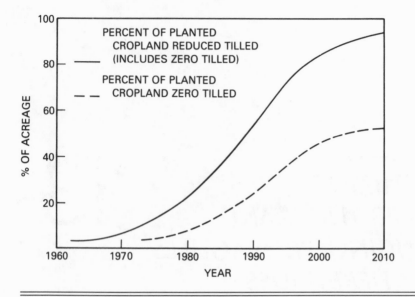

FIGURE 13–1. Estimated adoption of minimum and zero tillage in the United States to the year 2010.
Source: Back, 1975. Reproduced courtesy of USDA.

Application to destroy (burn down) weed (plant) top growth, rather than to kill the plants, is a special type of treatment to minimize competition. This approach to the use of herbicides and the attendant question concerning competition is growing in importance in view of its use in zero tillage that is increasing as a production system. As we see in Figure 13–1, zero tillage may be practiced on nearly 50% of U.S. cropland by the end of this century. The use of herbicides to check growth, of course, will likely be only minor. However, the point can be made that a search for herbicides specifically effective in checking growth might lead to some that are more effective in this respect than those we already have that were selected for their ability to kill plants.

MINIMIZING COMPETITION WITH THE GROWING CROP

Herbicide Application Methods

Herbicides may be applied in a number of different ways to reduce competition from weeds growing with a crop. Commonly used ways are shown in Figure 13–2.

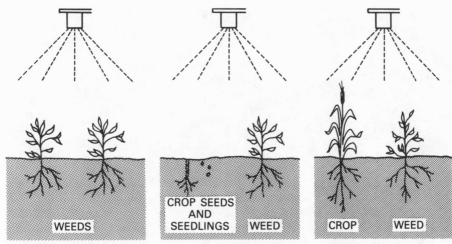

A. Application of herbicide to growing weed before crop has been planted

B. Application of herbicide to growing weeds after the crop has been planted

C. Application of herbicide to growing crop and weeds

FIGURE 13–2. Ways herbicides may be used to minimize competition from growing weeds.

The first two ways, application before planting the crop (Figures 13–2A) and application after planting the crop (Figure 13–2B), represent rather special uses and are based on a separation in time between the weed and the crop. Since the crop plant is not present, a rather broad spectrum of herbicides otherwise toxic to the crop may be safely used. The first way (Figure 13–2A) is commonly used in zero-tillage systems. In this usage, the crop is planted directly into the killed weeds with no seedbed preparation to bring new weed seeds to the surface. The second way (Figure 13–2B) may be used where the crop is planted so deeply that the shallow-germinating weeds emerge first. This method was the basis for selective control of weeds in potatoes with dinoseb (Aldrich et al., 1954). For both methods, crop damage is avoided by using herbicides not readily absorbed from the soil.

The most widespread usage by far is application to a mixture of weeds growing with a crop, as shown in Figure 13–2C. Control may be equally as striking as with soil applications. For example, we see in Figure 13–3 excellent control of a mixture of annual grass and broadleaf weeds in soybeans. Control was accomplished with a combination of 0.22 kilogram per hectare of the selective grass killer sethoxydim and 1.1 kilograms per hectare of bentazon.

Steps in herbicide action.   In minimizing competition from weeds growing with

A. Untreated soybeans

B. Soybeans treated with herbicides applied postemergence

FIGURE 13–3. Mixture of broadleaf and annual grass weeds selectively controlled with a combined application of bentazon and sethoxydim.

crops, the effect of the herbicide is the result of four steps or phases: (1) retention, (2) penetration, (3) translocation, and (4) biochemical reaction. The first three steps are of primary concern to us in weed management since they largely determine the effectiveness and extent of expression of inherent selectivity (biochemical reactions) of a given herbicide. That is, variations in retention, penetration, and translocation largely explain variations from what is expected based on the known mode and mechanism of action of a particular herbicide. Finally, retention, penetration, and translocation are the steps over which we have some control. As we turn to an examination of these three as factors affecting selectivity, we should keep in mind that these steps are not separate and self-standing but rather are links in a sequence of events. That is to say, they are mutually dependent, not mutually independent, processes.

Herbicide Selectivity

In order to clarify the roles of retention, penetration, and translocation in herbicide selectivity, we will assume that the effect of the herbicide on the crop and the weeds is a direct reflection of the amount each absorbs. Nevertheless, in the final analysis, it is what happens after the herbicide enters the symplast system and reaches the site of biochemical reaction that is the final determinant of herbicidal activity. Retention and penetration simply determine how much is taken up.

The quantity of herbicide retained per unit weight of plant tissue is the important differentiating measure in selectivity, rather than the amount per plant or per leaf, since both of the latter may vary a good deal in size. Just as was true for soil applications, selectivity with foliar applications may be based on physical or biological differences or both. However, these differences come into play at a very different point relative to the respective root and leaf structures. As we learned with soil application, uptake through the soil is not a very discriminating process. Thus, differentiation among species in effect begins with translocation. Uptake by the foliage, on the other hand, varies greatly among species due to differences in both retention and penetration of the applied herbicides. Therefore, it is helpful to understand the roles of retention and penetration in both physical and biological selectivity.

Retention. Differential retention of a herbicide by the foliage of weeds and crops influences the quantity of herbicide available for absorbtion. Such differential retention provides the basis for both physical and biological selectivity.

Physical basis. Physical selectivity based on differences in retention is accomplished by a separation in space between the weed and the crop—that is, on a difference in size. If the weed is either shorter or taller than the crop, methods of applying herbicides have been developed that provide effective contact with the weed without harmful dosages contacting the crop. In other words, selectivity is obtained by providing opportunity for weeds—but not the crop—to retain the herbicide.

If the crop is somewhat taller than the weeds, herbicides may be successfully used by directing spray beneath the crop foliage directly onto the weed foliage. This method is called *directed postemergence*. Many weed–crop situations have the size differential necessary for this approach to work, allowing selectivity with herbicides for which the crop may not possess adequate biological tolerance. These situations range from applications to weeds in fruit tree orchards to those in annual row crops such as cotton. Selectivity is predetermined because of a separation in space occupied by the weed and the crop. Nonetheless, other aspects of selectivity enter into success with this approach. The herbicide must be one that at the rate used will not damage the crop if it reaches the soil where it can be picked up by the crop's root system. Neither can it be so volatile as to present an opportunity for excessive uptake through the crop's foliage.

If the crop is somewhat shorter than the weeds, selectivity may also be attained by providing opportunity for weeds—but not the crop—to retain the herbicide. Two general types of equipment to accomplish such selective application are shown in Figure 13–4. Figure 13–4A is a recirculating sprayer that directs the spray horizontal to the ground and into a collecting box. The principle involved is that the weeds growing above the crop retain sufficient herbicide to be killed, and any unused or unabsorbed herbicide is caught by the box and recirculated. Figure 13–4B shows a selective application using a so-called rope-wick applicator. The principle here is one of actually wiping herbicide droplets onto the weeds that overtop the crop from a fabric (rope) surface wetted by capillary flow of the herbicide from its source in the plastic pipe. Either of these applications gains a measure of selectivity over sprays directed to weeds beneath the crop in that presumably in the former case, only as much chemical is actually applied as can be retained by the weed. Even so, if crop injury is to be avoided, the herbicide must not volatize in amounts toxic to the crop. Nor can it be one that is easily washed with rain from the weed foliage onto the crop or into the soil where the crop roots can pick it up. Peters and McKelvey (1982) have also found that a herbicide may carry over in the treated weeds to cause damage to other crops in subsequent years. Where they applied picloram selectively with a rope-wick to goldenrod overtopping a fescue pasture, soybeans grown the following year were severely damaged.

Biological basis. Through its gross morphology and leaf surface microstructure, the plant can influence the quantity of herbicide retained. It is important to understand that except with very small weeds, only a fraction—that is, commonly less than 25%—of the leaf surface on an area will actually be contacted by herbicide spray droplets. This fact serves to remind us that foliar applications fall far short of providing complete coverage of all the leaves on the plants we are trying to control. In such instances, the herbicide usually needs to move to the parts not contacted for satisfactory results to be obtained.

A. Recirculating sprayer directing spray horizontal to the ground. Spray not intercepted by weeds is caught in box opposite nozzles and recirculated.

B. Rope-wick applicator wiping herbicide droplets onto weeds. Rope-wick is continually wetted via capillary action by flow of herbicide from plastic pipe.

FIGURE 13–4. Equipment for selectively applying herbicides to weeds overtopping a growing crop; in this case, johnsongrass overtopping soybeans.
Source: Courtesy of C.G. McWhorter, USDA, Agricultural Research Service, Stoneville, Mississippi.

As already discussed, plants vary greatly in their aboveground growth form. It follows that the leaf surface area exposed to incoming spray droplets varies from species to species. This difference provides a basis for selectivity. As an example, the upright growth of cereals exposes less surface than the spreading growth with horizontal leaves of wild mustard. This difference, in part, was the basis for selective use of sulfuric acid and other phytotoxic chemicals for mustard control in cereals in the early 1900s.

Leaf arrangement may also affect the relative leaf surface area exposed to incoming spray droplets. This effect can best be explained by comparing one species with opposite leaves to another that has alternate leaves. When viewed directly from above and assuming leaves are the same size, the species with alternate leaves exposes twice the leaf area as the one having opposite leaves.

Leaf attitude also influences the extent of retention of an applied herbicide. The broadleaf weed in Figure 13–5, for example, retains more herbicide than does

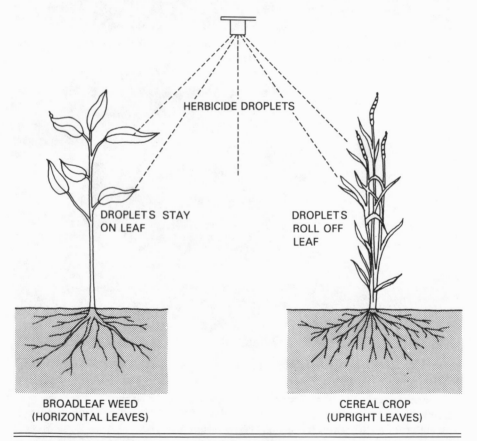

HERBICIDE DROPLETS

DROPLETS STAY
ON LEAF

DROPLETS
ROLL OFF
LEAF

BROADLEAF WEED
(HORIZONTAL LEAVES)

CEREAL CROP
(UPRIGHT LEAVES)

FIGURE 13–5. Influence of plant growth form and leaf attitude on herbicide retention.

the crop both because more leaf surface is exposed and because the horizontal leaves retain the spray droplets while the upright leaves of the crop do not.

The surface of leaves of different species differ in a number of ways, including differences in pubescence, waxiness, and surface roughness. Differences in pubescence and surface roughness can be seen in the appendix to Chapter 11. Each leaf characteristic may affect retention of a herbicide droplet. Pubescence can be visualized to either increase or decrease actual contact between the spray droplet and the leaf, depending upon the number of such hairs. If hairs are numerous, as with common milkweed (Chapter 11 Appendix) they may actually keep a spray droplet from reaching the leaf surface. If sparse, as with velvetleaf (Chapter 11 Appendix), they may serve to hold the droplet on the leaf surface against a contact angle that might otherwise allow the droplet to run off.

Differences in leaf size, leaf arrangement, leaf attitude, and the nature of the leaf surface itself, therefore, provide a basis for biological selectivity among species. The usual situation is for more than one of these factors to come into play in such biological selectivity. Table 13–1 shows differences in spray retention on leaves of five plant species. The amount retained, of course, is a consequence of all leaf attributes combined. For example, mustard leaves are numerous, comparatively small, form a fairly dense canopy, and are rough and pubescent. These characteristics combined account for the high retention observed. As can be seen, wild mustard retains approximately 8 times as much spray per gram of dry weight as does barley and 6 times as much as pea. Thus, for a given rate of application, mustard might be selectively controlled by a contact herbicide in these crops.

Penetration.   With respect to penetration, the basis for selectivity is the ease with which a species' leaves are penetrated. The extent of contact between the spray droplets and leaf is integrally related to penetration: the greater the contact, the larger the gradient force that can serve to move the herbicide through either the apoplast or symplast system.

TABLE 13-1

Plant species differing in retention of herbicide sprays.

Species	Stage of Growth	Retention in Milliliters per Gram Dry Weight of Shoot
White mustard	2 leaves, 5–7 cm high	2.5
Sunflower	2 leaves, 6 cm high	2.0
Linseed	2 leaves, 5 cm high	1.1
Pea	2 leaves, 5–7 cm high	0.4
Barley	3 leaves, 15–20 cm high	0.3

Source: Data from Blackman, et al., 1958.

Penetration, thus, cannot be neatly separated from retention, even though each is a distinct step in the sequence of events leading to ultimate effect from the herbicide. Anything that increases retention can be expected to increase penetration as well. Here, too, we must be reminded that although penetration is assumed to be synonymous with activity, it is what occurs within the plant that is the final determinant of effect. As we saw when we examined entry, transport, and biochemical action in detail in Chapter 11, leaves differ in their cuticle composition, numbers and location of stomata, and internal structure, all of which may influence herbicide penetration. Here we simply need to recognize that these characteristics are altered somewhat by the physical environment and may provide opportunities for selective use.

For herbicides not readily taken up through the leaves of otherwise susceptible weeds in crops tolerant to that herbicide, altering the spray so as to obtain penetration can provide selective control. For example, small amounts of naphthinic or paraffinic oils are added to wettable powder formulations of atrazine for selective postemergence control of weeds in growing corn. Without the addition of the oils, the atrazine does not penetrate the weeds in sufficient quantities to be effective, even though the weeds are susceptible once the atrazine enters. For its part, corn is tolerant of the atrazine because of its ability to detoxify the herbicide. Thus, it is not damaged, even though penetration may also be increased by addition of the oils.

Surfactants. Before leaving retention and penetration, we need to consider briefly their relationship to surface tension. In simple terms, *surface tension* is a measure of the force with which particles on a liquid surface are held together. This is commonly reported in dynes per centimeter but may also be reported in other units. A *dyne* is equal to the force required to impart an acceleration of 1 centimeter per second^{-2} to a mass of 1 gram. A high surface tension indicates that the particles on the surface are held tightly together. We say that a liquid with high surface tension does not *wet* another surface very well. Water has a relatively high surface tension of 71 to 72 dynes per centimeter. With such strong cohesiveness, water spray will form spheres on a surface such as a plant leaf, rather than spread out, even when droplets are relatively large.

Figure 13–6 shows that both droplet surface tension and droplet size influence retention. Droplets in the 100 micron range in Figure 13–6A are much more readily retained than larger droplets. Surface tension is shown in micronewtons (μN) in Figure 13–6B, but the measurement would be the same in dynes. As can be seen, very little of the spray would be retained if it had the surface tension of water (71 to 72 μN/mm). Thus, it is common practice to include an additive to reduce water surface tension if the herbicide formulation itself does not adequately do so. In view of the common usage of such substances, brief consideration of their action is in order.

Surfactant is the term applied to such substances and comes from the fact that the substances have surface activity. Surfactants include such materials as

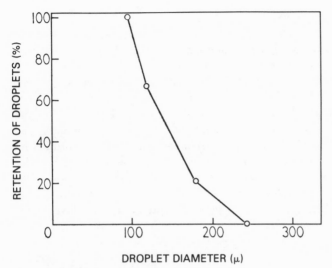

A. Droplet size inversely related to retention on leaf

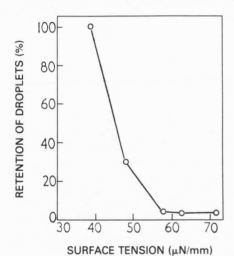

B. Droplet surface tension inversely related
to retention on leaf

**FIGURE 13–6. Effects of spray droplet size and surface
tension on herbicide retention on the leaf; in this case, pea
leaflets.**

Source: Holly, 1976. Reproduced with permission of Academic Press,
Inc.

emulsifiers, detergents, stickers, and wetting agents. Surfactants have other properties, but only their effect on surface tension is of interest to us here. A common characteristic is to have both lipophilic and hydrophilic properties. That is, one part of the surfactant is compatible with lipid and lipid-like materials and the other part is compatible with water. This compatibility tells us that surfactants are active at interfaces. The dual characteristic and its function relative to reducing surface tension are illustrated graphically in Figure 13–7A and Figure 13–7B, respectively. That part compatible with lipid or lipid-like substances—an oil droplet in this case—provides a bond with them, and that part compatible with water ties to water, thus serving to bond these two otherwise opposing liquids.

In effect, then, the surfactant serves to reduce the internal cohesiveness of the spray droplet by providing an interfacing capability of that droplet with the leaf surface. Rather than remaining as droplets, the spray spreads as a thin layer on the

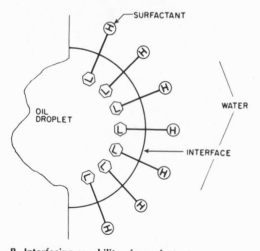

A. Lipophilic and hydrophilic properties of a surfactant

B. Interfacing capability of a surfactant

FIGURE 13–7. Schematic illustrations of the characteristics and function of a surfactant in increasing herbicide spray retention.

Source: Adapted from Behrens, 1964. Reproduced with permission of the Weed Science Society of America.

leaf. Both droplet size and surface tension affect physical selectivity as they interact with the plant surface. New application equipment allows droplet size to be rather precisely controlled and may provide opportunities for using this capability to obtain selectivity not possible with equipment previously available, which delivered droplets whose size varied over a wide range.

Translocation.   After the herbicide has penetrated the plant, translocation is the next step in the sequence of events. As discussed in Chapter 11, certain aspects of herbicide usage to minimize competition are influenced by or interact with translocation. Retention is one aspect. Retention plays the role of maintaining a sufficient concentration on the epidermis to assure a gradient force for movement into the leaf until it ultimately reaches the symplast. Once the herbicide is inside the symplast, it moves as a passenger with photosynthate from the leaf to the site of biochemical reaction. Thus, the state of photosynthetic activity influences results. Actively growing weeds may be selectively removed from dormant or relatively inactive crops.

Factors Affecting Success

Many elements can intervene to reduce control or selectivity with foliar-applied herbicides, just as was true with soil applications. In seeking an understanding of factors affecting success, the difference between soil and foliar applications is found in the fact that the main modifier of soil applications is the soil itself, whereas the plant is the primary modifier of foliar applications. Variations from the expected can be due to four general factors: (1) stage of development, (2) plant growth form, (3) plant growth rate, and (4) direct temperature and humidity effects.

Stage of development of crop and weeds.   The stage of development of the crop and of the weeds may influence both success in preventing competition from the weeds and the avoidance of herbicidal injury of the crop. As discussed in Chapter 6, weeds cannot grow with crops for very long without causing permanent loss in crop yield. It follows that herbicides must be applied before this loss occurs if they are to fully meet the objective of minimizing competition. Additionally, weeds commonly become progressively more difficult to control as they advance in maturity. At the same time, of course, sensitivity of the crop may also vary with stage of development. The most sensitive, or the most tolerant, stage is determined by the particular biochemical reaction or reactions involved. In a general way, stages of rapid differentiation and cell division may be particularly sensitive. Thus, 2,4–D and many other herbicides applied before tillering is completed in cereals may reduce tillering and cause abnormal seedheads. Flowering is also a time when many crops may be damaged by herbicides.

Growth form of weeds.   Chapter 2 discussed the fact that growth form is a very plastic characteristic in plants. The previous section pointed out that growth form very much influences contact and retention of spray droplets. Not surprisingly then, growing conditions prior to spray application may affect overall results. The extent of branching, leaf size, and leaf attitude may all be influenced by density of the weed–crop community. In a very dense stand of weeds with the crop, the weeds may be less branched and more upright than in a sparse stand. Low temperature preceding and during leaf development tends to cause the leaves to be small. Moisture stress during leaf development also leads to relatively smaller leaves. Pubescence tends to be greater under high temperature, high light intensity, and low moisture. Influenced by growing conditions, all of these aspects of growth form may modify the effects of the spray application.

Growth rate of weeds.   Growth rate, as affected by growing conditions, can best be visualized as having its effect on penetration, translocation, and ultimate biochemical reaction at the sites of activity. This general statement is predicated on the assumption that extent of penetration, translocation, and biochemical reaction is quite directly related to movement in the symplast system that in turn is influenced by the degree of photosynthetic activity in the leaf. There is ample evidence that herbicidal activity is related to photosynthetic activity.

Growth rate may also influence results from herbicide applications indirectly through its effect on the leaf cuticle. The slow growth associated with low temperature usually leads to less cuticle. Such plants are more easily penetrated by a herbicide. Slow growth as the result of extended drought, on the other hand, may lead to more cuticle, thus reducing penetration of a herbicide.

Temperature and humidity.   High humidity and high temperature commonly lead to an increase in stomatal aperture. Entry of herbicides through the stoma may be severalfold greater than through the cuticle itself. High humidity is commonly associated with an increase in transfer of the herbicide from the leaf surface to the phloem. Of course, we would expect temperature to affect activity of herbicides because of its effect on the rate of chemical reactions.

REDUCING WEED PROPAGULES

Eliminating the source of the weed problem—that is, seeds and perennating parts—is a goal quite possibly impractical for any but very special circumstances where conditions can be carefully controlled and the value of the crop can justify the expense. For example, the cost of total eradication of an introduced noxious weed might be warranted if the weed is restricted to relatively small areas, such as soil in pots, transplant beds, and the like. Furthermore, eradication of weeds common to major crops faces the nearly insurmountable task of eliminating seeds from extensive regions that have undergone pronounced changes in topography, climate, and plant cover over the ages.

Although elimination of such species may be impractical, the reduction of the reservoir of propagules on an individual farm may be within reach as a practical way of reducing losses from weeds and the cost of control entailed. The technology, in fact, has been demonstrated. Some of the earliest uses of chemicals were of soil sterilants and fumigants to eradicate certain specially troublesome perennial weeds, especially those confined to patches and to free potting soils and other specialty uses of soils of all seeds. Such usage continues to represent a minor place in the use of chemicals for reducing viable propagules in soil. This approach has not been used on a large scale in major crops because of the large bulk oftentimes required, because of residues that sometimes prevent crop production for a period of years after treatment, because of the high cost, and because of the frequent intricacies of application.

Advances in our knowledge of dormancy itself and the discovery of chemicals that stimulate germination have redirected attention to this use of chemicals for weed management. The steady trend towards reduced tillage also dramatically changes the prospects for this approach. Under reduced tillage, a new population of weed seeds is not being brought to the surface each year as is the case where plowing is a common practice. Furthermore, under reduced tillage, efforts can focus on the top 2.5 to 5 cm rather than on the 15 cm to 20 cm depth that must be dealt with when the entire plow layer is involved.

Reducing viable propagules in the soil requires effort in two areas: (1) reducing those propagules already present and (2) preventing the addition of new ones. As shown in Figure 13–8, chemicals have a place in both areas. Uses in each area are examined separately.

Reducing Propagules Present in the Soil

As mentioned previously, one of the earliest uses of chemicals for weed control was as a soil sterilant. Such usage was restricted mainly to patches of weeds in cropland or to industrial sites where no vegetation was desired. Chemicals were commonly those that persisted in the soil for months or even years. Soil sterilants still have a minor place in weed control. Soil fumigants also have a minor role. Such chemicals may effectively eliminate all weed propagules from treated soil, but because they are volatile, they rapidly dissipate from soil in the open. Because of costs, bulk, and intricacies of application, such uses are applicable to very special situations and small areas. Therefore, our concern here is not with control or with preventing germination but rather with what can be done to stimulate perennating parts and seeds to germinate.

Stimulation of germination involves chemistry new to weed science. What we

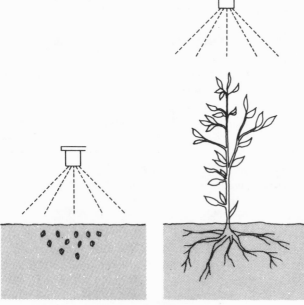

A. Application of chemicals to soil to (1) break dormancy of propagules, (2) hasten germination or regrowth of propagules, and (3) destroy all propagules

B. Application of chemicals to the growing weed to (1) prevent production of seed or of perennating parts and (2) prevent dormancy in such reproductive parts

FIGURE 13–8. Direct applications of chemicals to reduce the weed propagule bank in soil.

know about the mechanism of action and biochemical sites of action with herbicides may have little application. Rather, the use of chemicals to stimulate germination is integrally related to the chemistry of the development of dormancy in the seed and the reinitiation of growth, which we know as germination. The known chemistry is not covered here. For a detailed review of the chemistry, refer to *Dormancy and Developmental Arrest,* edited by Mary Clutter (1978). Note, however, that the chemistry of dormancy and germination is related to the water potential and membrane permeability of cells within the seed and perennating part, which, in turn, are controlled by inherent growth substances. Thus, as efforts to reduce propagules expand, it is to be expected that attention will focus on growth substances and activities that they control. The scope of treatment here identifies the potential for weed management using this approach and what is known about factors affecting results.

Buds. Figure 13–9 shows that new growth on leafy spurge can be greatly stimulated by gibberellic acid. Values are averages of 3 plants whose foliage was sprayed with the concentration of gibberellic acid in a 0.1% Tween 20 (surfactant) water solution. After 21 days, new growth on plants that received only 10 ppm of gibberellic acid was approximately 25 times that on check plants.

These results illustrate dramatically the potential influence of such substances for manipulating regrowth of perennial weeds. Such manipulation may offer opportunities for reducing the numbers of perennating parts already in the soil. In particular, it suggests such substances may be able to stimulate new growth of dormant perennating parts. Indeed, Shafer and Monson (1958) found that gibberellic acid stimulated growth of emerged dormant buds of leafy spurge. Although the potential has been demonstrated, little has been done to determine the

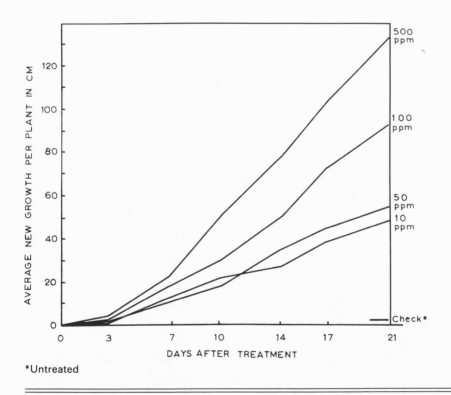

*Untreated

FIGURE 13–9. Effect of gibberellic acid on production of new growth by leafy spurge.
Source: Shafer and Monson, 1958. Reproduced with permission of the Weed Science Society of America.

feasibility of using plant growth-regulating substances to reduce the numbers of perennating parts of perennial weeds in soil. Furthermore, annual weeds are of much greater relative interest, both because of their greater numbers and because seed can retain viability for a much longer time than most perennating parts.

Seeds. Germination of dormant seeds of some weeds can be markedly increased by chemicals in the laboratory, as can be seen in Figure 13–10. The five species represent different types of dormancy: Wild oat seeds are usually dormant when released from the parent and the hull tends to inhibit germination somewhat; dormancy of wild mustard seed is due to a hard seed coat; curly dock and field pennycress seed require light, alternating temperatures, or both for best germination; and tansy phacelia *(Phacelia tanacetifolia)* seed germination is inhibited by

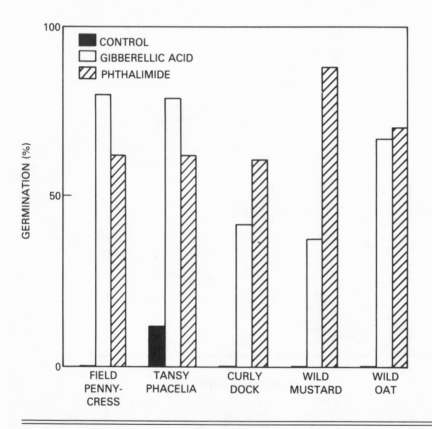

FIGURE 13–10. Increase in germination of dormant seeds of 5 weeds treated with gibberellic acid and a substituted phthalimide.
Source: Data from Metzger, 1983.

light. Germinations shown in Figure 13–10, determined after 2 weeks incubation, were obtained under the above conditions to assure dormancy of the seeds of the individual species. The chemicals were able to counteract all types of dormancy.

Stimulation of germination has also been documented for sodium azide on wild oat seed (Fay and Gorecki, 1978), ethylene on witchweed seed (Eplee, 1975) and on cocklebur and redroot pigweed seed (Egley, 1980), ethanol on several grass seeds (Taylorson, 1981), and nitrate on seeds of some broadleaf species (Hurtt and Taylorson, 1979). The number of different weeds affected and the number of different chemicals shown to stimulate their germination clearly demonstrate the potential in this approach.

Field results, however, have been erratic and generally less successful than the above results obtained under controlled conditions. There is insufficient work to justify anything other than rather general conclusions by way of explanation. One rather obvious condition for success is that moisture and temperature must be favorable for germination to proceed. If not, the seed is apt to revert to the dormant stage after the stimulant is gone. Also, the stimulant must be in contact with the seed. This condition represents a more stringent requirement than that faced by herbicides applied to the soil to prevent seedling establishment. Further, contact between the stimulant and the seed must persist for some time. For example, as shown in Figure 13–11, ethylene (C_2H_4) had to be in contact with cocklebur seed

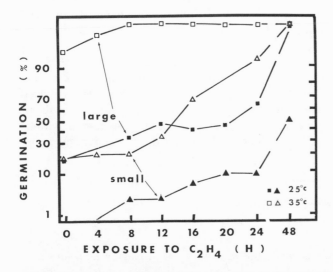

FIGURE 13–11. Length of exposure to ethylene and temperature influencing the degree of stimulation of germination in large and small common cocklebur seeds.

Source: Egley, 1980. Reproduced with permission of the Weed Science Society of America.

for several hours to promote germination. Large and small seeds were exposed to 10 microliters of ethylene per liter of atmosphere for 0, 4, 8, 12, 16, 20, 24, and 48 hours and then transferred to an ethylene-free atmosphere for the remainder of a 7-day dark period. The effects were compared under 25°C and 35°C. As can be seen, seeds whose germination was 20% or less without exposure to ethylene—small seeds at both temperatures and large seeds at 25°C—had to be exposed for 8 or more hours before germination was increased and for 48 hours for maximum germination. Even the large seeds at 35°C, whose germination was above 90% without ethylene, had to be exposed 8 hours for maximum stimulation. Also, poor field results with sodium azide in stimulating germination of wild oat were attributed to its being readily leached and rapidly dissipated from soil (Fay et al., 1980).

Factors affecting success.   From these bits of evidence, treatment to stimulate germination seems to be subjected to the same factors discussed in Chapter 12 as influencing the effectiveness of herbicides applied to the soil, plus some additional ones. Not only must the stimulant be in actual contact with the seed, but the nature of dormancy itself may represent a constraint on success. For example, work so far has shown that so-called hard seeds of some species are not vulnerable to this approach. In spite of the general lack of field success, with the possible exception of control of witchweed seed, the fact that the concept has been established and the potential benefit is so great suggests that this usage of chemicals in weed management will ultimately develop to the point where it is an important additional tool in our total weed management program.

An aspect yet to be explored but offering possibilities is that of manipulation of soil microorganisms to eliminate the seed's inherent protection against decay. Rice (1974) suggests and provides supportive evidence that seeds do indeed contain chemicals that prevent the growth of some microorganisms on them. Certainly, the persistence for many years of some seeds suggests that an antimicrobiological factor is involved. Ways to strip the seed of this protection seem to be worthy of examination.

Preventing the Addition of Viable Propagules

A distinction is made here between the prevention of propagule additions as a result of herbicides that destroy the weed and prevention as a result of chemicals applied for the express purpose of reducing production of propagules without killing the plant. Destruction of the weed seedling or growing plant prior to reproduction, of course, serves to prevent the weeds so treated from adding propagules to the reservoir in the soil. This result may be an important side benefit from herbicides used to prevent weed emergence with crops and those used to minimize competition from weeds growing with crops. Also, certain situations may justify the cost of applying chemicals to destroy weed plants for the sole purpose of preventing production of propagules.

Irrespective of the method employed, some way of preventing periodic additions to the propagule bank in soil must be found for a preventive approach to be successful. Eliminating only those propagules already present in the soil has limited value in agriculture unless addition of seeds or perennating parts can be prevented. On the other hand, by itself, preventing additions to the propagule bank in the soil in time reduces the population of even the most persistent weed to a level that does not interfere with normal crop production (Figure 3–6 and related discussion). Chemicals may be an especially valuable tool for this purpose. Mechanical methods frequently may be impractical because of the advanced stage of development of the crop at the time when action needs to be taken against the weed to prevent production of viable seed or perennating parts.

Concern for possible herbicide damage to crop seed prompted examination of direct effects of herbicides on seed viability soon after the growth regulator type herbicides were introduced in the 1940s (Aamisepp, 1966). The finding that herbicides indeed could affect viability and germination of crop seed encouraged research to determine if herbicides could be effectively used in this way against specific weeds. In the early 1950s, maleic hydrazide was found to be effective in preventing seed production of annual bluegrass (Engel and Aldrich, 1960) and wild oat (Carder, 1954; and Friesen and Walker, 1956). Maleic hydrazide applied at 1.1 kilograms per hectare (1 pound per acre) was enough to greatly reduce production of annual bluegrass seed heads in bentgrass turf. As little as 0.56 kilogram per hectare (1/2 pound per acre) was enough to reduce the production of viable wild oat seeds to less than 1%. The fluoro-substituted phenoxyacetic acids were found to be effective in preventing production of annual bluegrass and crabgrass seed without appreciable damage to the turf grasses (Anderson and McLane, 1958).

As suggested by Figure 13–12, complete prevention of seed production is possible in some weeds with sublethal rates of herbicides. In this case, 2,4–D was applied to curly dock at 1000 ppm at the indicated stages of flowering. This rate is too low to kill established curly dock plants. Treatment 12 days prior to anthesis (flowering period) completely prevented seed production. Although some seed was produced by plants treated at anthesis, none of the seed germinated. Further delay in treating resulted in proportionate increases in seed production and germination.

Factors affecting success.   Research in this area is too limited to justify more than limited general conclusions. It is clear that time of application is critical. As we saw with curly dock, treatment at or just before flowering was most effective. Further, the most sensitive period is from shortly before to shortly after flowering. Best results with maleic hydrazide were obtained when it was applied to wild oat in the milk stage (Friesen and Walker, 1956). Both amitrole and maleic hydrazide

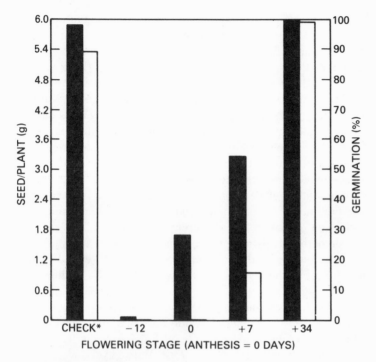

*Untreated

FIGURE 13–12. Effect of stage of flowering on reduction of seed production of curly dock treated with 2,4–D.
Source: Data from Maun and Cavers, 1969.

were most effective against medusahead when applied during the boot stage (Evans et al., 1963). The fluoro-substituted phenoxyacetic acids were effective against annual bluegrass and crabgrass when applied at the time the panicles were being differentiated (Anderson and McLane, 1958). Cacodylic acid was most effective against yellow foxtail and goosegrass *(Eleusine indica)* when applied during heading (Taylorson, 1966).

As we see, the effectiveness of herbicides to prevent weed seed production was well established early in the modern herbicide era. However, herbicides are not commonly used for this purpose. Chapter 15 examines the place for such usage in a weed management approach. At this point, we should recognize that the main reason herbicides are not used for this purpose is that we are not yet geared to weed management. Undoubtedly, prevention of viable propagules will always be used as part of a total program—that is, as an adjunct to other efforts in weed management.

Preventing dormancy.   Preventing dormancy is a special aspect of the prevention of viable propagules. As already mentioned, dormancy of seed and of perennating parts is common in most weeds. Dormancy assures the survival of weeds from the stress imposed by both tillage of the land and by the environment. The fact that a large part of the population of a given crop of weed seeds may, in fact, be dormant is a major reason means of preventing or controlling weeds are necessary every year crops are grown. If dormancy could be prevented, the problem of dealing with the particular weed would be very much simplified. There is evidence that treatment of plants can alter the development of dormancy in both buds and in seeds.

A number of growth regulator herbicides applied to wild garlic when the offset bulbs were forming in the spring resulted in the bulbs having little dormancy, whereas unsprayed plants had bulblets that were dormant for at least 6 months (Parker, 1976). Additional research with growth regulators has shown them to be effective against other species in reducing seed dormancy as well.

Growth regulator type herbicides have also been shown to affect dormancy in weed seeds. However, results have been inconsistent. In early work (Rojas-Garciduenas and Kommedahl, 1960), treatment with 2,4–D reduced dormancy in redroot pigweed seed. In later work (Fawcett and Slife, 1978a), 2,4–D and dalapon were found to affect dormancy in redroot pigweed, lambsquarters, and giant foxtail. But effects on initial dormancy were sometimes different than effects on dormancy after overwintering. Further, in this instance, initial dormancy of redroot pigweed seed was increased by 2,4–D.

Nitrogen fertilization of common lambsquarters plants resulted in seed with reduced dormancy (Fawcett and Slife, 1978b). Whereas germination of seed from unfertilized plants was 3%, that from plants fertilized with nitrate was 7 to 12 times greater. In this same study, velvetleaf was unaffected by nitrogen fertilization.

The magnitude of the reduction in dormancy of the rather limited work that has been done falls short of making this a practical way of completely preventing the carryover of viable seeds in the soil. Nevertheless, these studies have shown that chemicals can alter dormancy of seed and of perennating parts. As more is learned about the processes of dormancy development and the initiation of growth, and as more of the relatively large numbers of chemical moieties are examined for this effect, we can reasonably expect that this approach may also find a place in a total weed management program.

CONCEPTS AND CONCLUSIONS

1. For herbicides applied to growing crops and weeds, selectivity is determined by four linked phenomena acting in sequence: retention, penetration, translocation, and biochemical reactions.

2. For herbicides applied to growing crops and weeds, selectivity may be achieved by both physical and biological factors. Selectivity based on physical factors is accomplished by a separation in space between the weed and the crop. Selectivity based on biological factors is accomplished by gross morphological differences, differences in leaf surface microstructure, and differences in internal physiology and metabolism between the weed and the crop.
3. Reduction of the propagule seedbank in the soil may be accomplished both by preventing the addition of new propagules and by eliminating those already present in the soil. Herbicides may have a place in each.
4. Reducing dormancy of seed produced by weeds could hasten seedbank drawdown. Herbicides may have a place here also.
5. For propagule seedbank drawdown to be most useful in a weed prevention–weed management context, periodic additions must be prevented. By itself, effective prevention of seedbank renewal will be successful in time, whereas by itself, eliminating those propagules present will not.

REFERENCES

Aamisepp, A. 1966. Herbicide effects on plants from seeds from treated plants. Vaxtodling, 22:1–147.

Aldrich, R.J., G.R. Blake, and J.C. Campbell. 1954. Cultivation and chemical weed control in potatoes, circular 557. New Jersey Agricultural Experiment Station, New Brunswick, N.J.

Anderson, B.R., and S.R. McLane. 1958. Control of annual bluegrass and crabgrass in turf with fluorophenoxyacetic acids. Weeds 6 (1):52–58.

Anderson, O. 1958. Studies on the absorption and translocation of amitrol (3-amino-1,2,4-triazole) by nutgrass (C. rotundus). Weeds 6 (4):370–85.

Back, W.B. 1975. Minimum tillage: A preliminary assessment (part II). Prepared by USDA, Office of Planning and Evaluation, for the Committee on Agriculture, U.S. Senate, Washington, D.C.

Behrens, R.W. 1964. The physical and chemical properties of surfactants and their effects on formulated herbicides. Weeds 12 (4):255–58.

Blackman, G.E., R.S. Bruce, and K. Holly. 1958. Studies in the principles of phytotoxicity, V. Interrelationships between specific differences in spray retention and selective toxicity. J. Exp. Bot. 9:175–205.

Carder, A.C. 1954. The selective control of wild oats in cereal crops by use of maleic hydrazide, Research Report, vol. 11, p. 50. North Central Weed Control Conference, Fargo, N. Dak.

Clutter, M.F. 1978. Dormancy and developmental arrest. Experimental analysis in plants and animals. New York: Academic Press.

Egley, G.H. 1980. Stimulation of common cocklebur and redroot pigweed seed germination by injections of ethylene into soil. Weed Sci. 28 (5):510–14.

Engel, R.E., and R.J. Aldrich. 1960. Reduction of annual bluegrass, *Poa annua*, in bentgrass turf by the use of chemicals. Weeds 8 (1):26–28.

Eplee, R.E. 1975. Ethylene: A witchweed seed germination stimulant. Weed Sci. 23(5):433–36.

Evans, R.A., B.L. Kay, and C.M. McKell. 1963. Herbicides to prevent seed set or germination of medusahead. Weeds 11 (4):273–76.

Fawcett, R.S., and F.W. Slife. 1978a. Effects of 2,4–D and dalapon on weed seed production and dormancy. Weed Sci. 26(6):543–47.

———. 1978b. Effects of field applications of nitrate on weed seed germination and dormancy. Weed Sci. 26 (6):594–96.

Fay, P.K., and R.S. Gorecki. 1978. Stimulating germination of dormant wild oat seed with sodium azide. Weed Sci. 26 (4):323–26.

Fay, P.K., et al. 1980. Coating sodium azide granules to enhance seed germination. Weed Sci. 28 (6):674–77.

Friesen, H.G., and D.R. Walker. 1956. Selective control of wild oats in Olli barley with MH, Research Report, vol. 13, p. 54. North Central Weed Control Conference, Chicago, Ill.

Holly, K. 1976. Selectivity in relation to formulation and application methods. In L.J. Audus, ed., Herbicides: Physiology, biochemistry, ecology, 2nd ed., vol. 2, pp. 249–77. New York: Academic Press.

Hurtt, W., and R.B. Taylorson. 1979. Field studies on chemical promotion of weed emergence. In Abstract 178 of 1979 Meeting of WSSA, p. 83. San Francisco, Calif.

Maun, M.A., and P.B. Cavers. 1969. Effects of 2,4–D on seed production and embryo development of curly dock. Weed Sci. 17(4):533–36.

Metzger, J.D. 1983. Promotion of germination of dormant weed seeds by substituted phthalimides and gibberellic acid. Weed Sci. 31(3):285–89.

Parker, C. 1976. Effects on the dormancy of plant organs. In L.J. Audus, ed., Herbicides: Physiology, biochemistry, ecology, 2nd ed., vol. 1, pp. 165–90. New York: Academic Press.

Peters, E.J., and R. McKelvey. 1982. Residues of picloram and dicamba in pasture soils after weed treatment with a rope-wick applicator. In Abstract 75 of 1982 Meeting of WSSA, p. 41. Boston, Mass.

Rice, E.L. 1974. Allelopathy. New York: Academic Press.

Rojas-Garciduenas, M., and L. Kommedahl. 1960. The effect of 2,4–D on germination of pigweed seed. Weeds 8(1):1–5.

Shafer, N.E., and W.G. Monson. 1958. The role of gibberellic acid in overcoming bud dormancy in perennial weeds, I. Leafy spurge and ironweed *(Verronia baldwini Torr.)*. Weeds 6 (2):172–78.

Taylorson, R.B. 1966. Control of seed production in three annual grasses by dimethylarsinic acid. Weeds 14(3):207–10.

———. 1981. Dormant weed seeds due for a rude awakening. Weeds Today 12 (1):15.

CROP PRODUCTION PRACTICES AND WEEDS

14

In Chapter 2, reference was made to the changes in weed composition that have occurred in response to herbicides. In the intervening chapters, we have examined competition, weed reproduction, germination and dormancy, allelopathy, biological relationships and herbicides. One or more of these factors may be involved in shifts in the makeup of weeds important in crop production. With this background, we are ready to examine the interrelationships between these factors and crop production practices. This is a necessary first step in predicting future weed problems. Today's computer technology and systems modeling provide weed science the necessary tools to predict weed problems if the effects on weed composition are known and well documented. Thus, the student of weed science should approach the science with the expectation that prediction of changes in weeds and the design of programs for dealing with such changes will be an integral part of weed science in the future.

First, to develop an understanding of changes that production practices cause in weeds, it is desirable to review the three broad ways in which weeds change. In terms of weeds as a problem with which the farmer must deal, changes can occur as a result of: (1) introduction, (2) genetic and physiological modification of existing species, and (3) shifts within the community of weeds in response to changes in environment imposed by production practices. Humans are an integral force with respect to each of the ways weeds may change.

WEED INTRODUCTION AND SPREAD

Examination of the ways in which weeds are introduced and spread clearly shows the extent to which humans are involved. Possibly two-thirds of the problem weeds in the United States are species introduced from other countries. Europe has been a major contributor, coincidental with being the major source of early settlers. Table 14–1 shows the source by plant family of weeds introduced into North America from Europe. These families are recognized as being of relatively recent evolutionary origin. Is this not what we would expect based upon what we know about response to change—that is, for natural selection to result in species and populations adjusted to the new environment? A second speculation may be in order. Does the preponderance of weeds among families of relatively recent evolutionary origin suggest that the long-term trend is towards increasingly troublesome weeds?

Asia has also contributed some weeds to the United States. Japanese honeysuckle *(Lonicera japonica)* and Japanese knotweed are two examples. They were introduced as ornamentals and later escaped to become pests.

Introduction has not been a one-way street, however. Even though the United States has contributed far fewer species to other nations than it has received, horseweed, tumbling pigweed *(Amaranthus albus)*, and sunflower are three species apparently native to the United States that have been introduced to become problem weeds in Europe.

TABLE 14-1

Seven families whose species make up 60% of the 700 species of weeds introduced into eastern North America from Europe, with the number of such species in each.

Family	Number of Species
Compositae	112
Gramineae	65
Cruciferae	62
Labiatae	60
Leguminosae	54
Caryophyllaceae	37
Scrophulariaceae	30

Source: Data from Fogg, 1975, from Hill, 1977.

Weeds were introduced in a number of ways. The most important were as contaminants in crop seeds, with feed for livestock, in nursery stock, and in the days of colonization with sailing vessels, as contaminants of soil used for ballast. The ballast was dumped at any convenient port to make room for the return cargo.

Aliens

Why are so many U.S. weeds aliens? The answer is provided by ecology. First, clearing of the land on the new continent provided environments ecologically comparable to those of the old world where weeds had been provided an opportunity to become established and to evolve. Second, the new continent provided an environment free of some of the constraints imposed by that of the old world. In effect, this fact recognizes a basic concept discussed in connection with biological control. The search for biological control agents has concentrated in the country from which the weed species originated. This is so because the weed in its new environment can be expected to be relatively free of natural enemies. Thirdly, some aliens were successful weeds in a new environment simply because there were unfilled niches that the alien was able to fill.

This review of introduction leads to the conclusion that it will not be a major source of change in weeds in the future, partly because ample time and enough opportunities have been provided for most species to have been introduced, and partly because none of the vehicles for introduction are significant factors today. This does not mean that introduction can be ignored, only that the flush of introduction as a major source of change is past. Now, the appearance of each new species is noteworthy. For example, witchweed *(Striga lutea)*, a native of tropical and subtropical regions in the Eastern Hemisphere that was discovered in isolated areas in North Carolina and South Carolina in 1956, has been the subject of concerted efforts at eradication. Itchgrass, a native of India, found in Louisiana and Florida in the early 1970s, has been the subject of study to determine its potential spread. By 1981, common crupina *(Crupina vulgaris)*, a native of the Mediterranean region, had a known infestation of 23,000 acres in Idaho and is the subject of special containment efforts. However, these additions as a source of change will be a relatively much less important source than changes among species already present.

Mechanisms of Spread within the United States

The following is a list of mechanisms for weed seed dispersal within the United States over short distances:

Crop seed
Livestock feed
Birds and other animals
Machinery
Wind
Surface water
Crop and livestock waste

Before briefly examining each of these mechanisms, we need to remind ourselves that the movement of weeds was mainly from east to west with the pioneers, so much so, that the Indian name for plantain was White Man's Foot. We should also keep in mind that movement within the United States is important largely as a source of reinfestation rather than as a way of establishing a species previously not a problem. Our present spread, however, is extremely significant for any long-term weed management effort. Finally, we need also recognize that spread by birds and animals and by wind—relatively unimportant in total numbers—are the only mechanisms of the seven listed over which we have little or no control.

Crop seed.   Infested seed is by far the most important way in which weeds were spread in the past and is still a major source today. The potential is shown in results reported by Dunham (1972) of a survey of weed seeds in farmer's drills in Manitoba, Canada. In the survey, 28% of the farmers were planting seed too contaminated with weeds to pass inspection. Contamination of crop seed is the only mechanism of movement, with the possible exception of movement in irrigation water, that can cause appreciable economic loss in the crop in the planting year. With the availability of certified seed under the seed improvement programs in our several states, there is little reason now for crop seed to be a major source of weed infestation.

Livestock feed.   Since feed is not subjected to the same cleanup and regulation as is seed, it can be an important source of weed spread. Feed, even hay, commonly may be transported many miles from the point of production to where it is fed to livestock. It has been well established that seeds of many weeds can survive passage through the animal gut. Thus, weed seeds in feed can be expected to add to the seedbank when and wherever the manure is used.

Birds and other animals.   Birds and small animals may be a source of spread as a result both of seed ingestion and subsequent release in droppings and of seed attachment to feathers or hair. The spread of St. Johnswort seed in the western United States in the early part of this century was associated with the movement of cattle and sheep in the area. Similarly, the spread of johnsongrass was apparently associated with the movement of horses and their feed during the Civil War.

Machinery.   Machinery can be a particularly important source of spread over fairly short distances. As machinery moves from field to field, and in some cases even from farm to farm, weed seed, rhizomes, and so forth, may be moved with it in mud on the wheels or in trash attached to cultivator teeth, left in the combine, and in other such ways. Although no data are available to identify the effect, it seems likely that many weeds are moved over relatively great distances with the advent of custom combining that may involve movement of machines from the Gulf of Mexico into the Canadian provinces in North America.

Wind.   Wind is among the more obvious vehicles for weed seed dissemination. Dandelion seed with its parachute-like transport system is commonly observed to be moving with the wind. Many seeds like dandelion have special structures to assure dissemination of their seed (Figure 3–3).

Surface water.   Weed seeds may also move in significant quantities in surface water. Table 14–2 shows the number of seeds of selected weeds found in water from the Columbia River and in an irrigation lateral during the irrigation season. A

TABLE 14-2

Kind and number of weed seeds in water from the Columbia River and an irrigation lateral.

| Weed | Seeds per 254 Kiloliters Water[1] | | Percent Germination[2] |
	Columbia River	Irrigation Lateral	
Barnyardgrass	3.53	72.87	19
Cattail	0.12	8.87	34
Cutgrass, rice	0.69	8.99	9
Dandelion	0.12	1.24	65
Dock, curly	2.40	6.08	37
Dropseed, sand	0.79	6.89	66
Flixweed	1.01	22.66	52
Foxtail, green	0.69	7.56	2
Foxtail, yellow	0.12	4.97	52
Horseweed	3.76	15.20	80
Lambsquarters	21.72	307.24	5
Lettuce, prickly	8.18	16.83	57
Mustard, tumble	36.40	65.46	70
Pigweed, redroot	6.82	66.10	4
Quackgrass	0.00	10.97	80

[1] 254 kiloliters is equivalent to an irrigation of 2.47 inches per acre.

[2] Average of all sources.

Source: Adapted from Kelley and Bruns, 1975.

total of 137 different species were represented in weed seed in the irrigation lateral and 77 plant species in water from the Columbia River. The fact that more seeds are found in the irrigation lateral than in the Columbia River, which is the water source, is a reflection of the irrigation bank as a source of weed seed.

Crop and livestock waste.   Crop screenings and livestock waste may be the vehicle for spreading large numbers of weed seeds. In the handling of sugar beets, for example, dirt attached to beets delivered to a processing plant is normally returned to the farm. However, the dirt returned is not necessarily that associated with beets from that particular farm. Thus, weed seeds associated with beet production on one farm may be transferred to another farm. Centralized feed lots with local distribution of the associated manure also represents a potential source of weed spread.

The principles involved in dispersal are beyond the scope of our interest here. Refer to van der Pijl (1982) for a thorough treatment of such principles. Thus, introductions from long distances may be relatively unimportant, but local introductions are occasionally important sources of change in weed composition today.

GENETIC AND PHYSIOLOGICAL MODIFICATION OF WEEDS

Genetic and physiological alteration of existing species, although important, is a comparatively long-term process, as discussed in Chapter 2. Nevertheless, in our agricultural endeavors, we are continually providing forces necessary for speciation to occur, suggesting that genetic and physiological modification will be a constant but limited source of change in weeds.

EFFECTS OF CROP PRODUCTION PRACTICES ON WEED CHANGES

In terms of its implication for weed management, the most important source of change is the shifts in composition in response to production practices, including weed control practices. Like speciation, these ecologically caused changes are also occurring continuously. However, the time frame within which an effect can be manifested ordinarily will be much shorter—as soon as 3 to 5 years—than for speciation. Even so, the effects are subtle and inconstant from year to year because of the interactions with environmental factors that in themselves are not constant.

In this regard, remember that *each new production or managerial practice ultimately has its own complement of weeds*. Unless this fact is recognized and steps taken to deal with it, new production practices may fail to attain the potential envisioned for them. To a degree, this experience has occurred with minimum tillage. The merits of this production practice have been documented for a variety of crops, soils, and geographic locations. However, evidence now suggests that the weed problems are different and may be more difficult to deal with than under conventional tillage. The weed problems with minimum tillage serve to remind us that it is essential to have an understanding of the shifts that may be expected and why they occur with specific changes in crop production practices.

Production practices may be divided into three broad types: (1) cropping practices, (2) tillage practices, and (3) herbicide practices. Each is examined separately, although a change in one is usually associated with a change in one or both of the other practices. For example, the move to monoculture corn in the Corn Belt occurred in part because herbicides were available to effectively control weeds. The availability of effective herbicides was also partly responsible for a shift to corn production under reduced or minimum tillage. Examination of each of these categories develops an understanding of the underlying forces involved.

Cropping Practices

As discussed in Chapter 6, crop species and varieties differ in their competitiveness toward weeds. Thus, we would expect weed populations to change with changes in crops and varieties produced. Some of these specific ramifications are explored in conjunction with an examination of crop sequence and monoculture versus rotation.

Crop variety.   Most studies of the competitiveness of varieties have been concerned with crop yield rather than with effects on weeds and have been relatively short-term. Such studies provide only circumstantial evidence that variety influences weed composition over time. More importantly, since varieties are continually changing, it is difficult and somewhat academic to trace such effects. To the extent that changes in varieties represent a general change in growth form, the effect should be traceable. Over the years, plant breeders' objectives have changed, leading to the development of new varieties quite different in growth form from their predecessors. For example, a general shift towards shorter and stiffer strawed varieties of wheat leads us to expect a change in the makeup of the weed community associated with wheat production.

The effect on weediness of a change in crop growth form has been demonstrated in potato production on Long Island. A switch from the Green Mountain variety to the Katahdin variety was followed by a substantial increase in yellow nutsedge (Sweet, 1976). As discussed in Chapter 4, yellow nutsedge is relatively

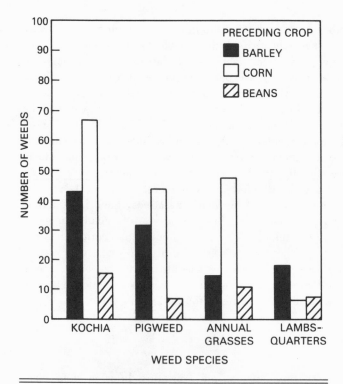

FIGURE 14–1. Effect of preceding crop on weed numbers and community composition. Weed numbers are those that germinated in a 400 g sample of soil following three years of each sequence.
Source: Data from Dotzenko et al., 1969.

sensitive to shading. Sweet found that in mid-July, the Katahdin variety intercepted only 25% of the incident light compared to 65% interception by Green Mountain. By the end of August, the interception percentage was 20% and 58%, respectively. Thus, the Katahdin variety provides less competition for light than the Green Mountain variety. Since this area of Long Island has been in monoculture potato production for many years, all other factors could be ruled out as explanations for the insurgence of yellow nutsedge.

Previous crop.   Where several crops are raised, the sequence in which they are grown may influence the makeup of the weed community over time. Dotzenko et al. (1969) found that the crop that preceded sugar beets in his studies in Colorado had a marked effect on weed numbers and community composition in beets. In this study, shown in Figure 14–1, the number of all weeds except lambsquarters was highest where corn was the preceding crop and least where beans was the preceding crop, with barley in between these two. The numbers are those that germinated in a 400 gram sample of soil after 3 years of each sequence. Lambsquarters was highest following barley. The explanation is found in the opportunity each preceding crop offers weeds to become established. Barley is the earliest planted in the spring and is seeded before soil temperatures are ideal for germination and growth of all species except lambsquarters. Thus, the total number of weeds is somewhat restricted, but lambsquarters is maximal. Corn is planted in mid-April when temperature is more optimum for weed germination and growth; as a result, weed numbers are high. Beans are planted in early June after the flush of germination of many summer annual weeds. Seedbed preparation thus destroys many of these weeds.

Monoculture and crop rotation.   The effects of a preceding crop are accentuated if continued for several years or for several complete rotations. This fact is shown in Figure 14–2 for corn, wheat, and soybeans after 6 years grown in monoculture and in rotation. Five of the more than 30 species identified are included in the figure. The area was in alfalfa for several years prior to establishing this study. Standard cultivation—but no herbicides—was used throughout the 6-year period. Thus, the results represent the accumulative effect of crops grown. Six years provided for 2 complete cycles of the multicrop sequences. In just 6 years, clear-cut and substantial differences in weed composition were apparent among the crop sequences. Velvetleaf and giant foxtail, which overtop soybeans, are favored by the continuous soybean rotation. Wild buckwheat, which germinates in the fall, is favored by continuous wheat, and even 1 year in 3 planted to wheat is sufficient for the weed to increase, compared with crop sequences that do not include wheat. Crabgrass is clearly discouraged by tillage since it decreased in all crop sequences that involved tillage every year. This conclusion is also supported by the fact that it, along with foxtail and panicum, increased substantially in continuous wheat.

Note also in Figure 14–2 that the number of instances in which the number of weed seeds increased is twice that for instances when the number of weed seeds decreased. In other words, the shift from alfalfa to annual crop production was followed by a general increase in weed seed numbers. This result is one more example of the fact that disturbed conditions increase the opportunities for weeds to increase.

The degree of change indicates the relative ecological stability of the individual cropping sequences. If we ignore the minus and plus signs and simply add the numbers for percent change in seven species that underwent major shifts (crabgrass, foxtail, panicum, pigweed, smartweed, velvetleaf, and wild buckwheat) in MacHoughton's (1973) study, the sum provides a measure of ecological stability. The resulting sums are 773, 1365, 869, 443, and 179 for continuous corn, continuous soybeans, continuous wheat, corn–corn–soybeans, and corn–

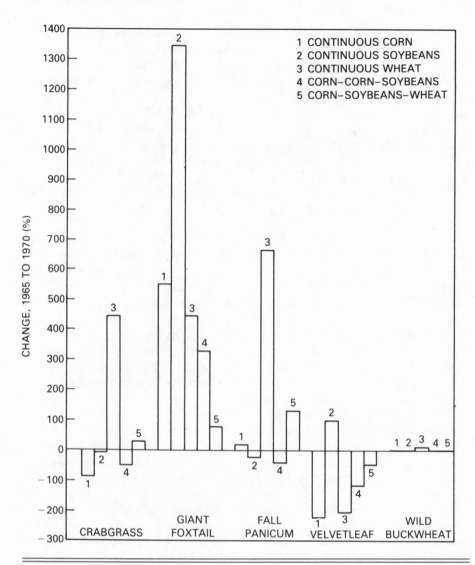

FIGURE 14–2. Effect of monoculture and crop rotation on weed seed composition of soil.

Source: Data from MacHoughton, 1973.

soybeans–wheat, respectively. In effect, each sum provides for the cropping system an index of the degree of change in weed numbers and rate. Greater changes occurred under monoculture than with a rotation. The explanation lies in the density relationships associated with disturbed environments, covered in Chapter 2. As discussed there, simple (annual row-crop) agroecosystems tend to have violent fluctuations in weed numbers and to have fewer species over time than undisturbed environments. In effect, the higher degree of change with monoculture than with the rotation simply reflects the fact that monoculture provided the maximum opportunity for the best-suited species to increase.

Intensity of crop production.   Intensity of the production enterprise may also affect weed composition. Figure 14–3 shows the effect on composition of seeds of selected weeds following a change from agronomic crop agriculture to vegetable crop agriculture in England. Prior to the initiation of the vegetable cropping study in 1953, the land had been in agronomic crops predominated by cereals for many years. The more intensive management associated with vegetable crops was reflected in an 87% reduction in weed seeds after 9 years. As can be seen, species varied greatly in their contribution to the overall reduction. Some actually increased.

Cropping history.   The shifts in weed populations identified in these examples are largely explained by the combined effect of tillage and competitiveness of the crops toward specific weeds. These examples serve as a reminder that at any point in time, the weed problem is a consequence of the cropping history of the land. The corollary is that reversion to the former agriculture and crop sequence can be expected to see a return of those weeds associated with the former crops. In other words, if the fields in vegetable crops in England were reverted to cereal crops in 1963, the weeds associated with cereals in 1953 would soon become the predominant ones again. Data such as these, when accumulated for sufficient locations and crop sequences, should make possible reasonably accurate predictions of weed problems for specific crop sequences in response to changes in them.

Crop seeding rate.   It is well known that density of the crop, as determined by seeding rate, is a factor in the competitiveness towards weeds. Although most of the work, including that with soybeans (Staniforth and Weber, 1956), cereals (Godel, 1935), and flax (Gruenhagen and Nalewaja, 1969), shows the depressing effects of increasing seeding rate on weeds, it does not examine composition of the weed community.

Moss and Hartwig (1980) did show lambsquarters to be reduced more than other weeds by competition from corn and soybean interseeded in the row. In their study, as the combined stand of corn and soybeans increased from 54,340 plants to 113,620 plants per hectare, the kilograms of dry matter of lambsquarters decreased from 2,211 to 760. The other weeds increased from 376 kg to 553 kg, respectively.

Marx and Hagedorn (1961), studying the effects on weeds of pea spacing in the row, observed a differential effect among the weed species. As spacing was increased from 3.6 cm to 8.7 cm, green foxtail increased 4.4 times, while the broadleaf species increased only 3 times. Thus, some evidence exists that crop seeding rate influences weed composition, but the data are insufficient for predictive purposes. The overall suppressing effect of increased seeding rate on weeds is quite clear-cut, however.

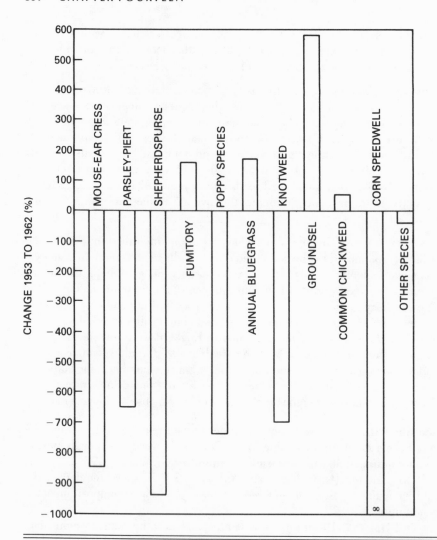

FIGURE 14–3. Changes in weed seed composition in soil under vegetable cropping begun in 1953.
Source: Data from Roberts and Stokes, 1965.

Crop pattern and spacing.   Plant spacing, of course, is affected by seeding rate. However, the effect of the *pattern* of crop spacing is an issue distinct from seeding rate. That is, the same seeding rate per land area can be obtained by either an equidistant planting pattern or by planting in rows. For example, a desired soybean stand of 500,000 plants per hectare can be obtained by spacing plants 20 cm apart in all directions or by spacing plants 2 cm apart in rows 100 cm apart. The greater competitiveness for light of the solid-planted (narrow-row) soybeans over those planted in wide rows was pointed out in Chapter 6. Because of the effect of row width on competitiveness, an effect on weed composition is to be expected.

Although studies of differential effects on weeds are limited, those that have been done indicate that weed species are affected differently. Wax and Pendelton (1968) showed that broadleaf weeds tended to be decreased and grassy weeds increased as row spacing of soybeans increased from 25.4 cm to 101.6 cm, as can be seen in Figure 14–4. No herbicide was used but the plots were cultivated. The weeds involved were giant foxtail, smooth pigweed, crabgrass, and prickly sida, plus a light infestation of velvetleaf.

Although there is some hazard in extrapolating from dry matter production to seed production because of compensation by individual plants, it is nevertheless realistic to predict higher seed production by the taller-growing broadleaf annual weeds, thus leading to their increase where soybeans are planted in narrow rows over a period of years. If the growth form of the weed, especially the height attained, is known for each weed in the community of weeds associated with a particular crop, it would seem that fairly accurate predictions of the shift in community makeup in response to plant spacing can be made for other crops. This

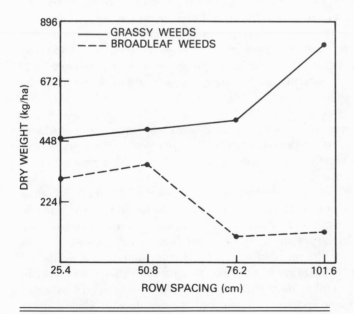

FIGURE 14–4. Different effects of crop row spacing on weeds.

Source: Data from Wax and Pendleton, 1968.

supposition assumes that light is the growth factor most usually competed for, particularly during the early part of the growing season. This is not to say that the weed problem is expected to be the same for a given row spacing in a given crop wherever that crop is grown since many other factors also affect shifts in composition of the weed community. What this statement does say, however, is that when the makeup of a weed community on a given area (field) is known at the time a shift in row spacing is planned, the shift in weed composition should be predictable.

Soil fertility. The fertility level is expected to affect composition of the weed community because of the differences in competitive ability among weeds. As stated in Chapter 2, early colonizers in ecological succession are those species whose survival strategy depends upon large numbers of seed. Later stages are represented by species of increasing competitive ability. Thus, we would expect that the most competitive species would be favored over the less competitive species by high fertility.

Research in pasture crops provides a good example that this expectation is the case. Studies of perennial ryegrass longevity in England (Smith and Allcock, 1978) showed that the relatively less aggressive grasses (bentgrass, *Agrostis tenuis* and *Poa trivialis*) invaded over time under low nitrogen (188 kilograms per hectare), while the more aggressive quackgrass was the most prevalent under high nitrogen (376 and 752 kilograms per hectare). Peters and Lowance (1974) found that broomsedge *(Andropogon virginicus)*, a frequent species in poor, rundown pastures, could be eliminated from permanent pastures in Missouri in 4 years by drilling in fescue, fertilizing with nitrogen, phosphorus, and potassium, and mowing each winter. Just fertilizing the bluegrass sod gradually reduced the broomsedge after 5 years.

Duration of crop cover. Intercropping and relay cropping, which are forms of *multiple cropping*—that is, the growing of two or more crops on the same field in one year—have been practiced for centuries, mainly in tropical regions with high rainfall. Pressures for more food and a reduction in capital investment in food production have pushed science to develop technology to extend multiple cropping to other areas. In the United States, growing a soybean crop in the year wheat is harvested has now become a standard practice on many farms south from the southern Corn Belt, and the practice is slowly moving northward. This practice has obvious implications for the makeup of the weed community since weeds are provided relatively less time to grow in the absence of competition from crops. In effect, the second crop is filling the niche that would otherwise be filled with one or more weed species. Those species that commonly germinate after wheat harvest can be expected to be discouraged in favor of winter annuals or perennial species that commonly germinate or make considerable growth in the fall following soybean harvest. Data are not yet available to identify the precise effects.

Planting cover crops to suppress weeds by filling the void in crop cover is a type of multiple cropping with potential for long-term weed management. While this idea is expanded upon in Chapter 15, we can appreciate here that such a cropping practice would be expected to lead to a change in the weed community.

Tillage Practices

In ecological terms, tillage influences primarily the physical environment of the weeds in a weed–crop ecosystem. Tillage can affect the physical distribution of weed seeds within the soil profile, the physical distribution of plant residues, and the moisture and temperature environment. All of these effects can serve to differentiate among weed species in their germination and establishment because of both different requirements and different chances offered for germination and establishment.

Tillage depth.   Plowing provides an excellent example of the effect tillage can have on the opportunity or chance for weeds to germinate and become established. Deep plowing (36 cm to 40 cm), shallow plowing (15 cm to 18 cm), shallow plowing plus subsoiling (40 cm to 46 cm), and rotary cultivation (15 cm to 18 cm) were compared in a study in England. As shown in Figure 14–5, plowing tends to

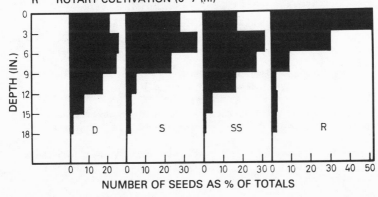

D   DEEP PLOWING (14–16 in.)
S   SHALLOW PLOWING (6–7 in.)
SS   SHALLOW PLOWING, PLUS SUBSOILING (16–18 in.)
R   ROTARY CULTIVATION (6–7 in.)

FIGURE 14–5. Effect of tillage on distribution of weed seeds in the soil. Distribution was determined after 9 years of differential primary tillage.

Source: Roberts and Stokes, 1965. Reproduced with permission of Blackwell Scientific Publications, Ltd.

distribute weed seeds throughout the plow layer. By contrast, rotary cultivation resulted in 50% of the weed seeds being in the top 7.6 cm (3 in.) and 80% in the top 15.2 cm (6 in.). There are approximately 2 1/2 times as many weed seeds in the top 7.6 cm (3 in.) under rotary cultivation than in that same depth under deep plowing. Because most weeds are successful in emerging only when in the top 7.6 cm (3 in.) or less, it follows that the potential population under deep plowing is only 40% of rotary cultivation. Even though there was no soil inversion with subsoiling, weed seeds were moved downward in the soil by this practice, as can be seen by comparison with shallow plowing.

The effect of tillage depth on weed seed distribution within the soil profile was utilized in a no-till continuous corn production system developed by Nebraska scientists (Wicks and Somerhalder, 1971) to reduce early competition. This system physically removes each year's weed seed crop from the corn row into the row middles, thus minimizing direct early competition of weeds towards the next corn crop. Figure 14–6 shows that after 3 years under this system, less than half as many weed seeds were in the top 7.6 cm immediately over the row than under conventional tillage. Thus, the source of weeds in the corn row is much less. They also found that plowing distributed weed seeds rather uniformly throughout the

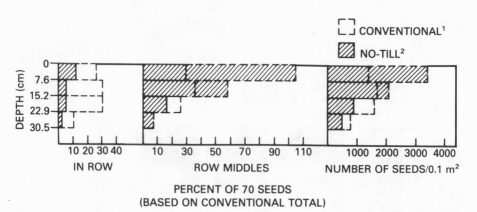

[1]Conventional tillage consisted of cutting the corn stalks, tandem discing, and harrowing to level the ridges created for furrow irrigation, plowing, pulling a sodbuster, and planting.

[2]No-till consisted of cutting the corn stalks, pushing the plant residues away from the row with a 40.7 cm flat sweep equipped with trash bars, and planting directly into the ridge along the old corn row.

FIGURE 14–6. Distribution of weed seed in soil at different depths within and between 101.6 cm corn rows after seedbed preparation under two planting systems at North Platte, Nebraska. Counts were taken the fourth year.
Source: Data from Wicks and Somerhalder, 1971.

plow layer, whereas no-till concentrated the seeds in the top 7.6 cm. Fifty percent of the total weed seed population was in the top 7.6 cm under no-till as compared with approximately 25% in that same soil zone under conventional tillage. Although the data do not provide a basis for identifying shifts in weed composition, it can be assumed that changes will occur over time.

Tillage amount.   A major purpose of tillage throughout the history of agriculture was to prevent or minimize losses from weeds. In fact, the main reason for planting many crops in rows has been to facilitate mechanical or manual control of weeds. From a maximum production standpoint, ample evidence suggests that the best arrangement often is equidistant spacing of crop plants. Beginning in the 1940s, widespread availability of increasingly selective and effective herbicides, by lessening the need for tillage to control weeds, has made reduced or conservation tillage feasible. The attendant reductions in soil losses and lower fossil fuel needs suggest this practice likely will, and indeed should, expand. Phillips et al. (1981) estimate that by the year 2000, 60% to 80% of the corn and soybeans grown in the mid-Atlantic and upper southeast regions of the United States will be produced under so-called no-till.

Since reduced tillage will probably continue to expand, weed scientists need to adjust their efforts to both meet the challenge of the new weed problems that can be anticipated and to further the successful use and expansion of this worthwhile major shift in tillage. If weed science is to meet the challenge and opportunity afforded by reduced tillage and by changes in other production practices, it must develop effective ways of predicting shifts in weeds caused by changes in production. At this time, only general shifts can be predicted, but even so, they do suggest the broad changes in approaches that are needed to deal with the weeds.

Effects of reduced tillage.   A number of shifts in weed composition are likely to be associated with reduced tillage. One such shift is for perennials to increase. This occurrence has been reported throughout the world and for many crops. For example, reduced tillage for cereal crop production in Germany (Schwerdtle, 1977) led to an increase in quackgrass. Reduced tillage in corn in the midwest and southeast portions of the United States led to an increase in honeyvine milkweed. This effect is simple ecology at work with respect to r- and K-strategy species. When tillage is reduced or eliminated, the competitive ability of the perennial weeds allows them to increase and become dominant. Thus, efforts for dealing with perennial weeds must increase in the coming years.

Among the annual weeds, reduced tillage favors the surface germinators and the early germinators. That is, species such as annual bluegrass, crabgrass, purslane, and tumbling mustard that germinate best at or very near the soil surface have relatively more of their seeds in a position favorable to germination than is true if tillage distributes them throughout the soil profile. Thus, reduced tillage provides them an opportunity to gain in numbers over species that germinate from

greater dep   id many others. The
early germi   e some of them will
have alread   ... pianted, thus giving them a
competitive   germinators. In the midwestern portion of the
United States, ine early germinators tend to be broadleaf species, so reduced
tillage can be expected to lead to an increase in such species over time. It should
not be too difficult to predict species that are apt to dominate for any crop and any
region. Weed research needs to adjust in line with such predictions.

Crop residue management.   An increase in crop residues on the soil surface is
a usual consequence of reduced or zero (no-till) tillage. The effects of such
residues on moisture and temperature at or near the soil surface can be expected to
influence the makeup of the weed community. In effect, residues provide a
different environment for weed seed germination and establishment than does a
conventional seedbed. The differential effects on germination and establishment
of downy brome *(Bromus tectorum)* and tumble mustard in Nevada rangeland
shown in Table 14–3 indicate that trash can indeed have a pronounced effect upon
weed species. Temperature and moisture relationships under bare ground and that
covered with litter were discussed earlier (Figures 2–5 and 2–6). These physical
aspects of the environment interacting with the seed characteristics of the species
account for the differences observed. The downy brome seed is large but light with
large awns. The better moisture environment provided by litter offers more safe
sites for its germination than does bare soil. The tumbling mustard has a small,
smooth, dense seed with a seed coat that surrounds itself with mucilage when
wetted. These seeds find proportionately more safe sites on a smooth, bare surface
than on one even partially covered with litter.

Time of seedbed preparation.   In view of what we know about periodicity of
weed seed germination, when the seedbed is prepared could be expected to affect

TABLE 14-3

**Frequency percentages of downy brome and tumble mustard the second
year after planting as affected by surface litter. Frequency was determined
at 100 random points in 5 transects of each plot.**

Species	Characteristics of Soil Surface	Date of Sampling		
		April 7	April 16	April 28
Downy brome	Litter-covered	50	34	48
	Smooth	7	6	6
Tumble mustard	Litter-covered	13	0	0
	Smooth	67	100	90

Source: Adapted from Evans and Young, 1970.

composition of the weed community. A study of the effect of tillage time on wild oat numbers, shown in Figure 14–7, indicates that indeed it does. Wild oat numbers increased about 400 times under 6 years of early tillage and decreased at about the same rate under later tillage. Of course, the effect of a preceding crop discussed earlier is essentially a reflection of tillage time.

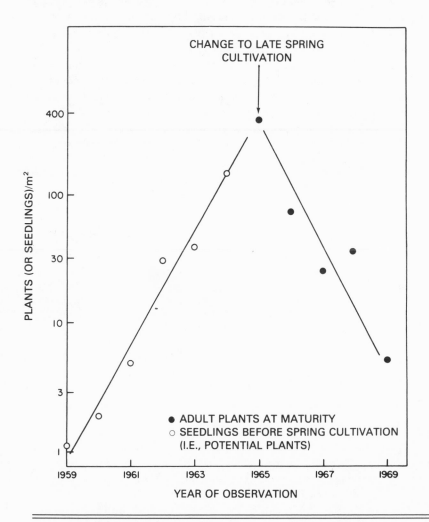

FIGURE 14–7. Effect of tillage time on weed composition. Results shown are for wild oat plants in continuous spring barley. During the period 1959–1964, cultivation was done in early spring; during the period 1965–1969, cultivation and sowing were done late.

Source: Harper, 1977. Reproduced courtesy J.L. Harper. © J.L. Harper.

The effect of tillage to encourage weed seed germination is utilized in a weed management practice called stale seedbed. *Stale seedbed* involves preparing the seedbed several weeks in advance of planting and then at planting destroying with a contact herbicide those weeds that have been encouraged to germinate, with no additional tillage to bring up new weed seeds. Wax (1972) has pointed out that the effectiveness of this approach is dependent upon the germination periodicity of the particular weeds in the weed community. Those weeds that germinate early, such as lambsquarters and smartweed, are effectively controlled in corn in the Corn Belt area in the United States. Foxtail and velvetleaf, which emerge both before and after planting, as well as pigweed and jimsonweed, which usually germinate after planting, are not effectively controlled. Thus, where the latter species are represented in the weed community, adoption of a stale seedbed practice could be expected over time to lead to a situation where foxtail, pigweed, velvetleaf, and jimson weed are the dominant species.

HERBICIDE PRACTICES

As a result of his review of the long-term effects of herbicides, Chancellor (1979) formulated a concept that we, as weed scientists, ought to keep in mind. He concluded that "it is unlikely any weed will ever be eliminated through the use of herbicides." The significance of this principle is the implication that the exclusive reliance on herbicides for managing weeds can be expected to create quite volatile conditions of weed composition. This anticipated result is due to the fact that environmental conditions supportive of a given weed community are kept from exerting their influence as long as the herbicide is used and is effective. However, those conditions remain and can again exert their effects if there is a herbicide failure or a change in herbicides with a change in crop.

Shifts in Weed Composition

Weed–weed competition in response to herbicide. For the most part, shifts occurring as the result of herbicide usage can be viewed as a response to competition within the community of weeds. It has been observed many times in many different crops that selective control of only some weeds in a community of species leads to a shift towards a community dominated by the uncontrolled species. As already discussed, this shift occurred in corn in the United States when effective control of broadleaf species by 2,4–D led to a weed community dominated by grasses, and later, following use of the s-triazine herbicide, to a community dominated by late-germinating weeds, such as panicum. In asparagus, lambsquarters was observed to build up under the use of chloramben and diphenamid, and redroot pigweed to build up under DCPA (Welker and Brogdon, 1972). In orchards (Schubert, 1972), weeds of a few species increased following continued use of certain herbicides. Pineapple production (Gowing and Lange, 1962), following the period from World War II to the early 1960s, has seen several shifts in response to changes in weed control methods. Prior to World War II, mechanical and manual labor were relied upon for weed control. Weather and development of the pineapple crop itself frequently interfered with timely control, thus resulting in a large number of a wide variety of weeds.

Herbicidal oils were used extensively in the 1940s. Because broadleaf weeds were covered more effectively, they tended to be selectively reduced, thus allowing for an increase in grass weeds. At the same time, the level of cultivation was reduced so that perennial species also increased. During the 1950s, the substituted ureas came into common usage. These herbicides were relatively more effective toward grass weeds, resulting in a relative increase in annual broadleaf and perennial species. In soybeans (Wax and Pendelton, 1968), trifluralin, which is widely used as a preemergence herbicide, is more effective against annual grasses than against annual broadleaf species. Where it has been used for a period of years, there has been an increase in broadleaf weeds.

Development of resistance in response to herbicide.   The only exception to shifts occurring in response to competition is shifts in response to the development of resistance to a given herbicide. Strictly speaking, this shift is the result of the buildup of resistant biotypes through natural selection. Biotype resistance has been reported for several weed–herbicide combinations (Putwain and Holliday, 1979). Where this combination occurs, we might expect the species with the ability to develop resistance to do so at the expense of other species, thus shifting the weed composition.

Even so, the development of resistant populations has occurred only in response to the s-triazine herbicides (Putwain and Holliday, 1979). A major factor no doubt limiting widespread and rapid development of resistant populations is the reservoir of seed in the soil. This seedbank contains seed produced during several preceding years, not just the previous year. Seed dormancy, depth of burial, and other factors assure that plants emerging any given year are a composite sample of that seedbank. It follows that a given herbicide has to be used each year for several years for resistance, if it occurs, to be fully manifested. Periodic changes in crops and in production practices serve to limit the instances where resistance might occur.

Ideally, a herbicide should control all weeds equally well. Practically, however, as the above examples indicate, most herbicides are somewhat more effective against some weeds than against others. Thus, continued use of a given herbicide can be expected to result in a shift in weed composition.

Herbicide Combinations

Shifts in weed composition as a consequence of differential effectiveness of herbicides have led to the now common practice of combining two or more herbicides. MacHoughton (1973) examined the effects of a single herbicide and a rotation of herbicides on weed seed composition of soil in a number of different crop sequence systems common to the Corn Belt in the United States. Figure 14–8, which shows some of the results in the continuous corn production system, indicates the extreme differences that can occur. In this case, the use of atrazine as the single herbicide for 6 years resulted in more than a fourfold increase in seeds of the three problem annual grasses. The rotation of herbicides resulted in a 48% to 95% reduction in seeds of these species in the soil. Broadleaf weeds collectively were reduced by both herbicide treatments but somewhat more by the rotation. Of course, the opposite can occur. If the single herbicide used is the most effective chemical towards certain species, using other less-effective herbicides in some of the years would lead to an increase. The important point here is that rotation of herbicides leads to less violent shifts in the weed community than use of a single herbicide.

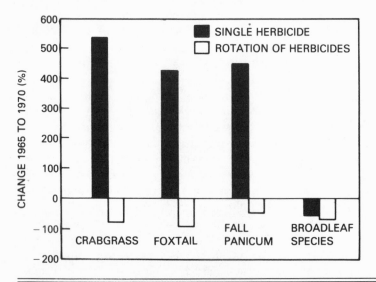

FIGURE 14–8. Weed seed composition in soil after 6-year treatment with a single herbicide or a rotation of herbicides in corn.
Source: Data from MacHoughton, 1973.

Crop Residues

In considering effects of herbicide usage on weed composition over time, the effect of crop residues associated with reduced or zero tillage must be borne in mind. Crop residues may intercept an appreciable part of the herbicide applied for weed control. Williams and Wicks (1978), referring to the Ph.D. dissertation by Bauman (1976), indicated that 30% of soil-applied atrazine failed to reach the soil surface during the first 90 days of a zero tillage system with 85% trash cover. Because of the nature of atrazine, most of that intercepted by plant residue is probably lost through volatilization or degradation. We can theorize that herbicides not subject to loss when intercepted by residue might be more effective against surface-germinating weed seeds by virtue of the fact that the residues retain them in the vicinity of the germinating seeds. In any case, trash normally associated with reduced tillage offers an additional source for shifts in weed populations as the result of its potential effect upon herbicide effectiveness.

COMBINED EFFECTS OF CROPPING, TILLAGE, AND HERBICIDE PRACTICES

The three production practices—that is, cropping, tillage, and herbicides—that influence weed composition are commonly exerting their effect simultaneously, not independently. This fact is summarized schematically in Figure 14–9.

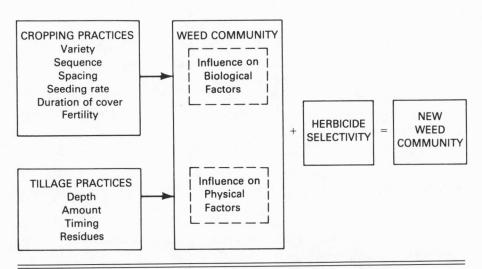

FIGURE 14–9. Schematic representation of simultaneous effects of the three types of production practices—cropping, tillage, and herbicides—on weed ecology.

Differential response of weeds to the herbicides used is viewed as being an override on the effects of cropping and tillage practices. This perspective recognizes that the impacts of cropping and tillage are not altered by herbicides, but their effects may well be masked.

Figure 14–9 also emphasizes the dominating effect of differential weed removal by herbicides. In this connection, recall that removal of a dominant (the objective in most herbicide usage) is in itself a disruptive influence. That is, removal provides a new environment (niche) for other species. Two points should be kept in mind, however. One point is that the three production aspects do not represent mutually independent decisions, at least not from the perspective of the farmer or other user of the production system. That is, the specific levels of the several aspects listed under tillage are influenced by one or more of those aspects listed under cropping practices.

Similarly, the choice of herbicide is influenced at least in part by the crop sequence, possibly by the variety chosen under cropping practices, and quite possibly by timing and residues chosen under tillage practices. The second point is that although their effects may be masked by the herbicide, both the influence of cropping and the influence of tillage practices remain as latent forces that may express themselves with a change in the herbicide. Thus, although herbicides may be the dominant influence, weed composition is the result of the combined influences of all aspects of the production system.

CONCEPTS AND CONCLUSIONS

1. Weeds on a given farm or field change as a result of introduction from outside, as a result of genetic and physiologic alteration within a species, and as a result of production practices followed.
2. In terms of numbers and the time in which marked changes may occur, changes brought about by production practices are the most important for weed management.
3. Each new crop production or managerial practice will ultimately have its own complement of weeds.
4. Cropping, tillage, and herbicide practices are aspects of production that influence weed composition, but the effects of herbicides commonly overshadow the other effects.
5. Effective ways of predicting shifts in weeds need to be developed in order to ensure the continued success and expansion of such new production approaches as reduced tillage.
6. A generally encountered response of weeds to reduced tillage is an increase in perennial species.

REFERENCES

Bauman, T.T. 1976. Movement and persistence of atrazine in soil with three tillage systems, Ph.D. dissertation. Purdue University, Lafayette, Ind.

Chancellor, R.J. 1979. A review of long-term effects of herbicides: The long-term effects of herbicides on weed populations. Ann. Appl. Biol. 91 (1):141–44.

Dotzenko, A.D., M. Ozkan, and K.R. Storer. 1969. Influence of crop sequence, nitrogen fertilizer, and herbicides on weed seed populations in sugar beet fields. Agron. J. 61 (1):34–37.

Dunham, R.S. 1972. The weed story. St. Paul: Agricultural Extension Service, University of Minnesota.

Evans, R.A., and J.A. Young. 1970. Plant litter and establishment of alien annual weed species in rangeland communities. Weed Sci. 18 (6):697–703.

Fogg, J.M., Jr. 1966. The silent travelers. Plants and Gardens 22:4–7.

Godel, G.L. 1935. Relation between rate of seeding and yield of cereal crops in competition with weeds. Sci. Agr. 16:165–68.

Gowing, D.P., and A.H. Lange. 1962. The impact of herbicide research on field practices in pineapple culture. Weeds 10 (2):118–20.

Gruenhagen, R.D., and J.D. Nalewaja. 1969. Competition between flax and wild buckwheat. Weed Sci. 17:380–84.

Harper, J.L. 1977. Population biology of plants. New York: Academic Press.

Kelley, A.D., and V.F. Bruns. 1975. Dissemination of weed seeds by irrigation water. Weed Sci. 23 (6):486–93.

MacHoughton, J. 1973. Ecological changes in weed populations as a result of crop rotations and herbicides, Ph.D. dissertation. University of Illinois, Urbana.

Marx, G.A., and D.J. Hagedorn. 1961. Plant population and weed growth relations in canning peas. Weeds 9 (3):494–96.

Moss, P.A., and N.L. Hartwig. 1980. Competitive control of common lambsquarters in a corn–soybean intercrop. In Proc. of NEWSS, vol. 34, pp. 21–28. Grossinger, N.Y.

Peters, E.J., and S.A. Lowance. 1974. Fertility and management treatments to control broomsedge in pastures. Weed Sci. 22 (3):201–05.

Phillips, S.H., et al. 1981. Multiple cropping systems using no-tillage techniques for crop production in humid temperate and humid tropical areas. In T. Kommedahl, ed., Proc. of Symposia, 9th International Congress of Plant Protection. Washington, D.C.: Entomological Society of America.

Putwain, P.D., and R.J. Holliday. 1979. Herbicide resistance in weeds. In T. Kommedahl, ed., Proc. of Symposia, 9th International Congress of Plant Protection, pp. 231–35. Washington, D.C.: Entomological Society of America.

Roberts, H.A., and F.G. Stokes. 1965. Studies on the weeds of vegetable crops, V. Final observations on an experiment with different primary cultivations. J. Appl. Ecol. 2:307–15.

Schubert, O.E. 1972. Plant cover changes following herbicide applications in orchards. Weed Sci. 20 (1):124–27.

Schwerdtle, F.V. 1977. The effect of direct sowing on the weed population. In W.

Koch et al., ed., Zeitschrift fur Pflanzenkrankheiten und Pflanzenochutz, Sondenheft 8, pp. 155–63. Stuttgart, Germany.

Smith, A., and P.J. Allcock. 1978. Hurley, England: Grassland Research Institute Annual Report, 1977.

Staniforth, D.W., and C.R. Weber. 1956. Effects of annual weeds on the growth and yield of soybeans. Agron. J. 48:467–71.

Sweet, R.D. 1976. When it comes to competing with weeds, some are more equal than others. Crops and Soils 28 (6):7–9.

van der Pijl, L. 1982. Principles of dispersal in higher plants, 3rd ed. New York: Springer-Verlag.

Wax, L.M. 1972. Weed control for close-drilled soybeans. Weed Sci. 20 (1):16–19.

————, and J.W. Pendelton. 1968. Effect of row spacing on weed control in soybeans. Weeds 16 (4):462–65.

Welker, W.V., Jr., and J.L. Brogdon. 1972. Effects of continued use of herbicides in asparagus plantings. Weed Sci. 20 (5):428–32.

Wicks, G.A., and B.R. Somerhalder. 1971. Effect of seedbed preparation for corn on distribution of weed seed. Weed Sci. 19 (6):666–68.

Williams, J.L., Jr., and G.A. Wicks. 1978. Weed control problems associated with crop residues systems. In Crop residues management systems, ASA Special Publication 31, pp. 165–72. Madison, Wis.: American Society of Agronomy.

A TOTAL
WEED MANAGEMENT
APPROACH

15

The preceding chapters have shown that enough information about weeds and their relationship to crops is now available to support an approach in which weed prevention and control have companion roles. We know weeds compete early. We know a great deal—but not enough—about what they compete for. Much has been learned about weeds themselves, including: knowledge of factors affecting production of seed and perennating parts; knowledge of factors affecting retention of viability of seeds and vegetative reproductive parts; and knowledge of factors that induce dormancy and resumption of growth of seeds and perennating parts. There is general knowledge of the shifts in weed composition that can be expected in response to changes in crop production practices. Our knowledge of allelopathy, with an associated increase in the potential for its use as a tool in weed management, is expanding. Expansion in the use of biological agents in weed management is slow but steady. Thus, the total body of knowledge is impressive, although much is yet to be learned in each of these areas.

In this chapter, what knowledge is known is brought together into what may be called a total weed management approach. A conceptual framework is developed to provide the necessary background for planning a weed management program for any given cropping system. The conceptual framework is then used to develop a weed management program for a hypothetical crop rotation. The conceptual framework is also examined in terms of recent developments in crop production. Finally, those areas urgently needing additional information in order to improve a total weed management effort are examined in detail.

For weed science to progress to a total management level, weed management must be viewed realistically. That is, care must be taken neither to oversell nor underestimate its potential and likely adoption.

Figure 15–1 serves as an excellent basis for developing a proper perspective of weed management. This figure shows the changes in weeds in a corn–corn–corn rotation in central Illinois. The pronounced reduction of weed seeds in soil in only 6 years with the rotation of herbicides shows what can be accomplished when seed production is largely prevented. The rotation of herbicides used is shown in Appendix Table 3. The total reduction of about 84 weed seeds per kilogram of soil represents a 70% reduction in the seedbank. However, the substantial reduction in numbers of seeds of broadleaf weeds by the single herbicide, atrazine, is more than offset by the increase in grass weed seeds. Thus, although prevention of weed seed production can be very worthwhile in weed management, unequal prevention among weed species may be counterproductive.

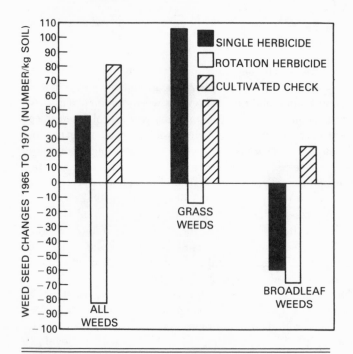

FIGURE 15–1. Effect of crop rotation and weed control type on weed seed numbers in soil after 6 years. Herbicides used are shown in Appendix Table 3.
Source: Data from MacHoughton, 1973.

WEED MANAGEMENT PROGRAM

Role of Weed Prevention

Prevention needs to be the foundation upon which a total weed management program is based. This point can be developed by reference to the *three stages in the development of a weed*—(1) emergence, (2) growth and maturation, and (3) reproduction—that offer individual opportunities for preventive approaches. The corresponding *approaches to weed prevention* during these stages are: (A) to reduce the number of weed propagules produced, (B) to reduce the emergence of weeds with the crop, and (C) to minimize the competition or interference of weeds growing with the crop. These stages and associated prevention approaches may be viewed sequentially in terms of the consequences of failure of the approach. Failure at A still leaves approaches B and C as ways to avoid crop loss. Failure under both A and B leaves only C as a means of avoiding crop loss. Another way of viewing the sequential relationship is to view modest success at A as removing some of the pressure for success at B and at C. Success at both A and B could very much reduce the pressure for success at C. Viewed in this way, prevention can be seen as the necessary foundation for a successful total weed management effort in order that all potential tools for dealing with weeds may be used.

Role of Weed Control

Weed control will continue to be an important part of a total weed management effort. However, it too needs to be seen as having an important place during each of the three stages of a weed's life cycle. That is, control of the weed plant can be accomplished to reduce propagules, weed emergence, and competition with the crop. Control will make its greatest contribution to a total management effort when viewed in this expanded context.

Complementary Relationship of Prevention and Control

Prevention and control can best be seen as complementary parts of a total program, not as alternatives. Success with one does not eliminate the need for the other but can be expected to improve results from the other. One way of visualizing this relationship is by adding control to the sequential relationship discussed under prevention:

	A. Reduce Weed Propagules	**B.** Prevent Weed Emergence	**C.** Minimize Competition/Interference
Prevention	Prevent additions to the propagule bank by tillage and cropping practices	Reduce the potential weed numbers by tillage and cropping practices	Minimize competition by cropping and tillage practices
Control	Treatment with chemicals to hasten germination	Preplant-incorporated and pre-emergence control with herbicides	Postemergence control

If we examine the relationships between control and prevention for only stage A, the mutual relationships can be seen. From what is known now, even a very successful treatment to hasten germination cannot be expected to eliminate a weed problem in the year of treatment because of seed dormancy, periodicity of germination, and other factors that protect some weed seeds from the treatment. However, even modest success can be expected to improve the effects of tillage and cropping practices in reducing production of propagules. Conversely, modest success in the prevention approaches can be expected to improve results with the hastening of germination approach by reducing the number of propagules to be dealt with. As mentioned for hastening germination, no matter how successful the approaches for preventing additions of new propagules, complete prevention is unrealistic. A comparable mutual dependency exists for stages B and C also. Similarly, there is a sequential, interactive relationship as we move from stage A to B and to C. Thus, success with prevention at A improves chances for control at B, and so on. In effect, using both prevention and control doubles the opportunities for reducing weed losses.

This view of prevention and control also helps to show why weed management necessitates a commitment to an on-going effort. That is to say, we must accept that weeds will be a factor to be reckoned with, each year and indefinitely on into the future. We may reduce the numbers through effective management, but it is unrealistic to expect we will ever eliminate a problem weed. Acceptance of this fact provides the necessary setting for long-term planning for steps to be taken at each stage.

Similarly, the relationship between prevention and control indicates why the focus of a weed management approach must be the production unit. That is, since this approach embraces an on-going effort with interactions among approaches to weeds in the entire crop production system or rotation, it necessarily involves the individual fields and crops on an individual production unit (farm). By contrast, a control approach that focuses on the complex of weeds in a given crop can be approached regionally and on a commodity basis.

Of course, we must always remember that the objective of an effective weed management program is maximum, sustainable crop production. This objective simply recognizes that weed management, weed prevention, and weed control by themselves have value only as they contribute to the purpose of the particular production enterprise. They are not ends in themselves. Thus, for any given contemplated weed management, weed prevention, or weed control effort, a decision of what to be done needs to be made in terms of this broader perspective.

PREVENTING WEED INTERFERENCE WITH THE CROP

This section identifies ways to utilize what has been learned about weed–crop relationships to prevent or minimize interference from weeds in a total management program. The concepts developed in the preceding chapters are used as a background and are listed in Table 15–1 for each of the ecological relationships studied. The ecological relationships include reproduction capacity, longevity, and germination and emergence of seed and perennating parts, competition, allelopathy, biological agents, and humans. Herbicides are included under humans since their use is entirely dependent upon them. The other phenomena, although influenced by humans, have effects that can be expressed independent of human efforts.

The concepts listed in the table are generalizations. Specific weed and crop situations may express different relationships from these generalizations. It is necessary to draw upon generalizations to develop an appreciation of how knowledge about ecological relationships can be used in the prevention component of weed management. With this knowledge as background, each of the following discussions concludes with a summary showing how control and prevention might fit together in weed management.

Because the reproduction unit (seed and perennating part) is central to a management approach, the discussion begins with ways to reduce propagules. The conceptual approaches to prevention are developed by considering each ecological relationship in turn. However, the desired degree of prevention cannot be attained from application of a single concept, but rather from the use of several concepts.

TABLE 15-1

Weed-crop ecological relationships and concepts that may be utilized in weed prevention.

Reproduction Capacity—Seed

a. Many weeds are capable of producing a normal seed crop even when their numbers are reduced.

b. Seed production commonly starts at an early age in weeds and may occur over an extended period.

c. Some very immature weed seeds may be viable.

d. Seed production of many weeds is curtailed by shade.

e. Influx from outside does not add significant numbers to the weed seedbank.

f. Weed seeds face many hazards before becoming a part of the seedbank.

Reproduction Capacity—Perennating Parts

a. Production commonly starts within a few weeks after emergence from either seed or an old perennating part.

b. Factors that encourage vegetative growth commonly discourage production of perennating parts.
   (1) High nitrogen levels
   (2) Shade
   (3) Ample to excessive water supply
   (4) Cool temperatures

c. Production is likely to be influenced by growth regulators.

d. Shading may reduce the size of the perennating part.

Longevity—Seed

a. Dormancy is common for some seeds of many weed species; such seeds are highly tolerant of temperature and moisture extremes.

b. A majority of weed seeds either germinate or deteriorate in 2 to 3 years after entering the soil, but a few may live much longer.

c. Longevity is commonly increased by burial in the soil.

d. Longevity is commonly reduced by tillage.

Longevity—Perennating Parts

a. Some dormancy is not uncommon, but it is less common and less pronounced than in seeds.

b. A majority of perennating parts either resume growth or die the year following their production, but some may live longer.

c. Perennating parts are vulnerable to desiccation and some to temperature extremes encountered in nature.

d. Longevity is commonly increased by burial in soil.

e. Tillage reduces longevity.

Germination and Emergence—Seed

a. Emergence is inversely related to depth of burial in soil; for many weed seeds, emergence falls sharply below 4 cm (1 in.). Germination will occur at any depth providing requirements have been met.

b. Many weed seeds have dormancy induced by burial in soil and some by leaf shade.

c. Alternating temperatures and several days of freezing or near-freezing temperatures frequently are needed for best germination.

d. Many weed seeds have chemical inhibitors of germination.

e. Many weed seeds require light for best germination.

f. Many weed seeds have the capacity to anticipate the best season in which to germinate and complete the life cycle.

g. The effects of factors are largely a matter of degree rather than being absolute.

Germination and Emergence—Perennating Parts

a. Emergence is inversely related to depth of burial in soil; successful emergence commonly occurs from greater depths than for seeds.

b. Emergence is directly related to the size of the perennating part.

c. Sprouting is directly related to N content.

d. Some form of correlative inhibition is common among buds on perennating parts; dominance by the apical meristem is most common.

(1) Separating the part from the parent often increases such dominance.

(2) Fragmenting the rhizome reduces but does not eliminate dominance.

(3) High N levels reduce dominance.

Competition

a. Weeds must be controlled early.

b. Weeds that emerge after about one-third of the crop growing period usually do not cut crop yields.

c. The effect of weed numbers on crop yield tends to be sigmoidal and that of weed weight tends to be linear.

d. Most annual weeds are relatively intolerant of competition.

e. Crop species and varieties differ in competitiveness.

f. Annual weeds tend to cause more losses in annual crops and perennial weeds more in perennial crops.

g. The leaf is the site of aboveground competition; factors that influence quantity and quality of light absorbed determine competition.

h. The root is the site of belowground competition; extent of competition is largely determined by root volume occupied.

i. The life cycle of many annual weeds is shorter than that of the crop with which it may be competing.

j. Competition for one growth factor frequently leads to competition for others.

k. Competition may influence both the production and activity of growth regulators by crops and weeds.

(continued)

TABLE 15-1 continued

Allelopathy

a. Chemicals are produced by some plants that prevent or inhibit germination and growth of others.
b. Chemicals may be produced in all plant parts.
   (1) Those in crop roots are likely to be the most significant in suppressing weeds in a crop.
   (2) Location in the crop plant is immaterial if the residue is used to suppress weeds.
c. Quantities produced seem to be directly related to stress.
d. Effects may be on any plant process or function and during any stage of development.
e. Allelochemicals enter the environment via volatilization, leaching, exudation, and decomposition of plant parts.
f. Allelochemicals embrace a wide variety of chemical compounds likely traceable to all basic processes of plant metabolism.
g. Crop species and genotypes vary in presence and in quantity.

Biological Agents

a. Natural enemies of weeds are present among plant-feeding insects, plant pathogens, and nematodes.
b. Some biotic agents selectively attack the flowers and seeds of weeds.
c. Greatest success with the inoculation approach is usually achieved with introduced pests of alien weeds.
d. Under the inoculation approach, 3 to 5 years or more may commonly be needed for a biological agent to build to an effective control level.
e. Results with a plant pathogen have shown that immediate control of a weed by a single application is practical.

Humans

a. Dependence on a single weed control approach over time leads to a community of weeds adapted to that approach.
b. Monoculture tends to narrow the weed base.
c. Reduced or zero tillage favors perennial species.
d. Among annual weeds, reduced or zero tillage favors the surface germinators (such as crabgrass) over those that germinate at greater depths (such as the morning-glories).
e. Depth of tillage determines the distribution of weed seeds in the soil profile; plowing distributes them more or less uniformly throughout the plow layer.
f. Plant residues on the soil surface can affect species composition in time.
g. Crops and crop varieties differ in competitiveness and can be expected to influence the composition of the weed community depending upon the number of years grown.
h. Increasing crop density through higher seeding rate and narrower rows can be expected to favor the taller-growing weed species.
i. The sequence in which crops are grown influences weed numbers and composition.
j. There is evidence of herbicidal specificity towards seed production and towards dormancy.

Reducing Weed Propagules

Reproduction capacity.   The concepts in Table 15–1 collectively point to the need for efforts aimed specifically at preventing reproduction. That is, it is clear that approaches designed only to control the weed plant itself are likely to be inadequate since any escapes from such practices may be expected to produce abundant seed or perennating parts. Several approaches might be used in response to the concept that seed and perennating parts of many weeds are curtailed by shade (concepts d and b, respectively). Among the possible approaches are: selection of crop varieties, and possibly species, for earliness and completeness of canopy; use of row and plant spacings that will develop a complete canopy as early as possible following planting; filling as many of the growing season niches as possible with crops.

Although information is incomplete for most effective use of each of these approaches, still, enough is known about each for reasoned decisions to be made that may reduce the production of propagules. For example, crop varieties and selections in breeding programs vary greatly in rate and form of growth. This information is usually recorded and, in fact, may be included in recommendations to growers to help them select a variety to plant. By choosing varieties and selections for their ability to compete for light, the production of weed propagules can be reduced.

Much information has accumulated on the appropriate seeding rate for both agronomic and horticultural crops. By planning the weed program for a several-year time frame, realistic projections of anticipated weed problems for any one year can be used to choose a seeding rate and row spacing that will maximize crop competition for light. For the most part, selection of varieties and plant spacings to maximize light competition may be viewed as no-cost approaches. That is, it should be possible to select varieties especially competitive for light from those already available for which no sacrifice in yield would be made to other varieties. Similarly, the use of narrow rows with soybeans, for example, as a means of increasing the competition of the crop for light does not represent an additional cost nor a potential loss in production capacity. Quite the contrary, there is reason to believe that solid-planted soybeans have a higher yielding potential than those in wide rows. Of course, for these approaches to be maximally effective, it may be necessary to select for the attributes in appropriate plant breeding programs and incorporate them into overall production programs. Nevertheless, utilization of these approaches may be viewed as relatively low cost in comparative terms.

Using cover crops to fill the niches not occupied by the crop is another way of utilizing concept d in Table 15–1. Many annual crops actually do not utilize much more than 50% of the growing season. For example, soybeans in mid-Missouri commonly occupy from 100 to 120 days of a 188-day growing season. Simply put, there is ample time both prior to planting soybeans and after they are harvested for weeds to emerge and produce seed or perennating parts. The long growing period

(90 to 120 days) available to weeds following wheat harvest in much of the Corn Belt provides a particularly good opportunity for weeds to multiply. In view of the sensitivity of annual weeds to competition, as well as the sensitivity of perennials to competition in the production of their perennating parts, judicious use of cover crops clearly offers the potential for reducing propagules.

Use of cover crops to fill the open niches in a cropping system offers the additional advantage of holding soil against erosion where that is a problem. Further, depending upon the cover crop used, this approach may also be a way of providing some of the nitrogen needed by the crop. Prior to the widespread availability of cheap fertilizer nitrogen, legumes were commonly used in this way as a source of nitrogen for such crops as corn, wheat, and other cereals. The escalation in fertilizer nitrogen cost may well provide a financial advantage to cover crops as an approach for providing some of the nitrogen needed. The so-called no-till, or zero-till, approach to crop production partially utilizes this concept, but without full consideration of the weed management aspects. By combining reduced tillage and cover cropping with full consideration of their impact on weeds, the advantage of this production system could be even greater.

Of course, the use of cover crops to fill the niches in the growing season not filled by the crop represents an additional cost. Further, although there is information on the use of cover crops in crop production, much of it may not be directly applicable to their use in preventing production of weed propagules. Nevertheless, this use of cover crops may well offer a relatively effective and inexpensive way of preventing propagule production.

The fact that high nitrogen levels may encourage vegetative rather than reproductive growth in perennials—concept b(1) under perennating parts—may be utilized to time nitrogen applications on crops in order to minimize reproductive parts. Although there are clear limits in the extent to which the time of nitrogen application can be changed to minimize production of perennating parts, nevertheless, there are certain crop and weed situations where this approach could be used. The most obvious possibility is with those crops for which it is common practice to top-dress with nitrogen. In those situations, it is simply a matter of considering the stage of development of both the weed and the crop in order to decide when to apply the nitrogen. Conceivably, there are times when changing the time of nitrogen application in order to minimize production of perennating parts by the weed would result in little or no sacrifice in crop yield.

Longevity.   Table 15–1 shows that longevity of both seed (concept c) and perennating parts (concepts c and d) is commonly extended by burial in the soil, and this information may be utilized to reduce propagules. The approach, of course, would be quite different with seeds than with perennating parts since seeds are on the soil surface to start with, whereas the perennating parts of perennials are commonly distributed through several centimeters of the soil, with some of them located at considerable depth in certain species. The specific aspect of burial depth we want to use is the sensitivity to exposure to temperature and moisture extremes at the soil surface. Thus, if a large weed seed crop of annuals is produced, delaying tillage until the following spring and then using only shallow tillage should reduce the number that become a part of the seedbank.

With perennial weeds, appropriate tillage implements can be used to bring reproductive parts to the surface to be destroyed by desiccation and lethal temperatures. Because such an approach means special or extra tillage, however, it is doubtful that it could be justified on large areas under extensive farming. Nevertheless, it might be a feasible approach in intensively grown crops. Further, since perennials frequently occur in patches rather than in uniform distribution across a field, such an approach might be usable by concentrating on such patches.

There may well be situations where tillage by itself (concept d for seeds and e for perennating parts) should be used to reduce propagules in the seedbank. For example, in the situation just mentioned, some shallow tillage for 2 to 3 years after production of a large weed seed crop should reduce the seedbank, compared to no tillage.

Germination and emergence.   The concepts in Table 15–1 are not directly applicable to reducing weed propagules. Indirectly, of course, concepts and associated management that reduce numbers of plants on a given area can be expected to reduce propagules.

Competition.   The concepts associated with competition in Table 15–1 provide little in the way of direct application for preventing the production of seeds and of vegetative reproductive parts. Indirectly, of course, reduced weed growth from the use of competitive crop species and varieties (concept e) could reduce production of propagules.

Allelopathy.   Table 15–1 shows that allelochemicals are effective against a wide variety of plant processes or functions (concept e). This fact suggests that crop selections may be available, or could be developed (according to concept g), that are specific in their inhibition of seed production or the production of vegetative perennating parts. For such crop selection to be effective in this regard, the allelochemicals produced need to be exuded through the crop root and readily translocated upward in the weed. This statement simply recognizes that leaching from leaves and stems and release as a result of decomposition of residues in the soil in all likelihood cannot be depended upon to match up with the time of reproduction in the weeds targeted. This use of allelopathy may not have enough potential to justify research and development exclusively for this purpose. However, it may be worthwhile to look for this special attribute in research already planned or underway to identify allelopathic effects on overall growth characteristics.

Biological agents.   Of the concepts listed in Table 15–1, the use of insects and plant pathogens (concept b) specifically to reduce the production of seeds appears to be especially promising. Such selective activity has already been identified with both types of biological agents. For annual weeds, potential usage may be best as a cleanup of weeds that escape the other weed management approaches. Often, one or only a few species escape to overtop the crop and thus offer the potential of producing a seed crop. As we learned, biological agents are likely to be most useful against single species rather than against a mixture of weeds.

For perennial weeds, this approach may be most usable against weeds that have not yet reached the economic threshold level (concept d in Table 15–1). Common milkweed in wheat in Missouri, shown in Figure 15–2, is an example. Milkweed has increased in much of the Midwest but likely is not yet a serious competitor. This is the case for a number of perennial weeds where minimum or reduced tillage is being practiced. Such situations provide the necessary time for the introduced pest to build to levels that will keep the perennial in check and prevent it from becoming a problem resolvable only by more costly approaches.

Humans.   The fact that chemicals have been shown to be selectively toxic towards seed production (concept j in Table 15–1) suggests that utilizing herbicides specifically for this purpose is likely to succeed. Although herbicides have been observed to have such specific effects, there really has not been a concerted evaluation of the broad spectrum of available chemicals in order to determine the potential with existing chemicals. Recent advances in application of herbicides offer additional possibilities for use of herbicides in this way. For example, both the rope-wick and recirculating sprayers provide a way of selectively applying herbicides to weeds that overtop the crop. The proper timing of such applications to stage of seed production might well be an effective way to minimize the number of viable seeds produced. A caution relative to this usage is in order. Delaying treatment of such weeds until they overtop the crop could entail serious competition with the crop before that time. Thus, it may well be that this approach has its greatest potential use in dealing with weeds that escape the normal weed program.

Relationship of prevention to control.   Figure 15–3 summarizes the cropping and tillage preventive approaches and adds the control practices that might be followed to fully implement weed management to reduce propagules in the seedbank. Although the technology has been identified for biological control, preventing seed production with herbicides, and hastening germination of seeds with chemicals, their application in a weed management context has yet to be demonstrated. The fifth control practice listed—that is, the manipulation of soil microorganisms—is only a theoretical possibility at present. Nevertheless, it should be apparent from the numerous approaches suggested that a reasonably effective weed management program could be developed to reduce the numbers of propagules in soil.

FIGURE 15–2. Common milkweed, often the only weed in wheat at harvest time in Missouri.
Source: Reproduced courtesy of Dr. L.E. Anderson, Department of Agronomy, University of Missouri, Columbia, Missouri.

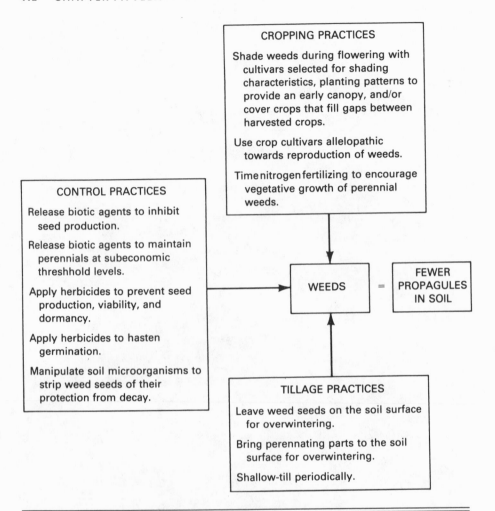

FIGURE 15–3. Summary of conceptual approaches for reducing numbers of propagules in the weed seedbank.

Preventing Weed Emergence with the Crop

Our interest in this section is in those ecological relationships and concepts in Table 15–1 that might be used to minimize the number of weeds that emerge with the crop.

Reproduction capacity. Those concepts developed for reproduction capacity in Table 15–1 are not directly applicable to preventing weed emergence.

Indirectly, of course, any success achieved in preventing the production of viable propagules helps reduce the number of weeds that emerge with the crop.

Longevity. The concepts developed for longevity in Table 15–1 are not directly applicable to preventing weed emergence. However, any steps that shorten the life of propagules in the soil ultimately reduce the number available to emerge with the crop.

Germination and emergence. The concepts in Table 15–1 relating to depth effect on germination and emergence (concept a) of both seeds and perennating parts offer opportunities for preventing their emergence with the crop. An approach for seeds is depicted in Figure 15–4. This approach buries the weed seeds so deeply in the soil that they cannot successfully emerge even if germination occurs. For many annual weeds common to row crops, placing the seed at the bottom of the plow layer, if this could be accomplished, would eliminate those seeds as a source of infestation with the crop that year. Only shallow tillage should be practiced in subsequent years to avoid bringing them to the surface where they could germinate and emerge.

There might be special situations where attempts to leach inhibitors (concept d in Table 15–1) from seeds are warranted. With irrigated crops, for example, it might be desirable to irrigate in the spring prior to tillage, both to leach out possible inhibitors as well as to provide the moisture necessary for early germination.

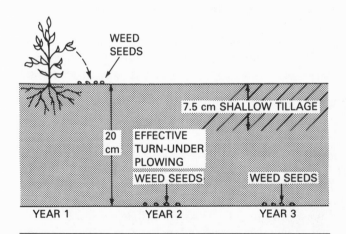

FIGURE 15–4. Use of tillage to minimize weed emergence following production of a large number of weed seeds.

The season-anticipating characteristic (concept f) offers possibilities of reducing emergence of weeds with the crop. Emergence can be reduced either by delaying seedbed preparation until the flush of germination has passed or by changing the crops grown to include either an early crop that precedes germination of most weeds or a late crop that is planted after most weed seeds have germinated.

Where perennial weeds are involved, the common occurrence of correlated inhibition (concept d) might be used to limit emergence of new plants. Limitation might be accomplished by deep plowing (30 cm or so) with only shallow tillage thereafter. The objective in this approach is to disrupt as little as possible the dominance effect of both the parent plant and the apical meristem. An alternative approach might be to till several times with a disk or other implement designed to accomplish as much fractionating of the rhizome or tuber chains as possible to minimize correlative inhibition and then, drawing upon concept b, plow them under to a depth from which successful emergence would be minimal.

Competition.   None of the concepts under competition in Table 15–1 would appear to be directly applicable in preventing weed emergence. Indirectly, the reduction of propagule production as a result of use of competitive crop species and varieties (concept e) would reduce the number of seeds available to germinate and emerge with the crop.

Allelopathy.   In Table 15–1, concepts a, b, e, and g for allelopathy may be usable in reducing weed emergence with the crop. In general terms, these concepts may be applicable to living crop plants and to the residues of crop plants. Where residues are the approach, it is desirable to concentrate them in the soil zone from which the major weeds are expected to originate. If shallow-germinating annual species are the major problems expected, then it is best to concentrate the residue in the surface soil layer (5 cm to 7.5 cm if possible). In this way, the allelochemical produced by the crop is concentrated in the zone from which the weeds originate. This is the same concept involved in the incorporation of herbicides. Of course, if we seek to inhibit a deep-rooted perennial or large-seeded annual, it would be necessary to distribute the residue throughout the plow layer. In either case, it might well be necessary to incorporate the plant material some weeks in advance of planting to allow time for microbial decomposition and release of the toxin.

Use of living crop plants to inhibit emergence may have its best potential against late-germinating weeds, such as fall panicum in corn in the central Corn Belt. By this time in the growing season, an allelopathic corn variety should have had sufficient time to produce enough allelochemicals to have the desired inhibitory effect. An additional incentive for looking to allelopathy to deal with such weeds is the fact that other approaches, such as applying herbicides, pose the hazard of mechanical damage to the crop.

Biological agents.   The possibilities for working with the concepts under biological agents in Table 15–1 are limited. One approach that may offer potential is the application of pathogenic spores to crop seeds to prevent emergence of weeds in the vicinity of the crop plant.

Humans.   Of the concepts identified under humans in Table 15–1, concept i might be utilized to reduce weed emergence by switching to later- or earlier-planted crops. Limits to this approach are obvious because climate, available machinery, markets, and the like restrict farmers' crop options. Still, we should be aware that occasional changes of this kind may reduce the numbers of weeds with which we must deal in any given year.

Relationship of prevention to control.   Figure 15–5 summarizes the cropping and tillage preventive approaches and adds the control practices that might be followed to fully implement weed management to minimize weed emergence with crops. Of course, the control practice of applying herbicides to soil is widely used. The technology for utilizing allelopathic plant residues, breaking dormancy and destroying emerged plants, and leaching germination inhibitors from weed seed then destroying weeds that emerge has been at least partially identified. Thus, there is a sizable array of approaches to make a weed management effort to minimize weed emergence with crops even more effective.

Minimizing Weed Competition

For the foreseeable future, herbicides or timely tillage will be needed to avoid serious losses once a weed problem exists. However, ways of managing production to minimize the competitiveness of weeds present with the crop are available. Reduction of weed competitiveness through management should serve to lessen the pressure on whatever control measures are followed. This is not to suggest that control will be less necessary, only that it may be more effective if those measures that can be taken to provide a competitive edge to the crop are in fact taken. Another way of viewing the importance of effective prevention to effective control is to recognize that without effective prevention to somewhat reduce the competitiveness of the weeds, failure to achieve success with the control effort is going to be more costly in terms of crop loss. From the discussion about the period of competition and the likelihood that competition for one factor leads to competition for another, we know that effective prevention and control provide a potential compounding effect towards weeds, thus preventing a corresponding compounding of competition on the part of the weed. With this information as background, let us examine possible ways to utilize the concepts developed for each of the ecological factors in Table 15–1 in terms of providing a competitive edge to the crop.

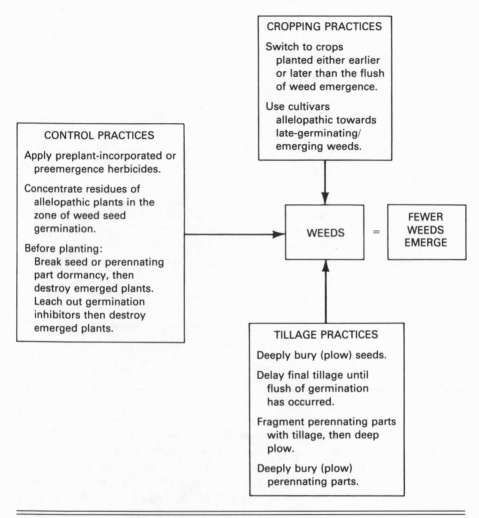

FIGURE 15–5. Summary of conceptual approaches for preventing weed emergence with crops.

Reproduction, longevity, and germination. There is no concept in Table 15–1 directly applicable to reducing competition in the areas of reproduction, longevity, and germination. However, success in preventing reproduction, as well as success in reducing the soil bank of propagules, indirectly reduces competition.

Competition. The key concept in Table 15–1 is that most annual weeds are relatively intolerant of competition (concept d). The fact that crop species and crop varieties differ in competitiveness (concept e) due likely to differences in their aboveground and belowground growth form (concepts g and h, respectively) suggests that selection for characteristics that contribute to early development of a complete canopy and rapid elaboration of root systems would be worthwhile in plant breeding programs.

As we have already learned, time is important in many ways in the weed–crop competition struggle. An advantage of only a few days in closing a canopy or in occupying the soil with roots can have a pronounced effect on competition. For most agronomic and horticultural crops, available germ plasm provides a wide range of growth characteristics from which to choose that which provides the desired type.

Differences in aboveground growth form and size are well known. Differences in root growth form and size may be at least as great. With soybeans, for example, the dry weight of roots (an indication of root volume) of eight varieties at maturity ranged from 1.52 to 5.94 grams per plant (Mitchell and Russell, 1971). Surface area of roots of two varieties differed by a factor of nearly 2 in other studies (Raper and Barber, 1970).

It should be recognized that those factors that contribute to high yields selected for in a breeding program may also coincidently contribute to competitiveness towards weeds. However, it seems reasonable to expect that selection for those attributes that would be most effective against the type of weed competition anticipated would be more successful than selection obtained coincidental to selection for yield. This statement simply recognizes that in a general way the differences in root/shoot ratios within the genetic material might be used to develop varieties especially competitive for soil factors or for light.

In situations where competition for water or nutrients is apt to be the basis of competition, selecting for early root elaboration would be advantageous. Conversely, where light is the factor most apt to be competed for, there would be an advantage in selecting for a high shoot/root ratio. For this approach to be most effective, however, the nature of competition between the weeds and the crop involved needs to be well understood. That is, we need to know what it is that the crop and weed are competing for, not just when they are competing.

Utilizing this approach to provide a competitive edge to our crops may not be as much of an additional burden to our present crop breeding programs as might at first be thought. Much of the data currently obtained on genetic material in a breeding program might well be usable in identifying that material most apt to contribute the desired competitiveness towards weeds. This fact can be seen in Figure 15–6 by examining samples of data sheets for recording information on each of three different commodities in a breeding program. In any case, selection for competitiveness towards weeds might well provide an important edge to the crop and one that might not be recognized in the selection process unless specifically identified as a goal. Thus, it may be advisable to include this as a goal in more of the plant breeding programs.

CORN

Plot	Stand	Lodging		Ears		Days to*			Root Pull*	Mois-ture	Yield
		Root	Stalk	Drop	Usable	Flower	Tassle	Silk			

FORAGE LEGUME

Plant Introduction number	Unifor-mity*	Habit (Erect/ Prostrate)*	Vigor	Plant*		Leaves*		Matur-ity*	Winter hardiness*
				Height	Width	No.	Texture		

SOYBEAN

Strain	Date*		Height*	Stem termination*		Branching*	Yield
	Flowered	Mature		Deter-minate	Indeter-minate		

FIGURE 15–6. Examples of data recorded for genetic material in a plant breeding program for selected crops. Starred (*) items identify data potentially useful in identifying material competitive towards weeds.

Crop planting pattern. The crop planting pattern, especially spacing, can also be managed to provide a time edge to the crop (concepts a, d, and g under competition in Table 15–1). An obvious example of this concept is the use of narrow (solid) rather than wide rows with soybeans. As we have already seen, a complete canopy is developed in much less time with narrow rows than with wide rows. In addition, closer spacing of plants also influences the time required for the crop roots to occupy a given soil zone (concept h). As our understanding grows of what factor or factors the weed and the crop are competing for in a given situation, we should be able to determine the best plant spacing to provide the necessary edge to the crop.

Crop seed treatments.   Under very special situations, such as in production of high acre value crops, it might be practical to presoak the crop seed or coat it with a hygroscopic material to shorten the time from planting to emergence. Germination 2 or 3 days earlier by such an approach could markedly reduce competition from weeds.

Allelopathy.   Concepts a and g under allelopathy in Table 15–1 can be drawn upon to develop and select cultivars inhibitory towards weeds. Because allelochemicals are somewhat selective in the plants affected, this approach may have its primary place against individual weeds. Further, the approach may be most usable against the dominant perennials, such as those occurring under reduced tillage programs. Where the objective is to suppress such a perennial, there might well be an advantage to releasing the allelochemical by leaching, exudation, and decomposition rather than by exudation only. This practice could serve to simplify the development of allelopathic breeding lines since only total quantities of allelochemicals would be of concern rather than location within the crop plant. Also, this method could serve to extend the duration of effect, which would be especially advantageous with perennials because of their common usage of a large part of the growing season.

The fact that quantities of allelochemicals produced are often greater under stress (concept c) suggests it should be possible to time the application of nitrogen to a crop to maximize the production of allelochemicals during the time when such chemicals would be most important as inhibitors of weeds. This approach might be particularly useful in such perennial crops as forages where there may be an option to apply fertilizer in either the spring or the fall of the year.

In those cropping programs where it is desirable to use the crop residue as the source of allelochemicals to suppress weeds, management of the residues needs to be done in such a way as to maximize the effect on the weed. For example, if the residue is intended to suppress a perennial that initiates growth in late spring or early summer, it is probably best to delay incorporation of the crop residue as long as possible prior to planting the crop to maximize the quantities of allelochemicals present when the weed initiates this first flush of growth. Nutsedges are good candidates for this situation. On the other hand, if the perennial is one that makes substantial early spring growth—for example, quackgrass—it might be best to incorporate the residue as early in the spring as possible. Similarly, the depth from which maximum regrowth of the perennial occurs should be taken into account when determining the depth to which the crop residue should be incorporated.

Biological agents.   The most useful role for biological agents may be against developing weed problems. Where a weed problem is developing but has not yet reached the point of seriously competing with the crop, the time needed for the biological agent to develop to a control level may be available (concept d in Table 15–1). This approach to the use of biological agents is limited by our inability to predict weed problems. As we learn more about the nature of competition and the response of weeds to changes in production practices, we will have the basis for anticipating those weeds likely to be associated with our crops. With enough advance warning, coupled with additional information about potential biological agents, satisfactory ways of utilizing biological agents to suppress emerging weeds can be developed.

Plant pathogens may offer a way to effectively deal with escapes by utilizing concept e. This approach is important because escapes may well be the most difficult problem to contend with in a total weed management program. Such escapes could contribute significant numbers to the propagule bank but in themselves not pose enough of a threat to the crop in which they occur to warrant control. It follows that the approach used against such weeds must be relatively low cost. The need for low cost, plus the fact that alternatives are limited, suggests that plant pathogens be carefully considered. Where there is a mixture of such weeds, it may be that a mixture of pathogens could be used. The suggestion that pathogens be considered is not meant to imply that this may be a low-cost approach. Rather, it is felt that all of the limited possibilities need to be explored.

Humans.   Farmers must understand the implications of such concepts in Table 15–1 as monoculture, rotation, and crop sequence for weeds (concepts b, g, and i). For some, such as a Great Plains wheat farmer, there may be little alternative to the one crop being produced. For many, at least some options are open concerning crops to be grown. Where options are available, occasional changes in crops may prevent, or at least delay, the development of a new and even more difficult weed problem. In another sense, there may be an advantage to growers in having the narrow weed base associated with monoculture. After all, the complications for effective weed management can be expected to increase as the number of species increases.

Thus, farmers interested in growing more than one crop might simplify weed management by raising only crop A on field 1, crop B on field 2, and so on. After a period of years, crops could be shifted among fields and the process repeated. Of course, factors other than weeds must be considered. Crop diseases and insects may increase under such a modified monoculture system, for example. Further, there must be effective ways to deal with the weeds encouraged by such a system. Nevertheless, this example serves to indicate the approaches growers may take if they fully understand the weed–crop ecological relationships.

Whenever a major change in the production program is contemplated (tillage, crop, growth form of crop, and so on), users need to draw upon concepts a, b, c, d, h, and i to anticipate what change it may cause in weed composition. This approach allows plans to be made for dealing with the new problem at the appropriate time.

It is helpful for users to know the effect of tillage depth and timing on weed seed distribution and plan accordingly (concept e). Any plan, no matter how good, can break down under adverse weather, machinery failures, and other similar factors. Thus, we can expect that there will occasionally be a year when a large number of weed seeds are produced or when a particular perennial weed is able to store large quantities of food reserves for its perennating parts. Understanding the weed and the factors affecting longevity of its parts can provide users with the information necessary to till in the right way at the right time and thus avoid tillage that might greatly magnify and extend the problem posed by such escapes.

Similarly, there will be times when users may not be able to manage their crop residues according to plan. A knowledge of the effect of such residues on weed seed longevity and germination (concept f) can help farmers choose the appropriate tillage practice to minimize the potential disruptive effects on the long-term weed management program.

Relationship of prevention to control.   Figure 15–7 summarizes the cropping and tillage preventive approaches and adds the control practices that might be followed in a weed management program to minimize competition from weeds growing with crops. The utility of postemergence herbicides and rotation of herbicides has been well established and both are widely used. Even so, weeds still cause an average loss in crop yield of 12% to 15%. This fact suggests the need to include the preventive approaches shown if this loss in crop yield is to be reduced significantly.

Summary

The underlying theme for our approach to weeds in the future must be the development of a long-term plan. Such a plan must have as its focus the production unit or possibly even the individual field. The latter might be particularly applicable for a monoculture cropping system. In either case, this approach to weeds must recognize the dynamic relationships that exist between weeds and crops at the individual field level. These relationships can best be observed and interpreted by the owner/operator on the land. Contingencies that are bound to arise can best be dealt with by this individual. That is, they cannot be effectively dealt with on a commodity or geographic area basis.

Viewed in this way, our program for the future can be most effective if it is founded on the principles of weed prevention, including a reduction in weed propagules, a reduction in emergence of weeds with our crops, and a lessening of competition from those weeds that are present. Such a plan for dealing with weeds can then embrace all tools available, including what is known about competition, about the weeds themselves, allelopathy, biological agents, and, of course, herbicides. In such a context, weed control becomes a capstone for an effective total weed management effort. Control will be relied upon to provide the final

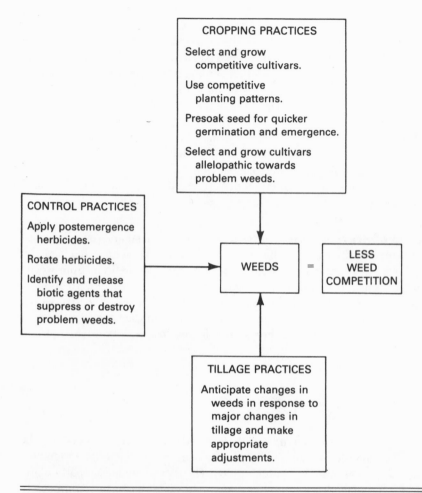

FIGURE 15–7. Summary of conceptual approaches for minimizing competition from weeds with crops.

measure of crop protection rather than the only measure, as is now frequently the case.

WEED MANAGEMENT FOR THE CROP PRODUCTION SYSTEM

In the previous section, we considered possible approaches to weed prevention in each of three broad stages in weeds' life cycles. In the course of our examination, the range of potential tools for dealing with weeds in a total management effort were identified. Here, these prevention approaches and control approaches are brought together and examined in terms of the entire crop production system. A hypothetical field example is useful for this purpose.

A producer plans to initiate a reduced-tillage production system involving soybeans, wheat, and corn. Let us assume that distributed uniformly in the plow layer is a large population of seeds of annual weeds—both grassy and broadleaf—common to the southern part of the Corn Belt in the United States. Also, there is a scattered stand of common milkweed that is not yet interfering with crop yields. To simplify the example, practices are identified that might be followed each year for 7 years on only one field. This procedure allows us to consider approaches in each crop twice plus consider a change in crops grown. After careful study of this program, it should be possible to use the concepts involved to develop comparable programs for other crops and other production practices.

At the outset, the producer needs to make a projection of what the weed problems will be during the first few years. Five years may be a convenient period. Based on what is known about weed seed longevity, the effects of reduced tillage on weeds, and of wheat as a potential source of weed renewal, these general projections are justified: (1) Common milkweed will increase during the 5 years unless something is done to check it; (2) annual weeds will compete during the period even if their seed production is prevented during this time; and (3) annual grasses, especially late germinators, will increase. The practices identified for each year are based on these projections.

Year 1: Soybeans

Because there is a large initial population of annual weed seeds uniformly distributed throughout the soil, effort should be made to limit those weeds that might pose a problem. This task might be accomplished by preparing a shallow seedbed (tillage to about 7.5 cm) as early as possible, allowing it to stand until time to plant soybeans, and then destroying the emerged weeds either with a burndown herbicide—for example, paraquat or glyphosate—or with shallow tillage. By direct-drilling the soybeans into the killed weeds, no new weed seeds would be brought to the surface. However, a preemergence herbicide should probably be used because of the large number of weed seeds in the soil. There are several to choose from, including alachlor, chloramben, linuron, metolachlor, metribuzin, and oryzalin. The soybean variety should be one that develops a canopy quickly and yields well when planted in narrow rows.

The follow-up weed control needed will be determined by the extent of control from the soil treatment. One of the selective postemergence herbicides, such as acifluorfen, fluaziflop, or others, can be used if there is a competing population of weeds. If there are some escapes but not a competing infestation, a rope-wick or recirculating sprayer application of glyphosate can be made to prevent their production of seed and to check growth of the milkweed. Steps should be taken to determine whether there is genetic material known to be allelopathic towards the new perennial weed, if one is anticipated, as well as to determine whether any biological agents have been successfully used against it. If such genetic material or biological agents are available, plans can be made to use them at the appropriate time.

During this first year, all weed species present should be identified in order that a projection can be made of the shift in weed species that may be expected after 5 years under this new production and weed management system. Once the species are known, information can be gathered on their growth form and life cycle, relative response to the herbicides being used, and relative response to the tillage planned. With this information, a first projection of weed composition 5 years hence should be made. A check of weed composition each following year will allow the projection to be modified as needed.

Immediately following soybean harvest, the field should be shallowly tilled with an implement such as a field cultivator to minimize storage of carbohydrate reserves by the milkweed.

Year 2: Wheat

The weed management efforts should focus on checking the milkweed and on preventing seed production of annual weeds following wheat harvest. One approach for dealing with both might be the use of a legume cover crop. It could be broadcast into the wheat in late winter to provide cover for the period from wheat harvest until the field is returned to corn the next year. Following wheat harvest, it may be necessary to mow the stubble to prevent production of seed of the fall panicum and summer-germinating broadleaf species and to prevent carbohydrate storage on the part of the milkweed and other perennial weeds. Whether or not this treatment is needed will be determined by the effectiveness of the cover crop in keeping these weeds in check. An alternative would be application of an appropriate herbicide or combination of herbicides with a rope-wick applicator.

Year 3: Corn

Since it likely will be desirable to plow under the cover crop, a large number of annual weeds should be expected as a result of new seeds being brought to the surface. Therefore, plans should be made to apply either a preplant-incorporated or a preemergence herbicide. Here, too, several are available, including alachlor, atrazine, cyanazine, metolachor, and others. Since no cultivation is planned, consideration should be given to planting the corn in 50 cm (20 in.) rows to provide the earliest possible canopy, as well as rapid occupancy of the soil zone by corn roots. The producer should be prepared to apply an appropriate herbicide postemergence as needed to prevent seed production of the annual weeds and to check the milkweed. Several appropriate herbicides are available. In mid-August, the producer should broadcast-seed a cover crop to further check the milkweed and late-germinating annual weeds.

Year 4: Soybeans

The seedbed should be prepared in late April to early May using only shallow tillage (7.5 cm) to avoid bringing up any new seeds. By tilling as late as possible, maximum benefit can be obtained from the cover crop in checking weed germination and growth. An alternative to tilling would be either to burn down the cover with a chemical such as glyphosate or mow it closely before direct-drilling the soybeans. Plans should be made for an early postemergence application of herbicides to control the annual weeds. Also, a later application with a rope-wick may be needed to prevent seed production of the annual weeds and to check the milkweed. The weed composition should be checked to see if the shifts projected in year 1 are taking place. If they are, planning should be started for the management, including the herbicides, to be used against the new weeds a year hence.

Years 5 and 6: Corn—Corn or Corn—Soybeans Rotation

These two years might be appropriate ones to change the crop rotation to either corn to be followed by corn, or corn to be followed by soybeans. This change could provide additional opportunity to check the milkweed and other perennial species, as well as to avoid or at least slow down a shift in weed composition. In any case, only shallow tillage (7.5 cm) should be used to avoid bringing more weed seeds to the surface.

Year 7: Wheat

Depending upon the success of efforts to find allelopathic crop germ plasm and biological agents, this might be the year in which these approaches could be initiated to serve as a check against the new perennial, if one is developing. Also, if efforts to prevent weed seed production have been successful to this point in time, the seedbank will have been drawn down sufficiently to warrant modifying the overall weed management program. The main change would be to eliminate the soil application of herbicides and rely upon postemergence applications to control escapes and prevent seed production.

WEED MANAGEMENT AND CHANGING TECHNOLOGY

As the approach to weeds changes from one based essentially on control to one based on prevention, the place of weed science relative to the other disciplines involved in production systems must also change. If weed science is to make its full contribution, weed scientists must have a part in shaping the total production system. That is, it will not be enough for weed science merely to adapt to new production systems developed by agronomists, horticulturists, and agricultural engineers. Indeed, as indicated in the previous two sections, some major changes in crop production practices are needed for the potential in weed management to be realized. Weed scientists, as partners in the total team of agricultural scientists, must provide the initiative for bringing about these changes. In this same context, changes in production practices can be expected to call for changes in farm machinery. Here, too, weed scientists must be willing to work with the engineers to help translate the desired concept into an appropriate mechanical design.

New Equipment

The development of machinery to facilitate reduced tillage demonstrates the adaptability and ingenuity of the farm machinery industry. Drills and planters have been especially designed for planting directly into sod and untilled ground. Some examples are shown in Figure 15–8. Attachments and special features like those shown in Figure 15–9A make precision planting possible even in heavy residues. Precision planting is accomplished by building into one machine (Figure 15–9A) the essential elements of the several machines commonly involved in preparing a complete seedbed. A single pass over the field results in a miniseedbed (Figure 15–9B). From what we have learned about weed seed survival and longevity and about reproduction in perennial weeds, it is clear these practices will have an influence on weed composition and numbers. Research is needed to identify and quantify the specific changes.

Tillage equipment has also undergone change. The chisel plow shown in Figure 15–10 is now widely used throughout agriculture as a way to disrupt hardpans without turning under crop residues that serve to hold the soil against erosion. The traditional moldboard plow, as can be seen in Figure 15–11, is available in different forms to facilitate desired depth of plowing, among other things.

A. Tye stubble drill

B. Buffalo till planter

C. Marliss no-till drill

FIGURE 15–8. Drills available for planting directly into sod and untilled ground.

Source: Part A reproduced with permission of the Tye Company; Part B reproduced with permission of Fleischer Manufacturing, Inc.; Part C reproduced with permission of Marliss Industries.

A. Hiniker Econ-O-Till planter

B. Miniseedbed

FIGURE 15–9. Precision planting in heavy residues by preparation of a miniseedbed.
Source: Reproduced courtesy of Hiniker Company.

The NU (New Universal) 36 cm (14 in.) bottoms have a long, slow-turning moldboard. They are primarily for sod, alfalfa, and grassland at speeds upward from 4 kph (2 1/2 mph) and depths of 13 cm to 20 cm (5 in. to 8 in.). Gentle inversion of the furrow slice reduces buckling and leaves a ribbon-like look. The NU 41 cm (16 in.) bottoms are designed for speeds ranging up to 8 kph (5 mph) and

FIGURE 15–10. Chisel plow for soil penetration without mixing.
Source: Reproduced with permission of John Deere and Company.

depths to 30 cm (12 in.). Features include unusually light draft, easy scouring, and effective tillage in stalk, bean, and stubble fields. The NU 46 cm (18 in.) bottoms for general-purpose plowing offer light draft, good scouring, and moldboard capacity to handle big furrow slices at speeds to 9.6 kph (6 mph) depending on conditions. They plow to 36 cm (14 in.) deep and leave a wide furrow floor for large tractor tires. Proper plow selection, setting, speed, and soil moisture should make it possible to place nearly all of the weed seeds deposited on the soil surface at the bottom of the plow furrow. Thus, plows are available to utilize what is known about the effects of burial depth on survival and emergence of seeds and of perennating parts to minimize or reduce weed interference.

Progress has also been made in designing cultivators for narrow rows and for heavy residues. Figure 15–12 shows a cultivator designed for use in heavy residues. A depth-control disk between each row cuts through the residue and maintains uniform penetration. Precise control on the depth of cultivation will be needed in many instances if the objectives of a long-term weed management plan are to be fully met. Thus, this feature needs to be taken into account in the development of narrow-row cultivators and other tillage equipment.

In a larger sense, weed scientists must help all of agricultural science, including the agricultural industry, look into the future to the time when weeds are indeed effectively managed. Adjustments are needed in all aspects of production. In view of the time it takes to develop, design, and manufacture new equipment, the machinery industry in particular must have adequate lead time to make the

A. NU 14 in. New Universal bottoms   **B. NU 16 in. New Universal bottoms**

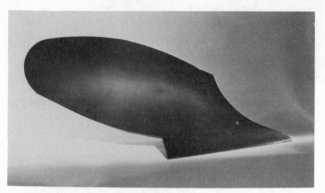

C. NU 18 in. New Universal bottoms

FIGURE 15–11. Moldboard plow bottoms designed for different soils, plant cover, plowing depths, and tractor speeds.
Source: Reproduced with permission of John Deere and Company.

changes needed in machinery. It is possible to visualize a time when all or nearly all machinery operations will be accomplished with a single tool-bar implement. Figure 15–13 shows an experimental machine that goes partway towards providing all operations in a single implement. It can be used to apply herbicides, broadcast seed and fertilizer, and do some tillage and cultivation at almost any stage of crop development and under most field conditions—features important to weed management in conservation tillage systems.

A phenomenon of modern agriculture in the United States with implications for weed science is that many farmers modify commercially available equipment to meet their specific situation. Such entrepreneurship is likely to continue to be a part of the American agriculture scene. Thus, weed scientists must be prepared for a future in which there are relatively more variations, both in how a given crop is produced and in the weed management approaches needed, than has been true in the past. In particular, weed scientists will need to help farmers understand the

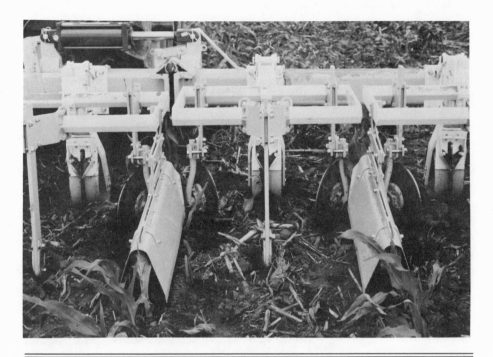

FIGURE 15–12. Cultivators designed to handle heavy residues found in conservation tillage systems.
Source: Reproduced with permission of Fleischer Manufacturing, Inc.

weed–crop ecological relationships so that farmers' weed management programs will fit the circumstances.

Research Needs

Weed science must also expand knowledge in several areas before weed management can be fully effective. Some of the most important needs are briefly discussed.

1. More precise information is needed about competition. There are nagging, unanswered questions about this subject that put serious constraints on weed management. For example, why are crop yields sometimes reduced when weeds are present for only the first two or three weeks after crop emergence? Knowing what we do about the plasticity of most of our crops, it is difficult to understand why they would not fully compensate for any competition that might have occurred during this brief, early period. However, the fact remains that such brief exposure to weeds does sometimes cause losses in yield. Can the loss be accounted for by

FIGURE 15–13. Experimental tractor designed to track on permanent sod strips.
Source: Gebhardt et al., 1982. Reproduced with permission of the American Society of Agricultural Engineers.

competition for a minor element in scarce supply? Can it be accounted for by the effect of competition during this early time on the production of the crop's inherent growth regulators? At this time, we can only speculate. However, in view of the pervasiveness of growth regulators within a plant, more clearly needs to be known about their relationship to weed–crop relationships and to competition. Of course, there is an urgent need for more precise information on what it is the weed and the crop are competing for at a particular point in time in their co-development. Until we have such precise information, our plans for dealing with competition over time will be less specific than they could and should be.

2. Ways to predict future weed problems are needed. Weed prediction is fundamental to an effective long-term weed management approach. Only when we

are able to predict the weeds likely to be present following a change in our production system will we be able to develop a fully effective plan for dealing with them. The problem is basically one of determining for any given production system the numbers of propagules of individual species already present, the numbers added to the seedbank annually, and their survival—that is, their dormancy, germination, and longevity. Extrapolation of trend lines drawn from data accumulated for a series of years could be used to predict future levels of infestation. Of course, accuracy of the projections would increase with years. Even so, early projections (after two to three years) could be very useful. They could provide advance warning of the weed problem likely to be faced at some future date. Advance warning would allow plans to be made for dealing with the problem before it becomes severe. To be fully effective, predictions would need to embrace competition as well as composition. That is, we would need to know what constitutes a competing level of infestation. As just indicated, much is yet to be learned about competition. Thus, we must view precise prediction as an ideal. Because we are dealing with a dynamic system containing many variables, prediction is not likely to ever be a precise science. However, even as an estimative science, it has much to offer a weed management approach.

3. There is a need for ways to determine when control is necessary. Although there is an obvious relationship between the number of weeds and their weight and the potential for reducing crop yield, the farmer/producer does not have adequate guidelines for evaluating when control is needed. In the absence of such discrete guidelines, the farmer/producer's only safe approach is the complete elimination of the weeds. Although there is nothing wrong with this in terms of a weed management objective, implementing it may be unduly costly. Indeed, in some instances, producers might better spend their money making sure that the weeds do not produce seed or perennating parts rather than on control. For these kinds of judgments to be made, however, we must know when weeds constitute a control problem.

4. More information is needed about dormancy. Dormancy of both seeds and perennating parts is an obvious obstacle to more effective management of weeds. More needs to be learned about the factors causing both the onset and the release from dormancy, especially the effects of agricultural production practices.

5. The effects of tillage need to be determined. There is general knowledge of the shifts in weed composition to be expected under a reduced tillage production system. More discrete data are needed for it to be most effectively used in a predictive model. Further, the precise effects of tillage time, type, and depth on longevity and emergence of weed seeds and perennating parts need to be determined for the implements commercially available. Much of what is now known was learned in controlled studies using experimental procedures and machines.

6. Cover crops need to be evaluated for weed management. Much is known about the attributes of selected cover crops for preventing soil loss, improving soil

tilth, and adding nitrogen. Weed science must add to this information on specific effects of cover crops on weed numbers and composition. Further, cover crops may provide a convenient way to utilize allelopathy to check weeds. For this technique to work, information is needed on the allelopathic effects of existing germ plasm. Appropriate lines can then be used or new ones developed.

7. The interactive effects of different crop pests need to be determined. Very little is known about the combined effects of weeds, insects, plant diseases, and other pests on our crop plants. More specifically, are the effects usually additive or are they commonly synergistic? As was mentioned in Chapter 14, the answer has far-reaching implications for our approach to pest management.

8. Ways to evaluate long-term programs are needed. What is it worth to reduce the seedbank a given percentage? What is it worth to have a competitive crop variety developed by the plant breeders? What is it worth to have an allelopathic variety developed? These are important questions in weed management and ones that cannot be adequately answered in terms of crop yield in any one year. Quite clearly, the answer has to be determined over several years. Answers to these and similar questions are needed for these approaches to weed management to find their proper place in a total weed management program.

A PHILOSOPHY FOR WEED MANAGEMENT

Full integration of weed prevention and weed control tactics should be our goal in weed management. Only then will its potential benefits be realized. To achieve this goal, we need a complete understanding of weed–crop relationships. Although much is known about these relationships, it is also true that our knowledge is incomplete. Thus, we should expect to build towards that goal through evolutionary, not revolutionary, changes. Viewed in this way, development and utilization of each bit of new information can be translated into some unit of progress in our struggle with weeds.

CONCEPTS AND CONCLUSIONS

1. Enough information is available about the weed–crop environmental relationship to plan a weed management program for a production system.
2. The weed management program should be based upon weed prevention.
3. The focus of a weed management program must be the individual production unit.
4. Weed control with herbicides will continue to be an important part of the weed management program.

5. Adoption of a management approach to weeds could bring about major changes in production practices as a whole and in farm machinery in particular.
6. For weed management to be fully effective, more information is needed about competition, dormancy, when control is necessary, and interactions with other pests. Further, effective ways must be found for evaluating long-term programs and for predicting weed problems.

REFERENCES

Gebhardt, M.R., et al. 1982. A high wide tractor for controlled traffic research. Transactions of the ASAE 1982:77–80.

MacHoughton, J. 1973. Ecological changes in weed populations as a result of crop rotations and herbicides, Ph.D. dissertation. University of Illinois, Urbana.

Mitchell, R.L., and W.J. Russell. 1971. Root development and rooting patterns of soybean (*Glycine Max* L. Merrill) evaluated under field conditions. Agron. J. 63:313–16.

Raper, C.D., and S.A. Barber. 1970. Rooting systems of soybeans, I. Differences in root morphology among varieties. Agron. J. 62:581–84.

APPENDIX
TABLES

Common and Scientific Names of Weeds Referred to in Text

Common and Chemical Names of Herbicides

Herbicides Used in the Study That Provided Data for Figure 15–1

APPENDIX TABLE 1

Common and scientific names of weeds referred to in text.

Common Name	Scientific Name	Common Name	Scientific Name
African feathergrass	*Pennisetum macrourum* Trin.	Bluegrass, annual	*Poa annua* L.
Amaranth, Palmer	*Amaranthus Palmeri* S. Wats.	Bristly foxtail	*Setaria verticillata* (L.) Beauv.
Annual bluegrass	*Poa annua* L.	Broadleaf plantain	*Plantago major* L.
Annual morning-glory	*Ipomoea spp.* L.	Broadleaved dock	*Rumex obtusifolius* L.
Annual sowthistle	*Sonchus oleraceus* L.	Broomsedge	*Andropogon virginicus* L.
Anoda, spurred	*Anoda cristata* (L.) Schlect.	Buckhorn plantain	*Plantago lanceolata* L.
Barley,		Buckwheat, wild	*Polygonum convolvulus* L.
foxtail	*Hordeum jubatum* L.	Buffalobur	*Solanum rostratum* Dunal
little	*Hordeum pusillum* Nutt.	Bull thistle	*Cirsium vulgare* (Savi) Tenore
Barnyardgrass	*Echinochloa crusgalli* (L.) Beauv.	Bulrush, hardstem	*Scirpus acutus* Muhl.
Beach cocklebur	*Xanthium echinatum* Murr.	Buttercup, creeping	*Ranunculus repens* L.
Bedstraw,		Cactus, prickly pear	*Opuntia spp.* Mill.
catchweed, cleavers	*Galium Aparine* L.	Canada thistle	*Cirsium arvense* (L.) Scop.
yellow	*Galium verum* L.	Carline thistle	*Carlina vulgaris* L.
Beggarticks,		Carrot, wild	*Daucus Carota* L.
devils	*Bidens frondosa* L.	Catchfly, nightflowering	*Silene noctiflora* L.
hairy	*Bidens pilosa* L.	Catchweed bedstraw	*Galium Aparine* L.
Beggarweed, Florida	*Desmodium tortuosum* (Sw.) DC.	Cattail	*Typha spp.* L.
Bermudagrass	*Cynodon Dactylon* (L.) Pers.	Chamomile, wild	*Matricaria sp.* L.
Bindweed, field	*Convolvulus arvensis* L.	Chickweed, common	*Stellaria media* (L.) Cyrillo
Birdseye speedwell	*Veronica persica* Poir.	mouse-ear	*Cerastium vulgatum* L. variety *holosteoides* Fries
Blackgrass	*Alopecurus myosuroides* Huds.	Cinquefoil	*Potentilla canadensis* L.
Black knapweed	*Centaurea nigra* L.	Clover, stinking	*Cleome serrulata* Pursh.
Black medic	*Medicago lupulina.* L.	Cockle,	
Black mustard	*Brassica nigra* (L.) Koch	corn	*Agrostemma Githago* L.
Black nightshade	*Solanum nigrum* L.		
Bladder-Campion	*Silene cucubalus* Wibel.		

(continued)

APPENDIX TABLE 1 continued

Common Name	Scientific Name	Common Name	Scientific Name
cow	*Vaccaria segetalis* (Neck.) Garcke	Cress, corn	*Lepidium compestre* (L.) R. Br.
white	*Lychnis alba* Mill.	hoary	*Cardaria Draba* (L.) Desv.
Cocklebur, common	*Xanthium strumarium* L.	mouse-ear	*Arabidopsis Thaliana* (L.) Heynk.
beach	*Xanthium echinatum* Murr	rock	Arabis hirsuta (L.) Scop.
Common chickweed	*Stellaria media* (L.) Cyrillo	Crunchweed	*Brassica Kaber* (D.C.) L.C. Wheeler, var. *pinnatifida* (Stokes) L. L. Wheeler
Common cocklebur	*Xanthium strumarium* L.		
Common crupina	*Crupina vulgaris* Cass		
Common milkweed	*Asclepias syriaca* L.	Crupina, common	*Crupina vulgaris* Cass.
Common mullein	*Verbascum Thapsus* L.	Curly dock	*Rumex crispus* L.
Common purslane	*Portulaca oleracea* L.	Cutgrass, rice	*Leersia oryzoides* (L.) Swartz
Common ragweed	*Ambrosia artemisiifolia* L.	Daisy, ox-eye	*Chrysanthemum Leucanthemum* L.
Common reed	*Phragmites communis* Trin.	Dalmation toadfax	*Linaria dalmatica* (L.) Mill.
Common yarrow	*Achillea millefolium* L.	Dandelion	*Taraxacum officinale* Weber
Corn		Devil's beggarticks	*Bidens frondosa* L.
cockle	*Agrostemma Githoga* L.	Dock, broadleaf	*Rumex obtusifolius* L.
cress	*Lepidium compestre* (L.) R. Br.	curly	*Rumex crispus* L.
marigold	*Chrysanthemum segetum* L.	Mexican	*Rumex mexicanus* Meissn.
poppy	*Papaver Rhoeas* L.	Dodder, field	*Cuscuta campestris* Yunck.
speedwell	*Veronica arvensis* L.		
spurry	*Spergula arvensis* L.	Dog mustard	*Erucastrum gallicum* (Willd.) O.E. Schulz
Couch grass	*Digitaria scalarum* (Schweinf.) Chiov.		
Cow		Dogbane, hemp	*Apocynum cannabinum* L.
cockle	*Vaccaria segetalis* (Neck.) Garcke	Downy brome	*Bromus tectorum* L.
cress	*Lepidium compestre* (L.) R. Br.	Dropseed, sand	*Sporobolus cryptandrus* (Torr.) Gray
Crabgrass	*Digitaria sanguinalis* (L.) Scop.		
Creeping buttercup	*Ranunculus repens* L.	Eulalia	*Miscanthus sinensis* Anderss.

Common Name	Scientific Name	Common Name	Scientific Name
European sticktight	*Lappula echinata* Gilib.	Galinsoga, smallflower	*Galinsoga parviflora* Cav.
Evening primrose	*Oenothera biennis* L.	Garden orach	*Atriplex hortensis* L.
Fall panicum	*Panicum dichotomiflorum* Michx.	Garden sorrel	*Rumex acetosella* L.
		Garlic, wild	*Allium vineale* L.
Falseflax,		Giant foxtail	*Setaria faberii* Herrm.
flatseed	*Camelina dentata* Pers.	Giant ragweed	*Ambrosia trifida* L.
		Goldenrod spp.	*Solidago spp.* L.
largeseed	*Camelina sativa* (L.) Crantz	Goosefoot, manyseeded	*Chenopodium polyspernum* L.
smallseed	*Camelina microcarpa* Andrz.	Goosegrass	*Eleusine indica* (L.) Gaertn.
Field		Goutweed	*Aegopodium Podagraria* L.
bindweed	*Convolvulus arvense* L.	Greenflower pepperweed	*Lepidium densiflorum* Schrad.
dodder	*Cuscuta campestris* Yunck.		
pennycress	*Thlaspi arvense* L.	Green foxtail	*Setaria viridis* (L.) Beauv.
Fingergrass spp.	*Chloris spp.* Sw.	Groundcherry	*Physalis spp.* L.
Flatseed falseflax	*Camelina dentata* Pers.	Groundsel	*Senecio vulgaris* L.
Fleabane	*Erigeron spp.* L.	Gumweed spp.	*Grindelia squarrosa* Willd.
Flixweed	*Descurainia Sophia* (L.) Webb.	Halberleaf orach	*Atriplex hastata* L.
Florida beggarweed	*Desmodium tortuosum* (SW.) DC.	Hardstem bulrush	*Scirpus acutus* Muhl.
		Hare's ear mustard	*Conringia orientalis* (L.) Dumort
Florida pusley	*Richardia scabra* L.	Hawkbit	*Leontodon hispidus* L.
Flowering spurge	*Euphorbia corollata* L.	Healall	*Prunella vulgaris* L.
Foxtail		Hedge mustard	*Sisymbrium officinale* (L.) Scop.
bristly	*Setaria verticillata* (L.) Beauv.	Hempnettle	*Galeopis tetrahit* L.
giant	*Setaria faberii* Herrm.	Hemp dogbane	*Apocynum cannabinum* L.
green	*Setaria viridis* (L.) Beauv.	sesbania	*Sesbania exaltata* (Raf.) Cory
yellow	*Setaria lutescens* (Weigel) Hubb.	Hoary	
Foxtail barley	*Hordeum jubatum* L.	cress	*Cardaria draba* (L.) Desv.
Foxtail millet	*Setaria italica* (L.) Beauv.	plantain	*Plantago media* L.
Fumitory	*Fumaria officinalis* L.	Hogweed (common ragweed)	*Ambrosia artemisiifolia* (L.) var. *elatior* (L.) Descourtils

(continued)

APPENDIX TABLE 1 continued

Common Name	Scientific Name	Common Name	Scientific Name
Honeysuckle, Japanese	*Lonicera japonica* Thumb.	prostrate	*Polygonum neglectum* Bess.
Honeyvine milkweed	*Ampelamus albidus* (Nutt.) Britt.		*Polygonum aviculare* L.
Horse-radish	*Armoracia rusticana* (Lam.) Gaertn., Mey. & Scherb.	Kochia	*Kochia scoparia* (L.) Schrad.
		Ladysthumb	*Polygonum persicaria* L.
Horseweed	*Conyza canadensis* (L.) Cronq.	Lambsquarters	*Chenopodium album* L.
Indian mustard	*Brassica juncea* (L.) Coss.	Largeseed falseflax	*Camelina sativa* (L.) Crantz
Ironweed, western	*Vernonia Baldwini* Torr.	Leafy spurge	*Euphorbia Esula* L.
Itchgrass	*Rottboellia exaltata* L.F.	Lettuce, prickly	*Lactuca serriola* L.
		Little barley	*Hordeum pusillum* Nutt.
Ivyleaf morning-glory	*Ipomoea hederacea* (L.) Jaeq.	Manyseeded goosefoot	*Chenopodium polyspermum* L.
Ivyleaf speedwell	*Veronica hederaefolia* L.	Marigold, corn	*Chrysanthemum segetum* L.
Japanese honeysuckle	*Lonicera japonica* Thumb.	Marijuana	*Cannabis sativa* L.
Japanese knotweed	*Polygonum cuspidatum* Sieb. & Zucc.	Marjoram, wild	*Origanum vulgare* L.
		Marshelder	*Iva xanthifolia* Nutt.
Jimsonweed	*Datura stramonium* L.	Medic, black	*Medicago lupulina* L.
Johnsongrass	*Sorghum halepense* (L.) Pers.	Mediterranean sage	*Salvia aethiopis* L.
Jointvetch	*Aeschynomene virginca* (L.) BSP.	Medusahead	*Taeniatherum asperum* (Sim.) Nevski
Kikuyu grass	*Pennisetum clandestinum* Hoch. St. ex chiov.	Mexican dock	*Rumex mexicanus* Meissn.
		Milkweed,	
Klamath weed	*Hypericum perforatum* L.	common	*Asclepias syriaea* L.
		honeyvine	*Ampelamus albidus* (Nutt.) Britt.
Knapweed, black	*Centaurea nigra* L.	showy	*Asclepias speciosa* Torr.
Russian	*Centaurea repens* L.	western whorled	*Asclepias subverticillata* (Gray) Vail
Knotweed Japanese	*Polygonum cuspidatum* Sieb. & Zucc.	Millet, foxtail	*Setaria italica* (L.) Beauv.
		Moonflower, purple	*Ipomoea turbinata* Lagasea y Segura

Common Name	Scientific Name	Common Name	Scientific Name
Morning-glory,		Nightflowering	*Silene*
annual	*Ipomoea spp.* L.	catchfly	*noctiflora* L.
ivyleaf	*Ipomoea hederacea*	Nightshade, black	*Solanum nigrum* L.
	(L.) Jacq.	Nutsedge,	
pitted	*Ipomoea lacunosa*	purple	*Cyperus rotundus* L.
	f. *purpurata* L.	yellow	*Cyperus*
tall	*Ipomoea purpurea*		*esculentus* L.
	(L.) Roth	Oat,	
Mouse-ear chickweed	*Cerastium*	wild	*Avena fatua* L.
	vulgatum L.	winter wild	*Avena*
	variety		*ludoviciano* Dur.
	holosteoides	Oat-grass	*Arrhenatherum*
	Fries		*elatius*
Mouse-ear cress	*Arabidopsis*		(L.) Presl.
	Thaliana		
	(L.) Heynk.	Orach,	
Mullein, common	*Verbascum*	garden	*Atriplex hortensis* L.
	Thapsus L.	halberleaf	*Atriplex hastata* L.
Musk thistle	*Carduus spp.* L.	spreading	*Atriplex patula* L.
Mustard,		Oxalis	*Oxalis spp.* L.
black	*Brassica nigra*	Ox-eye daisy	*Chrysanthemum*
	(L.) Koch		*Leucanthemum* L.
dog	*Erucastrum gallicum*	Palmer amaranth	*Amaranthus*
	(Willd.)		*Palmeri* S. Wats.
	O.E. Schulz	Panicum, fall	*Panicum*
hare's ear	*Conringia orientalis*		*dichotomiflorum*
	(L.) Dumort		Michx.
hedge	*Sisymbrium*	Panicum, Texas	*Panicum texanum*
	officinale		Buckl.
	(L.) Scop.	Parsley-piert	*Aphanes arvensis*
Indian	*Brassica juncea*		(L.) Scop.
	(L.) Coss.	Parsnip	*Pastinaca sativa* L.
tumble	*Sisymbrium*	Pennsylvania	*Polygonum*
	altissimum L.	smartweed	*pensylvanicum* L.
wild	*Brassica Kaber*	Pepperweed,	
	(DC.)	greenflower	*Lepidium*
	L.C. Wheeler var.		*densiflorum*
	pinnatifida		Schrad.
	(Stokes)	Virginia	*Lepidium*
	L.C. Wheeler		*virginicum* L.
wormseed	*Erysimum*	yellowflower	*Lepidium*
	cheiranthoides L.		*perfoliatum* L.
Naiad, slender	*Naja flexilis*	Perennial sowthistle	*Sonchus arvensis* L.
	(Willd.)	Pigweed,	
	Rostk. & Schmidt	prostrate	*Amaranthus blitoides*
			S. Wats.

(continued)

APPENDIX TABLE 1 continued

Common Name	Scientific Name	Common Name	Scientific Name
redroot	*Amaranthus retroflexus* L.	Redroot pigweed	*Amaranthus retroflexus* L.
Russian	*Axyris amaranthoides* L.	Redvine	*Brunnichia cirrhosa* Gaertn.
tumble	*Amaranthus albus* L. *Amaranthus graecizans* L.	Rice cutgrass	*Leersia oryzoides* (L.) Swartz.
tumbling	*Amaranthus albus* L.	Rock cress	*Arabis hirsuta* (L.) Scop.
Pimpernel, scarlet	*Anagallis arvensis* L.	Rocket, yellow	*Barbarea vulgaris* R. Br.
Pitted morning-glory	*Ipomoea lacunosa* f. *purpurata* L.	Russian knapweed	*Centaurea repens* L.
Plantain,		Russian pigweed	*Axyris amaranthoides* L.
broadleaf	*Plantago major* L.		
buckhorn	*Plantago lanceolata* L.	Russian thistle	*Salsola Kali* L. var. *tenuifolia* Tausch *Salsola pestifer* Nels.
hoary	*Plantago media* L.		
Poppy, corn	*Papaver Rhoeas* L.		
Porcupinegrass	*Stipa spartea* Trin.	Sage, Mediterranean	*Salvia aethiopis* L.
Povertyweed	*Monolepis Nuttaliana* (R. & S.) Greene	Salsify, western	*Tragopogon dubius* Scop.
Prickly lettuce	*Lactuca Serriola* L.	Sandbur,	*Cenchrus incertus* M.A. Curtis
Prickly pear cactus	*Opuntia* spp. Mill.	longspine	*Cenchrus longispinus* (Hack.) Fern.
Prickly sida	*Sida spinosa* L.		
Primrose, evening	*Oenothera biennis* L.	Sand dropseed	*Sporobolus cryptandrus* (Torr.) Gray
Prostrate knotweed	*Polygonum aviculare* L.		
Prostrate pigweed	*Amaranthus blitoides* S. Wats.	Sandwort, thyme-leaved	*Arenaria serpyllifolia* L.
Prostrate spurge	*Euphorbia supina* Raf.	Scarlet pimpernel	*Anagallis arvensis* L.
		Sesbania, hemp	*Sesbania exaltata* (Raf.) Cory
Puncturevine	*Tribulus terrestris* L.		
Purple moonflower	*Ipomea turbinata* Lagasca y Segura	Shepherdspurse	*Capsella bursa-pastoris* (L.) Medic.
Purple nutsedge	*Cyperus rotundus* L.		
Purslane, common	*Portulaca oleracea* L.	Showy milkweed	*Asclepias speciosa* Torr.
Pusley, Florida	*Richardia scabra* L.		
Quackgrass	*Agropyron repens* (L.) Beauv.	Sicklepod	*Cassia obtusifolia* L.
		Sida, prickly	*Sida spinosa* L.
Radish, wild	*Raphanus Raphanistrum* L.	Skeleton weed	*Lygodesmia juncea* (Pursh) D. Don
Ragweed,		Slender naiad	*Najas flexilis* (Willd.) Rostk. & Schmidt
common	*Ambrosia artemisiifolia* L.		
giant	*Ambrosia trifida* L.	Smallflower galinsoga	*Galinsoga parviflora* Cav.
Ragwort, tansy	*Senecio jacobaea* L.		

Common Name	Scientific Name	Common Name	Scientific Name
Smallseed falseflax	*Camelina microcarpa* Andrz.	Thistle, bull	*Cirsium vulgare (Savi)* Tenore
Smartweed, Pennsylvania	*Polygonum pensylvanicum* L.	Canada	*Cirsium arvense* (L.) Scop.
Smooth crabgrass	*Digitaria Ischaemum* (Schreb.) Muhl.	carline	*Carlina vulgaris* (L.)
		musk	*Carduus spp.* L.
Soapwort	*Saponaria officinalis* L.	Russian	*Salsola Kali* L. var. *tenuifolia* Tausch
Sorrel, garden	*Rumex acetosa* L.		
Sowthistle, perennial	*Sonchus arvensis* L.	Thyme-leaved sandwort	*Arenaria serpyllifolia* L.
Speedwell, birdseye	*Veronica persica* Poir.	Tickseed	*Coreopsis, spp.* L.
		Toadflax, dalmation	*Linaria dalmatica* (L.) Mill.
corn	*Veronica arvense* L.	yellow	*Linaria vulgaris* Hill
ivyleaf	*Veronica hederaefolia* L.	Triple-awned grass	*Aristida oligantha* Michx.
Spreading orach	*Atriplex patula* L.	Triple-awned grass spp.	*Aristida adscensionis* L.
Spurge, flowering	*Euphorbia corollata* L.	Trumpetcreeper	*Campsis radicans* (L.) Seem.
leafy	*Euphorbia Esula* L.		
prostrate	*Euphorbia supina* Raf.	Tumblegrass	*Schedonnardus paniculatus* (Nutt.) Trel.
Spurred anoda	*Anoda cristata* (L.) Schlecht.	Tumble mustard	*Sisymbrium altissimum* L.
Spurry, corn	*Spergula arvensis* L.	Tumble pigweed	*Amaranthus albus* L. *Amaranthus graecizans* L.
Starthistle, yellow	*Centaurea solstitialis* L.		
Sticktight, European	*Lappula echinata* Gilib.	Tumbling pigweed	*Amaranthus albus* L.
Stinkgrass	*Eragrostis cilianensis* (All.) Lutati	Velvetleaf	*Abutilon theophrasti* Medic
Stinking clover	*Cleome serrulata* Pursh.	Virginia pepperweed	*Lepidium virginicum* L.
St. Johnswort (Klamath weed)	*Hypericum perforatum* L.	Waterhyacinth	*Eichornia crassipes* (Mart.) Solms
Strangler vine	*Morrenia odorata* Lindl.	Waterprimrose, winged	*Jussiaea decurrens* (Walt.) DC.
Sunflower, wild	*Helianthus spp.* L.	starthistle	*Centaurea solstitialis* L.
Tall morning-glory	*Ipomoea purpurea* (L.) Roth	toadflax	*Linaria vulgaris* Hill
Tansy ragwort	*Senecio jacobaea* L.	Yellowflower pepperweed	*Lepidium perfoliatum* L.
Texas panicum	*Panicum texanum* Buckl.		

(continued)

APPENDIX TABLE 1 continued

Common Name	Scientific Name	Common Name	Scientific Name
Western ironweed	*Vernonia Baldwinii* Torr.	Winter wild oat	*Avena sterilis* var. *Iudaviciano* (Duriem) Husnot
Western salsify	*Tragopogon dubius* Scop.	Witchweed	*Striga lutea* Lour.
Western whorled milkweed	*Asclepias subverticillata* (Gray) Vail	Woodsorrel	*Oxalis spp.* L.
White cockle	*Lychnis alba* Mill.	Wormseed mustard	*Cheirinia cheiranthoides* Link *Erysimum cheiranthoides* L.
Wild			
buckwheat	*Polygonum convolvulus* L.	Yarrow, common	*Achillea Milliefolium* L.
carrot	*Daucus carota* L.		
chamomile	*Matricaria spp.* L.	Yellow	
garlic	*Allium vineale* L.	bedstraw	*Galium verum* L.
marjoram	*Origanum vulgare* L.	foxtail	*Setaria lutescens* (Weigel) Hubb.
mustard	*Brassica Kaber* (DC.) L.C. Wheeler var. *pinnatifida* (Stokes) L.C. Wheeler	nutsedge	*Cyperus esculentus* L.
		rocket	*Barbarea vulgaris* R. Br.
oat	*Avena fatua* L.		
radish	*Raphanus Raphanistrum* L.		
sunflower	*Helianthus spp.* L.		

APPENDIX TABLE 2

Common and chemical names of herbicides.*

Common Name	Chemical Name
Acifluorfen	5-[2-chloro-4-(trifluoromethyl)phenoxy]-2-nitrobenzoic acid
Alachlor	2-chloro-2-2,6-diethyl-*N*-(methoxymethyl)acetanilide
Ametryn	2-(ethylamino)-4-(isopropylamino)-6-(methylthio)-*s*-triazine
Amiben	(See *Chloramben*)
Amitrole	3-amino-*s*-triazole
Asulam	methyl sulfanilylcarbamate
Atrazine	2-chloro-4-(ethylamino)-6-(isopropylamino)-*s*-triazine
Barban	4-chloro-2-butynyl *m*-chlorocarbanilate
Benefin	*N*-butyl-*N*-ethyl-*α,α,α*-trifluoro-2,6-dinitro-*p*-toluidine
Bensulide	*O,O*-diisopropyl phosphorodithioate *S*-ester with *N*-(2-mercaptoethyl)benzenesulfonamide
Bentazon	3-isopropyl-1*H*-2,1,3-benzothiadiazin-4(3*H*)-one 2,2-dioxide
Benzadox	(benzamidooxy) acetic acid
Bifenox	methyl 5-(2,4-dichlorophenoxy)-2-nitrobenzoate
Bromoxynil	3,5-dibromo-4-hydroxybenzonitrile
Butachlor	*N*-(butoxymethyl)-2-chloro-2,6-diethylacetanilide
Butam	2,2-dimethyl-*N*-(1-methylethyl)-*N*-(phenylmethyl)propanamide
Butralin	4-(1,1-dimethylethyl)-*N*-(1-methylpropyl)-2,6-dinitrobenzenamine
Butylate	*S*-ethyl diisobutylthiocarbamate
Cacodylic acid	hydroxydimethylarsine oxide
CDAA	*N*-*N*-diallyl-2-chloroacetamide
CDEC	2-chloroallyl diethyldithiocarbamate
Chloramben	3-amino-2,5-dichlorobenzoic acid
Chlorbromuron	3-(4-bromo-3-chlorophenyl)-1-methoxy-1-methylurea
Chloridazon	(See *Pyrazon*)
Chloroxuron	3-[*p*-(*p*-chlorophenoxy)phenyl]-1,1-dimethylurea
Chlorpropham	isopropyl *m*-chlorocarbanilate
Chlorsulfuron	2-chloro-*N*-[[4-methoxy-6-methyl-1,3,5 -triazin-2-yl)amino]carbonyl]benzenesulfonamide
CIPC	(See *Chlorpropham*)
Cisanalide	*cis*-2,5-dimethyl-*N*-phenyl-1-pyrrolidinecarboxamide
Cyanazine	2-[[4-chloro-6-(ethylamino)-*s*-triazin-2-yl]amino]-2-methylpropionitrile
Cycloate	*S*-ethyl *N*-ethylthiocyclohexanecarbamate
Cyprazine	2-chloro-4-(cyclopropylamino)-6-(isopropylamino)-*s*-triazine
Cypromid	3,4-dichlorocyclopropanecarboxanilide
Dalapon	2,2-dichloropropionic acid
DCPA	dimethyl tetrachloroterephthalate
Desmedipham	ethyl *m*-hydroxycarbanilate carbanilate (ester)
Diallate	*S*-(2,3-dichloroallyl) diisopropylthiocarbamate
Dicamba	3,6-dichloro-*o*-anisic acid
Dichlobenil	2,6-dichlorobenzonitrile
Dichlorobenil	(See *Dichlobenil*)
Difenzoquat	1,2-dimethyl-3,5-diphenyl-1*H*-pyrazolium

(continued)

* Accepted by the Weed Science Society of America.

APPENDIX TABLE 2 continued

Common Name	Chemical Name
Dinitramine	N^4, N^4-diethyl-α,α,α-trifluoro-3,5-dinitrotoluene-2,4-diamine
Dinoben	2,5-dichloro-3-nitro benzoic acid
Dinoseb	2-*sec*-butyl-4,6-dinitrophenol
Diphenamid	*N,N*-dimethyl-2,2-diphenylacetamide
Dipropetryn	2-(ethylthio)-4,6-bis (isopropylamino)-*s*-triazine
Diquat	6,7-dihydrodipyrido[1,2-*a*:2,1-*c*] pyrazinediium ion
Diuron	3-(3,4-dichlorophenyl)-1,1-dimethylurea
DSMA	disodium methanearsonate
Endothall	7-oxabicyclo[2.2.1]heptane-2,3-dicarboxylic acid
EPTC	*S*-ethyl dipropylthiocarbamate
Ethalfluralin	*N*-ethyl-*N*-(2-methyl-2-propenyl)-2,6-dinitro-4-(trifluoromethyl) benzenamine
Fenac	(2,3,6-trichlorophenyl)acetic acid
Fluaziflop-butyl	butyl 2-[4-(5-trifluoromethyl-2-pyridyloxy)phenoxy]propionate
Fluchloralin	*N*-(2-chlorsethyl)-2,6-dinitro-*N*-propyl-4-(trifluoromethyl)aniline
Fluometuron	1,1-dimethyl-3-(α,α,α-trifluoro-*m*-tolyl)urea
Fluorodifen	*p*-nitrophenyl α,α,α-trifluoro-2-nitro-*p*-tolyl) urea
Flurenol	*n*-butyl-9-hydroxyfluorene-(9)-carboxylate
Fosamine	ethyl hydrogen (aminocarbonyl)phosphonate
Glyphosate	*N*-(phosphonomethyl)glycine
Ioxynil	4-hydroxy-3,5-diiodobenzonitrile
IPC	(See *Propham*)
Isocil	5-bromo-3-isopropyl-6-methyluracil
Isopropalin	2,6-dinitro-*N,N*-dipropylcumidine
Karbutilate	*tert*-butylcarbamic acid ester with 3(*m*-hydroxyphenyl)-1,1-dimethylurea
Lenacil	3-cyclohexyl-6,7-dihydro-1*H*-cyclopentapyrimidine-2,4(3*H*,5*H*)-dione
Linuron	3-(3,4-dichlorophenyl)-1-methoxy-1-methylurea
Maleic Hydrazide	1,2-dihydro-3,6-pyridazinedione
MCPA	[(4-chloro-*o*-tolyl)oxy]acetic acid
MCPB	4-[4-chloro-*o*-tolyl]butyric acid
Mefluidide	*N*-[2,4-dimethyl-5-[[(trifluoromethyl)sulfonyl]amino]phenyl]acetamide
Metham	sodium methyldithiocarbamate
Methazole	2-(3,4-dichlorophenyl)-4-methyl-1,2,4-oxadiazolidine-3,5-dione
Metolachlor	2-chloro-*N*-(2-ethyl-6-methylphenyl)-*N*-(2-methoxy-1-methylethyl)acetamide
Metribuzin	4-amino-6-*tert*-butyl-3-(methylthio)-*as*-triazin-5(4*H*)-one
Molinate	*S*-ethyl hexahydro-1*H*-azepine-1-carbothioate
Monuron	3-(*p*-chlorophenyl)-1,1-dimethylurea
MSMA	monosodium methanearsonate
NPA	(See *Naptalam*)
Napropamide	2-(α-napthoxy)-*N,N*-diethylpropionamide
Naptalam	*N*-1-naphthylphthalamic acid
Nitralin	4-(methylsulfonyl)-2,6-dinitro-*N,N*-dipropylaniline
Nitrofen	2,4-dichlorophenyl *p*-nitrophenyl ether
Norea	3-(hexahydro-4,7-methanoindan-5-yl)-1,1-dimethylurea
Norflurazon	4-chloro-5-(methylamino)-2-(α,α,α-trifluro-*m*-tolyl)-3(2*H*)-pyridazinone

Common Name	Chemical Name
Oryzalin	3,5–dinitro–N^4,N^4–dipropylsulfanilamide
Oxyfluorfen	2–chloro–1–(3–ethoxy–4–nitrophenoxy)–4–(trifluoromethyl)benzene
Paraquat	1,1–dimethyl–4,4–bipyridinium ion
PCP	pentachlorophenol
PEBC (Pebulate)	S–propyl butylethylthiocarbamate
Pebulate	S–propyl butylethylthiocarbamate
Pendimethalin	N–(1–ethylpropyl)–3,4–dimethyl–2,6–dinitrobenzenamine
Perfluidone	1,1,1–trifluoro–N–[2–methyl–4–(phenyl-sulfonyl)-phenyl]methanesulfon-amide
Phenmedipham	methyl m–hydroxycarbanilate m–methyl–carbanilate
Phthalimide	
Picloram	4–amino–3,5,6–trichloropicolinic acid
Potassium Azide	
PPTC	S–propyl dipropylthiocarbamate
Prodiamine	2,4–dinitro–N^3,N^3–dipropyl–6–(trifluromethyl)–1,3–benzenediamine
Profluralin	N–(cyclopropylmethyl)–α,α,α–trifluoro–2,6–dinitro–N–propyl–p–toluidine
Prometon	2,4–bis(isopropylamino)–6–methoxy–s–triazine
Prometryn	2,4–bis(isopropylamino)–6–(methylthio)–s–triazine
Pronamide	3,5–dichloro(N–1,1–dimethyl–2–propynyl)benzamide
Propachlor	2–chloro–N–isopropylacetanilide
Propanil	3,4–dichloropropionanilide
Propazine	2–chloro–4,6–bis(isopropylamino)–s–triazine
Propham	isopropyl carbanilate
Prosulfalin	N–[[4–(dipropylamino)–3,5–dinitrophenyl]sulfonyl]–S,S–dimethylsulfilimine
Pyrazon	5–amino–4–chloro–2–phenyl–3–(2H)–pyridazinone
Secbumeton	N–ethyl–6–methoxy–N(1–methylpropyl)–1,3,5–triazine–2,4–diamine
Sethoxydim	2–[1–(ethoxyimino)butyl]–5–[2–(ethylthio)propyl]–3–hydroxy–2–cyclohexen–1–one
Siduron	1–(2–methylcyclohexyl)–3–phenylurea
Silvex	2–(2,4,5–trichlorophenoxy)propionic acid
Simazine	2–chloro–4,6–bis(ethylamino)–s–triazine
Sodium Azide	
TCA	trichloroacetic acid
TCBC	trichlorobenzyl chloride
Terbacil	3–tert–butyl–5–chloro–6–methyluracil
Terbutryn	2–(tert–butylamino)–4–(ethylamino)–6–(methylthio)–s–triazine
Thiobencarb	S–[(4–chlorophenyl)–methyl]diethylcarbamothioate
Triallate	S–(2,3,3–trichloroallyl)diisopropylthiocarbamate
Trifluralin	α,α,α–trifluoro–2,6–dinitro–N,N–dipropyl–p–toluidine
2,3,6–TBA	2,3,6–trichlorobenzoic acid
2,4–D	(2,4–dichlorophenoxy)acetic acid
2,4–DB	4–(2,4–dichlorophenoxy)butyric acid
2,4,5–T	(2,4,5–trichlorophenoxy)acetic acid
Vernolate	S–propyl dipropylthiocarbamate

APPENDIX TABLE 3

Herbicides used in the study that provided data for Figure 15-1.

	Corn	Soybeans	Wheat
Single herbicide			
	atrazine	chloramben	dicamba
	(3.4 kg/ha)	(3.4 kg/ha)	(0.3 kg/ha)
Rotation herbicide			
1965	propachlor	trifluralin	2,4–D
	(4.5 kg/ha)	(1.1 kg/ha)	(0.3 kg/ha)
1966	CDAA (3.9 kg/ha)	NPA (3.4 kg/ha) +	2,4–D
	+ trichloroben-	CIPC (2.2 kg/ha)	(0.3 kg/ha)
	zyl chloride		
	(7.8 kg/ha)		
1967	atrazine	vernalate	2,4–D
	(1.7 kg/ha) +	(3.4 kg/ha)	(0.3 kg/ha)
	propachlor		
	(3.4 kg/ha)		
1968	propachlor	trifluralin	bromoxynil
	(4.5 kg/ha)	(1.1 kg/ha)	(0.6 kg/ha)
1969	atrazine	alachlor	MCPA
	(1.1 kg/ha) +	(2.2 kg/ha)	(0.6 kg/ha)
	butylate		
	(3.4 kg/ha)		
1970	alachlor	trifluralin	2,4–D
	(2.2 kg/ha)	(1.1 kg/ha)	(0.6 kg/ha)

Source: From MacHoughton, 1973.

GLOSSARY

Abiotic: The nonliving portion of the environment.

Abscisic acid: A naturally occurring, plant growth inhibitor; commonly considered to be a key factor in stomatal control, leaf senescence, and bud and seed dormancy.

Achene: A dry, single-seeded, indehiscent fruit whose pericarp and seed coat are not fused.

Acropetal: Plant structures produced in succession toward the apex; also, translocation toward the apex.

Additive design: With respect to studies of effects of weed infestation level on crops, experimental designs in which the total number of plants on a given area (weeds + crops) is either increased or decreased as their proportion changes. (See *replacement design*.)

Absorption: Penetration of a substance into the body of an organism or particle.

Adsorption: Retention of a substance on a surface.

Adventitious (bud or root): One originating from mature rather than from meristematic tissue.

Agroecosystem: The agricultural species and production practices functioning together in a production system.

Allelopathy: Any harmful effect of one plant on another from the production of chemical compounds that escape into the environment.

Allopatry: Speciation resulting from the compensation for environmental conditions of geographically separated segments of a species.

Amphoteric: A chemical capable of reacting either as an acid or as a base.

Annidation: The complementary use of resources by two or more plant species occupying a given area.

Annual: A plant that completes its life cycle in one year or less. A summer annual germinates in the spring or summer, flowers, produces seed, and dies that growing season. A winter annual germinates in late summer or fall, overwinters, then flowers, produces seed, and dies the following spring.

Antidote (herbicidal): A chemical used to protect a desired plant from an herbicide.

Apical dominance: Inhibition by the apical meristem of growth of buds on a rhizome or along the meristem.

Apoplast: The translocation pathway of a plant that involves nonliving cells.

Assimilation: The incorporation or conversion of absorbed substances into living matter.

Augmentation: Modifying the environment or supplementing the population of a native biotic agent to increase its effectiveness in biological control.

Auxin: See *plant growth regulator*.

Axillary bud: One originating at the angle between the stem and a branch or leaf petiole.

Basipetal: Structures produced in succession toward the base; also, translocation toward the base.

Biennial: A plant that requires more than one but less than two years to complete its life cycle.

Binomial: With reference to taxonomy, the two-part Latin name used in the scientific identification of plants (e.g., *Chenopodium album* = lambsquarters).

Biochemical site of action: The single reaction affected at a concentration lower than any other reaction, or first affected at a given low concentration.

Bioherbicide (mass exposure): A biological agent effective in controlling a weed at the applied concentration.

Biomass: The total quantity of plant tops and roots produced on a given area.

Biosystem (weed—crop): Regularly interacting and interdependent weeds and crops in a plant community.

Biotic: The living portion of the environment.

Biotic agent: A biological organism used to suppress or control weeds.

Bulb: A specialized underground organ consisting of a short, fleshy, usually vertical stem axis (basal plate) bearing at its apex a growing point or a flower primordium that is enclosed by thick fleshy leaves.

Canopy: The cover of leaves and stems formed by the tops of plants as viewed from above.

Carrying capacity: The maximum biomass that can be maintained on an area over time.

Casparian strip: A continuous, impermeable, waxy band in cell walls of the root endodermis that serves as a barrier to free passage of water and solutes to vascular tissue.

Chlorosis: Lack of green color in foliage caused either by loss of chlorophyll or by its failure to develop.

Climax: A stabilized ecosystem in ecological succession.

Clone: A group of organisms descended by asexual reproduction from a common ancestor.

Coexistence: Persistence on a given area over time of two or more plant species sharing common resources.

Coleoptile: Sheath surrounding the plumule in a grass seedling.

Coma: A tuft of hairs attached to a seed.

Community: The assemblage of plant populations on a given area.

Competition: Relationship between two or more plants in which the supply of a growth factor falls below their combined demands.

Competitive exclusion principle: An ecological separation of closely related and similar species in response to competition.

Contact herbicide: A chemical that kills plants mainly by contact with tissue rather than as a result of translocation to another site.

Control: That part of weed management which focuses on the reduction of a given weed infestation for a specified period of time, usually part of a crop growing season.

Corm: The swollen base of a stem axis enclosed by dry, scale-like leaves. Distinguished from a bulb by its solid stem structure with distinct nodes and internodes.

Correlative inhibition: The inhibiting effect of one bud on the growth of another as on rhizomes of a perennial weed.

Cover crop: A close-growing crop grown primarily to protect soil between periods of regular crop production.

Creeping rootstock: Laterally growing roots whose tissue commonly stores carbohydrates and may form adventitious buds for regeneration of growth, such as in bindweed.

Culm: The jointed, usually hollow, stem of various grasses.

Cultivation: The mechanical loosening or tilling of soil around growing plants.

Day length: See *photoperiod*.

Density: Number of plants on a specified area.

Depletion zone: The volume of soil in which the supply of a growth factor is reduced by plant roots.

Dermal tissue: The outer system of cells of a plant.

Dicot (dicotyledonous): Those plants having two cotyledons, as in broad-leaf weeds. (See *monocot*.)

Diffusion: With respect to a soil-supplied nutrient, its movement in response to uniform mixing (equalizing concentrations) in the soil solution.

Directed application: Application of an herbicide to a specific area, or plant part, commonly the base of plants.

Dispersal: The movement of a reproductive unit (seed or perennating part) from its place of production.

Diurnal: A daily event or process usually associated with changes from day to night.

Dockage: Reduction in the price paid for a farm product as a result of contamination with weeds or weed parts.

Dominants: Species in a community that exert the major controlling influence on energy flow and on the environment of other species in the ecosystem.

Dormancy: State in which growth of a specific plant part is not resumed even though the environment supports germination, seedling growth, or development of other, apparently identical, tissues of the same species or plant. (See *enforced dormancy, induced dormancy,* and *innate dormancy*.)

Ecological (biological) niche: See *niche*.

Ecological succession: See *succession*.

Ecology: The study of the relationship between living organisms and their environment.

Ecosystem: Any unit that includes the living and nonliving environment regularly interacting to form a unified whole with clearly defined trophic structure, biotic diversity, and materials cycles.

Ecotone: The juncture zone of two or more ecological communities.

Ecotype: A locally adapted population of a species.

Edge effect: Tendency for greater species diversity at the juncture of ecological communities.

Emergence: The stage in plant development when the seedling is first visible above the soil surface.

Enforced dormancy: Failure to germinate and grow because conditions necessary to support growth are lacking.

Epinasty: The twisting or curling of leaves and stems caused by uneven growth of cells.

Epithet: With reference to the binomial nomenclature, the second part of the species' Latin name (e.g., *album* in *Chenopodium album*).

Eradication: The complete elimination of all live plants, perennating parts, and seeds of a weed from a given area.

Escapes: Individual specimens or species of plants not controlled by a specific control practice.

Factor compensation: Modification of plant growth form and of the physical environment by a plant that serves to limit the effect of the physical conditions to which it is exposed.

Fallowing: Allowing cropland to lie idle, either tilled or untilled, for the entire or most of the growing season.

Fibrous root system: A root system having a large number of small, finely branched, spreading roots but no large individual roots or central root.

Fundamental tissue: The tissue within which the vascular tissue is imbedded and from which the various plant parts originate.

General-purpose genotype: Genotypes that survive over a wide range of climatic conditions while still maintaining the ability to evolve new forms through genetic recombinations.

Genus: With reference to the binomial nomenclature, the first part of a species' Latin name; it provides generic identity to the taxonomic group between family and species within the plant kingdom.

Germination: Resumption of growth of a seed or of a vegetative perennating part.

Gibberellins: A specific, naturally occurring group of plant growth regulators that stimulate growth.

Growth factor: Any one of the five factors—light, carbon dioxide, water, nutrients, and oxygen—required for plant growth.

Growth form: A plant's aboveground general shape, including its height, leaf type, leaf arrangement, and attitude towards light.

Growth substance: See *plant growth regulator*.

Gymnosperm: A plant that does not have flowers in the ordinary sense, but is naked seeded, such as ground hemlock *(Taxus canadensis)*.

Habitat: Place where a plant lives.

Herbaceous perennial: A vascular plant that lives for more than two years and does not develop woody tissue.

Homeostasis: Tendency of a biological system to resist change and remain in a state of equilibrium.

Hybrid: A plant resulting from a cross between parents of different species, subspecies, or ecotypes.

Hydrophilic: With respect to surfactants, that portion of the molecule soluble in water.

Hydrophobic: See *lipophilic*.

Incorporation: The mechanical mixing of an herbicide in the surface 2.5 cm to 7.5 cm of soil.

Induced (secondary) dormancy: Creation of the dormant state as a result of conditions to which the reproductive part is exposed after separation from the parent.

Inflorescence: The flowering part of a plant.

Innate (primary) dormancy: Presence of the dormant state in the reproductive part when released from the parent.

Inoculation: Release of a biotic agent to build to levels sufficient to hold a weed infestation below an economic threshold level.

Interference: The deleterious effect of one plant on another.

Juvenile period: That stage in the early development of a plant before initiation of reproduction (of seed or perennating parts).

K-strategy: With respect to survival, a weed that depends upon strong competitive ability, such as is found with many perennial species. (See *r-strategy*.)

Land equivalent ratio: The land area required to produce a given total yield in monoculture compared to the area needed to produce the same total yield in intercrops.

Leaching: The movement, most commonly downward, of an herbicide in soil with percolating water; also, the introduction of an allelochemical into the plant environment as a result of dissolution from living or dead plant parts.

Leaf area index: The blade area of a leaf, or leaves, relative to the given soil surface area it covers.

Life cycle: The life span of a plant from germination of the seed, to growth, maturation, reproduction, senescence, and death.

Limits of tolerance: Range of supply of a growth factor or environmental attribute within which an organism will exist.

Lipophilic: With respect to surfactants, that portion of the molecule soluble in oil.

Longevity: The time, after being produced, a seed or vegetative perennating part retains its ability to resume growth.

Manipulative method: With respect to biological control, steps taken to conserve or augment the number of individuals of a biotic control agent present so as to attain the desired weed control level.

Mass exposure: See *bioherbicide*.

Mass flow: Movement of a soil-supplied nutrient or herbicide by movement of the soil water.

Mechanism of action: The biochemical and biophysical responses of a plant to an herbicide.

Mode of action: The total phytotoxic effects and fate of an herbicide on or in a plant.

Moisture extraction profile: The cross-section profile of lateral and vertical extraction of water from soil by plant roots.

Monocarpy: The production of only one seed per carpel (seed-bearing structure).

Monocot (monocotyledon): Any seed plant having only one seed leaf.

Mutually exclusive: With respect to weed control in a crop with herbicides, the separation of the herbicidal effect, if any, from the effect of interspecific competition.

Mycorrhizae: Fungal association with the roots of higher plants, which may be a factor in nutrient or water uptake in weed–crop situations.

Niche: Physical space, functional role in the community, and position in environmental gradients of temperature, moisture, pH, soils, and other conditions of existence occupied by an organism (what an organism does).

Ontogeny: The developmental history of an individual plant.

Organism: See *species*.

Pappus: The modified calyx limb forming a crown at the summit of the achene in Compositae and other plants.

Patch: The concentration of individuals of a single weed species, commonly perennials, to a specific site or portion of a crop field.

Penumbra: With respect to reception of light by a given plant, the extent of shading of one leaf by another over the total photoperiod.

Perennating part: A specialized structure for vegetative regrowth of perennial plants.

Perennial: A vascular plant that lives for more than two years. (See *herbaceous perennial* and *woody perennial*.)

Periodicity: The tendency for seeds or perennating parts of an individual species to have a flush of resumption of growth at a certain time in the growing season.

Persistence: The duration of toxic levels of an herbicide in soil.

Phloem: The food- (photosynthate-) conducting tissue of vascular plants.

Photoperiod (day length): Period of photosynthetically active radiation.

Photosynthate: The primary product of photosynthesis, mainly carbohydrates.

Phytochrome: A light-absorbing pigment that affects plant morphogenesis; especially important in weed seed germination.

Plagiotropic: With respect to light reception of an individual leaf, change in inclination towards the sun to maximize light capture throughout the photoperiod.

Plant growth regulator: Any synthetic or naturally occurring organic compound that in very low concentrations affects plant growth and development.

Plant hormone: See *plant growth regulator*.

Plasmodesmata: Minute tubules through pores in plant cell walls.

Plasticity: The extent to which any aspect of plant growth changes in response to changes in the environment.

Polycarpy: The production of two or more seeds per carpel (seed-bearing structure).

Polymorphism (seed): Production by an individual plant of seeds differing in color, form, dormancy, or other characteristics.

Polyploidy: Having more than two times the basic chromosome number.

Population: Collective group of organisms of the same species.

Postemergence: Application of an herbicide after the specified weed or crop plants emerge.

Preemergence: Application of an herbicide prior to emergence of a specified weed or seeded crop.

Prevention: The part of weed management that focuses on preventing influx and reproduction of weeds and on practices to minimize their competitive effects. (See *control*.)

Protectant: See *antidote*.

Ramet: An individual reproductive unit of clonal growth that may develop independently if severed from the parent.

Recirculating sprayer: A type of application equipment designed to apply a spray horizontal to the ground and to catch that spray not intercepted by the plants in a receptacle for recirculation.

Relative yield total: The sum of the yields of each species in a mixture divided by its yield in pure stand.

Replacement design: With respect to studies of effects of weed infestation level on crops, experimental designs in which the total number of plants (crop + weeds) is kept constant as their proportion is changed. (See *additive design*.)

Resources allocation: The portion of photosynthate or minerals utilized in the production of distinct plant parts. Commonly applied to partitioning of photosynthate or minerals to production of reproductive versus vegetative growth.

Rhizome: A specialized horizontal stem that grows belowground or just at the soil surface.

Rootstock: Root tissue that commonly stores carbohydrates and may form adventitious buds for regeneration of growth. (See *creeping rootstock* and *taproot*.)

Root depletion zone: The soil area surrounding a root or root system in which the quantity of a soil-supplied growth factor has been reduced through root uptake.

Root volume: The soil volume occupied by a plant's roots.

Rope-wick: An applicator for herbicides in which the herbicide in solution moves by capillary action to an applying surface (commonly a rope or fabric) where it is wiped onto the weed leaves.

r-strategy: With respect to survival, a weed that depends upon large numbers of reproductive units, such as is found with most annual species. (See *K-strategy*.)

Secondary plant compounds: Those having no physiological function essential for the maintenance of life.

Seed: A fertilized, mature ovule having an embryonic plant, stored food material (rarely missing), and a protective coat or coats.

Seedbank: The reservoir of viable weed seeds in soil.

Seedling establishment: The stage in the life cycle of a plant when the newly emerged plant becomes independent of the parent or seed.

Selectivity: The extent of tolerance of desired plants to the amount of herbicide needed to control specified weeds.

Speciation: The product of natural selection and genetic mutation resulting in a new gene pool.

Species: A biological unit that shares a common gene pool.

Stability index: A number that indicates the extent of changes in weed numbers of a given cropping system. It can be found by summing percentage changes in numbers of individual weed species at any specified time following initiation.

Stale seedbed: A weed management practice that involves seedbed preparation enough in advance of crop planting to ensure germination of many weed seeds that are then destroyed by herbicides.

Stolon: A general term for any of several specialized horizontal stems (e.g., tubers and rhizomes). In weed science, it is best to restrict the term to aboveground structures to distinguish them from rhizomes.

Succession: Orderly process of community development involving changes in species with time.

Surfactant: A material that improves the emulsifying, dispersing, spreading, wetting, and other surface-modifying properties of an herbicide formulation.

Survival strategy: See *r-strategy* and *K-strategy*.

Sympatry: Speciation under very local conditions, such as a result of polyploidy, hybridization, self-fertilization, and asexual reproduction.

Symplast: The part of a plant's transport pathway consisting of phloem and living matter of the fundamental tissue.

Synergistic: Complementary effect of one plant on another so that the collective growth exceeds either one alone. Also, complementary action of two or more herbicides (chemicals) resulting in a greater combined effect than the sum of the independent effects.

Systemic: An herbicide readily translocated within the plant that commonly has its effect at a site other than the point of entry.

Taproot: A central, dominant root that normally grows vertically and from which most or all of the smaller roots spread out laterally; also, root tissue that commonly stores carbohydrates and may form adventitious buds for regeneration of growth, such as in dandelion.

Threshold level (value): That point in infestation by weeds (numbers or weight) at which crop yield begins to be reduced.

Tillage: The mechanical manipulation of soil, with *conventional* being the combined primary and secondary tillage commonly performed in preparing a seedbed for a given crop and area; *minimum* being the least amount of soil manipulation necessary for crop production or to meet tillage requirements under the existing soil and climatic conditions; *primary* being the initial major soil-working operation commonly designed to loosen or reduce soil strength; *reduced* being any combination of tillage operations designed to lessen the total amount of tillage; and *secondary* being any soil-working operation following primary tillage, commonly designed to refine the seedbed for crop planting.

Tiller: An erect or semierect branch arising from a bud in the axils of leaves at the base of a plant, as in johnsongrass.

Tissue system: One of the three broad types of tissues common to vascular plants (e.g., dermal, vascular, and fundamental).

Tuber: A relatively short, thickened stem structure that develops belowground as a consequence of the swelling of the subapical portion of a rhizome and subsequent accumulation of reserve materials.

Vascular tissue: The conducting tissue of vascular plants.

Viability: The extent to which seed or perennating parts retain the capability to resume growth when provided conditions favorable to growth.

Weed: A plant that originated under a natural environment and, in response to imposed and natural environments, evolved, and continues to do so as an interfering associate with our crops and activities.

Weed composition: The makeup or the proportion of weed species in a weed community.

Weed—crop ecology: The study of the interrelationships between crops and weeds and their environment.

Weediness: The extent of weed abundance in a field, lawn, garden, and other areas used by humans.

Weed management: The approach to weeds in which prevention and control have companion roles.

Woody perennial: A vascular plant that lives for more than two years and develops woody tissue.

Xylem: The principle conducting tissue for water and mineral nutrients in plants.

INDEX